**In every band of brothers, there is always one
who looks out for the others. . . .**

They were Easy Company, 101st Army Airborne—a fighting unit whose members became legendary in the annals of World War II combat for their bravery, their ability to get the job done against nearly insurmountable odds, and their loyalty to one another in the face of death. Every soldier in this band of brothers looked to one man for leadership, devotion to duty, and the embodiment of courage: Major Dick Winters.

This is the riveting story of an ordinary man who became an extraordinary hero. After Winters enlisted in the army's arduous new Airborne division, his natural combat leadership helped him rise through the ranks, but he was never far from his men. Decades later, Stephen E. Ambrose's *Band of Brothers* made him famous around the world.

Full of never-before-published photographs, interviews, and Winters' candid insights, *Biggest Brother* is the fascinating, inspirational story of a man who became a soldier, a leader, and a living testament to the valor of the human spirit—and of America.

BIGGEST

BROTHER

The Life of Major Dick Winters,

the Man Who Led the Band of Brothers

LARRY ALEXANDER

NAL
CALIBER

NAL Caliber
Published by New American Library, a division of
Penguin Group (USA) Inc., 375 Hudson Street,
New York, New York 10014, USA
Penguin Group (Canada), 90 Eglinton Avenue East, Suite 700, Toronto,
Ontario M4P 2Y3, Canada (a division of Pearson Penguin Canada Inc.)
Penguin Books Ltd., 80 Strand, London WC2R 0RL, England
Penguin Ireland, 25 St. Stephen's Green, Dublin 2,
Ireland (a division of Penguin Books Ltd.)
Penguin Group (Australia), 250 Camberwell Road, Camberwell, Victoria 3124,
Australia (a division of Pearson Australia Group Pty. Ltd.)
Penguin Books India Pvt. Ltd., 11 Community Centre, Panchsheel Park,
New Delhi - 110 017, India
Penguin Group (NZ), cnr Airborne and Rosedale Roads, Albany,
Auckland 1310, New Zealand (a division of Pearson New Zealand Ltd.)
Penguin Books (South Africa) (Pty.) Ltd., 24 Sturdee Avenue,
Rosebank, Johannesburg 2196, South Africa

Penguin Books Ltd., Registered Offices: ·
80 Strand, London WC2R 0RL, England

Published by NAL Caliber, an imprint of New American Library, a division of Penguin Group (USA) Inc.
Previously published in an NAL Caliber hardcover edition.

First NAL Caliber Trade Paperback Printing, May 2006
10 9 8 7 6 5 4 3 2

Copyright © Larry Alexander, 2005
All rights reserved

NAL CALIBER and the "C" logo are trademarks of Penguin Group (USA) Inc.

NAL CALIBER Trade Paperback ISBN: 0-451-21839-6

The Library of Congress has cataloged the hardcover edition of this title as follows:

Alexander, Larry, 1951–
     Biggest brother: the life of Major D. Winters—the man who led the band of brothers / by Larry
Alexander.
        p. cm.
     ISBN 0-451-21510-9
     1. Winters, Richard D.   2. United States. Army. Parachute Infantry Regiment, 506th. Company E—
History.   3. United States. Army—Biography.   4. World War, 1939–1945—Regimental histories—
United States.   5. World War, 1939–1945—Campaigns—Western Front.   6. Soldiers—United
States—Biography.   I. Title.
     D769.348506th.A43   2005
     940.54'2142'092—dc22   2004027330

Set in Bodoni
Designed by Ginger Legato

Printed in the United States of America

This book is dedicated to the memory of
Israel and Dorothy Gockley and
Adam and Cora Burkholder,
and to all other Americans who either
served their country during a time of war
or awaited the return of a loved one.

CONTENTS

Author's Note ⋆ ix

Preface by Damian Lewis ⋆ xv

Prologue: Shrine Auditorium, Hollywood ⋆ xix

1. The $10,000 Jump ⋆ 1

2. "$21 a Day, Once a Month." ⋆ 20

3. "I'll Meet You at the North Star." ⋆ 39

4. "A Very, Very Tough Day." ⋆ 65

5. "I Just Knew You'd Do Well." ⋆ 81

6. "We Took a Hell of a Licking." ⋆ 96

7. "My Luck Is Still Holding . . ." ⋆ 114

8. "Here We Go Again." ⋆ 131

9. "You Can't Leave Us, Sir." ⋆ 151

10. "Their Guys Are Probably Dumber Than Ours." ⋆ 166

11. "Now I Know Why I'm Here." ⋆ 178

12. "The Spoils of War." ⋆ 195

13. "I'll Bet You Thought I Was Gonna Shoot You." ⋆ 215

14. "I'll See You After I Make the Final Jump." ⋆ 231

15. "I Think E Company Has a Story to Tell." ⋆ 242

16. "This Is Our Last Hurrah." ⋆ 255

Epilogue: "Everybody Wants a Piece of You." ⋆ 272

Appendix: Dick Winters on Leadership ⋆ 282

Acknowledgments ⋆ 286

Glossary ⋆ 288

Bibliography ⋆ 290

Index ⋆ 291

AUTHOR'S NOTE

An author probably should not admit this, but the idea for this book was not my own. It resulted from a suggestion by my boss, Charles Raymond Shaw, which might be only fair since he is the one who had me get in touch with Dick Winters in the first place.

It all began in September of 2001 when Shaw, editor of the *Lancaster Intelligencer Journal*, in Lancaster County, Pennsylvania, where I work as a reporter and weekly humor columnist, approached my desk. The miniseries *Band of Brothers* had been airing for several weeks on HBO, and Shaw, who knew I had a Bachelor of Arts degree in history and was very knowledgeable on World War II, had an assignment for me. He asked if I had been watching the miniseries. I told him I had, a fact which I am sure came as no revelation.

"You know, according to the book, Dick Winters lives in Hershey," Shaw told me. "Why don't you try to look him up? It'd make a good story."

Good, hell. It'd be a *great* story, so I hurried over to a shelf in the newsroom where we kept phone books. You'd think a newspaper would keep current phone books, but that is not the case. Our collection was so old that one book still had a listing for Thomas Edison. So it came as no surprise when I picked up the Hershey phone book, dialed the number and found it was not the Winters' residence as the book indicated. The veteran had wisely changed his number. I don't know who the poor soul is who had it reassigned to him, but I'm sure he has since gone mad.

I wasn't sure where to go next when fate intervened. Stopping at a bookstore next day I stumbled across a special "Band of Brothers" edition of *World War II* magazine and, lo and behold, inside was contact information for the 506th Parachute Infantry Regiment Association. I called the number in

Michigan and, after identifying myself, was told by the gentleman on the other end of the line that he had no information on Winters to give me. However, he did have the phone number of one of Winters' men, William "Wild Bill" Guarnere, who was still living in Philadelphia. I dialed the number.

Guarnere was the same type of guy depicted in the film; gruff, with a South Philly twang and salty as hell. I loved it. Guarnere told me he could not hand out Winters' phone number, but did give me his post office box address. Then he added some advice. "One more thing," Guarnere told me. "He won't talk to you if you haven't read the book. So if you haven't read the goddamn thing, don't bother."

No problem there. I had read the book once and listened to the audio version at least twice. I wrote Winters that same evening but didn't mail the letter until next day, so when I addressed the envelope, I used my home address in Ephrata, Pennsylvania, for my return address, rather than my Lancaster work address.

Three days later my work phone rang. The conversation went something like this.

"Newsroom, Larry Alexander."

"Hello," a quiet voice said on the other end of the line. "This is Dick Winters from Hershey."

Excitement coursed through me. "Oh, my," I stammered. "Thank you for calling. This is an honor."

What he said next puzzled me. "Where in Ephrata do you live?"

I told him.

Then he added, "I lived in Ephrata, too. On East Fulton Street."

"My God," I replied. "I grew up on East Fulton Street. Where did you live?"

"Next to the stockyard," he said.

"That big, wood frame house? I know it," I said, thoroughly amazed. "I lived on the other end of the block, at the corner of Fulton and Lake. I saw your house every day of my life."

"I lived there in the twenties," he said. "We later moved to Lancaster." (Somehow I had missed the reference to Lancaster near the end of episode two of the HBO series, "Day of Days.") "Did you know Lottie Gardner?"

"Sure I knew Lottie," I told him. "That was our favorite place to go trick-or-treating when I was a kid. She gave dimes instead of candy. A dime bought two plain Hershey bars back then."

Winters chuckled. "It's a small world."

Our first interview and meeting was a few days later. I took along my colleague, photographer Dan Marschka, who was almost as excited as I was to meet Winters. We met in the second-floor office at his home, and I sat in the same creaky leather chair once used by author Stephen E. Ambrose and actor Damian Lewis (although not at the same time). Our interview lasted about an hour, but Dan and I spent another two hours there, enthralled by the man, his stories, indeed, his very presence.

The article ran next day and was entitled "Biggest Brother," a phrase I used in my first paragraph, where I wrote, "If the men of Easy Company, 506th Parachute Infantry Regiment of the 101st Airborne are a 'Band of Brothers,' then Dick Winters is the Biggest Brother." The editor loved it. Unfortunately, he pulled it for the title and changed my reference to "Winters is the Big Brother." Editors! Ya gotta love 'em. (Later, when I told people about this book and its title, some thought I swiped it from Steven Spielberg, who used the same term to describe Winters at the Emmys in September 2002, when actually I had used it a year earlier.) Winters called me that day.

"I have been interviewed by a lot of newspapers and magazines," he said. "But that was the best article about me I have ever seen. You did a helluva job. And the picture was terrific."

Although that made me happy, what thrilled me even more was when he reproduced copies of the article, including photos, and sent them along in replies to any fan who requested an autograph. Better yet, I quickly became Winters' favorite reporter and Dan became his favorite photographer.

That meeting sparked a long and happy friendship with Winters. Over the next few months, we spoke often and I visited him when I had the chance. In April 2002, HBO rereleased the series and I again interviewed Winters, on how it feels to be an eighty-four-year-old media celebrity. For this article I also interviewed Forrest Guth and Bill Guarnere. Dan again went along as my photographer and his picture of Winters sifting through a stack of mail, with a whole box of other letters sitting beside him, became one of Winters' favorites. That photo appears in this book.

This book came about in the spring of 2003. I had been in Ray Shaw's office, talking about Winters' hectic public appearance schedule.

"You and he have become pretty close," Shaw said. "Have you thought about writing his biography? I'm sure there's a market out there for it."

Actually, I hadn't thought about it, and even if I had, it is unlikely I would have suggested it to Winters as I felt it would have been imposing on our friendship. Also, I was very busy myself and a book is a major undertaking. But the more I thought about it, the more I realized that someone was going to write a book about him someday, so why not me, someone who knew him and had a deep and abiding respect for the man and his deeds. So the next time I was at Dick's home, I broached the idea, adding that if he did not like it, all he had to do was say "no" and that'd be that.

"Let me think about it," he said.

A few days later he called me.

"I've been thinking about that project we talked about," he told me. "Let's do it."

We got together a few days later and Winters had prepared for me a plastic crate containing four looseleaf binders bulging with reports, diary entries, letters, photographs, maps and so forth.

"This is the same material I gave to Hanks and Ambrose," he told me.

That was good, but my idea was not to rewrite *Band of Brothers,* which Ambrose had already so eloquently done, but to look at Winters' life, not just during the war years, but both before and after. Winters knew what I wanted and added to the crate his collection of "Letters to DeEtta," a binder with over 100 letters written between 1942 and 1945 to DeEtta Almon, a woman he met while in training at Camp Croft. DeEtta became his pen pal throughout the war, and the letters gave deep insight to what was going on inside the young man's head, and heart, while he was dodging German bullets in Europe. These letters proved especially valuable because of what they said not about the other men he served with—he seldom discussed them to any depth—but what the letters revealed about himself.

Dick and I began a series of interviews that eventually totaled between twenty-five and thirty hours. Sometimes we'd break and go out for lunch, particularly to one deli where everyone seemed to know Dick and would say, "Hello, Major," when he entered.

Other treasures supplied to me during this research and writing phase included actual transcripts of his first meetings with Ambrose, a copy of that author's first draft of Chapter One of *Band of Brothers* and some of Ambrose's handwritten notes on the men of Easy.

But what Winters gave me most of all was encouragement and confidence. Initially, I had begun writing in the first person, wanting the reader to see what Winters saw, and feel what Winters felt. The last thing I wanted was a dry biography. Having written rough drafts of the first two chapters, I sent them to Dick for his input. He loved them at first, but in November 2003 had second thoughts. He was "uncomfortable" with the first-person use of "I" and "me." But even more, he feared that associating himself that closely with the book would open a new floodgate of fan mail and media attention that he said he would be unable to cope with.

So I changed the tense, but not the style. My goal was to still make the action come alive. I wanted the reader to see his life through his eyes, to feel as though they were in the jump seat beside Winters on June 6, 1944. I wanted them to feel the thrill of launching themselves from the bucking airplane into a night sky filled with whizzing tracers. It was my goal to have the reader run alongside of Winters as he crossed the open field at the crossroad in Holland, to hear the pounding of feet on the ground, the puffing of their breath and the rustle of grass crushed down by jump boots. The incidents in this book are all true and the dialogue, if not words actually spoken, is based on Dick Winters' own writings and thoughts.

Dick liked my treatment of his story. As my first chapters were finished, I sent them to him for commentary to make sure I was presenting his story in a way that pleased him. Using a red felt-tip pen, he made some adjustments, but his overall remarks were complimentary. Words like "Excellent," and "Takes my breath away" were scrawled on the tops of the first pages of these chapters.

Dick Winters is an American success story; a humble man, coming as he did from humble beginnings. Like many of his generation, he went off to war, did his duty in the service of his country, and was one of the lucky ones to come home relatively unscathed. Back in the States, he got a job, found a wonderful woman to share his life, raised two fine children and ran a successful business. By a quirk of fate, he rose to national prominence and on one fine, glittering evening, received a standing ovation from the biggest names in Hollywood at the 2002 Emmy Awards.

This book, written out of respect and admiration, is a tribute to Major Richard D. Winters, an exceptional leader, a good man and my friend.

Larry Alexander
May 2005

PREFACE

W ho's playing Winters? Who's playing Winters?"
This whisper was caught on the wind and ricocheted off the barrack walls of Longmoor Camp. It was March 2000. Myself and forty-nine other men were at boot camp, in training for what was to become one of the most successful TV series of all time, *Band of Brothers*. It followed Easy Company of the 506th regiment of the 101st Airborne Division from the jump into Normandy on D-Day, 6 June 1944, until VE-Day, almost a year later. This band of brothers had had a leader, a man whose skills as a soldier were second to none, a hero to his men and to subsequent generations, and the boys in the barracks that day we all first met were keen to know who was going to play him. Well, it was me.

Every young actor wanted to be in *Band of Brothers*. Steven Spielberg and Tom Hanks were producing for HBO and it quickly became the project that everyone had to be "seen" for. But it wasn't just the high profile of the producers that excited everyone. It was the story—a true story about real people and the extraordinarily heroic things they did in the Second World War. And we'd been asked to tell it.

I remember, as I arrived at Longmoor Camp for training that first day, I still wasn't fully aware of the enormity of what I was being asked to do. Everyone had been telling me, "You're the guy. He's the main guy." But I hadn't seen all the scripts (they weren't all written yet), and was equally being told it was an ensemble piece. It was. But Winters was its spine.

Two things then happened that made me sit up.

I discovered that the actors living in the States (as opposed to those cast out of the UK) had made contact with the veterans they were going to portray, and had already formed considerable friendships. They'd had a few whiskies (depends on your definition of a few!), shared many stories, laughed and cried. The actors were ready to tell the vets' stories and ready to do justice to the achievements of their new friends. It was infectious.

The second thing that shook me was a conversation I had with Donnie Wahlberg, who was playing Sergeant Carwood Lipton, a man also decorated for his bravery. We'd been yelled at and driven relentlessly on our first day's training out in the field. No concessions were made to us being actors; in fact, the opposite was true, and we were exhausted. It was nighttime, a few minutes before lights out, and I found myself and Donnie in the first moment of peace we'd had since arriving, leaning out of the top-floor windows of our barracks, facing each other across the concrete of the parade ground, discussing our fears and anxieties about doing these men justice in the nine long months ahead of us. The night was still and Donnie said in a calm voice, "I don't know you, but the fact they've asked you to portray this man means you have my respect already." And in that moment I knew. I knew what Dick Winters meant to people. He was a hero, an icon.

Dick kept diaries in the war. He wrote letters home. He had several folders of memories. And I had them all for research. But I had never met him. At boot camp I called him for the first time, and through a series of phone calls I set about slowly trying to earn his trust. What emerged as I got to know him was a man not given to late nights in bars, reminiscing, not given to romanticizing his past glories. He was a man whose recollections were analytical, pragmatically ordered, not emotional, a man who was much happier answering questions on technical maneuvers or what boot he wore his knife on (the left by the way), than what he felt, as he found himself isolated from his men, staring at a whole company of Germans, on top of that dyke in Holland, for example. "I was always just concentrating on getting the job done," would be his typical reply. It dawned on me what a happy coincidence it was that I had felt slightly removed from the "hype" at the beginning of the job, a little detached. For it was precisely this ability to distance himself from any hysteria and to remain calm and lucid in moments of danger that made Dick Winters a natural leader of men. But not only that. Once I had his trust, I found a warmth, a wickedly dry sense of humor and a willingness to listen that is not often found in men of power.

After the series had been filmed I went and visited Dick and Ethel at home in Hershey, Pennsylvania. We chatted and joked as he showed me some of his mementos and walked me around their beautiful farm (another major achievement in his life). He treated me like a son and told me that he thought I'd done a pretty good job portraying him, although he was unsure at first! I thought, yup, that's him. Authoritative, nurturing and honest all at once. I felt immensely proud that I'd had the opportunity to portray this man, a decorated war hero whose story I'd been entrusted with. It had needed a precision and an unfailing commitment to the truth. It's what Dick always demanded, of himself and others.

And as I sit in my trailer on another film set writing this now, the big band sound of "Chattanooga Choo Choo" swingin' in the background on my stereo, I'm reminded of what Dick used to say to me during filming, "Just hang tough!" but always with a twinkle in his eye. . . .

Damian Lewis
September 22, 2004

Shrine Auditorium, Hollywood

September 22, 2002

A ctor Martin Sheen stepped up to the microphone, looking out through the hot stage and TV lights at the tuxedoed and evening-gowned audience. The envelope clutched in Sheen's hand held the name of the winner in the Best Miniseries category here at the Fifty-Fourth Annual Emmy Awards ceremony.

This was the moment the eighty-four-year-old man seated uneasily in the third row had been awaiting for the past several hours. Up until this point, Dick Winters felt he and his wife Ethel, seated to his right, were out of place in Hollywood's Shrine Auditorium, surrounded by filmdom's finest and brightest.

Directly in front of him were cast members of the hit TV series, *Friends*, including David Schwimmer who portrayed Captain Herbert Sobel in *Band of Brothers*. Directly to Winters' left was actress Rita Wilson and, next to her, her husband Tom Hanks. Directly behind Hanks sat Steven Spielberg, one of the finest, if not *the* finest, directors in Hollywood. Beside Spielberg was his wife, actress Kate Capshaw.

What in the hell was a retired high-nutritional animal feed salesman from Hershey, Pennsylvania, doing here?

In another life, Dick Winters had been Major Richard D. Winters, commander of Company E, and later of 2nd Battalion, of the 506th Parachute Infantry Regiment, 101st Airborne Division, which, through a combination of hard training, firm discipline, superb leadership and a good deal of luck, fought through and survived some of the most hellish battles of World War II in Europe. He had led his men into Normandy on D-Day, fought beside them in Holland, held them together during the harsh winter outside Bastogne and celebrated the end of the war with them on the balcony of Adolf Hitler's mountaintop hideaway, the Eagle's Nest. During those eleven months, they had fought and suffered together through terrible hardships. They had witnessed horrible destruction and human atrocities, seen their friends killed and maimed, and had taken the lives of other young men.

After the guns had ceased firing, they came home, married, took jobs, raised families and tried to blend back into everyday life. In the decades that followed, their bodies aged, their hair grayed, their quick, youthful movements slowed, and the memories of their war years, tucked back into the recesses of their minds, began to fade. Some of the men passed on while the rest slipped quietly into retirement.

Then, in the late 1980s, author/historian Stephen E. Ambrose, researching a book on D-Day, was introduced to the men of Easy Company. After hearing their stories he astutely recognized the unit for what it was—a microcosm of the entire last year of the war in Europe; a story every soldier who served in the ETO would recognize and identify with, and one that future generations of Americans should know. From that, in 1992, came Ambrose's World War II classic work, *Band of Brothers*, and the lives of Winters and his men would never be the same.

In 1999, around the same time Spielberg's landmark World War II film *Saving Private Ryan*, in which Hanks starred, was making a sensation in theaters across the country, Winters received a phone call from Ambrose. Hanks wanted to buy the film rights to *Band of Brothers*.

A collaboration between Hanks' production company, Playtone, and Spielberg's Dreamworks, the project was envisioned as a twelve-part miniseries for Home Box Office. The final production was pared down to ten parts and cost $125 million, making it the most expensive miniseries ever produced. It debuted on HBO in September 2001 and was watched by some nine million viewers. Not only did the series prove a stunning success, but it propelled Winters and the men of Easy Company from a set of obscure retirees with their quietly shared memories to international celebrities with incessant demands for autographs, personal appearances and interviews.

In 2002 *Band of Brothers* was nominated for nineteen Emmys, including Best Miniseries, which is how Winters found himself being flown to Hollywood, fitted for a tuxedo, courtesy of HBO, and sitting amid a veritable galaxy of stars.

Now that the moment for the announcement had arrived, however, Winters was uneasy. *Band of Brothers* was up against some stiff competition in the form of *Dinotopia*, *The Mists of Avalon* and *Shackleton*.

Winters held his breath as he watched Sheen open the envelope.

"The Emmy goes to *Band of Brothers*," Sheen announced.

The auditorium erupted in applause as Hanks and Spielberg rose from their seats, turned to face each other and shook hands. Winters also rose, leaning on his cane. Hanks extended a hand and helped the aging veteran out into the aisle, then steadied him as they walked toward the stage.

Unsteady on a pair of legs that were once powerful enough to run six miles up and down a Georgia mountain and propel him out of airplanes, Winters had originally hoped to be able to walk onto the stage from the wings and not have to negotiate the tricky steps now looming before him. However, buoyed by Hanks and his own decisive willpower, the few steps proved no challenge. Now on stage, Winters, Hanks and Spielberg, along with a growing mass of the film's writers, directors and cast members, walked to the podium. Hanks had planned to speak, but with Winters on his right arm, the emotion of the moment left the actor speechless. Spielberg accepted the golden statuette and stepped up to the microphone.

"Thank you very much, members of the academy," he said. "Thank you very much for this wonderful appreciation. But we didn't win this. The men of Easy Company won this in 1944."

This drew the entire audience to its feet in a rousing standing ovation. The applause increased as cameras cut away to the grand ballroom of the St. Regis Hotel. There, surviving members of Easy Company, now elderly men in various degrees of health and flown to Hollywood at HBO's expense, as well as the widows and children of men no longer living, watched the proceedings on a closed-circuit TV hookup. The faces of the men radiated the same joy Winters felt as he accepted the crowd's gratitude.

"These are the real men who were the boys of Easy Company," Spielberg announced by way of introduction.

When the applause died away and the audience had resumed their seats, Spielberg continued. He thanked "the great historian," Stephen Ambrose, who, suffering from the lung cancer that would take his life twenty-one days later, was unable to attend.

Then Spielberg said, "May I now introduce our biggest brother of *Band of Brothers*, Major Dick Winters."

The auditorium again exploded in applause as Hanks led Winters forward to the microphone so the first soldier of Easy Company could address not just Hollywood's finest gathered before him, but millions of viewers on TV.

"Thank you very much," Winters began in his quiet, slow Pennsylvania Dutch drawl. "I want to represent myself here as representing all the men of Company E that are present and accounted for, and on behalf of all the men who have passed before us."

The camera cut back to the St. Regis to pan the faces of the veterans as they listened to their commander speak.

"We want to thank Steve Ambrose for listening to our stories and our memories." He stopped briefly to choke back emotion. "And for telling the story of *Band of Brothers.*

"We don't want to forget Tom Hanks and Steven Spielberg and their entire crew who did such a wonderful job in telling our memories. And I want to thank every one of you," he told the audience, "for your support."

He snapped his right hand to his forehead. "I salute you," he said.

Hanks reclaimed Winters' arm and, with the entire hall ringing with applause, the old soldier faded from the stage to resume a life that would never be quiet and peaceful again.

CHAPTER 1

The $10,000 Jump

June 6, 1944, 0100–2200

The sudden, deafening crack of the antiaircraft shell bursting outside caused First Lieutenant Richard D. Winters to flinch as he stood poised in the doorway of the C-47 transport plane. Shrapnel from the exploded shell rattled off the fuselage like hailstones. Outside in the night sky, Winters could see other paratrooper-laden planes, madly bobbing and weaving through puffs of smoke from ack-ack shells. Between the planes, ribbons of colored fire spewed out from unseen gun emplacements on the ground arced upward as if the earth itself were outraged by the presence of these aerial invaders.

Winters turned and nodded reassuringly at the sixteen men nervously lined up on both sides of the plane's interior, their parachute static lines clipped to the overhead cable, eyes glued on the two lights by the hatch. One light was red, indicating they were nearing their drop zone. The other, a green light, was the "go" signal. Despite the hell outside and the men's eagerness to get out of this lumbering target of an airplane, neither light was yet lit.

It had been just two hours since the air armada left England, the vanguard of the long-awaited Allied invasion of Europe. As his 33,000-pound transport plane glided through the night air over the English Channel, Winters sat just inside the humming, vibrating fuselage, next to the open hatch, staring absently into the darkness. In the jump seats around him sat the rest of Stick 67, a total of seventeen men, all crammed tightly together, yet each eerily alone with his thoughts and fears.

How will I react when I first come under fire, Winters asked himself. Can I handle it? Will I make the right decisions? Or will I end up getting myself and my men killed?

At age twenty-six, Winters was the commanding officer of the first platoon of Easy Company, 506th Parachute Infantry Regiment of the 101st Airborne Division, and on that unforgettable June morning they were winging their way toward their first combat at 150 miles per hour.

From the open doorway, Winters looked down in awe at the Allied invasion fleet, five thousand ships silently knifing through the black waters of the English Channel. Flying just five hundred feet above the water to stay below German radar, the paratroopers had the best seat in the house for the greatest show on earth. Watching the fleet, heavily laden with men and equipment, pass beneath the plane's wings, Winters felt absolute astonishment at the enormity of the operation in which he, a lowly boy from tranquil Lancaster County, Pennsylvania, was now an integral part. Being in that aircraft, surrounded by one half of his platoon, Winters had taken a personalized view of the war. Glancing out the door at the ships blanketing the Channel, and feeling the closeness of the other transports flying in their tight V formations in the sky around him, brought welcomed reassurance.

When the men had first loaded onto the planes at the Upottery airfield, there was the soldiers' usual pissing and moaning, mostly directed at the discomfort caused by the approximately 125 pounds of gear each man had to carry.

As the flight monotonously droned on, the men became more subdued. Some prayed, others dragged on cigarettes and gazed reflectively through the curls of smoke, while still others dozed, possibly from lack of sleep the evening before, or as a result of the motion sickness pills they'd been issued prior to takeoff. Even Winters was feeling the effects of the pills.

"My God, stay awake," he thought, mentally slapping himself around. "You can't go to sleep tonight."

Conversations were short and held in a low murmur. Three seats to Winters' left, Private Joseph E. Hogan began singing softly. Winters appreciated his attempt to break the tension and joined in. So did a few others, but all soon tired of trying to be heard above the thrumming of the two Pratt and Whitney engines, and lapsed back into silence.

*   *   *

Twenty minutes earlier, around 12:40 A.M., two large, dark shapes appeared on the water below. The plane's crew chief worked his way back through the fuselage over a tangle of sprawled legs to stand beside Winters.

"Jersey and Guernsey," he hollered above the engine roar, leaning close and pointing at the looming shapes. "We're twenty minutes out."

Winters nodded. Jersey and Guernsey were British islands that an emasculated English army had been unable to defend following Dunkirk and the defeat in France. Since 1940 they had become advanced bases for the Nazis, and as the air armada passed overhead a smattering of ineffectual antiaircraft fire rose up to greet them, the first hostile fire the men had seen.

As the Channel Islands faded into the distance, a more ominous shape began to take form ahead: Occupied France. Passing over the French coastline, the planes began climbing to fifteen hundred feet. The $10,000 jump, as it was wryly dubbed because of their GI life insurance, was near. Final cigarettes were lit. Although still miles from the drop zone, Winters decided to prepare the men.

"We've go to be ready to jump any time now, so let's get up and hook up," he said to Private First Class Burt Christenson, seated next to him, and the other men within earshot. "If we get hit, at least we won't be taking it sitting down."

Winters rose and, facing the men, called out above the engine roar, "Stand up." They struggled to their feet. "Hook up!" he called, and the click of sixteen static lines being connected to the overhead guide cable rang out. "Equipment check!" he yelled, and soon the men sounded back, "seventeen okay," "sixteen okay," "fifteen okay," "fourteen okay" and so on until it reached him. "One okay," he said, and turned to face the door, snapping his static line to the cable.

Taking one more look around the plane's interior, Winters smiled reassuringly to Corporal Denver "Bull" Randleman, the number seventeen man in the stick. A highly reliable, solidly built man with a good sense of humor, Bull was assigned the last seat by Winters for a very good reason. With Randleman bringing up the rear, no man was going to freeze in the doorway.

As the planes continued inland they ran into an unexpected fog bank. With their visibility drastically cut, the transports began spreading out to lessen the threat of a midair collision. The fog also obscured the visual guides pilots use to stay together at night—flames from the engine exhausts of other aircraft, and a small blue light on each plane where the right wing met the fuselage—and the formations began to break up.

Attempting to spot familiar landmarks on the ground that might lead them to the drop areas, pilots brought their planes down to seven hundred feet or lower. Tense minutes passed. Even though over enemy-held territory, the Germans had yet to react.

"I can't understand this," Winters said to Christenson. "No ack-ack."

"You don't hear me complaining, do you?" Christenson replied.

Winters smiled. He liked Christenson, who was not only a capable soldier, but an excellent artist who could handle paper and charcoal as well as he could an M1.

As if the Nazis had heard Winters' comment, bursts of antiaircraft fire suddenly began illuminating the clouds ahead like Roman candles. At first it was sparse and poorly aimed. The lead planes had caught the Germans napping, leaving bleary-eyed crews to scramble for their weapons. Soon the fire intensified as the gunners settled down and began their work in earnest. Trails of blue, green and red tracers split the night. Winters knew that every seventh shell was a tracer, leaving six unseen rounds in between. It was not a reassuring thought. Oddly, the German fire seemed to move in slow motion, coming straight at Winters' plane, then falling off behind.

"They're shooting wild," he told Christenson. "They're not leading us."

Again, as if his criticism had been heard, the enemy gunners adjusted their fire, and the distinct crack of the bursting rounds outside made a formidable noise. It was 1:10 A.M. by Winters' watch when the red light blazed to life. Ten minutes! The men braced themselves, knowing that once the light went from red to green, they had to get out rapidly. If just thirty seconds elapsed from the time the first man jumped until the last man was out the two would land a mile apart.

On they flew through the thickening ground fire. The sky outside was a Fourth of July celebration gone mad, and planes began taking evasive action, against orders. More tracers streaked upward. Winters' plane was buffeted as several rounds pierced its tail.

An antiaircraft shell exploded below the C-47, sending out a shower of shrapnel. One chunk sliced through the fuselage and struck the pilot, Lieutenant William M. Sammons, in the foot. Partly in terror, partly at the shock of being hit, Sammons reached out and flipped on the jump light. "Jesus Christ," Winters thought when he saw the green light blaze. Without hesitation, he shoved the heavy equipment bag containing machine guns and ammunition out the door. As he watched it fall away Winters realized the plane hadn't slowed. "We're going too fast," he yelled to Christenson. Then, knowing he had no choice, Winters stepped into the doorway, fingers on the outside of the plane. Four hundred feet below he saw a town with a building afire, an antlike line of civilians formed up in a bucket brigade, trying to douse the flames.

Winters took a deep breath and steeled himself for what he knew was going to be a difficult jump into an even more difficult war. In those final seconds, the young lieutenant's thoughts turned to General William Lee, the 101st Airborne's first commander. Tough, yet popular with his men, Lee had formed the division, trained it, and led it to England, only to suffer a heart attack and be forced to give up command.

"Bill Lee!" Winters yelled, and launched himself into the violent night.

*   *   *

The jolt of the parachute opening at that speed, coupled with the fierce propeller blast, was the worst Winters ever experienced, and would leave his arms and legs bruised for weeks. Far more disturbing, however, was that the musette bag, which was strapped across his chest, and his leg bag, both of which carried nearly all his gear, including his M1 Garand rifle and ammunition bandoliers, were torn away by the shock. Dangling from the chute's risers, Winters tried to keep an eye on his falling leg bag, all the while cursing the last-minute idea that foisted the leg bag on the men with no chance to experiment. Now, except for his jump knife and whatever he had thought to jam into his pockets, everything he owned was plummeting toward earth. At the same time he was trying to track his equipment, Winters' attention was diverted by a German 20 mm battery firing skyward. He could hear the rounds whirring past in the dark and thought, "Jesus Christ, they're trying to pick me up with that machine gun. There, my bag dropped in that field by that tree line. Goddamn that machine gun."

Winters hoped to land in the same field as his gear. Instead, he drifted left, over a road and another line of trees, and thudded down in the adjacent field. Recovering quickly, he collapsed his canopy and began freeing himself from his parachute harness. Machine gun bullets from an unseen MG-42 zipped overhead as Winters struggled with the tangled lines. The enemy gun crew had yet to zero in on his location, but Winters knew it was only a matter of time before the lead flying across that field found him. Finally wrenching himself free, Winters was confronted with the fact that he had no idea where he was or where his men were, and didn't even know which way to go to reach the rally point. Ordinarily, to reach the rally point, the first men to jump began walking in the direction the plane was flying and the last ones out headed back the way from which it came and, if all went well, they would meet somewhere in between. In the mass of confusion that was D-Day, this proved impossible. Needing to collect his thoughts, Winters stepped up to a tree and took a leak, both to relieve himself and as a means of taking a second to relax and gather his thoughts.

Before Winters jumped, he had considered slicing off a strip of his camouflaged parachute to use as a raincoat. But now, with bullets cutting through the air, his only thought was to retrieve his gear and get the hell away from that machine gun and that town. Slipping his jump knife from its boot scabbard, he was just about to do that when another paratrooper landed nearby. Racing to the man's side, Winters helped cut him out of his harness and recognized him as a supply sergeant from F Company. Since the sergeant was armed with a Tommy gun, Winters relieved him of a hand grenade, then said, "I need to recover my gear. It's in my leg bag in the next field." Winters indicated that the armed sergeant was to take the lead. The sergeant, unenthused by the prospect, balked, so Winters said, "Follow me," and headed off into the night.

The two cautiously made their way around the German 20 mm battery in the direction of the road that separated Winters from his possessions. From out in the darkness, an enemy machine gun opened up, firing down the road they had to cross.

"To hell with it," Winters told the trooper, doubtless much to the man's relief. "Let's get out of here."

They walked quietly through the darkened countryside, the rustle of their boots in the grass drowned out by the rumble of German flak batteries and the drone of a new wave of C-47s carrying the 82nd Airborne into battle. Having most of the Germans' attention focused upward was a blessing for those already on the ground, lost and confused, for there were no familiar landmarks to be seen despite weeks of studying maps and sand tables back in England. Still, Winters kept walking, looking for something—anything—that would give him a clue as to where he was.

Winters heard a rustling sound in the darkness. Taking out his cricket, a small toy the troopers had been issued before departing England, he clicked it once and was relieved when the two-click reply came back. He was even happier to find it was one of his sergeants, Carwood Lipton, and about twelve men, including several 82nd Airborne stragglers. Lipton, whom Winters considered one of Easy's most capable noncommissioned officers, said he'd spotted an old Roman road sign indicating that the town with the blazing building was Ste. Mere-Eglise.

"Who's got a poncho?" Winters asked. A man handed him one.

Winters hunched on the ground, stuck his trench knife into the earth, then crawled under the poncho. Taking his flashlight off his belt, he turned it on, laid out his map and placed a compass on it. Within moments Winters not only knew exactly where he was, but, thanks to those sand tables, he also knew where the German positions were that he would have to avoid. The bad news was, he and his men were four miles from their objective, Ste. Marie-du-Mont, as the crow flies. And they weren't crows. By foot, it was closer to eight miles.

Winters crawled out from under the poncho and reached for his knife but it was gone. He rose slowly and glared at the men, anger welling inside. The 82nd boys looked nervous and sweaty, but no one confessed to lifting the knife. Winters knew this was neither the time nor the place to raise hell, so he tersely said, "I know where we are. This way," and led them northeastward toward the beach.

By 0230 the group was well away from Ste. Mere-Eglise and a few more Easy Company men had latched on, including Lieutenant Lynn "Buck" Compton, Sergeant Bill Guarnere and Corporal Don Malarkey. Like Winters, Lipton, Compton and Guarnere had lost their weapons in the jump. Lipton had managed to pick up an M1 carbine, but Compton and Guarnere were armed only with jump knives. Earlier that night, Guarnere, toughened from growing up on the streets of South Philadelphia, had jumped a man in the darkness and, holding the knife to his throat, hissed, "Whose side are you on?"

"I'm an American," the frightened man squealed.

"Yeah," Guarnere said, "but whose side are you on?"

The man finally convinced Guarnere he was a friend.

With Compton was Corporal Joseph Toye, sporting a bandaged right hand and in obvious pain.

"What happened, Joe?" Winters asked, indicating the wound.

"Stupidity," the tough ex-coal miner from Pittston, Pennsylvania, replied. "I thought I could get out of the plane easier if I wrapped the rope from my leg bag around my hand. When I jumped, the goddamned bag fell away and the rope bit into my hand. Cut it clean to the bone. But I can still fire a weapon, Lieutenant. I didn't come here to sit in no aid station."

"Glad you're here," Winters said. "But the first chance we have, you get that taken care of. You're more help to me if you have two hands."

About 0300 the group came across Lieutenant Colonel Robert Cole, commander of the 3rd Battalion of the 502nd with about fifty men. Cole was leading his column toward his objective, Causeway 3 and the coastal batteries at Ste. Martin-de-Varreville. Since that was roughly the same direction Winters and his fifteen men were going, they fell in line. Groping their way through the predawn darkness, Winters watched in disbelief as Cole studied his map with the aid of an unshielded flashlight. Winters knew Cole and considered him a man who felt invincible, that he could never be hit, and he doubtless would have scoffed at the young lieutenant's discomfort over his blatant breach of normal safety and common sense. Cole's bravado would earn him the Congressional Medal of Honor a few days later but would cost him his life in Holland.

Within minutes of joining Cole's group, they were stopped by the approaching sound of clopping horses' hooves and the creak of wooden wheels and leather harness moving toward them along the dark Norman road. At Cole's signal, the men dispersed along both sides of the road, hunching down among the underbrush. The men who had lost their weapons in the jump,

Winters, Guarnere, Compton and Lipton, stayed back. Four horse-drawn German supply wagons now appeared on the road, accompanied by a platoon of infantry. As they drew near, Cole's trap was prematurely sprung when his men opened fire too soon. In the brief but violent blaze of gunfire, men yelled, cursed and screamed, horses whinnied, and bullets whistled through the air and thudded into flesh. Two of the wagons managed to get turned around and tore away, but the drivers of the other two, plus several of the infantrymen, were cut down. When the shooting stopped a number of Germans lay dead and ten had surrendered. But the Americans had not come through it unscathed. One of Cole's officers, Major J. W. Vaughn, had been killed.

With the fight over, there was a wild scramble for guns and souvenirs. Winters and Guarnere joined the macabre scavenger hunt, each coming away with a pistol. The guns were small and almost toylike, but at least the two men were now armed and felt less helpless.

The first blue-gray streaks of dawn were tinting the eastern sky as the column reached an intersection with a road Winters knew to be the D-14, the one he'd been seeking. Bidding Cole farewell and good luck, Winters and his men wearily peeled off, each column now heading for its assigned objective. Half an hour or so later, Winters and his men stumbled upon another German supply wagon. It had been recently shot up, probably by Allied fighters prowling overhead, and sat abandoned by the roadside, its dead driver slumped across the seat. Hoping to find a more effective weapon than the scrawny pistol he'd picked up earlier, Winters searched the wagon and was amazed to find an M1 Garand. Evidently the German had also been collecting souvenirs before the Army Air Forces ended his career. Bumming ammo clips from some of the other men, Winters now felt ready to fight for the first time since he'd jumped into France.

Shortly after daybreak, the distant booming of large naval guns rumbled across the fields, the first indication that the amphibious landings were underway. American shells began streaking inland, unseen but loudly splitting the air as they passed overhead. Winters and his men felt comfort in that they were no longer alone.

The closer they got to their objective, the more friends they came across, including about twenty-five men from D Company, led by Captain Jerre S. Gross, whom Winters knew to be a capable and talented officer. No sooner had Dog Company fallen in than the column caught up to 2nd Battalion headquarters; forty men led by Lieutenant Colonel Robert Strayer. Along with Strayer was Major Oliver Horton, the battalion's executive officer, and Captains Clarence Hester, the competent battalion S3, and Winters' good friend, Lewis Nixon, who was Strayer's S2.

"Glad to see you, Winters," Strayer greeted him as the lieutenant reported in.

"Thank you, sir," he replied. "It took us a while to figure out where we were."

Winters asked about First Lieutenant Thomas Meehan, Easy's commander, whom he had last seen at the airstrip in England.

"No one has seen Meehan, nor anyone else from Easy's HQ," Horton responded. "Until we do, it's your company, Dick."

Second Battalion now consisted of about eighty officers and men. Easy Company was made up of two officers, nine enlisted men, two light .30 caliber machine guns, a bazooka for which there was no ammo, and a 60 mm mortar.

Still three kilometers from Ste. Marie-du-Mont by 0930, the battalion filed through the small village of le Grand Chemin, weapons held at the ready. Most of the inhabitants of this hamlet were farmworkers from a large estate called Brecourt Manor, whose buildings could be seen ahead. The estate was owned by a retired French Army colonel named de Vallavieille, a veteran of the Marne and Verdun thirty years earlier. This war had cost him two of his sons, a captain and a sergeant, both lost during the Battle of France in 1940. Now sixty-nine, the old army officer hid with the rest of his family, including his two surviving sons, Louis, nineteen, and Michel, twenty-four, inside their large home, along with two of his farmworkers, their wives and a baby.

Located just a few miles inland from Utah Beach, Brecourt's roads were dotted with dead horses and abandoned German equipment, victims of aerial strafing. Some of the Americans felt a tinge of sorrow for the horses, caught up in the fury of war, killed simply because men had not learned to live together in peace.

Outside the village, near where the D-913 met the D-14, the advancing column was greeted by the distinct rapid staccato of a German MG-42 machine gun. Men instinctively scrambled for cover by the road embankment, which was high enough to offer protection from the flying lead. Safe in this sunken road, Winters relaxed against the embankment, taking a breather for the first time since he'd landed. The harassing fire was coming from a tree line about 350 yards to the battalion's right. Strayer ordered D Company to silence the gun. Gross handed the job over to the young Lieutenant John Kelly, who inexpertly deployed his men and launched a frontal assault without first reconnoitering the ground. The company ran headlong into heavy fire and was pinned down for several minutes before working its way back to the road, luckily without casualties.

Winters was still resting when Lieutenant George Lavenson, Strayer's aide, found him.

"Strayer wants you up front," Lavenson said.

Winters found Strayer and Hester talking with a harried Lieutenant Kelly. Winters stood silently near the small group. Hester soon turned to him.

"There's a battery of 88s along a tree line in a field to our right, with a direct line of fire on Causeway Two," Hester said without preamble. "Colonel Strayer wants you to take Easy and knock them out."

Hester then turned and walked away without any further instructions.

Blessed with a keen tactical mind, Winters did not want to repeat Kelly's mistake; he planned to see what he was up against. Creeping cautiously along a small hedgerow, he moved within sight of the German position. The enemy was located in an L-shaped trench about 400 yards long, with three 105 mm guns, which the Americans mistook for 88s, facing northwest toward Causeway 2, and a fourth 105 turned in the direction of Causeway 3. The guns were heavily camouflaged, which explained why Allied fighter-bombers hadn't spotted them and knocked them out in the preinvasion attacks. In the bend of the L, between the first and second guns, was the MG-42 that had taken the battalion under fire. Across the field in front of the guns, hidden in another hedgerow, three more machine guns were set up to cover the artillery in case of an attack from the beach. However, with the threat currently coming from behind, those weapons were now facing the road. To Winters' right, he spotted two long hedgerows that ran parallel to the one he was now in, and perpendicular to the German position. These hedges almost, but not quite, intersected the German position. He would use these for his approach.

Making his way back to the road, Winters gathered Easy Company. Besides Compton, he had ten men; Sergeants Lipton, Toye and Guarnere, Corporals Malarkey and Robert "Popeye" Wynn, and Privates Mike Ranney, Cleveland O. Petty, Joseph D. Liebgott, Walter Hendrix and John Plesha Jr. Winters outlined the mission.

"How many Krauts are we lookin' at?" Guarnere asked, glancing around.

"Don't know, Bill," Winters replied. "Why?"

"No reason." The feisty sergeant shrugged.

Private Gerald Lorraine, Colonel Sink's driver, but currently jeepless since he'd been unable to find the colonel, was standing nearby. He hurried up to Winters.

"Lieutenant," he said. "I'd like to go along if you can use me."

"Certainly can," Winters replied. "Glad for the help."

Laying out his assault plan, Winters said, "This will be a double envelopment. Buck, you take Lipton, Toye, Lorraine, Popeye and Ranney along that first hedgerow. Everyone else is on me. We'll move along the second hedgerow; that way we can't all get pinned down at once."

Turning to the two machine gun crews, Petty and Liebgott on one, and Hendrix and Plesha on the second, Winters said, "When we get out there, you'll position your guns to give us a base of fire. Lipton, you and Ranney move to the right and secure that flank. Lip, you have a demolition kit in that musette bag, right?" Lipton nodded. "When you see we've taken the first gun, bring it up fast." Winters next turned to Compton. "Buck, Malarkey, Popeye. Get close to that machine gun and put grenades on it. Then we all run like hell for the trench. Speed is everything. We've got to hit them hard and fast, and get into that trench before they can react. Then we'll concentrate on the first gun, take it, then go after the rest one by one. Questions? Okay, drop everything except your weapons and ammo. Stay alert. Don't do anything foolish. Follow me."

Hunched over and moving quickly, the two groups moved along the hedgerows undetected. Once in position, Winters saw that Petty and Liebgott's machine gun could fire point-blank on the first artillery piece. He crawled over to his gunners.

"You're in a good spot," he told them. "Hold your fire until you have a definite target. Don't give away your position too soon."

Ranney and Lipton got to their assigned spot near the rusted hulk of an abandoned truck. Visibility was poor, so Lipton slung his carbine around his neck and climbed a young tree. Perched precariously on thin branches and in front of the slender trunk, the position provided him a clean line of sight, but soon exposed him to German return fire. It was a rookie mistake that, luckily, Lipton would live to learn from.

Once everyone was set, Winters took a deep breath. This was it, his first experience leading men in combat. Resolved, he signaled Liebgott to open fire. The machine gun blazed to life, its .30 caliber slugs raking the trench and kicking up plumes of dirt. The rest of the men joined in, providing cover fire for Compton and his group. The enemy machine gun responded, and Germans in the trench opened up with their Mauser rifles. A German helmet poked up above the trench. Winters aimed his M1 and squeezed off a round. The helmet dropped out of sight. He later found a pool of blood at the spot but no sign of the German.

Compton finally got his team into position. The three men slipped grenades from their web gear, yanked out the pins and hurled the "pineapples" at the gun. Seeing that, Winters yelled, "Come on! Follow me!" He leaped to his feet and ran forward, the others close behind. The exploding grenades knocked out the MG-42 and its crew, but bullets from Germans in the trench and the machine guns in the distant tree line buzzed around the Americans like hornets, kicking up dirt devils at their feet as they charged. Reaching the trench, the GIs leaped into it safe, but not sound. As he dove for cover, Wynn yelped when a bullet struck him in the buttocks. Writhing on the bottom of the trench, and bleeding into his ripped trousers, he kept apologizing to Winters.

"I'm sorry, sir. I goofed," he cried. "I messed up. I'm sorry, Lieutenant."

A German potato masher grenade thrown from the nearby artillery position landed among the men, almost at Toye's feet.

"Grenade!" Winters yelled. "Move, for Christ's sake, move!"

Men dove in all directions. Toye flopped over backward as the grenade went off, shattering the stock of his M1. The Americans tossed grenades back. As they exploded, Lorraine, Guarnere and Winters stormed the gun position, weapons blazing. Three Germans leaped from the trench and ran toward their comrades in the opposite tree line.

"Nail 'em," Winters yelled and swung his rifle up to his shoulder.

The M1 bucked and a single round caught one man in the back of the head. He fell like a rag doll. A burst from Lorraine's Thompson killed a second German, but Guarnere missed his man. Winters raised his rifle, fired, and hit the fleeing soldier in the back. Guarnere let loose with a burst that struck the wounded man yet failed to kill him.

"*Hilfe, hilfe,*" the wounded German called over and over, yelling for help.

Winters turned to Malarkey, who'd just caught up, and said, "Finish him." Malarkey aimed and put a bullet through the man's head. A fourth German leaped from the trench and ran for the distant hedgerow. Winters took careful aim and fired. The fleeing man spun to the ground as if punched by an invisible fist and lay still. Only about twenty seconds had elapsed since Easy Company had gained the trench, and they had already silenced one gun. Quickly assessing his situation, Winters thought, "Jesus Christ. Somebody will cut loose any minute now from farther up the trench." Keeping his head low, he scouted ahead and found a pair of Germans setting up a machine gun. Winters squeezed off two quick shots, striking the gunner in the hip and the other man in the shoulder.

"Buck, Joe," Winters called to Compton and Toye. He pointed toward the next gun emplacement. "Put fire on that position." Their weapons immediately blazed to life. Suddenly Malarkey leaped out of the trench and Winters watched horror stricken as he raced toward the bodies sprawled in the field. Malarkey had often talked about picking up a Luger as a souvenir, and he thought he'd seen one on one of the dead men.

"Get back here, you idiot," Winters yelled. "This area is lousy with Krauts!"

Luck was with Malarkey. The Germans let up their fire, possibly thinking only a medic would dare expose himself like that. Malarkey reached the dead man only to find the "Luger" was in fact a gun sight for one of the 105s. Now aware of his vulnerable predicament, Malarkey jumped up and raced madly back to the trench as bullets chewed angrily at the ground near his feet. In the trench, Guarnere and others laid down covering fire. Leaping into the first gun emplacement, Malarkey crawled under the silent 105 as bullets twanged off the metal. He lay there several minutes until he was able to move to a more protected part of the trench. Malarkey had survived the Germans, but now had to face his lieutenant.

"Dammit, Don, what the hell's the matter with you?" Winters yelled, furious at the lapse in training shown by this usually superb NCO. "You ever pull a bonehead stunt like that again and it won't be the Germans you'll have to worry about."

Winters sent the chagrined Malarkey out to the right, beyond the first gun, to secure that flank, and moved back to where Wynn lay, still apologizing for getting hit. "I can't spare anyone to help you back, Popeye," Winters told him. "Can you make it on your own?" Wynn said he could, so Winters and Compton hoisted their wounded friend out of the trench, warned him to keep low, and sent him on his way. He was no sooner gone than Compton yelled, "Look out! Grenade!" He'd yanked a pin from a grenade and was about to toss it when it slipped from his hand.

In the narrow confines of the trench, there was nowhere to go but down, so the men hit the dirt as the grenade went off, again near Toye.

"Jesus Christ," he muttered, shaken but unhurt by this second brush with death.

Toye wasn't the only one rattled by the explosion. A German hiding nearby came running forward, his hands in the air. He was the Americans' first prisoner. Winters tried to point the man to the rear but they could not communicate, since no one in the group spoke German. Lorraine slipped on a set of brass knuckles and belted the man.

Winters detested such treatment of prisoners. "That's enough, Lorraine," he ordered.

Lorraine backed off. The Nazi soldier lay moaning, and Winters kicked him in the behind. He rose to his feet and again Winters indicated he was to go to the rear. Winters did not approve of Lorraine's action, but the sock to the jaw had evidently broken down the language barrier, and the prisoner headed rearward.

Three more Germans now approached, all armed.

"Set your range for two hundred yards," Winters quietly told the men.

At about 225 yards, an overeager Lorraine opened up with his Thompson. The enemy returned fire. One German was wounded in the short firefight, but all got away.

Winters now prepared to attack the second gun. After first making prisoners of the two German machine gunners he'd wounded earlier, he left three men to hold the first 105 and moved the rest closer to the second, keeping low to avoid the enemy fire still coming from the opposing hedgerow and from another machine gun near the manor house that had just joined in. On Winters' signal, the Americans attacked quickly, firing their weapons and tossing grenades as they charged. The enemy fled except for six men who walked forward, hands over their heads and saying in stilted English, "No make me dead."

After a delay caused in part by Lipton stopping to apply sulfa powder to Wynn's wounded backside, Lipton and Ranney finally caught up to Winters. However, Lipton soon realized he'd left the demolition kit with the explosives, fuses and percussion caps in his musette bag back at the road when the men had dumped their excess gear. Embarrassed, he quickly crawled away to retrieve the bag.

As Winters turned his attention to the third gun, he got a modicum of help in the form of two men from other companies. While he did not recognize one of them, the other was Private First Class John D. Hall of A Company, whom Winters knew from his days of coaching the regiment's basketball team.

"We thought maybe you could use some help, Coach," Hall said.

"I certainly can, Hall. Thanks," Winters replied earnestly, and quickly briefed the two on what had been done so far and what was next.

In taking the first two guns, Winters and his men had made one concerted push each time, moving rapidly through the trench with the always-aggressive Guarnere leading the way. Just before they'd left England, Guarnere had learned that his brother Henry, a medic, had been killed in Italy. Anger burned inside him, and he eagerly took to his role, although Winters worried that it led Guarnere to take dangerous and unnecessary chances.

To take this third gun, Winters opted on a quick, three-pronged attack, sending Hall up the trench while he, Compton and Guarnere would attack on the outside, with Winters on the left, and Compton and Guarnere on the right, even though this would briefly expose all to fire from across the field. At Winters' signal, the four men charged, firing as they ran. Guarnere sprayed the emplacement with his Tommy gun, killing several of the crew. Six more Germans surrendered, but Hall was killed. This was a blow to Winters, who had liked Hall's ambition. Kneeling over the body as it lay sprawled in the trench, Winters felt twinges of sorrow. Up until then the war had not been completely real for him. But now, leaning over the battered body of his young friend, retrieving the dog tags that he knew would be used in order to notify Hall's family of his death, Winters began to fully understand the true horror of combat.

Winters rose. Hall was the first, but would not be the last. Winters would grieve for them all more completely when there was time. For now, though, he turned his attention to the third gun emplacement, where he'd noticed a command center with radio and direction-finding equipment. Poking through the papers left behind by the fleeing enemy, he discovered maps that denoted gun positions. It took just a few moments for Winters to realize this map pinpointed artillery and machine gun emplacements all over the Cotentin Peninsula. He had to get it back to Strayer. After ordering the radios destroyed, Winters spotted the man who had arrived with Hall and handed him the maps.

"Tell my machine guns to come up and join me," he told the soldier, wondering why they hadn't already done so. "Then take these to battalion. Tell Colonel Strayer we've taken three guns but, in order to take the fourth, we must have reinforcements and more ammo."

The man nodded and left. Winters waited. And waited. After a while Buck Compton joined him.

"We're spread awfully thin, Dick," he said. "If the Krauts get their shit together and attack us, they'll plow us under."

"I'm fully aware of that, Buck," Winters replied. "I sent a man back for help, but so far, nothing."

"Maybe he didn't make it," Compton said.

"Maybe." Winters paused, then added, "Take over here. I'm going myself."

Slipping over the rim of the trench, he crawled rearward through the grass, keeping as flat as possible to avoid the machine gun bullets flying by just overhead. Winters came across the body of an American. Drawing closer he recognized the man as Warrant Officer Andrew Hill. Earlier in the fight, while working his way around behind the trench to join Easy Company, Hill had met Lipton and Ranney. Crawling forward together the three ran into the man Winters had sent to the rear with the maps, who asked, "Where's HQ?" Lipton looked back at Hill, who raised his head to reply. Before he could utter a word, however, a German machine gun bullet punched through his helmet and into his forehead. When Winters came across Hill, the young man lay on his back, his right arm extended upward. Crawling past the body, Winters noted a watch on Hill's right arm. For some reason the watch played on Winters' mind and, after he was several yards beyond the body, Winters thought, "Hell, I could use that watch," and turned around. Heading back another thought struck him. "You're nuts!" he chided himself. "This watch isn't worth it." Reaching Hill, Winters unstrapped the watch, pocketed it and again crawled toward battalion.

At the road, Winters found Strayer and his staff sitting unconcernedly, studying the captured maps. Tired, sweaty and with the adrenaline of battle pumping through his blood, the sight of this seeming indifference by his superior officer while he and his men were hanging on to the trench by their fingernails, caused the usually soft-spoken Winters to erupt.

"Goddamit!" he yelled at the officers who now stared at him, mouths agape. "When I send for ammunition and help, I mean now! Not when you get around to it!"

None of them had ever seen Winters that mad. Standing there in the road, hand tightly clutching his Garand, his sweaty uniform streaked with dirt and grass stains, a smear of Hall's blood on his sleeve, Winters was a ferocious figure. The image had the desired effect. Bandoliers of ammo were suddenly being heaped on him. Hester said he'd send up Lieutenant Ronald Speirs of D Company with some reinforcements, and that he himself would bring more explosives.

Private Len Hicks of F Company heard the exchange and said, "Lieutenant Winters, I'd like to help."

"Okay, Hicks," Winters said. "See if anyone else from Fox Company wants to come along, and bring them."

With assurances that help was coming, Winters returned to his men.

Hester was as good as his word. He brought the TNT charges plus new instructions from Strayer.

"The battalion is moving on to Ste. Marie-du-Mont," he said. "Strayer sent Nixon to the beach with those maps you found. The colonel wants you to mop up here, then catch up."

Winters and Hester slipped the TNT charges down the barrels of the three 105s and set them off with incendiary grenades. The blasts split the barrels like banana peels. By now a dismayed Lipton had returned with his TNT satchel, only to see the guns had already been disabled.

Speirs arrived, bringing along Hicks, Sergeant Julian "Rusty" Houch, the F Company clerk, and privates Jumbo DiMarzio, Ray Taylor and another man. They immediately set about knocking out the fourth gun. Houch and Hicks crawled through the grass toward the Germans. Hicks nodded and Houch rose to throw a grenade. From somewhere, a Schmeisser machine gun opened up, its slugs tearing into Houch, who fell dead. Speirs, an aggressive leader, jumped up and led his men forward. Hicks fell, struck in the leg, and a second man was severely wounded. Speirs leaped into the gun pit alone, causing the startled Germans to flee. Speirs cut them down with fire from his Tommy gun.

After dispatching this gun as they had the other three, with TNT and a grenade, and with ammo running low, Winters decided it was time to leave.

"Can you make it back okay?" Winters asked the injured Hicks. When Hicks said he could, Winters ordered his machine guns to lay down covering fire as the Americans began pulling back to the road. As was his custom, Winters was the last man out. Leaving the trench, he spotted the two Germans he'd first wounded. Left behind, they again began setting up their machine gun. Winters shot them both dead.

Once the company had reassembled at the road, Winters ordered Malarkey to drop mortar rounds on the Germans at the Brecourt Manor house. Malarkey, who did not have the base plate or bipod for the 60 mm mortar, bore-sighted the weapon. He dropped fifteen rounds on the farm with remarkable accuracy, eventually breaking every window in the building, despite the fact that the mortar burrowed itself in the dirt with each recoil. Winters was impressed by Malarkey's "God-given touch" with the mortar. After he ceased fire, Malarkey set about trying to disinter his mortar. An elderly French man ran out of a nearby building carrying a shovel and helped Malarkey dig out the tube.

Winters began contemplating his next move in what Strayer referred to as a "mop-up," when he heard a rumble of engines and the clank of treads on the road. Two Sherman tanks from the 4th Division appeared with Nixon riding the lead one.

"Brought you a present," Nixon said, jumping down, a huge grin on his handsome face. "The first two tanks to come off Utah Beach. I thought you could use some help."

"I think I can find something for them to do," Winters said. "Thanks, Nix."

As the tanks drew to a halt, more help arrived in the form of Lieutenant Harry Welsh and about thirty men. Winters told Welsh, his assistant platoon leader, to have his men stand by in case they were needed, then crawled up on the lead tank. Getting nose to nose with the commander in order to be heard over the engine, he briefed the man on what needed to be done. Winters jumped down from the tank and instructed the same men who'd accompanied him in the earlier attack, minus the wounded Wynn, to follow along behind for support. The Shermans clanked toward the German positions, Winters guiding them with hand signals. At Winters' direction, the tanks opened up, sweeping the tree line with their .50 and .30 caliber machine guns. The impact of the heavy slugs chewed through the hedges and trees with devastating effect, convincing the Germans it was time to leave. Winters next had the tanks turn their weapons on the manor itself. Again, the machine guns roared. The added punch of American armor drove the last of the enemy away. Causeway 2 was now clear. Thanking the tank commander, Winters surveyed the field once more, then turned and led Easy Company toward Ste. Marie-du-Mont.

★   ★   ★

The fight at Brecourt had taken about three hours, during which Winters' small band had attacked a position held by about fifty Germans of the 6th Battery, 90th Regiment. Fifteen enemy had been killed and twelve captured. All four 105s had been destroyed. Winters listed his losses as two wounded and four dead, although he later learned that the one man of Speirs' group whom he thought had been killed had, in fact, survived.

Weeks later, just before the regiment was returned to England, Colonel Sink called on Winters at his headquarters tent. "I've just been going through your after-action report from Brecourt," he said. "That was a fine piece of soldiering, Dick. I'm recommending you for the Congressional Medal of Honor. I think you deserve it. I'll also accept any award recommendations you have for the men who were with you. Have them on my desk by tomorrow."

For their action at Brecourt on June 6, 1944, Winters nominated Guarnere for a Distinguished Service Cross, which Strayer downgraded to the Silver Star. Compton, Lorraine and Toye also received the Silver Star; Lipton, Malarkey, Ranney, Liebgott, Hendrix, Plesha, Petty and Wynn each received the Bronze Star. As for Winters' Medal of Honor nomination, General Maxwell Taylor, the division commander, had decreed that only one be awarded to the 101st. It went to Colonel Cole, downgrading Winters to the Distinguished Service Cross. He received it from General Omar Bradley during a parade ground ceremony on July 1.

Later, Winters discovered that during the whole fight at Brecourt, a French family had been hiding in a large, deep sink hole, out in the middle of the field. They'd taken shelter there when they heard the rumble of shells coming from the shore and cowered in the hole during the entire battle as bullets zipped by overhead. Knowing the anxiety he felt that day, Winters later said he could only imagine the terror that family must have experienced. To his regret, he also learned that Michel De Vallavielle had been shot in the back while surrendering to a paratrooper who incorrectly assumed that since the guns were on his family's land, he was a collaborator. The teenager survived.

★   ★   ★

The 506th spent its first full night in France dug in along a hedgerow outside Ste. Marie-du-Mont. Winters remained in command of Easy as there was still no word of Lieutenant Meehan. Concern for his commander's fate was not alleviated by Harry Welsh.

"When I was coming down this morning," Welsh said, "I drifted over a burning C-47 lying in a field outside of Ste. Mere-Eglise. Think that might've been Meehan's?"

"God, I hope not, Harry," Winters replied sincerely, remembering the last time he saw the smiling Irishman, as they boarded the planes in England. "I keep hoping he'll show up."

Winters thought about Meehan, whom he had known for such a short time, and about Meehan's young wife, Anne.

"Thank God I'm not married," he thought.

"But you don't think he'll catch up, do you?" Welsh asked, breaking Winters' reverie.

"What concerns me is that it isn't just Meehan," Winters replied. "No one's seen anyone from that plane; not Sergeant Evans or Carl Riggs, Dick Owens, Herm Collins. None of them. That's not good."

Winters settled down and tried to sleep, exhausted by the day's exertions, both physical and mental. But German infantry in another hedgerow across an open field kept firing their weapons into the dark and shouting. Unable to sleep, Winters decided to get up and make a personal reconnaissance. Walking quietly along a footpath in the dark, he heard the approaching clatter of hob-nailed boots and froze.

"Krauts," he thought. Dropping into a ditch, he huddled there quietly as a German patrol walked by, passing so close that Winters caught a whiff of strong German tobacco. As the enemy moved away he blessed the U.S. Army for using rubber-soled boots.

Back safely with the company, Winters lay on the ground by Welsh. Having no blanket to cover himself—his was still in some farmer's field inside his lost leg bag—Winters took some newspaper he'd liberated earlier in the day and formed a small tent over his face and upper body. This was less for warmth than it was to keep away the mosquitoes he could hear bouncing off the newspaper.

Before closing his eyes that night, Winters realized he hadn't said his prayers, so he rolled over and got to his knees. Welsh watched somberly.

"Dick," he said following Winters' amen, "I'm Catholic, and when I get back home, I'll go to church every Sunday and pray. But I won't pray here."

Welsh kept his word. But Winters prayed, and that night he thanked God for surviving this first, terrible day, and asked Him to watch over him the next day. He also made a vow that after the war he would settle down in some quiet place and live the remainder of his life in peace.

CHAPTER 2

"$21 a Day, Once a Month."

January 21, 1918–August 25, 1942

Richard Davis Winters was born in Lancaster General Hospital in Lancaster, Pennsylvania, on Monday, January 21, 1918, during a week-long stretch of intense winter cold that would culminate the next day with a crippling snowstorm that paralyzed much of the East Coast.

His father, Richard Nagle Winters, was twenty-six when his son arrived. Born on August 29, 1891, he was the sixth generation of a family that could trace its American roots back to Timothy Winters, an Englishman who immigrated to colonial Pennsylvania in the late 1760s. In 1778, three years after the Revolutionary War broke out in Massachusetts, Timothy Winters enlisted in the 1st Pennsylvania Regiment. Nicknamed the "First Defenders," the regiment was commanded by Lieutenant Colonel Thomas Robinson. Timothy Winters evidently served with distinction, as evidenced by his promotion to corporal on September 1, 1780. He served with the regiment in its numerous engagements, including the last one, the Battle of Yorktown in October 1781, when British forces, hemmed in by land and sea, surrendered to General George Washington.

One hundred forty years after Timothy Winters arrived back home and hung up his Brown Bess on pegs over the fireplace, young Dick Winters' father worked as a general foreman for Edison Electric Company, with an office on the third floor of what still is Lancaster's tallest structure, the thirteen-story Greist Building. The boy's mother, Edith Esbenshade Winters, was a housewife, tending the home and raising her children with a loving, yet firm hand. Born August 26, 1896, Edith Winters was raised in the Lancaster County Mennonite traditions of respect, discipline and hard work, traits her young son learned well and would embrace throughout his life.

For the first three years after Dick Winters' birth, the family lived in the small town of New Holland, near where Edith had been raised. Her father, Serenus Herr Esbenshade, had been born in Paradise, Pennsylvania, on April 13, 1857, and spent most of his life as a farmer in Strasburg Township, tilling the rich, black earth of the fertile Mill Creek Valley. He retired from farming in 1912 and moved to Lancaster, taking a job as an attendant at a city parking lot. Emma Neff Casky Esbenshade, Edith's mother, was born April 26, 1861. A friendly but reserved woman, at family gatherings she and young Dick would quietly sit and cast smiles back and forth at the boisterous talk and laughter of the rest of the clan.

In 1921 Richard Winters moved his small family to Ephrata, a bustling town about eight miles northwest of New Holland. Here they shared a large, two-and-a-half-story wooden frame house that still stands at 41 East Fulton Street with the boy's paternal grandmother, Catherine A. "Kate" Shirk Winters. Born in 1862, Kate was the widow of William Davis Winters, one of Lancaster County's most prominent hotel men. William Winters had carved a name for himself in the community years earlier as owner of the Ephrata House, a three-story hotel at 46 East Main Street. Built between 1864 and 1866 by a carriage maker named George S. Wise, who had his shop at the rear, the building changed hands three times before being bought in 1877 by Barton N. Winters, William's uncle. Ten years later, Barton sold the business to his nephew, who extensively remodeled the structure. He removed the old Wise carriage shop and added a distinctive mansard roof, traces of which can still be seen today. With his renovations, the local newspaper, the *Ephrata Review*, said the building "almost lost all trace of its former plan." Winters added a poolroom in 1897, which quickly became a popular gathering place for the town's male population. Two years later the property left the Winters family when it was sold for $20,000. Now William Winters, who had taken to strong drink, briefly owned and operated a liquor store in Lancaster. However, he soon returned to Ephrata to manage the Hotel Cocalico, which stood at Main and Lake streets in Ephrata and was one of the most luxurious hotels in eastern Pennsylvania. Four years later, on June 22, 1910, William Davis Winters' alcohol consumption caught up to him and he died at his home.

The 1920s were an enjoyable time for young Dick Winters, growing up in a small, rural town. Living on the edge of the borough, he played in adjacent fields and explored the woods behind his home. Immediately west of the house was a railroad line, and the boy spent many hours watching with keen interest as steam locomotives chugged past, smoke billowing from their stacks. Sometimes they pulled passenger cars filled with travelers, possibly heading for a seaside excursion to Atlantic City. More often, the trains hauled open cars heaped with coal or boxcars of freight or livestock. Between Winters' house and the tracks stood a small stockyard where beef and dairy cattle were housed while being shipped in to local farmers, or out for market. Horses also passed through the stockyards, since Ephrata boasted two large commercial stables. The boy spent many a day climbing on the weathered wooden fence rails to watch the animals chomping on the hay that was stored in a nearby barn. If he was lucky, a careless attendant would leave the hay barn unlocked, and Winters would sneak inside to play among the stacked bales.

The presence of the stockyard provided the young boy with an outlet for his vivid imagination and perhaps piqued his later interest in farming. Tying string around long, wooden sticks, he would then drag them around his backyard.

"What do you have there?" his father would ask.

"These are my cows," the boy replied, and proceeded to tell him about each and every "animal" in the herd. His father was highly amused by this, and in later life often teased his son with this memory of his days as an imaginary cattleman.

When he wasn't haunting the stockyards, or the nearby lumberyard and coal yards that also lined the railroad tracks near his home, Winters would cross Fulton Street to his father's sister's house. Charlotte Winters Gardner was the young boy's favorite aunt, and he spent many happy hours with her. A petite woman and mother of two children, Lottie was saddled with the huge task of having to attend her husband. Charles C. Gardner, a captain in the U.S. Army during what was then called the Great War, had been gassed late in the conflict. Now seriously ill, he was bedridden. Despite this burden, Lottie never lost her sense of humor, and always had time for her young nephew. Hand in hand, the two often walked downtown to the Grand Theater, where they enjoyed the silent cowboy movies.

Behind Lottie's house flowed the small trickle known as Gross Run. With abundant optimism, Winters would tie a safety pin to a string, attach it to a pole and go fishing in the run. His two favorite fishing holes were directly behind Lottie's house by a railroad trestle or four houses to the east, behind the home of a widow named Nettie Hull. Here by this stream, which was about four feet wide and seldom more than twelve inches deep, he and his makeshift fishing pole spent many patient hours in hopes of landing a fish. His parents thought the scene was funny as hell, but the boy was intent and serious.

To help make ends meet, Kate Winters rented out a small, two-story building behind the main house. Called the Summer House, it was inhabited during this time by a family named Fassnacht, and young Winters became good friends with their son, Hank. The two boys spent a great deal of their youth together. Both would serve in the army during the war, although not in the same unit. Winters later recalled how Fassnacht visited him in camp one day and was impressed by the spit-and-polish atmosphere of the airborne. Fassnacht also showed up in Holland just after Winters and his men arrived back from several weeks on the line. The paratroopers startled Fassnacht since, in Winters' words, they were "a pretty tough-looking bunch." The boyhood pals would never meet again.

On Sundays, the Winters family attended the Bethany Reformed Church on East Main Street, where the boy was enrolled in Sunday School. Winters' most vivid boyhood recollection of those days was the annual Christmas pageant staged by the youth of the church. Unaccustomed to public speaking, he broke out in a cold sweat whenever he had to stand up and speak before the congregation.

By contrast, Winters' maternal grandfather, Serenus, whose most memorable features were his full white beard and sideburns, and his round, wire-rimmed spectacles, sometimes took the boy to church with him. He was a member of an older order Mennonite sect, where congregants sat on hard, backless wooden benches. Serenus and the boy sat on one side of the aisle with the men, while his Grandma Emma and the women sat on the other side, a typical seating arrangement in Lancaster County's plain Mennonite community.

When it came time for school, Winters entered the first grade at Franklin Street Elementary School, an austere two-story brick structure with a heavy, iron school bell that clanged from its belfry. Located just two blocks from his home, it was an easy walk for the boy. While his memories of this time have faded with the years, Winters vividly recalled his first-grade teacher, Miss Killian, whom he fondly remembered as "a wonderfully kind woman who was great with young children." One especially crisp memory was the day she spotted Winters writing on a piece of paper and holding the pencil in his left hand. Being left-handed was often frowned upon, and it was not uncommon for teachers and parents to smack a child's left hand if he or she showed tendencies of being a southpaw. Miss Killian walked up to the boy, removed the pencil from his left hand and placed it in the other.

"Why don't you try writing with your right hand, Dick," she said. Winters admired Miss Killian and was so afraid to disappoint her that he never again held the pencil in his left hand.

In the summer of 1927 Winters' father moved his family from Ephrata to Lancaster to be closer to his work and avoid the twenty-eight-mile round-trip trolley ride each day. He purchased half a double house at 418 South West End Ave. for $7,200, and young Winters was enrolled at the nearby Lancaster Township Junior High School which, despite its name, included grades one to eight.

Weeks later, on August 20, 1927, Great War vet Charles Gardner died, and Winters traveled back to Ephrata with his family to attend the funeral and give what comfort he could to Lottie.

Unfortunately for Winters' father, two years after he bought the house, the New York Stock Exchange nose-dived with unprecedented losses, heralding the Great Depression. The elder Winters managed to keep his job throughout the economic chaos that now swept the nation, sparing the family the severe hardship felt by millions of others as the Depression deepened. Richard Winters brought home about fifty dollars per week, so there was always food on the table. To bring in extra needed income, Edith made corsets in her home and sold them door-to-door. Despite those efforts, money was tight and while the struggling family could pay its bills and make the interest payments due on the house, there was little or nothing left to put on the principal. It would not be until Dick Winters entered the airborne and could send home extra money, including his jump pay, that the family had the $6,900 still needed to pay off the mortgage.

That same year, 1929, Edith gave birth to a daughter, Beatrice, who died shortly after birth. Winters never saw his baby sister, but her loss cast a profound sadness over the household. This gloom was lifted immensely in 1931 when his mother gave birth to another girl, Ann. After thirteen years, Winters was no longer an only child.

By that time, Kate Winters had sold her Ephrata home and divided her time after her husband's death between Lottie's home in Ephrata and the Winterses' home in Lancaster. Having his grandmother living in his house again provided good times for young Dick. Not only did they thoroughly enjoy each other's company, but it was economically enriching. As a boy, Winters received an allowance of ten cents a week. To make a little extra money, each spring he and Kate would wander around in fields behind their house, cutting fresh dandelions. After washing the cuttings, Winters would sell them door-to-door in the mornings before going off to school. Whether people bought from him because they liked to eat cooked dandelion, or because they took pity on the boy, he never knew. Either way, it gave him a few more pennies to spend, although not enough to indulge himself in extra activities. When he was twelve, Winters contemplated joining the Boy Scouts, but decided he could afford neither the uniform nor the dues of ten cents per week.

Academically, Winters was doing fairly well at school in spite of himself.

Never a studious child, most of his public school career was spent doing only what was needed in order to pass. Yet he made such a positive impression that principal Elizabeth Martin, who had a reputation for being strict and having little patience for children who failed to put forth an honest effort, took a liking to the boy and he became one of her favorite students. She appointed him the captain of the school safety patrol—his first commission.

In 1934 Winters moved on to Boys High School, where he took an active part in sports, playing guard in basketball and halfback on the football team. His favorite sport, though, was wrestling. He excelled in a technique called leg wrestling, where he would get his opponent down on the mat and then use his legs in a scissors grip. Winters never competed on a wrestling team in school, but on occasion students were sent to individual meets in York or Harrisburg and he'd go along. Winters' love for this sport carried over into his army life. As an officer, he was prohibited from wrestling with the men, so he would leg wrestle with them, thereby having fun without technically laying a hand on them.

Winters' tendency to underachieve in school dismayed his father, who expected his son to go to college, a point he consistently drove home. No one in the family knew how this education would be paid for, but his father was determined it would happen. Edith had expectations for her son. "I want you to become a doctor," she'd tell him. Winters never had the heart to tell his mother that medicine held no appeal.

Since college seemed to be preordained, the increasingly cost-conscious Dick Winters selected Franklin & Marshall, mainly for one sound economic reason; it was located within walking distance of his home, allowing him to save money by not living on campus. To help pay for college, Winters, now eighteen, took a job at Cohen's grocery store at Manor Street and West End Avenue, near his home. When customers entered the small neighborhood grocery store, Winters issued them a card. As they picked up items around the store, other clerks marked the card, which was then presented to the cashier at the checkout. Winters split his work time with another store owned by Mr. Cohen, located in downtown Lancaster on Prince Street. Winters stocked shelves for twenty-five cents an hour, which seemed like a lot of money to the youth until he took his lunch break at a small nearby restaurant where he paid twenty-five cents, an hour's wage, for a hot dog and a plate of beans.

During the summer between high school and college, Winters' father got him a job with Edison Electric, which by now had changed its name to Pennsylvania Power and Light. Always a hard worker, Dick's job involved tree trimming and digging postholes at twenty-five cents a foot, for which he earned an average of twenty-eight dollars per week. Looking for something that paid a little better, in July he convinced his father to get him assigned to a maintenance crew. Winters' father supervised these work crews, and attached his son to a four-man team assigned to paint the tall metal towers supporting high-tension wires along the fifteen-mile stretch from the southern end of Lancaster to the Susquehanna River. The men scaled the towers to the top, then painted their way down. For this job, Winters was paid big money, forty cents an hour, more if he worked weekends. That was when the crew painted the arms supporting the thick wires. Power would be shut off on one side of the tower on one weekend, and on the other side the next. This work earned Winters time and a half, sixty cents an hour, and he was pulling down between thirty-three dollars and forty dollars a week.

Winters, now old enough to drive, chauffered his mother in the family car while she made her corset deliveries. In the evenings, the house on South West End Avenue would be filled with music as Winters' father would sit down and bang out songs on the piano, and he and his son would regale the family with duets.

After graduating from Boys High School, Winters entered F&M in September 1937. Through his job he had scraped together the $192 for tuition and $15 for textbooks; all used, of course—he was not prepared to pay two or three times that amount for new ones. Cracking open his first college textbook, Winters suddenly realized the extent of his academic skills, or lack of them. After years of doing no more than the bare minimum, Winters was now going to have to knuckle down and study. That meant no time for sports. Now, when he wasn't working at his job, he was poring over textbooks. Reinforcing Winters' newfound work ethic was the sobering realization that he was paying for his education with his own sweat. Bearing that fact in mind, in four years of college, Dick Winters never missed a day of class.

Keenly sensitive to his slender financial base, Winters became almost fanatical in documenting his income and expenses, painstakingly keeping tabs on every penny spent. In 1940, for example, besides normal living expenses, his outlay included seven pairs of socks for three dollars, five dollars for gym shoes, thirteen dollars and fifty cents for the dentist (he had one tooth pulled, four filled and a cleaning that year), one dollar and twenty cents for a sweater and six dollars for a pair of pants. He spent two dollars on a date to Hershey, eighty cents on school supplies and one dollar to attend the PP&L employees picnic.

Despite his tightfisted personal financial policy, he did occasionally allow himself to splurge, spending twenty-five dollars for a trip to New York City in 1940 and two dollars to go see a popular singing group, the Ink Spots, at Hershey in 1938. In a typical year, Winters spent about fifteen dollars on what he called "amusements." These amusements did not include drinking or smoking. As a youth his father, recalling his own father's alcoholism, took the boy aside for a heart-to-heart talk.

"Dick," his dad said. "If at any time you feel you need to have a drink of beer or whiskey, you may, but I want you to do it here at home. And the same for tobacco. If you get the urge to try a cigarette or cigar, that's okay. But again, do it here at home. But if you do take up drinking or smoking, just remember you might not live to grow up."

It was a talk that stuck with Winters the remainder of his life. He also seldom swore, finding he generally didn't need foul language in order to make a point.

Winters' compulsion of accounting for every penny is probably the reason he enrolled in college as a business major and took courses in accounting, advertising and business administration. Yet his actual future goals were far from certain. His favorite courses, the ones he excelled in, were religion and philosophy, because they made him think, and he enjoyed mental exercises. But more importantly, it was these courses that made Winters realize that it would be himself and no one else who would set the standards for his life. His actions and attitudes toward work, toward life and toward other people, would mark his path into the future. This understanding laid within him the foundation for the philosophy that would guide him throughout his life—to go out every day and do the best he could in everything he tried. Winters considered this the most important lesson he took away from F&M.

Naturally, he didn't learn all that at first, and in the beginning, at least, he tried to be one of the "fellas" by joining the Delta Sigma Phi fraternity in 1940. Unfortunately, his frat "buddies" discovered that he had never dated, and set him up with a brunette, convincing him to bring her to a fraternity dance.

"I don't know how to dance," the socially awkward Winters told them. "I don't even know how to hold the girl."

"Just take her out on the floor and walk to the music," was their advice. He did, but spent more time on her feet than on his own.

"I'm sure she recalls that dance even to this day," he said years later.

The two went on one more date, this time to an ice skating rink. Winters loved ice skating, but it proved a painful night for the girl, who could not keep her feet. It was their last date.

Winters soon dropped out of the fraternity. Membership cost eleven dollars and he didn't have the money to spare.

His experience at the frat dance did not mean Winters gave up dating. Following one date with a blond-haired girl that included a trip to an ice hockey game in Hershey, his focus turned to redheads. The first was a nurse, a very intelligent girl, he recalled, who "had something between her ears and could carry on an interesting conversation." He also had a few dates with her roommate, another redhead. By his senior year, though, the academic pressure was so intense that Winters added women to his "do later" list.

The death of Dick's grandmother, Kate Winters, in 1938 affected the twenty-year-old college sophomore profoundly, taking from him one of his most favorite people. Her death was soon followed by another. Serenus Esbenshade had been in poor health for two years. He and Emma had been living with his daughter and son-in-law at 614 Manor Street, an easy walk from the Winters' Lancaster home. In early January 1940, Serenus suffered a stroke that paralyzed him. Four weeks later, on February 8, he died at the age of eighty-two and was laid to rest in the Strasburg Mennonite Cemetery in a plain wooden coffin, in accordance with his older Mennonite tradition.

*   *   *

By the spring of 1941, two thoughts began to dominate young Winters' mind: his upcoming graduation from college, and the ominous situation in Europe. Since the invasion of Poland in 1939, German forces had overrun most of Europe. Even France, once thought to have the finest army on the Continent, fell in just six weeks as a stunned world watched. In the months that followed, Adolf Hitler's hordes, coming to the aid of their faltering Italian ally, had subdued the Balkans and swept across North Africa. England alone had withstood the storm.

About the same time Winters was being handed his diploma at F&M College in June 1941, an amazed world saw Hitler hurl his armies against Russia, scoring one victory after another as they drove across the steppes into the Soviet heartland. And, of course, that wasn't even taking into account Japan and its aggressions in the Far East.

In America, its military emasculated by years of living with the fallacy of isolationism to the point where the size of its armed forces ranked sixteenth in the world—behind Romania—only the most optimistic still believed the United States was not going to be sucked into this maelstrom. President Franklin D. Roosevelt, foreseeing the grim future, began retooling the nation for war, quietly at first, until 1940, when he instituted the first peacetime draft in American history.

For young men like Dick Winters, graduating from college in that summer of uncertainty and of prime military age, the choice was simple: go into the job market and wait for someone to pluck his draft number from that huge bowl in Washington, D.C., or beat them to the punch and enlist, and satisfy his one-year military obligation to his country. Winters chose the latter, although at first he hated the very idea of going into the army. At one point he considered drawing on his Mennonite background and declaring himself a conscientious objector. Friends of his had already done this to avoid military service, and were getting jobs in hospitals. Winters soon realized, though, that he was not a conscientious objector and to say so would be a lie, so he decided to enlist in the army and put in his one year of service.

Surprisingly, his parents not only did not object, but supported this decision. Even his mother, with her pacifist background, agreed. Within days of his graduation, where he received a Bachelor of Science degree in economics and achieved the highest grade point average in the department, Dick Winters visited the army recruiting office in downtown Lancaster. There he signed the papers that would have such a profound effect on his life, well beyond his years of actual service.

Between drafts and enlistments during that final summer of peace, the army's ranks were full to the brim. This gave Winters another two months to work before his call-up. Inexplicably, the thought of going into the army caused Winters to slip back into his lackadaisical public school mentality. He boasted to his coworkers that he was going to cruise through army life by doing what he had to do to get by and nothing more. This rankled his foreman, a veteran sergeant from the Great War who, like a good NCO, got nose-to-nose with Winters.

"Let me tell you something, boy," he said in a firm, drill sergeant tone. "The army is a job, just like the one you got here. Once you put on that uniform, you do not goof off. You get in there and you do your best. Don't you ever forget that, not for a minute."

It was a stern message, delivered in a no-nonsense tone that stuck with Winters. For the rest of his life he not only lived by that message, but made it a point to pass it on to younger generations. (In 2001, upon being selected by two elementary school students from Lebanon, Pennsylvania, as a hero they wanted to write about, Winters sent them copies of the *Band of Brothers* book, in which he wrote, "Follow me, Dick Winters." Recalling that, he said, "I hope those words sink in for them like that foreman's did for me, so that maybe I can help the next generation to 'follow me.'")

Winters' call-up orders came and on August 25, 1941, he was inducted into the U.S. Army at New Cumberland, Pennsylvania. His parents, sister and Aunt Lottie saw him off at the Lancaster train station as he headed for basic training at Camp Croft, South Carolina. Lottie gave her nephew a five-year diary that he kept diligently.

Camp Croft was one of the original Replacement Training Centers established

by the army in 1940. Here Winters would spend the next thirteen weeks under the tutelage of a sergeant named Slusher, who drilled the fundamentals of
being a soldier into the raw recruit.

For Winters, basic training was anything but a hardship. With his love of
physical exertion, he enjoyed scaling walls and poles, the running and calisthenics. He had run regularly in civilian life and was in fine shape. His only
admitted weakness was swimming, a sport he had never embraced. In addition, the rigid study regimen he adopted in college made the book learning
part of his training a snap. Under Slusher's guidance Winters and his class-
mates learned to stand at attention, perform close order drill and to instantly
obey orders. They took long marches, both with and without heavy field
packs, and learned the rudiments of self-defense and bayonet tactics. They
also were issued rifles, 1903 bolt-action Springfields, leftovers from the Great
War, and Winters, who practiced his marksmanship evenings and weekends
while others knocked off for the day, soon qualified as an expert marksman,
one of the very few in his class.

His salary, however, dropped significantly from what he was paid to climb
towers for PP&L. In the army he earned, as was often said, "$21 a day, once a
month." Luckily, Winters' needs were few since the army provided most of his
wants. Accustomed to living on a shoestring from his college days, he allowed
himself a dollar a week allowance, saving the rest. This was plenty since he
didn't drink, didn't smoke and the "ice cream in camp was lousy." His main
expense was buying stationery to write home.

Basic training also gave the young man a chance to make new friends, including Ed Wolf from Pottsville, Pennsylvania, and a fellow named Zerbe
from Adamstown in Lancaster County, just twenty miles north of Lancaster.
Winters' best friend, however, was a fellow Lancaster boy named Triesta
Trenta. The two formed a close-knit friendship.

Winters and Trent, as he was called, usually went on weekend passes together, which included one excursion in late November 1941 to Asheville,
North Carolina, seventy miles from Croft. The two soldiers took accommodations at the YMCA, which offered the cheapest beds in town. There they
struck up an acquaintance with a man named Hazard who ran the local Red
Cross. A likable fellow, Hazard and the two young soldiers chatted the night
away. Next morning, Sunday, Winters had planned to sleep in, a rare luxury
for a soldier, when Hazard shook him awake.

"Get up, Dick," he said. "I want you to go to church with me."

Winters rose groggily from the bed, envying Trent, who was Catholic and
therefore immune to Hazard's invitation. Hazard belonged to a Christian Sci-
entist church, which proved a totally new experience for Winters. He wasn't

used to the informality of a service where people seemed to rise at random, walk to the front and speak. The congregants seemed pleasant, though, and Hazard and he—both bachelors—were invited to a family's home for dinner. This had never happened to Winters before, and he was mightily impressed with his first exposure to Southern hospitality.

The next week Hazard had another surprise for his young friends. Two local girls, Annie DeEtta Almon and Frances Johnson, approached him and said they'd baked a batch of brownies. They asked if he knew any soldiers who'd be glad to have them. Naturally Hazard thought of Trent and Winters, and the two men soon got a package of the most delightful brownies either had ever eaten. Courtesy demanded the two soldiers thank the girls so, being the letter writer, Winters responded with a note on their behalf and asked if they could thank the girls personally on their next pass to Asheville. Meeting the girls a week or so later, Winters was instantly taken by DeEtta, a short, pretty redhead. Winters and Trent began seeing the girls regularly, both as couples and in foursomes, and for the next five years DeEtta would be Winters' best friend, pen pal and confidante.

★   ★   ★

Near the end of the thirteen weeks of basic training, Sergeant Slusher called Winters and Trent into his office. The two had impressed the drill sergeant.

"You men know your stuff," he told them as they stood at ease in front of his desk. "You've worked hard and learned well. After graduation, this class is being shipped down to Panama. I'd like you guys to consider staying on and helping to train the next batch of recruits. Do well, and you'll soon be wearing corporal stripes."

It was an easy decision. When the class shipped out on November 27, 1941, Winters and Trent remained at Croft.

"Naturally we jumped at the chance," Winters wrote DeEtta that evening. "For who wants to go down Panama way and wear yourself out fighting mosquitoes when you can stay down south and enjoy the good old traditional hospitality."

Winters finagled a weekend pass in Asheville to keep a date he'd set with DeEtta for Sunday, December 7. DeEtta had arranged for them to go horseback riding at the Biltmore Estate. Galloping through the fall countryside on that pleasantly brisk Sunday afternoon, they had a long, invigorating ride. Upon arriving back in town, he and DeEtta learned about the Japanese attack on Pearl Harbor. It was like a slap in the face, Winters recalled.

Like most Americans, Winters knew war was coming. Yet part of him felt secure behind the two oceans that separated the United States from Europe and Asia. "You take care of your side of the ocean," he mentally told the leaders of the nations now at war, "and I'll take care of mine."

That dream was over. Winters now knew he'd be going to war, and that his anticipated one-year military obligation was ended. He was in for the duration.

With the outbreak of war, the pace of activities around Croft increased as the need for men and officers took on a new urgency. Men who enlisted or were drafted no longer waited for induction, but were almost immediately sent to camps like Croft, where instructors like Winters and Trent tried to make soldiers out of a "bunch of dopes from Chicago," as Winters called his first class.

Not only was the country now preparing for war, but Winters was starting to mentally get himself on a war footing. On December 9, he wrote DeEtta, "The sooner we sail into those little brown men and the rest of the motley crew, the quicker it'll be over. We've got the stuff to do it and by gosh we will."

Besides training, Winters occasionally drew MP duty, hanging around the PX ordering soldiers to fasten their jackets or straighten their ties. If they had too much beer and became rowdy or boisterous, he quickly evicted them. He enjoyed the duty. Other times, Winters was assigned to Change of Quarters, which he considered to be a glorified errand boy job. He had to oversee lights out at nine, do a bed check at eleven, then clean the orderly room. Since the war, the CQ was always on call, so Winters spent the night sleeping fully dressed, including a necktie. He had to rouse the KP crew at 4:45 A.M., make sure reveille sounded at 5:15 A.M. and do roll call. Afternoons were supposed to be free time, but seldom were.

The early days of World War II, especially with the series of stunning Japanese victories in the Pacific that left American and British forces reeling, led to war hysteria in the nation. Cities and towns all across the land began holding air raid drills, and there was even discussion about painting the Capitol rotunda in Washington, D.C., black to hide it from enemy bombers. This frenzy was especially keen on the West Coast, where a Japanese submarine had actually shelled a California oil refinery. In response to this widespread concern and fear, on December 17 Winters helped prepare a shipment of army gas masks to be distributed in California. People were in a panic and false alarms were numerous. Invasion, or at the least a gas attack, seemed like a very real threat. Winters didn't see what the masks would accomplish as they were training masks, wholly inadequate in a real emergency. But the army sent them anyway. It was hoped their mere presence would help comfort people.

On December 21, Winters started a ten-day furlough and began hitchhiking the 530 miles from Croft to Lancaster. Winters enjoyed hitchhiking because it was cheaper than a train or bus, which was important for a soldier making twenty-one dollars a month and appealed to his frugal nature. But also, in hitchhiking, he usually got rides from local people who would take it on themselves to act as tour guides, showing him points of interest and bragging about local history and culture.

Winters rose at 6:30 A.M. on December 21 and was along the highway, thumb in the air, by 7:30. However by 8:45 he had only made ten miles. Cold and exasperated, he was so eager for a ride that when a woman stopped and said she was going to Louisville, Kentucky, he agreed, even though it was out of his way. She dropped Winters at the YMCA, where he was treated to a chicken dinner. After checking into his room, he walked the town, admiring its clean, wide streets and modern buildings. Standing on the bank of the Ohio River, he watched as it flowed swiftly on its way to merge with the Mississippi.

Next day Winters was up by 6 A.M. and on the road by 7. He grabbed a bus and rode to the edge of town, then stuck out his thumb. He almost immediately got a ride that carried him to Charles Town, West Virginia, arriving there by 4:30. It was starting to get dark, but he wanted to reach Clarksburg if possible, which would still give him three hundred miles to cover to get home. His luck was in, and Winters got another ride. Winters recalled that the driver was a "nice enough looking fellow" and a good conversationalist. Until he laid his hand on Winters' leg.

"We can find a nice hotel up ahead and have a good dinner," the man said. "Then I can make you feel happy."

"Here's a better idea," Winters said, lifting the man's hand away. "Do you see that crossroad up ahead? I'll be happy if you just stop right there so I can get out."

The man didn't argue and Winters found himself standing alone on a dark highway in the West Virginia mountains, miserable, cold and somewhat shaken by his unfamiliar experience with the car driver. After about fifteen minutes a logging truck rumbled down the road, picked him up, and took him seventeen miles to Spencer.

Rain fell the next day and Winters spent thirty cold and wet minutes waiting for his first ride. Arriving in Chambersburg, Pennsylvania, around midday, he hitchhiked east along Route 30. The famous Lincoln Highway was heavily traveled, yet rides were hard to come by and Winters, even though back in his home state, began to sour on Yankee hospitality. It was almost midnight on December 23 when a wet, disgusted and dead-tired Private Winters stepped up on the porch of 418 South West End Avenue and back into the welcoming arms of his family. Settling into the familiar environs of his bedroom, he stripped off his damp uniform, took a luxurious hot bath, fell into his nice, clean bed and slept for fourteen hours.

Winters had hoped to spend the next day, Christmas Eve, relaxing, but he had to run out and get his uniform cleaned and pressed. Worse, his parents, glad to have their son back with them, proudly dragged him around to relatives and friends to show him off. That evening Winters took his sister Ann to see a play, *The Chocolate Soldier,* at a local theater.

Winters' father delighted in showing his son the latest gadget he'd purchased, which allowed him to connect the record player to the family radio so he could play his collection of 78 rpm records through the radio's speakers. "It sure is neat," Winters wrote DeEtta that night.

The first few days of his Christmas leave proved hectic. "These folks at home have me about nuts," he confided in a letter to DeEtta. He had hoped to find time to take a long hike in the countryside, sit in a comfy chair and read, or just listen to the radio, and simply enjoy the soft life for a while. The family always seemed to have other plans. Winters had also hoped for a little time to go ice skating, his favorite winter sport, but a spell of warm weather kept local ponds ice free.

Taking leave of his family on December 31, Winters hit the road back to Camp Croft. The end of that first day found him in Rocky Mount, Virginia, where he spent New Year's Eve alone in a dumpy little lodge called the Rocky Mount Hotel, well off the beaten track and difficult to find. Winters wrote that the poorly lighted hotel was one of those "quaint old places one reads about or laughs at in the movies."

As Winters entered the hotel he noticed the desk clerk trying to look busy even though Winters felt convinced the place "hadn't seen a cash customer in days."

"I'd like a room for the night," Winters said. The man nodded and handed Winters a book to sign in. After he did so and paid for the room, Winters asked, "Could I have a receipt?"

"Beg pardon?"

"A receipt." No response. "For the room." The man still looked clueless. "Just take a piece of paper, write down how much I paid for the room and the name of the hotel and sign it please."

After teaching the man what a receipt was, Winters was led to his room. Like the lobby, the room was "old and crummy." Its furnishings consisted of a few beat-up chairs, a bed and a lone table, which had only three legs. In order to write to DeEtta, Winters had to remove the mirror from the wall, lay it glass-side down on the bed, pull up a chair and use the bed as a desk. Miraculously, the hotel had electric lights and running water.

Winters felt the need to get out and grab a bite to eat, then realized the clerk had not left him a room key. He returned to the desk.

"You didn't leave me a key," Winters told the clerk.

"Oh, that's all right," the man said. "You have a bolt on the inside."

"But I want to go out. Do I take my luggage along, or just leave the door unlocked and trust you?"

Winters never got the key. Returning after his dinner, he was relieved to find his possessions unmolested.

⋆   ⋆   ⋆

On January 22, 1942, shortly after Winters brought his platoon of trainees in from the rifle range, the commanding officer of the training battalion called him into his office.

"I've been watching you, Winters," he said. "You're good with the men and have leadership potential. Right now the army needs that. Would you be interested in Officer Candidate School?"

It was as if he'd read Winters' mind. He had been thinking about applying for OCS ever since he saw some of the new, young officers come into camp, and how ineffectual they seemed. What finally convinced him to apply was the day he laid out a new M1 Garand rifle and a 1903 Springfield on a table so a young lieutenant could brief his men on the operation of both. As the lecture began, Winters watched in disbelief as the lieutenant picked up the Garand and began referring to it as the '03 Springfield.

"Hell, this is ridiculous," Winters thought. "I can do better than that."

So Winters jumped at the opportunity to attend OCS, and that evening he wrote DeEtta, "If anything ever comes of it or not, of course, remains to be seen. But if they give me the chance, I'll show them how I can work when I want to. That's something I want, and by gosh, I'll get it."

OCS, though, meant leaving Croft and moving to Fort Benning, Georgia. It also meant leaving his friend Trent, but Trent had his own ideas involving Benning.

"Dick," he said that evening. "I don't think I want to stick with the infantry. I'm thinking of putting in for the paratroops. It's new. It looks exciting. I think I'd like it."

Winters thought the notion idiotic and told his friend so.

"Are you nuts?" Winters asked in words that would come back to haunt him. "The paratroops? That's a suicide outfit. Trust me, you don't want any part of that."

In the end, Trent stuck with the infantry and in February was transferred to Fort McClellan, Alabama, where he got his corporal's stripes. The move left

Winters without a roommate. By that time, though, Winters was too sick to care. Flu swept Croft that month and fifteen of the fifty-five men in Winters' barracks ended up in the hospital.

Back on his feet after the flu, Winters had his physical exam for OCS on February 16, followed ten days later by an oral interview. He'd only been given an hour's advance notice about the interview, which he felt was fortunate since it gave him little chance to get nervous, and he breezed through it.

The competition for OCS was stiff, especially since Winters was the only private among a bevy of sergeants and corporals taking the written test. This seemed to work to Winters' benefit. Calling on the study skills he honed at college, and with his old PP&L foreman's words still ringing in his ears, Winters crammed for the exam while many of the others seemed to assume that, as NCOs, they already knew everything.

Winters was ecstatic when the news came down that he had passed, and he soon joined the rest of the successful candidates in a four-week, pre-OCS class. Ironically, the class was placed under the command of a new shavetail lieutenant who barely knew his left from his right. Seeing this man wearing officer's bars assured Winters that he would do just fine.

On March 10, 1942, Winters received his corporal's stripes. The boost in rank excited him, not just because of the promotion, but for the fifty percent hike in pay that accompanied it. On that same day Winters was offered the option of taking OCS at Fort Knox, Kentucky, after which he would be placed in an armored unit. He turned it down, preferring to remain in the infantry. He felt his seven months army experience, plus the thirteen weeks of training he would get at Benning, would give him the self-assuredness to serve as an infantry officer. As a tanker, Winters felt he'd be starting from scratch.

On April 6, 1942, Winters shipped out for Benning.

Compared to Croft, Benning was a slice of heaven with brick barracks that were airy, roomy and clean. There were modern furniture, reading rooms, sidewalks and streetlights. Winters loved it.

In preparing for OCS, Winters recalled with great irony his derogatory remarks to Trent two months earlier, for now his own thoughts were turning more and more toward the airborne. For it was at Benning that Winters first saw paratroopers up close. They were everything he'd always envisioned a soldier to be: lean, hard, well trained and disciplined, bronzed and tough. The men bore a fierce pride, and the more Winters saw them, the more he told himself that if he had to go to war, these were the guys he wanted to fight with. Besides, as a second lieutenant, he'd make $268 per month.

Only two things held Winters back: his less than proficient swimming ability, and his parents. One he had the power to correct, the other would be more difficult. His parents knew and accepted the risk he would be running as a soldier during time of war, but they did not share his enthusiasm over the paratroops. They used the same arguments he'd used on Trent, calling it foolhardy and dangerous. They also enlisted friends and neighbors in their cause. Winters, who had always taken his parents' advice in the past, decided this time to trust his own judgment. "They think it's the money and glamour that seems attractive to me," he wrote DeEtta on May 10. "In a way it is, but the main thing is it looks like interesting work and something I'll enjoy. So I still think I'll take a try at it."

Officer Candidate School was thirteen weeks of hard work. Winters learned the basics of being an officer, and there was intense training in weapons, interlocking fire, map reading and small unit tactics. This latter was Winters' favorite, giving him free rein to use his head and his instincts. The candidates saw demonstrations on handling supplies, administration, manning or attacking fortifications, troop deployment on all levels from the squad through division, and use of tanks and trucks. There was machine gun practice detailing how to safely shoot over the heads of one's own troops, aiming at one target and hitting another, and hitting a target despite a smoke screen. Classes were held on how to call in mortar and artillery support, and how to set up strong bases of covering fire.

During this time Winters mentally established a code of conduct for himself, setting himself up as an example for his men, not just in combat by leading from the front, but in his attention to training and by his personal demeanor in camp. It would be a twenty-four-hour-a-day job, he decided.

On May 30, the OCS class observed war maneuvers and watched a battalion storm a creek under fire and aerial attack. The engineers threw down a footbridge and established a ferry under the cover of smoke shells. Winters found it an impressive show.

During his three months at Benning, Winters never set foot off the post, for to miss a formation was to flunk out of OCS. Transportation in the area was poor and he was not about to take the chance of losing this opportunity. Besides, the ice cream in camp was good, so he stayed and studied.

By the end of June, graduation from OCS was drawing near. New uniforms began arriving, along with shiny gold bars and decorations. As Winters looked at his new rank insignia, he felt a pride of accomplishment that he could barely contain.

"Here we are, about to reach that charmed class, a distinct social class," he wrote DeEtta on Tuesday evening, June 30, pride flowing from every stroke of his pen. "We'll command respect and authority. It's the dream of every rookie from the day he comes into the army and we are just about to reach out and grasp it. At times it's hard to convince yourself that it's true."

On Thursday, July 2, 1942, Winters was discharged from the U.S. Army as a corporal in the first company, third student training regiment, and reinstated as a second lieutenant. But instead of being shipped out to the airborne as he expected, he found himself reassigned to Camp Croft to resume his role as an instructor of new recruits. The move proved temporary. Winters had been accepted to a newly forming regiment of paratroopers and had only to await his new orders.

Until then, newly minted Second Lieutenant Winters had a class of recruits to train. Meeting them for the first time he quickly discovered that not only did it contain three men from his hometown of Lancaster, but also an F&M College classmate. Rick Burgess was a handsome fellow from Shamokin, Pennsylvania, who was a member of the college's varsity wrestling team. The two were amazed to come across each other at Croft. Winters and Burgess spent a lot time together over the next several weeks, and Winters even loaned his friend a spare uniform and $125 so he could get married. Ordinarily, the army frowns on close fraternization between officers and enlisted men, and Winters was careful to keep that distance on the training grounds. But after hours, and knowing he'd be gone soon, he mingled freely with the men. Winters later admitted he might have felt differently if he had gotten his gold bars at West Point, but, until a few weeks earlier, he had been an enlisted man, and that bond lingered.

In late August Winters' new orders came. He was to report to Camp Toombs, Georgia, near a town called Toccoa. There he would join the 506th Parachute Infantry Regiment. On the eve of his departure, Burgess and the men threw Winters a going-away party and presented him with a shiny new Schaeffer pen set. The camaraderie the men had forged in such a short time had been strong, so much so that four of the men in this class would follow Winters into the paratroops after basic training, including Burgess, who would serve with the 101st Airborne artillery. This group also included Al Krochka, who would be the official photographer of the 501st during the war.

The next day Winters packed his bags, said his good-byes and left Camp Croft behind.

CHAPTER 3

"I'll Meet You at the North Star."

August 31, 1942–June 5, 1944

Sunday Services had ended at St. Michael's Church by the Green in Aldbourne, England. Lieutenant Richard Winters stepped outside into the brilliant morning sunlight. Placing his hat squarely upon his head, he slowly meandered along the cobblestone walkway leading from the church to the street, stopping when he reached the end. Parishioners leaving the austere thirteenth-century church flowed around him like a stream around a rock. Some continued down the narrow street past rustic cottages; others strolled across the lush village green, still damp from the dew—all headed for their homes. Winters knew he should be heading for his home, too, a makeshift camp on the edge of the town, but his feet were unwilling. He and several thousand other soldiers had just spent weeks sealed in an embarkation camp in the States, and then packed themselves tightly into a troopship like olives in a jar for the ten-day Atlantic crossing. Arriving in Liverpool, the GIs were crammed aboard a train for the trip to southern England, and then loaded onto trucks. Now they were shoehorned into an overcrowded camp.

It all left Winters seeking solitude, which is why he went to church. He knew no other soldiers would attend. Putting off going back to camp, Winters wandered around the side of the church and into the cemetery. The quiet graveyard was set on a small hill, and a pair of benches atop the hill seemed to call out to him. He walked among the graves, some dating back almost as far as the seven-hundred-year-old church itself, whose tall, Norman tower stood the silent vigil of the centuries. Most of these older stones were badly weathered, condemning their occupants to the anonymity of the ages.

Selecting one of the benches, Winters sat and stretched out his legs. He had begun feeling pretty damned sorry for himself. He was homesick, and missed his family, his house, his bed and his life, all of which he was keenly aware he might never see again. Those grim thoughts were made all the more ironic by his surroundings, for in these headstones Winters could foresee his own future.

While wallowing in this self-pity, Winters noticed an older couple enter the cemetery. Stopping by a fresh grave, the woman bent down and laid some flowers. Straightening, they both looked somberly down at the grave. In a few moments the man glanced up and noticed the solitary American. He spoke briefly to his wife, and they sauntered in Winters' direction.

"Good morning, Yank," the man said as they approached. "Fine day. Hope we're not disturbing you."

"Certainly not," Winters told him, glad to have company to keep away the gloom.

"Barnes is the name, Francis Barnes," he said. "I'm the village grocer. This is my wife, Louie May. You must be with those Yanks that just arrived."

"Yes," Winters said. "I'm Dick Winters. Please, have a seat."

The couple sat on the remaining empty bench and began chatting. Winters spoke admiringly about the quiet, picturesque charm of the village, the Gothic beauty of the church. In fact, everything he'd seen so far during his brief time in England was lovely, and belied the fact that the war had ever touched this country.

"It has, leftenant, very much so," Mrs. Barnes assured him. She pointed in the direction of the fresh grave. "That's our son. He was with the Royal Air Force. We lost him a year ago."

"I'm so sorry," Winters replied, but the couple gave him no chance to slip back into the gloominess the situation almost demanded.

"Would you care to come have tea with us today? Say, four o'clock?" Mr. Barnes asked suddenly.

Lonely and miserable, Winters was overjoyed by the opportunity to mingle with someone not wearing olive drab. He replied, "Thank you. I'd like that."

★   ★   ★

So much had happened from the day Winters left Camp Croft until that Sunday morning in Aldbourne, almost a year later. The assignment papers that took him from Croft came within five weeks of his graduation from OCS. The very next day Winters was headed for the newly established Camp Toombs, Georgia, tucked into the foothills of the Blue Mountains.

Camp Toombs had a morbid air that matched its dreary name. En route to the camp, soldiers traveled down Highway 13, passing a casket company on the way. This doom and gloom combination wasn't just felt by Winters. Shortly after his arrival the regimental commander, Colonel Robert F. Sink, ordered the name changed to Camp Toccoa, after the nearest town, six miles down the road.

In that summer of 1942 Camp Toccoa was still under construction. Accommodations were makeshift, with enlisted men bivouacked in tents. Officers like Winters were billeted in unfinished tarpaper shacks with glassless windows gaping open. Initially, the only electricity was in the latrines. There were few paved areas, meaning there was plenty of thick, red Georgia mud when the rains swept up from the Gulf of Mexico. The humidity was thick as a bowl of grits and the men ran around in shorts. By contrast, two wool blankets were needed to contend with the cold nights.

In many ways this new camp was a reflection of the paratroopers themselves. Parachute infantry was a new concept in the U.S. Army. The Germans had used parachutists to good effect at the war's outset in Poland, Holland, France and especially Belgium, where a pinpoint landing swiftly overwhelmed the defenders of Fort Eban Emael, once thought to be impregnable.

Taking their lead from the Germans, the British organized their own airborne divisions. This caught the Americans' attention, and in June 1942 General William "Bill" Lee was sent to England to study British training and tactics. It was Lee's notes and observations that led to the formation of the 82nd Airborne Division and its offspring, the 101st. Eventually Lee was given command of the 101st. He oversaw the raising, training and equipping of the division, and in September 1943 led it to England in preparation for the invasion of Europe. However, in February 1944 Lee suffered a heart attack and was forced to relinquish command. Having been instrumental in the birth of the elite airborne arm, he would never lead it into combat.

★   ★   ★

The 506th Parachute Infantry Regiment, to which Winters was now reporting, was activated July 26, 1942. Its commander, Colonel Sink, was a 1927 graduate of West Point. At age thirty-seven, Sink was nearly old enough to be the father of some of the young men he now led. A military professional, Sink did not feel the need for the haughty attitude that so many academy men felt they had to project in order to command. An innovator in a U.S. Army still mired in the static ideas of the past, Sink was one of the first men to volunteer in 1940 when General Lee formed the First Parachute Battalion, which evolved into the 501st Parachute Infantry Regiment. Sink went on to command Company B of the 501st and later became the regimental executive officer. After a brief stint in command of the 503rd PIR, Sink was handed the job of forming the 506th.

Winters admired Sink's earthiness. He mingled freely with his men and consumed alcohol freely when not on duty. He was gruff, yet not overbearing, and he made both the officers and men feel they were truly part of a team. He respected his junior officers and they returned the sentiment. Winters held his colonel in awe, a feeling he did not extend to his battalion commander.

Robert Strayer was a fine administrator and a good man. He knew how to set a training schedule and get the troops fit for action, and while he liked the man personally and showed him no signs of disrespect during the war or in the years after, Winters did not feel Strayer was an effective combat leader. His map-reading skills were lacking, partly since he did not see a need to attend the training classes, and he seemed all but incapable of making a firm decision under pressure. What Strayer excelled at was selecting top-notch staff officers, particularly Major Oliver Horton, the battalion's executive officer, whom Winters considered a far more capable leader than the commander himself. Men like lieutenants Clarence Hester, Lewis Nixon and George Lavenson also contributed immensely to Strayer's success.

However, Strayer did prove he was innovative. When put in charge of acquiring physical training gear, especially clothing, for the men, Strayer discovered that there was none to be had. He even traveled to bases in Atlanta without success. Then he met a supply officer who, for a monetary consideration, arranged for an army train running from Atlanta to Greenville, South Carolina, to stop near Toccoa. While the crew was in town enjoying some of the entertainment that springs up around military bases, Strayer's 2nd Battalion raided the train only to find that the entire cargo consisted of crates of blue shorts. From that day forward, the regiment's official PT uniform was white T-shirts and blue shorts.

But, leadership-wise, Strayer was Patton compared to Winters' company commander. Almost from the day Winters met Lieutenant Herbert M. Sobel, he knew they would not get along. Sobel lacked almost all the skills Winters felt a leader must exude. Cold and impersonal, Sobel treated the men under him with utter disdain. He was exceedingly harsh and unfair, Winters noted, and as time went on and his inadequacies became more and more glaring he became, in Winters' description, "downright mean." Winters believed that, in the eyes of the enlisted men, a junior officer should reflect his company commander. In Easy Company, that was impossible.

Excellent when it came to physical training, calisthenics and drill, Sobel, from Chicago, was hopelessly out of his depth in the field. During one night exercise, the company lay in a strong defensive position in a wooded area waiting for the "enemy" to walk into their carefully set ambush. In the silence of the woods, a breeze stirred the leaves. Springing to his feet, Sobel, his nerves taut, yelled, "Here they come! Here they come!"

"Jesus Christ," Winters heard a nearby soldier mutter. "I'm going into combat with this man? He'll get us all killed."

It was, perhaps, because of his ineptness that Sobel's Jewish background became a focal point of insult and derision.

Sobel certainly had a military bearing. He had attended Culver Military Academy as a boy and knew the routine, but he became the master of chickenshit—the fine art of blowing even the smallest detail out of proportion—both at Culver and in the army. Winters knew the army would be no bed of roses, but Sobel loaded men down with extra duties and handed out harsh disciplines far in excess of what was required. The men suffered under him, but the worst victim of his tyranny would be Sobel himself.

Sobel was the first junior officer assigned to the new company, followed by Hester, who later transferred to battalion staff. Thus Winters became the third officer to join Easy Company, 2nd Battalion of the 506th PIR. The regiment had yet to be assigned to a division—at this point there was only one airborne division, the 82nd—so the unit patches worn on their left sleeves were red, white and blue stripes inside a circle, indicating a training unit.

Sobel placed Winters in command of 2nd Platoon. Fresh from basic training, all thirty-four men he would lead were privates, so Winters began by selecting temporary noncommissioned officers.

"Heads up!" Winters shouted to the men. "Fall in to my left, tallest to smallest." The soldiers complied. Winters then pointed to the man on the far left.

"You're acting platoon sergeant," he said.

Working his way down the line, man by man, Winters soon had all of his NCOs. These promotions would last only a few days. Time and training would show who among these men would finally wear stripes.

One who rose quickly to the top was James L. "Punchy" Diel, whom Winters soon made his permanent platoon sergeant. A skinny Ohioan with a boyish face and disarming smile, Diel nonetheless had a commanding presence. He could be one of the fellows and joke with the best of them, but when it came down to business, his voice oozed command and he got the men's attention. Also among those upon whom Winters soon bestowed stripes were sergeants John W. Martin, William J. Guarnere, Myron Ranney and Robert J. Rader, and corporals Joseph J. Toye and Denver "Bull" Randleman.

Winters broke the platoon into four squads of seven men each, giving him three rifle squads and a mortar squad of six men. Besides himself, there was now one other officer in the platoon, Lewis Nixon.

The son of a wealthy industrialist, his family owned the Nixon Nitration Works—a plastic manufacturing company—in the aptly named Nixon, New Jersey. In many ways, Winters' new assistant platoon leader was the proverbial spoiled rich kid who never had to do a day's work in his life. Worse, Nixon suffered from an alcohol habit that would cause him numerous problems throughout his military and personal life.

Everything about Nixon was in stark contrast to Winters. Where Nixon drank to excess, Winters was a teetotaler. Where Winters was a stickler for getting things done on time and in good order, Nixon tended to goof off. Yet the two got along famously. Their friendship and devotion were beyond question, and while Winters in some ways considered Nixon the most unreliable man he had ever met, he also knew he could always count on Nixon when there was an important job to be done. Not that Nixon always did that job himself. He was good at delegating responsibilities, and an expert at retaining and passing along critical information. Winters' biggest gripe with Nixon was that he loved to argue, and when they'd get into a heated discussion, Winters would simply let him spout off.

Within weeks of arriving at Toccoa, however, Nixon would transfer to battalion staff to be replaced by Second Lieutenant Harry F. Welsh. Despite that move, Nixon could generally be found by Winters' side throughout the war.

*   *   *

The most dominant feature of Toccoa was a mountain—a large hill, really—that loomed 1,200 feet over the camp. The mountain was named Currahee, a Cherokee term for "Stands alone," which the 506th adapted into their motto, "We Stand Alone." Upon his arrival at the camp, Winters took one look at the mountain and rightly predicted that he and his men would have to scale it.

The training regimen at Toccoa began with reveille at 0500, followed by breakfast at 0600. Physical training was next on the menu, followed by School of the Soldier, where the men were instructed on close order drill, standing at attention and facings. On rainy days, training often moved indoors with map- and compass-reading classes. In between there were roll calls and barracks inspections, when Sobel ruthlessly searched men's footlockers, seizing items such as magazines, letters from home and anything else he could label as "contraband." Often, these inspections occurred while the men were out in the field.

Everything at Toccoa was done at the double-quick, a foot-long shuffling stride where all the weight was put on the ball of the foot. When they weren't drilling or running the obstacle course, the men underwent intensive weapons training, learning to break down, clean and reassemble everything from the M1 Garand rifle and the Colt .45 automatic to the .30 caliber machine gun and 81 mm mortar. Then it was off to the ROTC firing range at Clemson University to learn to shoot those weapons. Training was also given in communications, demolitions and judo.

Winters seemed to excel in training; not just PT, but also in tactical exercises. During nighttime problems, where some officers got lost, causing delays in time and unwelcomed extra marching by the weary men under them, Winters was blessed with a superb sense of direction, a point his soldiers appreciated. His abilities did not go unnoticed. During his first week at Toccoa, Winters was leading the company in calisthenics while Sink was observing the camp. The colonel stopped to watch, then asked, "Lieutenant. How many times have these men had PT?"

"Three, sir," Winters replied.

"Thank you very much," Sink said. "Carry on."

Nothing more was said, but when Sink returned to his office, he promoted Winters to first lieutenant. Winters received his new bars from Sobel, who had been elevated to the rank of captain.

One of the most memorable training exercises occurred in November 1942, in what would forever be called the "hog innards problem." Sink ordered that hog entrails from a local meat-packing company be scattered over an area twenty feet wide and fifty to sixty feet long. Barbed wire was strung from stakes eighteen inches off the ground. Machine guns loaded with live ammo were mounted on two-by-four wooden supports with the tripod legs sandbagged down so the guns remained stable. The men were required to crawl through the bloody gore as .30 caliber bullets whizzed by overhead. While the exercise drew plenty of gripes from the rank and file, it drew none from Winters, who felt it set up a true combat atmosphere.

"The use of live ammunition gave the men the incentive to keep head and butt down in the hog guts," he wrote.

But what was universally remembered by all the men who went through Toccoa were the six-mile round-trip runs up and down Currahee. The trek was usually made at double time, with the last mile being at quick time, sometimes in PT gear, and sometimes in full uniform with field packs. While Currahee was an ordeal for some, Winters thought it a challenge. The 506th's record for running up Currahee and back was forty-two minutes. It was held by Sergeant Joseph Reed of C Company. Winters ran it in forty-four.

As training continued throughout 1942, Sobel never tired of pushing the men to the brink of exhaustion, running them over the obstacle course and taking them on nine-mile runs with full packs, rifles and machine guns. Sobel's favorite exercise was the Friday-night thirty-five-mile nonstop hike with full gear. He would order canteens to be filled with water at the start of the hike, and expected them to still be full when they got back. Harsh punishment awaited any man who sneaked a sip.

Winters grew disgusted with Sobel's increasingly harsh treatment of the men. Walking the ranks during inspection, Sobel would bark out, "dirty stacking swivel," "dirty gun sight" or "dirty ears," and dock the men leave time. Sometimes the punishments were just, sometimes they were not and other times they were sheer fantasy. It didn't matter to Sobel, but it did to Winters, who was often ordered to come up with a list of infractions, real or imagined.

Sobel's habit of canceling leaves as punishment was not a hardship for the socially reserved Winters. While many of the men crossed the street to the Wagon Wheel or walked a short distance down the highway to the Hi-Dee-Ho to tip a few beers, Winters was just as happy remaining on the base.

When he did go into Toccoa, it was often to attend church, where he was usually invited for dinner at the Sunday School superintendent's home. Winters did take a short leave to meet his mother who, in what Winters felt was probably the biggest single adventure of her life, came to visit her son at camp.

* * *

As the weeks dragged on, training intensified. If a man tired of the rigorous routine, he was free to quit, at which time he moved his gear into a section of the camp reserved for W Company. Known also as Cow Company, this part of the camp was the first stop for new men coming into Toccoa, and the last stop for men shipping out. A stay in Cow Company was roundly hated by the soldiers who experienced it. The ground flooded easily in rain and men often awoke to the gurgling sound of running water just inches from their faces, as their cots had sunk deeply into the muck.

While some gave up, most endured, discovering, Winters wrote, that they could go "farther and do more than they ever dared to dream."

As demanding as the training schedule was for the enlisted men, it was worse for the officers. Just one lesson ahead of the men they commanded, and knowing, as Winters said, that they were "not that damned smart" themselves, the officers were under intense pressure. They studied late into the night, making sure they grasped the lessons they expected their men to learn the next day.

Easy's ordeal under Sobel was magnified when the men looked at the other two companies in second battalion, Dog and Fox. Whereas the rosters of those two companies remained relatively stable, men came and went from Easy with frightening rapidity, especially officers. Hester, Nixon and S. L. Matheson all transferred out, in most cases moving into battalion or regimental slots. Others simply dropped out of the airborne. Only Winters stuck with the company.

In September 1942 the men began preparing for jump training, with the first lesson being a two-day course on how to pack a parachute. Sink expected his officers to qualify first. Initially, Sink had hoped to qualify the entire 506th at Toccoa by building his own airstrip. The job was done by R. G. Letourneau, a somewhat flamboyant multimillionaire industrialist who had his own airplane that was every bit as big as a C-47. Letourneau owned heavy equipment factories in Toccoa and in Peoria, Illinois, and built the field for Sink by bulldozing the top off a nearby hill. The airfield was naturally dubbed Le Tourneau. To complete Sink's training plans, the army gave him one C-47 Skytrain.

The problem with Le Tourneau Airfield was that the runway was not long enough for a C-47 to land or take off, especially when fully loaded. Pilots taking off were forced to dive parallel to the slope of the hill to gain flying speed. When landing, pilots reaching the end of the airstrip had to cut left or right and run along the edge of the hill. It made for a hellish ride for paratroopers and flight crews alike. Winters commented that it was safer to jump out of the plane than to land in it.

As the officers prepared for their first of five qualifying jumps, Sink organized a Junior Officers' Olympics in order to determine which man would have the honor of being the first out of the plane. There were push-up, chin-up and obstacle course competitions, culminating in a race to see who could make the best time up and down Currahee. Winters won and was awarded the first seat in the first stick for the first jump.

After a hair-raising takeoff, the C-47 circled the drop zone. As jumpmaster, Winters stood by the door, a mixture of excitement and fear coursing through his mind. He was anxious to go, yet he asked himself, "Am I nuts? What the hell am I doing here?" Pushing his fears aside, he jumped, coming down in a cornstalk-stubbled field.

That night Nixon asked Winters, "How'd it go? Were you nervous?"

"No," Winters replied. "But I questioned my own sanity. Then I just told myself that if I want to be a paratrooper, I'm going, and it overcame my common sense."

The fifth and final qualifying jump for the 506th's officers was a morning exercise, after which Sink made a plane available for anyone wanting to go into Atlanta to celebrate. Winters decided to go and shop for a new jacket and uniform items, but on this landmark day, Sink decided to make things even more memorable. At his direction, the sergeant flying the C-47 took the plane down to treetop level, hedge-hopping over farms and fields and houses, sending people scattering and chickens flying. It was the most nightmarish flight Winters had ever experienced to date.

Next came the qualifying jumps for the enlisted men. The first went off without a hitch, but before the next jump the C-47, coming back to base after unloading its stick of paratroopers, overshot the airstrip and crashed. The pilot and crew escaped serious injury, but it marked the end of qualifying jumps at Toccoa, and the training was shifted to Fort Benning.

As he was readying the 506th for its move from Toccoa to Benning, Sink read an article in *Reader's Digest* about a Japanese unit in Malaya that marched one hundred miles in seventy-two hours. Determined to prove his men were better than anything the Emperor could field, Sink ordered that his regiment walk to Atlanta. The trek began on December 1. The next day a cold winter rain swept in, forcing the men to make their beds that night in a muddy field. Lacking a tent, Winters rolled out his sleeping bag on the ground, removed his wet boots and tried to settle in as best he could. Temperatures dropped below freezing overnight and Winters awoke to find his sleeping bag frozen to the mud and his boots stiff to the point where he could barely get them on, even with the laces totally undone.

The cold, wet clothes and boots, and more rain mixed with snow, made the third day of the march by far the worst, yet when the regiment arrived at Benning on December 4, only twelve of the 586 men who started had failed to finish. They had marched 118 miles in seventy-five hours, fifteen minutes (actual marching time, thirty-three hours, thirty minutes) and earned a unit citation.

At Benning, the men learned how to land properly by jumping into piles of sawdust from dummy plane fuselages, and were dropped under a deployed parachute from a 250-foot tower, like the Lifesaver's Parachute Jump ride at the 1939 World's Fair. Finally, it was time for the real thing.

For most, the first jump was the toughest, yet few refused to leap from the plane, knowing that to do so meant an instant washout. When a man did freeze in the door, a member of the plane's crew clutched the overhead cable, lifted himself off the floor, and kicked the soldier out from behind. That usually cured the man's fear.

One whose endurance surprised Winters was Sobel, who was cursed with what Winters called "big flat feet" that caused him to "run like a duck in distress." Winters was certain that landings were painful for Sobel, and some-

times those landings became the butt of company jokes. On one jump, as Sobel neared the ground, his feet seemed to send out a distress signal to his
brain, causing him to have a last minute knee-jerk reaction, and he landed
hard on his ass. Sobel was sore for several days and the men had a private
laugh at their commander's expense.

*   *   *

With jump training now behind him, Winters took a ten-day leave and headed
for Pennsylvania, arriving home at 7:30 P.M. on New Year's Eve. The home-
coming was not what Winters expected. Although glad to be back with his
family, his experience in the wartime army had so drastically changed him
that he felt out of place and isolated in this once-familiar world that had now
grown so foreign.

"Home is still a wonderful place, but nowadays I am a stranger among
friends," he complained to DeEtta on January 15, 1943, after returning to
camp. "It's good to get away from there. They don't even know there's a war
going on."

In early March the 506th moved to Camp MacKall, North Carolina, where
the troops underwent the most extensive maneuvers they had yet experienced. Emphasis now shifted from just learning how to jump and land, to
quick movements and operating behind enemy lines. Within Easy Company,
though, the increased field training seemed to heighten the tension as Sobel's
leadership deficiencies became more and more apparent, and his treatment of
the men grew correspondingly harsher. They, in turn, retaliated with a host of
pranks. His maps were "mislaid" so he got lost on field exercises, and once
medics, as part of an exercise on treating the wounded, put Sobel under anes-
thesia and performed a fake appendectomy, complete with an actual scar. He
never discovered who was responsible.

Winters was also growing frustrated. More and more he was doing the duties of the executive officer, but without the official title.

"For the past few weeks I have been running the company, yes sir, company commander," he wrote DeEtta on March 28. "The darndest part of it all
is that we've had the hardest part of our training in those weeks." Winters expected to be named executive officer, a job he was already performing unofficially. That prophesy came true a few weeks later when Winters was
appointed executive officer for Company E, 506th. "My job is to take charge
of the company when the captain is not around, which he never is, and do the
paperwork," he wrote DeEtta on Easter Sunday, April 15. "Don't ask me what
the captain does."

The 506th left MacKall to take part in army maneuvers in Kentucky and

Tennessee, jumping from C-47s that also towed gliders along behind them. At Camp Breckinridge, Kentucky, they crossed the swiftly flowing Cumberland River in rubber boats. It became obvious to all that they were preparing for deployment overseas.

Even though Winters was aware that each day, each drill and each maneuver brought him nearer to combat with all its dangers, he optimistically thought beyond the war to a future that was anything but guaranteed.

"I've sent word home to buy a farm after they get done paying off the house with the money I send home each month," Winters wrote DeEtta. "I want a good investment and a place to go after this war's over. I'd sure like to see what they pick out, but I guess any place in Lancaster County would be OK by me."

On August 22, the 506th arrived at Camp Shanks, an embarkation center nicknamed "Last Stop USA" near Orangeburg in Rockland County, New York. Amid this final preparation, Winters was given a special assignment. Sink had ordered all officers to buy a new overcoat; plus the officers' club stock was low on whiskey. Each officer was assessed the price of the coat and a share of the booze, but Sink needed an officer he could trust, especially with the whiskey detail. Who better to send than a man who did not drink? So Winters was sent off to Philadelphia.

Buying the coats was simple since Winters had a list of names and sizes, and they were duly purchased and shipped. Getting the whiskey was a different matter. Sink ordered Winters to buy a truckload of Southern Comfort, evidently forgetting that almost everything in the nation, including alcohol, was rationed. After converting his wad of cash to money orders, Winters spent a day riding around Philadelphia in a taxi but came up empty. Exasperated, he caught a train home to Lancaster and called his regimental headquarters at Camp Shanks.

"Colonel, I have been all over Philly looking for the whiskey, and I've run into a brick wall," he told Lieutenant Colonel Charles H. Chase, the regimental executive officer. "I have called or visited every distributor I could find. I've asked almost everybody I've met. I don't know where else to turn."

"Stay near a phone, Lieutenant," Chase told him. "I'll call you back."

Next day, Chase phoned and gave Winters the name of Schenley's, a large liquor distributor headquartered in the Empire State Building in New York City. Winters boarded a train and set out to complete his mission. At Schenley's Winters was ushered into an office and introduced to a pudgy man seated in a chair, his gout-ridden foot propped up on a stool. Swarming around the man were "more beautiful, well-groomed secretaries than I'd ever seen in my life," Winters later wrote. Winters felt ill at ease in this "totally foreign atmosphere," but knew he had to succeed or go back without the whiskey and, he feared, face a firing squad.

"Jesus," Winters later told Nixon. "There I was, just a kid from a Mennonite family background, and I was facing this bloated executive with all these beautiful secretaries, and he was the only man who could save me."

He told the man what he needed.

"Yes, I can take care of that order," the man instantly replied. Ecstatic, Winters felt the "bloated executive" had just helped to win the war.

✱ ✱ ✱

The S.S. *Samaria*, an old, fatigued Cunard passenger liner now pressed into service as a troop transport, slipped away from Piermunt Pier and out of New York harbor the morning of September 5. On board the ship, equipped to carry one thousand passengers, Winters and five thousand other GIs somberly watched the Statue of Liberty glide by to starboard. Standing with Winters, Lieutenant Frederick T. "Moose" Heyliger of headquarters company stared at the fading statue with special intentness. Just prior to departure, he received word that his wife had given birth to a "Little Moose." Once at sea, Heyliger, Winters and their friends celebrated with a night of singing.

The ship's cramped conditions made the ten-day passage miserable. Fresh drinking water was only available at fifteen-minute intervals. Shaving time was limited and the men took saltwater showers, using a special soap that left them feeling sticky. It was only slightly better for the officers.

The threat of prowling German U-boats meant all ranks had to wear life jackets and sleep in their clothes. The coffee was horrible, and the men ate meals twice a day in a crowded, unventilated mess hall on the lower deck. Luckily the trip across the unpredictable North Atlantic was relatively calm, yet by the time they docked in Liverpool, Winters felt as though he had lost all of his muscle tone, especially in his legs.

✱ ✱ ✱

Aldbourne, a picturesque hamlet in Wiltshire, lies fifty miles west of London. Here Sink kicked the regiment back into shape with fifteen-, twenty- and twenty-five-mile hikes with full field pack. Training exercises included lessons in street fighting, combat team training and map reading. Plus there were training jumps on company, battalion and regimental scale. During one of these jumps, on March 8, 1944, the company suffered its first loss. Private Rudolph R. Dittrich was killed when his parachute failed. The death of a man they had trained with for over a year cast a pall of sorrow over the men of Easy. Winters knew the men had to shake off this tragedy and move on. Dittrich might have been the first death, but he would not be the last, and the troops had to learn to live with the distinct possibility that any of them, even the officers, could be next.

At Aldbourne, the men lived in Nissen huts but officers were farmed out to the community to ease overcrowding. The Barnes family, whom Winters had befriended that Sunday morning, agreed to house two men provided one be their young American friend.

Besides being the town grocer, Francis Barnes was a lay minister at the Methodist Chapel on Lottage Road. Louie May was the church organist. The couple welcomed Winters into their home, along with his assistant platoon leader, Harry Welsh, giving the two officers a second-floor room overlooking the street. They still slept on army cots, but at least they were away from the crowded camp.

While Welsh, product of a Pennsylvania coal mining town, was usually out on the town, Winters used the quiet time to study and reflect on his job and himself. In later life, he felt living with the Barnes family was one of the luckiest breaks of his life, allowing him the needed time to mature as a man and build the strong sense of character that he would carry with him for the remainder of his life.

Besides privacy, the Barnes family also presented Winters with a new "sister." At thirteen, Elaine Stevens was the same age as Ann Winters back in Lancaster. Blond, five feet tall, and chipper despite being separated from her family, Elaine was one of thousands of children evacuated from London to the countryside where German bombers seldom roamed. Winters felt bad for the child and eagerly took to the role of big brother. From a poor, working-class family background, Elaine came to the Barnes poorly dressed. With wartime rationing, there was little available in the way of new clothes, so Winters enhanced Elaine's wardrobe by having some of his shirts retailored to fit her. He bought her a sweater, gloves, scarves and shoes with some of his ration coupons, and took her to shows, shopping and out to eat. One of their favorite dining spots was the officers' mess hall for Sunday dinner.

Life at the Barneses' residence was not too unlike life at home. Around nine each evening, Mother Barnes would climb the stairs and knock on Winters' room door and ask, "Leftenant, would you like to come downstairs and listen to the news on the radio?"

Often he joined the family around the dining room table, where Mr. Barnes would read Bible verses while Louie May cut up bread for snacks and served tea.

"They don't put butter or jam on toast, and they don't have popcorn, marshmallows or hot dogs," Winters complained in a letter home, not about the Barnes family, but the British in general. "They never heard of the stuff. Man, what I wouldn't give for a milkshake, some eggs, a couple quarts of milk and ice cream."

That done, around ten, Mr. Barnes would announce authoritatively that it was time for bed.

Winters enjoyed his quiet life in Aldbourne. He made many friends in the village, especially among the kids who tagged along with him when he went for walks, giving him the "thumbs-up" sign or asking, "Any gum, Yank?"

There were aspects of British life Winters had to adjust to, such as phrases that had two meanings and were taken one way by an Englishman and a completely different way by a GI. One evening over tea, Winters was relating his exhausting day to Mr. and Mrs. Barnes; the drills, the field problems and the chore of getting men ready for war. A weary Louie Barnes also had a busy day and sighed, "Oh, I am all knocked up."

Winters recalled that he nearly choked on a mouthful of tea.

Though in the warm presence of an adopted family, Winters still valued his solitary lifestyle. While the other officers and men took leave in London or elsewhere, he remained in Aldbourne to read or study. He took well-intentioned ribbing from his men, but it was teasing borne of respect. His hermitlike lifestyle carried a certain loneliness.

On March 29, 1944, he wrote DeEtta, "I am a half-breed; an officer, yet part enlisted man. So I work and do my duty as I should, but when it comes to play, I am in a bad position and only in athletics with the men do I enjoy myself. The happiest days of my army career were at Croft, making $21 a month, yet always a little money at the end of the month. I traveled more, did more and had more fun than at any time since."

It was in this same letter that he told DeEtta about his father's response to buying a farm. His father, Winters said, advised his son to postpone the farm idea and first take time to "rest and play" before settling down.

Winters contemplated taking a job as a deckhand on a tramp steamer or on a liner and sail around the world. When he tired of traveling, he would settle down and look for a job. "It's not practical, fantastic and all that, but brother, I know this idea of thinking you can go home and adjust yourself to that old type of life by just changing uniforms is wrong," he wrote DeEtta. "And I don't want to be around home while I am adjusting myself."

Insistent on keeping in shape, Winters slipped out of the Barneses' house early each morning for a five-mile run. During free time he coached the 506th basketball team with Lieutenant Lynn "Buck" Compton, newly assigned to the company, as his assistant. A no-frills operation, the team had no basketball court, hence no practices, no offensive or defensive strategies, and all their games were "away." They also had no uniforms, so when the team played the spit-and-polish Army Air Force's teams, Winters' players in shorts or long johns were in stark contrast to their opponents, whose new uniforms and sweat suits had been brought over from the States.

Their shabby dress notwithstanding, Winters had a solid team consisting of Sergeant Robert J. Rader, Sergeant Floyd Talbert, Corporal Lavon P. Reese, Corporal Gordon F. Carson, all of E Company and Private First Class John D. Hall at center, Private First Class Donald Harms at forward and a Sergeant Barlow as guard.

In a military camp, men gamble on almost everything, and these inter-regimental games were fertile ground for those looking to make extra leave money. Prior to a match against the 501st, Sink told Winters, "Just remember, Lieutenant, the 506th's payroll is riding on this game, so just go out and win."

"Yes, sir," he said, although his mind was cynically adding, "Nothing to it."

Luckily Winters did not disappoint his commander. With the game tied in the final seconds, Winters noticed Barlow, his top playmaker, was wearing down. He pulled Barlow out and replaced him with Carson, who got the ball, moved rapidly down court and fired a long shot that dropped in for the game-winning points.

"From today on, you are my hero," he told Carson afterward.

"Great," Carson replied jokingly. "How about rewarding me with a transfer back to the States?"

"Sorry, Gordy," Winters said. "I need all the heroes I can get right here."

As the invasion drew near, playtime was getting harder to come by as the 506th took part in more extensive exercises. Operation Beaver on March 27–31 involved seaborne troops storming ashore at a simulated Utah Beach at Torquay, Devonshire, while airborne forces "dropped" at nearby Slapton, usually by jumping off the backs of moving trucks due to a lack of aircraft. Operation Tiger, April 23–30, a division-size exercise, took place in the same vicinity and Operation Eagle, May 9–12, the largest exercise of all, saw airborne troops take off from the same airfields and, if possible, on the same planes they would use on D-Day.

The training was cold, dirty work, and a bone-weariness settled in among the troops. Winters' philosophy of dealing with his men and keeping up morale and fighting spirit was to move among them. One damp, dreary morning he noticed Private Clarence S. Howell manning a machine gun outpost and looking thoroughly miserable. The men had been marching and fighting mock battles for twenty-four hours nonstop. Howell, like the rest, was tired, wet, cold and hungry. As Winters watched, Howell fished a photograph from a pocket and stared down at it.

"How's it going, Shep?" Winters asked, kneeling next to the young soldier.

"Fine, sir," he replied, still looking at the photo.

"What's that?" Winters asked. "A picture from home?"

"Yes, sir," Howell said, showing it to Winters. It was a young woman. "My girl," he added, as if he felt he had to explain.

"She's very pretty, Shep," Winters said, examining the smiling young face. "You must miss her. Are you two planning to tie the knot?"

"Yes, sir," he answered, studying the photo again. "I was just wondering how long it'll be until I can get back to her, or even if I'll ever see her again."

"You will," Winters said, patting the man's shoulder. "Just keep your mind focused on your job. You're a good man, Shep. Hang tough."

Walking away, Winters reflected on the young private's fears and his hopes for the future. The brief exchange with this lonely youngster reinforced the heavy burden of command placed on Winters' shoulders. The survival of these men depended, in large part, on his own knowledge and skills as a teacher and a leader. It was a sobering moment.

"In three years, I've aged a great deal," he wrote that night. "It seems as if the college days and the days of civilian life when I did as I pleased are long gone. It must have been a dream, a small, short, but beautiful part of my life. All I do is work to improve myself as an officer, and them as fighters and as men, make them work to improve themselves. As a result, I am old before my time. Not old physically, but hardened to the point where I can make the rest of them look like undeveloped high school boys. Old to the extent where I can keep going after my men fall over and go to sleep from exhaustion, and I can keep going like a mother who works on after her sick and exhausted child has fallen asleep. Old to the extent where if it's a decision or advice needed, my decisions are taken as if the wisdom behind them was infallible. Yes, I feel old and tired from training these men to the point where they are efficient fighters. I hope it means some will return to that girl back home."

* * *

One weight that had been lifted from Winters' shoulders was Herbert Sobel. The simmering dispute between the two had boiled over the previous October. Winters had been ordered by Sobel to inspect the company latrines an hour prior to an 11 A.M. inspection by Colonel Sink. After spending the morning, at Strayer's direction, in the orderly room censoring the men's outgoing mail, Winters pedaled his bicycle to the latrines, parking it outside at 10 A.M. on the dot. Entering, he found Sobel already inspecting the facility. Sobel brushed by Winters, head down, as if his lieutenant did not exist. Private Joachim Melo, the latrine orderly trailed along behind Sobel, mop in hand. Melo's clothes were soaking wet, his face unshaven, his hair uncombed. To Winters he looked like "a man who had just finished a dirty job." Completing his inspection, Sobel made some notations, then left without uttering a word. Winters proceeded to conduct his own inspection, finding that Melo had done an excellent job.

Forty-five minutes later, as Winters prepared for the inspection, First Sergeant William S. Evans found him.

"Lieutenant Winters," Evans said, holding out a piece of paper. "Captain Sobel's compliments, sir."

Winters took the paper and unfolded it. He couldn't believe what he was reading.

> Subject: Punishment Under 104th AW
> To: 1st Lt. R.D. Winters
>
> 1. You will indicate by indorsement *(Author's note: The mis-spelling was Evans')* below whether you desire punishment under 104th AW or trial by Courts Martial for failure to inspect the latrine at 0945 this date as instructed by me.
>
> > Herbert M. Sobel, Capt.
> > Commanding

Taken aback, Winters hurried to Sobel's office to confront his commander, who told him he had changed the time to 9:45 and had both tried to phone Winters about the change and had sent a runner with the new time. Winters knew Sobel was trying to "gig" him; that no runner had been dispatched and that Sobel knew there was no phone in the orderly room. "Bullshit!" Winters told himself, anger welling up. "This is it." After the inspection he returned to the orderly room and wrote "I request trial by Courts Martial for failure to inspect the latrines at 0945 this date" on the bottom of Sobel's memo, signed and returned it.

Next day Evans handed Winters a second note:

> 1. You will be denied a 48-hour pass until after Dec. 15, 1943.
> 2. In accordance with the procedure outlined in the Court Mar-

tial Manual you will institute your own letter of appeal with your reasons for objection and also a request for trial by courts martial.
3. Unless set aside by superior authority the above punishment will be enforced.

Relinquishing his pass was no punishment for Winters since he seldom left Aldbourne, preferring, as he wrote, to "loaf around camp on weekends" and read, run or play football. But the unwarranted attack infuriated him and he wrote in his November 4 appeal:

1. Under the provisions of Article of War 104 appeal is requested on punishment rendered by Captain Herbert M. Sobel on Lt. Richard D. Winters for failure to inspect latrines on Oct. 30, 1943 at 0945 hrs.
2. On October 30, 1943 I was ordered by Captain Herbert M. Sobel to inspect the latrines at 1000 hr. Until that hour I was engaged in supervision or work relegated to me by Lt. Col. Strayer at about 0930 hr. I did inspect the latrines at 1000 hr. and never received the latter order of Capt. Sobel moving up the time to 0945 hr. as I was on detail as previously explained.

The war on paper continued. On November 8, Sobel wrote to Winters, saying:

1. Punishment for the above offense given by the undersigned will not be lifted by him.
2. You will recall that in a telephone conversation about 0915 on Oct. 30, I talked with you and told you to be here at 0940 and to have Lt. Davis be here also then.
3. When given another task to perform by a ranking officer to myself you should have delegated your task to another officer to inspect the latrine and not let it go until such time that there was little time for corrective measures to be taken before the arrival of the General Officer about 10 minutes later.

On November 11, an exasperated Strayer intervened, writing that "Punishment under 104th A.W. of Lt. R.D. Winters is hereby set aside, as per authority contained in Court Martial manual. Papers will be returned to the appellants' commanding officer for file with the record in the case."

The argument settled for him, a disgruntled Sobel fired a parting volley at Winters:

1. You will reply by indorsement hereon your reason for failure to instruct Pvt. J. Melo in his duties as latrine orderly.
2. You will further reply why he was permitted to be on duty at 1030 this date in need of a shave.

Winters' reply to both accusations was "No excuse."

"I'm guilty," he thought bitterly. "So shoot me."

Despite the "acquittal," Strayer transferred Winters out of Easy and made him battalion mess officer. This incensed Winters, who felt mess duty was only given to men "who were goof offs you don't know what to do with." Winters felt crushed. It was the first time since being in the army that he was not in the field with the men.

The departure of Winters and the fact that Sobel remained in command of the company stirred the deepest resentment among the noncommissioned officers. Winters discovered how deep one Saturday afternoon when he was invited to a meeting of the noncoms in the orderly room.

Sergeant Myron "Mike" Ranney led the meeting.

"We have decided we've had enough of Sobel and his bullshit," he told Winters. "We don't want to serve as NCOs in any company led by that man, so we've decided to write letters to Sink, turning in our stripes."

Winters considered this for a moment, realizing the seriousness of what these sergeants were contemplating.

"You're talking mutiny," he told them. "I can't condone that action. Sink could have you all shot. Do yourselves a favor. Don't even think about it."

At that moment Sobel walked in. All eyes turned to him and he stared back at the men. It was Ranney who first regained his composure.

"Now, how can we improve our athletic program?" he asked.

Sobel picked up a book and left, but Winters was convinced Sobel knew something was afoot.

The NCOs were resolved and, despite Winters' words of caution, they presented their letters to their commander. Sink was furious at the sergeants' ultimatum. He immediately busted Ranney to private and had Sergeant Terrence C. Harris transferred, but the poisoned atmosphere now plainly visible within Easy finally moved Sink to action. Sobel was reassigned to the jump school at Chilton Foliat and First Lieutenant Thomas Meehan was brought in from Baker Company to take command, with First Lieutenant Patrick J. Sweeney of Able Company temporarily transferred in as executive officer. Winters was brought back to the company and put in command of 1st Platoon, reclaiming his old job as executive officer after Sweeney's departure.

When the dust had settled, Major Horton, regimental XO, stopped Winters.

"You gave me one hell of a problem trying to figure out how to quash that court-martial," he said. "Sink was on my ass the whole damned time. We had the court-martial manual out and were doing a lot of reading for a couple of days."

"Sorry to give such trouble, sir," Winters said. "But I had all of that S.O.B. I could take."

"Well, I'm just glad to have you back," Horton said. "And so is the colonel."

*   *   *

By late May 1944 the 101st was making preparations for its part in the invasion of Europe. Duffel bags were packed, and personal items stored. The final social event Winters and his men enjoyed before leaving for the marshaling area on May 29 occurred nine days earlier, when Sergeant Leo Boyle married an Aldbourne girl. Winifred "Wyn" Hawkins was an attractive and vivacious girl, and Winters found it quite easy to see how Boyle could fall in love with her. Winifred sprang from a deeply religious family, so it came as no surprise to Winters when Boyle became a regular churchgoer. He'd soon gained her family's approval and worked up the courage to ask for her hand in marriage.

For Winters, it was the first church wedding he had ever attended, and he found the experience unnerving to the point where he said he'd rather jump out of a plane. "My legs were quivering and I was just an onlooker," he wrote. The wedding was not without its share of pranks, including when Boyle's buddies dropped smoke grenades as the happy couple was leaving the church, then kidnapped the bride during the confusion. They returned Wyn thirty minutes later. "If time hadn't been so valuable," Winters wrote a few days later, "I'll bet that she'd still be missing."

Just as it had become necessary to bid farewell to his real family in America, Winters now said good-bye to his English family. Many of the townspeople, some weeping, waved farewell to their Yanks. Hoisting themselves into the deuce-and-a-halves that lined the cobblestone road, the regiment began its journey to war. As the trucks moved out, Winters saw Elaine and waved what he hoped would not be a final good-bye.

The 506th was taken to Upottery. Here, on May 31, the men learned for the first time that they were bound for Normandy. For the next several days they rigorously studied the area's defenses, towns and landmarks so that, before they took off, they could sketch the road networks around their drop zones from memory. On June 3 Winters led his men to the supply dump to draw ammo and grenades. They took hot showers, the last they would have for weeks, and stocked up on candy and cigarettes.

Unaware of these preparations for war, DeEtta had been hoping Winters could get a furlough home and planned a boat ride for the two. On June 2, Winters dashed that dream. But he had another suggestion.

"Every night at taps, I'll meet you at the North Star," he wrote. "The old North Star is a soldier's guiding light when he's lost, alone, and feeling mighty funny in the pit of his stomach. That's when he feels good, when he can look up and know that there is somebody else looking up there also."

On June 4, the 101st moved to its assigned airfields and made a final check of their gear. Each trooper was issued $10 in French francs, newly minted in Washington, D.C., and a map of the Normandy area, printed on silk. That evening the cooks served up a feast of steak, mashed potatoes, white bread, peas, ice cream and coffee. The meal was accompanied by the usual cracks about "fattening us up for the kill."

General Maxwell Taylor, who had succeeded Lee as division commander, took the opportunity to give the men a pep talk that would later be recalled with wry humor. "Give me three days of hard fighting," he said, "and then you'll be withdrawn."

Tension got the best of Lieutenant Raymond Schmitz, who challenged Winters to a boxing match. Winters refused but Schmitz kept haranguing him, finally daring Winters, "Okay, let's wrestle." This was right up Winters' alley, so the match was short and painful, especially for Schmitz, who ended up with two cracked vertebrae. He would miss the jump. For the next twenty-four hours men asked Winters, "Will you break my arm for five dollars?"

That evening the 506th was trucked to the airfield. There Winters had his men spread out their gear for one last equipment check. Besides his weapon, each man carried GI socks and underwear, a brass compass, canteen, first-aid kit (which included one morphine syrette, sulfa powder and a tourniquet), horsehide gloves, jump knife, pocketknife, entrenching tool, ninety-six rounds of ammo, matches, four grenades, pistol or cartridge belt, gas mask, four K rations, three D rations, at least two cartons of cigarettes (to smoke or barter once in France) and Halizone tablets to purify water, rain poncho, toiletry set, thirty feet of rope and everything else a man might require in the field. A Mae West life jacket completed the ensemble.

As jumpmaster of his stick, Winters was handed two packets of papers to hand out once they got to the planes. After synchronizing their watches, Winters ordered, "Load up," and the men climbed into trucks to be whisked off to the hardstand. There, eighty-one parked C-47s, many with bundles of ammunition strapped to their underbellies, awaited the regiment.

Winters' platoon was divided into two groups, or sticks, with him in command of one, and Welsh taking charge of the other. Two men from headquarters company, Robert Burr Smith and Joseph E. Hogan, were reassigned to Winters' two planes after Meehan found his C-47 overloaded. The trucks carrying Winters and stick #67 halted by plane 42-100646, their ride to the war. "Everybody out," Winters said, jumping from the truck to the tarmac. Hauling themselves out of the truck, the men were allowed to relax before the order came to climb aboard. With double daylight savings, it didn't get dark until 10:30 P.M., so the troops sat in clumps on the ground or under the wings of the planes, chatting and watching the sun go down.

Then bad weather closed in over the Channel, and a fierce wind kicked up. Shortly afterward, Meehan stood up in the back of a jeep and told the men they had been ordered to stand down. The invasion was postponed. A loud moan interspersed with colorful language swept over the field. After working themselves up into a high state of readiness, the delay came as a hell of a letdown for Winters and the rest.

On the afternoon of June 5, preparations began again. Winters spent the afternoon getting ready, then grabbed a fitful two-hour nap. At 8:30 P.M., the 506th once more headed for the airfield. Columns of men passed buddies marching in other directions, but in the somber air few words were exchanged, just a silent nod of greeting or a simple, "Good luck" or "See you over there." As Winters led his men past a British antiaircraft gun crew, he noticed the Tommies had tears in their eyes. Walking quietly across the field toward their aircraft, Winters spotted some flowers in bloom and wondered if he'd see the flowers blossom next spring.

At the C-47 Skytrain, Winters handed out the "poop sheets" he'd been given the day before. One carried the letterhead of the Supreme Headquarters Allied Expeditionary Force, or SHAEF, and was signed by General Dwight D. Eisenhower. It said they were "about to embark on a great crusade, toward which we have striven these many months." It continued, "The eyes of the world are upon you. The hopes and prayers of liberty-loving people everywhere march with you." At the end it wished them, "Good luck! And let us all beseech the blessing of Almighty God upon this great and noble undertaking."

Its words rang somewhat hollowly in the ears of the men about to jump into Occupied France, yet there was a general feeling of pride and anticipation.

The second note was from Colonel Sink, who wrote that they were heading for the "great adventure for which you have trained for over two years."

"Tonight is the night of nights," Sink's memo read. "Tomorrow throughout the whole of our homeland and the Allied world, the bells will ring out the tidings that you have arrived and the invasion for liberation has begun."

Winters folded his two letters and tucked them inside his helmet liner.

The timetable called for the men to begin loading into the planes at 10:15 P.M., with takeoff about 11:10 P.M. The drop was slated for 1:20 A.M.

As ten o'clock approached, the soldiers began the arduous task of climbing into their gear. Winters noticed Private Robert T. Leonard was missing something.

"Jeeter," Winters said. "How come you only have one bandolier of ammo? You're supposed to have two."

"Yes, sir, I know," he replied. "It's all I could carry."

Winters had spare ammo to give him, but agreed that the man was weighed down.

"See me in the assembly area," Winters told him. "I'll give you more."

He never saw Leonard again. The young private would be badly wounded before the day was out and the next Winters heard from him was in a letter from a hospital in England, letting him know what happened and fretting that Winters might still be toting around that extra bandolier, looking for him.

Adding to the burden the men had to carry was the fact that their uniforms had been impregnated with a chemical to make them resistant to a gas attack. Unfortunately, this also had the effect of making the clothes stiff and heavy, and they stank like hell. Plus, the chemical irritated the skin. Winters' treated uniform was in his footlocker. Even the possibility of death by lethal gas could not entice him to wear it.

"I figured if I'm going to die, I'm going to die, but I wasn't about to be miserable while I was doing it," he later said. "I wondered if anyone else had left his chemical-laden uniform behind, but I didn't ask."

Something else that was dreamed up by the boys who would not be making the jump was the issuance of motion sickness pills. These had never been used during practice jumps, and one of the side effects, the men sadly discovered, was drowsiness, a soldier's worst enemy in combat next to the Germans.

But the worst fiasco Winters and the rest had to contend with was a British innovation: the leg bag. Strapped to the right leg and around the instep of the boot, the large canvas bag was a place to store extra gear. In his, Winters carried his disassembled M1 Garand rifle, grenades, ammunition, blanket, clothes, mess gear, pistol, binoculars; in short, almost everything he needed upon landing. The leg bag wasn't bad in theory. When leaving the plane, the trooper swung his right leg out of the doorway and let gravity take over. Once out and after the chute had deployed, the soldier pulled a metal pin on the bag, which caused it to drop on the end of a twenty-foot rope. Thus, the bag hit first, helping to warn the man of the approaching ground and softening his own impact. It was a good idea if it worked right. Most didn't.

One thing Winters would've liked to have worn but had to leave behind was his reserve parachute. With a musette bag strapped across his chest and stuffed with all the gear he couldn't get into his leg bag, plus his Mae West, he simply couldn't get the reserve chute on. He prayed the main chute was packed correctly.

At 10:15 the order came, "Load up!"

Burdened by 125 pounds of equipment, the simplest of movements became a major chore. Men helped each other to stand up. Waddling ducklike to the plane, the soldier was hoisted inside with one man shoving from the rear and two crewmen pulling from above. Once aboard, the soldier took his preassigned seat.

Before Winters boarded, Meehan stopped by. The two officers shook hands and nodded good luck. No words were exchanged. None were needed. Winters turned and climbed into the aircraft, taking his place at the door.

Around eleven, the pilots flipped the ignition switches and their engines began to turn over. Even inside the fuselage, the growing roar of the Pratt & Whitneys was deafening. Winters' plane rattled and vibrated as its motors built up speed. Normal conversations had to be delivered via shouts. Then the plane began to roll forward.

At 11:13 P.M. the lead Skytrain roared down the runway. The pilot, Lieutenant Colonel Charles H. Young, commander of the 439th Transport Group, leaned back on the wheel and pulled the C-47 into the air. Its propellers bit into the night, fighting to gain altitude. He was followed by plane after plane in rapid succession until all were aloft.

After Winters' plane was airborne, one of the transport's crewmembers removed the hatch and shoved the large equipment bag, containing the heavier weapons, into the doorway. When the green "jump" light went on, Winters was to push out the equipment bag before following it as rapidly as possible. Once on the ground, the men would retrieve the bag and the weapons. In a day jump this would be easy; a night jump was another matter. Anticipating this difficulty, during one practice jump Winters tried what seemed like a good idea at the time, but could have been fatal. He attached a thirty-foot rope to the equipment bag, tying the other end to himself. The theory was that, once he landed, all he had to do was follow the rope to find the bag. However, during his descent, the wind caused the rope to swirl and spiral high over his head, and he feared it might wrap around and collapse his canopy, sending him plummeting to the earth like a lead weight. That ended the rope experiment.

Aloft, the transports carrying the 506th divided into two serials, with forty-five planes led by Young in the first, and thirty-six in the second, ten miles to the rear. This group of thirty-six C-47s included the eight planes carrying Dick Winters and the 139 men of Easy Company. On the ground, men watched somberly as the air armada turned on a southeasterly heading and disappeared into the gathering darkness.

CHAPTER 4

"A Very, Very Tough Day."

June 7–July 12, 1944

Through the binoculars, the rooftops of the village of Vierville, about a mile and a half away, came crisply into focus despite the hedgerows that crisscrossed the marshy, flat fields. Yesterday, D-Day, a reconnaissance patrol from the 506th had scouted the ground and found no Germans. At 0400 on D-plus 1, units of the 1st Battalion of the 506th Regiment, with tank support, passed through Vierville, brushing aside token resistance. It was now about 0600, and no one had any clear idea of what might be lying in wait up ahead. Winters lowered the binoculars and handed them back to Captain Hester.

"The battalion's moving out shortly," Hester said. "I hate to do this to you after yesterday's fight, Dick, but your company's got the point."

"So all we have to do is walk straight down this road and knock on the front door," Winters said grimly.

"Not my idea, Dick. Talk to Strayer."

"Sure I will," Winters said to Hester with a wink, then returned to his company. With Lieutenant Meehan still missing, Winters retained command of Easy, which had grown overnight as men showed up in dribs and drabs. Winters handed command of first platoon over to Harry Welsh. Buck Compton kept second platoon, and Warren Rousch remained in charge of third. To replace the missing First Sergeant Evans, Winters tapped Punchy Diel.

"Gather round," Winters told his officers. "Here's the deal. We're point on the advance into Vierville. There's no telling what we're likely to encounter, but if we meet resistance, Harry, you deploy to the left of the road. Buck, you take the right. Rousch, third platoon'll be in reserve with the mortars. Any questions? Good. Get your men ready and keep alert."

Shortly after 0600, Winters got the order to move and Easy Company filed down the road. Walking with weapons at the ready, they hadn't gone a half mile when German small arms fire crackled from ahead. Their own guns blazing a reply, the men fanned out and dove to the ground. Easy had discovered the hard way that paratroopers of Colonel Frederick von der Heydte's 6th Fallschirmjager Regiment had reoccupied Vierville and taken up strong positions directly in front of the 506th.

Reacting to this sudden setback, Colonel Strayer ordered F Company to deploy on Easy's left. Captain Thomas Mulvey led his men into the action, but ran into heavy resistance and made no better progress than Winters had done. With the attack quickly bogging down, Strayer sent his reserves, Dog Company, around Fox's left, but Captain Gross ran into equally stiff German fire and was stopped.

Meanwhile, Winters' men and the German paratroopers continued to exchange fire. The barrels of the M1s and Thompsons grew hot as the GIs fed clip after clip into the smoking breeches. Behind the infantry line, Sergeant Guarnere was barking out ranges as the company's 60 mm mortars dropped rounds on the Germans, yet the well-entrenched enemy held. Shouting encouragement, Winters edged his men slowly forward, their progress measured in inches.

"Keep firing! Don't let up!" Winters yelled, snapping off several rounds from his Garand. "Pour it on 'em, boys. That's it. Reload! Keep at 'em."

The deadly contest continued well into midmorning, with the paratroopers making small gains. Still, the roar of gunfire and the deadly whir of bullets cutting through the air did not abate. At around nine, troops of Lieutenant Colonel Robert L. Turner's 1st Battalion began arriving, several tanks rolling along with them. Winters knew Turner and considered the West Pointer to be cocky, a point he proved today by riding in the lead Sherman, standing up in the open hatch, his arms resting on the rim. Turner was giving directions to the tank commander below him, inside the vehicle.

Winters, a believer that men in command need to take chances, but not act foolhardy, saw Turner and shook his head in disapproval.

Bullets now clanged off the armored sides of the tanks as the Germans swung their machine guns on the Shermans. The tanks halted, turrets swiveling as the gunners sought targets. With an ear-shattering roar they opened fire, their 76 mm cannons ripping the German position with canister shells. Yet even as their rounds blasted the enemy, a German bullet found Turner, who dropped back into the tank, dead.

On the far left, Jerre Gross managed to work Dog Company around the German flank and into Vierville. Under pressure from front and flank, the firing gradually flickered out as the battered Germans pulled back, leaving the town to the Americans. It would be the first of many clashes between the 101st and the 6th Fallschirmsjagers before the war's end.

*   *   *

Colonel Sink established regimental headquarters at the farming hamlet of Angoville-au-Plain, pulling Winters' company off the line to provide security. The rest of the 2nd Battalion continued the fight south of Vierville the next day, closing in on St. Come du Mont. From HQ, Winters and his men could see the smoke and hear the distant rumble of the fierce fight taking place around the intersection of D-913 and Route Nationale 13. A wrecked American tank, its slain commander draped over the hatch, had given this intersection the grisly nom de guerre of Dead Man's Corner. In a field near the intersection, Dog Company lost Captain Gross, killed by shrapnel from an exploding artillery round. He was replaced by Lieutenant Joseph F. McMillen.

Being behind the front line did not exclude Easy Company from the action. "Krauts!" one of Winters' men yelled. "Krauts in the open!"

Winters ran from his command post and saw an entire battalion of Germans scampering across the swampy field between his position and St. Come du Mont.

"Machine guns, open fire," he shouted. "Give it to 'em, Liebgott."

The company's two .30 calibers spat a stream of lead at the Germans, who scattered in disarray. Some wisely headed south, but most sprinted west toward the road, where they ran into GIs of the 3rd Battalion. Those Germans who weren't shot down were taken prisoner. Of nearly eight hundred men only twenty-seven men made it back to their lines.

Easy Company spent three days at Angoville-au-Plain, listening to the distant roll of the guns, watching the billowing smoke and scrambling for cover when the occasional German plane, risking Allied air superiority, made a token strafing run. Winters' biggest problem occurred when some of his men discovered a hidden cache of wine and freely imbibed. Winters had the alcohol seized and sternly reprimanded the offenders for their lapse of discipline.

*   *   *

With a peacetime population of about four thousand, Carentan was the largest French town in the Utah Beach sector of the Cotentin Peninsula. The town sat astride the Cherbourg/Caen/St. Lô highway, as well as the Cherbourg/Paris railroad. Its distinction as a transportation hub made Carentan the main objective for the 101st Airborne now that the causeways from the beaches were open and secure. The town's fall would clear the way for a linkup between U.S. troops now pouring ashore at Utah and Omaha beaches.

Initial attacks on Carentan by the 101st began on June 8. The Germans had blown the bridges leading into the town and set up heavily fortified road-blocks that the Americans found costly to clear. In Carentan, von der Heydte's situation was precarious at best. He was outnumbered, out of communication with his headquarters and seriously low on supplies and ammunition, thanks to Allied fighters that made German airdrops almost suicidal. On June 10 General Taylor sent von der Heydte a surrender message, which the German rejected by writing back, "What would you do if you were in my position?" It was a warrior's rebuff. The fighting continued.

On June 11, Easy Company rejoined 2nd Battalion, which was headed south along Nationale 13 toward Carentan. Outside the town, the battalion swung right, across swampy fields heading toward Nationale 803, which entered Carentan to the west. It was one of the Germans' escape routes if they had to pull out.

"Our objective is this intersection leading out of town," Strayer had told Winters earlier. "We take it, and we can cut off the German retreat. They'll be forced through this swampy, flooded area, or be trapped. You'll take Easy directly into the town along the road. F Company will be on your left, Dog in reserve. We don't know how many Krauts are in the town. They've been very quiet, not giving away their positions."

Lit only by the eerie glow of burning vehicles from earlier fighting, the flooded field made for difficult traveling in the dark. The stench of dead flesh lingered over the field as Winters and his men stepped over contorted bodies and weaved around shattered equipment. As they plodded laboriously over marshland, the muck sucked at their boots. Passing through tangled stands of trees, units became separated and lost contact. Winters felt disgust at the disorganization, blaming not the junior officers so much as the battalion's ranking officers, who had skipped nighttime field problems back in England and at Toccoa. Radio contact between units was sporadic and, when contact was made, conversation was carried on in muffled tones. It was rumored that German armor was near; luckily, none showed up.

The plan called for being in position by 0530 with jump-off thirty minutes later, but by 0530 the men were far from prepared. The march had been long and hard, and the troops were exhausted. Worse, from Winters' point of view, there was no time for reconnaissance. Despite Allied air strength, there would be no air cover, nor was any artillery available. The attack seemed hastily thrown together and it pissed Winters off.

As the men awaited the assault, Lieutenant Lavenson, battalion S1, went off into a field, hiked down his trousers and squatted. His white buttocks gleamed in the moonlight, making him an inviting target. A shot rang out and

Lavenson yelped in pain as a bullet struck his behind. He was dragged to safety.

Route 803 entered Carentan as a gentle downward slope, with shallow ditches to both sides of the roadway. In town, it merged with another street to the right at a forty-five-degree angle. Together, they formed a slanted T intersection, dominated by a hotel that sat straight ahead, looking down the 803. Houses and shops lined both sides of the village street. That intersection was Winters' objective.

After taking all this in, Winters gathered his platoon leaders.

"What do you think?" Welsh said.

"I don't know, but I don't like it. The men are tired, the road exposed and there could be a thousand Krauts up ahead for all I know. Anyway, you've got the honors, Harry. Take first platoon straight in. Second platoon will follow, then third. Mortars and machine guns will provide covering fire. Get in there fast, all of you. When you hit the intersection, secure it and fan out to the right. Fox will handle our left."

Welsh got his men in position behind the crest of the hill. Winters knelt beside him. At 0600 Winters looked back at battalion HQ, located on the road to the rear, and saw Strayer and his staff watching. He signaled his machine guns to open fire, then turned to Welsh.

"Okay, Harry. Move out," he said. "Go!"

Welsh led his men forward and Winters signaled Compton to get second platoon ready. No sooner had Welsh jumped off than a German machine gun in the hotel ahead came to life. In perfect position to dominate the road, the MG-42 spat flame and death at the charging GIs. Welsh and his first six men braved the hail of lead and made it into the town, taking cover behind the nearest buildings. However, the next man in line, Sergeant Robert J. Rader, "simply put his head down and froze," as Winters recalled. Like cars in traffic, the rest of the platoon backed up behind him and, suddenly, on both sides of the road, men hunkered down in the ditches, heads low, immobile. Winters was horrified. Not only did he now have seven men on their own in the enemy-held town, but the rest were in danger as well. Stopping under fire was the worst thing they could do; it converted them from men into targets.

"Move!" Winters yelled above the racket. "Move. Don't stop."

Heads stayed low as his words went unheeded. From behind, he could hear Strayer shouting, "Move out, Winters. Get those men moving."

Winters blew his cork. Oblivious to his own safety, he leaped to his feet and ran into the middle of the road.

"Go forward," he yelled. "You can't stay here. Move! Move!"

Winters was a sitting duck for the German gunners, and he knew it. He had become the only visible target, and the machine gunner did not neglect the opportunity. Bullets churned up the ground at Winters' feet and buzzed around his ears like mosquitoes as he bounced back and forth across the road, frantically grabbing men, yanking them to their feet and pushing them forward.

"Get going!" Winters yelled. "You're gonna die here. Move!"

The men were stunned, less by the German fire than by the sight of their mild-mannered lieutenant suddenly transformed into a raving madman. At first they gaped at him in awe, then, at last, the discipline they'd forged during two years of training returned. Rader moved out, followed by another man, then another, until all were charging ahead under the withering fire. Winters ran with them, encouraging them forward. Several men were hit and fell, but the rest were soon pouring into the streets of Carentan.

While the German gunners were focused on Winters and the men attacking down the road, Welsh closed in on the machine gun position. Yanking the pin from a grenade, he lobbed it through the hotel window. The explosion silenced the gun.

Fanning out across the intersection, GIs tossed grenades into windows and kicked open doors of houses, firing into the interiors. German fire slackened as the enemy was rooted from its hiding places.

"Secure this intersection," Winters ordered. "Clear those buildings to the right."

As Strayer expected, the Germans' only means of escape was across the marshy fields. A stream of American fire followed them, cutting several down as they fled. Just then, without warning, an explosion rocked a nearby building.

"Mortars," Winters yelled. "Take cover!"

The Germans had the intersection zeroed in and, as houses were ripped apart, flying chunks of steel and masonry struck several men. One private was killed outright. Edward J. Tipper was severely wounded in the head and both his legs were broken when a mortar shell blasted a building he was securing. Welsh got to Tipper quickly and yelled for a medic. Lipton was struck in the upper thigh and crotch by shrapnel. He was scooped up and carried to safety by Sergeant Floyd Talbert, who first checked the frightened man to make sure "everything was okay." The injured were taken to the aid station that Lieutenant Jackson Neavles, one of the regimental surgeons, had set up in the first building on the northwest corner of the intersection.

The rain of mortar shells ceased as suddenly as it had begun. Fearing the lull might signal a counterattack, Winters decided to check the company's ammo supply. Walking by the hotel at the intersection, where the dead German machine gun crew lay sprawled, a voice called, "Lieutenant Winters. Is it safe to cross?"

It was Strayer. The battalion commander and his staff, less the wounded Lavenson, were directly across from Winters, crouched by the wall of a building.

"Yes, sir," Winters replied, irked by Strayer's question in light of the fact that his men had just bled to secure the area. To emphasize the point, Winters stepped into the middle of the street. Strayer nodded, then hurried across, his staff trailing behind. Winters smiled and shook his head in disgust. That was typical of Strayer, he thought. Don't lead the way if someone else can do it instead.

Strayer was no sooner out of sight than something slammed into Winters' left shin with the impact of being hit by a baseball bat. He involuntarily gasped in pain and hobbled to the side of the road.

"Goddamit," he said, less from pain than out of anger for knowing he had stupidly exposed himself to show up Strayer. Welsh ran to Winters and helped him into a sitting position on the sidewalk.

"Let's get that boot off," Welsh said. Doing so, he examined the wound. "It's not deep. Maybe I can get it."

He drew out his trench knife and began probing.

"Ouch! Dammit, Harry, you're all thumbs." Winters winced. "Just help me to the aid station."

At the makeshift hospital Doc Neavles hurried over and helped Welsh ease Winters onto a tabletop. "You're not supposed to be here," Neavles joked. "At least, not as a customer."

"Sorry, Doc, I forgot that," Winters replied.

Neavles grabbed a few instruments and effortlessly dug out a piece of a bullet. The broken slug was bent and misshapen.

"You're lucky, Lieutenant," Neavles said. "It was a ricochet. It'll hurt like hell and get stiff on you, but you'll live. Any chance you can keep off of it for a while?"

"I doubt it," Winters replied.

Neavles shrugged as he applied sulfa powder and wrapped the wound with a bandage. Winters put his boot back on, noting a small hole in the tongue. He did not lace the boot to the top.

Easy had suffered ten casualties in the attack on Carentan, most of them wounded and now in the aid station. Neavles, along with company medics Eugene G. Roe, Ralph F. Spina and John R. Holland, moved among the men, tending their needs and addressing their injuries. Winters got off the table and limped around the room, speaking briefly to Lipton and other wounded men. Then he saw Private Albert Blithe sitting with his back against a wall, seemingly unhurt.

"He said he can't see," Neavles said, noting Winters' questioning gaze. "I believe him. It's called hysterical blindness. I've heard of it, but I've never seen it 'til now."

Winters knelt in front of the young man.

"Blithe," he said. "It's Lieutenant Winters. Can you tell me what's the matter?"

"Everything just went black, sir. I can't see a thing. I'm sorry. I'm truly sorry."

Winters patted the distressed young man's shoulder. "Don't you worry about a thing, son," he said. "We'll get you out of here and back to England. You just hang tough." He rose and limped away. He'd barely taken five steps when Blithe called to him.

"Lieutenant Winters," Blithe said, slowly rising to his feet, swiping the back of his sleeve across his eyes. "I can see. It's okay. I can see. I think I'll be all right."

Winters walked back to him. Blithe looked into Winters' eyes, and the lieutenant said gently, "That's good, Blithe. But why don't we send you back with the rest and get you checked out properly to make sure you're okay."

"No, sir," he replied. "I'd like to stay here with the fellas, if that's okay."

Winters would have preferred to send him back, but relented. "All right. Rest here a bit first, just to make sure you're fit. Then report back to your platoon."

Blithe nodded. As Winters walked away he felt enormous pride in Blithe. The young man was so terrified he literally lost his eyesight. Yet, once given a few reassuring words, he had snapped out of it and was ready to return to duty. Winters appreciated that Blithe could've taken the easy way out, but chose to stick with his friends.

Winters soon had another reason to be proud. Hester sought him out and said that he, Strayer and Sink had been in a position to watch the regiment attack the town.

"Yours wasn't the only company to come under heavy fire, Dick," he said. "And it wasn't the only one that froze. But you were the only one that quickly recovered and got the job done. Some of the others got chewed up pretty badly. Colonel Sink was impressed."

Carentan was secure. Now Winters prepared his men for a possible counterattack. The rumored attack seemed likely when the distinct rumble of an approaching German armored vehicle reverberated through the village streets. A Panzer tank rolled into view and halted, its forty-three-ton bulk squatting menacingly in the street. The turret traversed slowly as the tank's 75 mm cannon pumped shells into buildings and at the American position. Shrapnel from one round caught Sergeant Boyle in the left leg. Easy's bazooka team crept up on the iron beast. The gunner aimed and fired. The three-pound rocket streaked at the tank, bouncing harmlessly off the sloped forward armor. Unhurt but rattled, the enemy crew considered discretion to be the better part of valor and the tank withdrew the way it had come.

$$\star \quad \star \quad \star$$

The 101st was given a brief rest after seizing Carentan, but with the threat of a German counterattack still looming, the men were roused to their feet and marched into the countryside to form a protective perimeter around the strategic town. Easy Company was on the division's far right, their line ending at a railroad track with nothing but swampland beyond. Approaching a hedgerow on high ground two miles outside of Carentan, German mortar and small arms fire hit the company, stopping the men as if they'd struck a brick wall. Holding the elevated ground gave the enemy an excellent field of fire. The company returned fire as Winters quickly deployed the men along the tangle of a hedgerow just to their front. Keeping his head under the flying lead, Winters crawled along the line, giving encouragement to the men.

Recalling the fight years later, Winters said, "The most important thing you can do as a leader is to move around and let the men know you're there, that you're watching out for them, and that they're not alone. You have to keep your own head down, pop up and take a shot or two, and then keep moving."

Dusk brought a lull to the fight, but the night was far from quiet. Just after midnight a German patrol began firing weapons and shouting insults at the Americans. Winters cautioned his men to be alert for a possible night attack. None developed. A few hours later the darkness was pierced by a shriek as Sergeant Talbert, wearing a captured German rain poncho, was bayoneted by Private George H. Smith Jr. Talbert had attempted to wake Smith up for guard duty but, emerging from the haze of sleep, Smith mistook Talbert for an enemy soldier.

"How is he, Doc?" Winters asked Roe as the medic hunched over a squirming Talbert.

"It hurts like hell," Talbert gasped, answering for Roe.

"I don't think it's life-threatening," Roe said. "But I need to get him to the rear."

"I'm sorry, I'm sorry," Smith kept moaning. "He looked like a Kraut."

"Calm down, son," Winters said. "Doc's got him. You just watch the line."

After seeing that Talbert was attended to and that men in nearby foxholes remained calm, Winters returned to his makeshift HQ, where he was joined by Nixon.

"Headquarters thinks we've run into a German counterattack heading toward Carentan," Nixon said. "We're going to attack them at 0530 if they don't hit us first." Winters nodded and told Diel, who was also present, to alert the platoon leaders. He was comforted by the fact that the men had just been resupplied with food, water and ammunition.

Following a fitful night's sleep interrupted by spurts of harassment fire, Winters had his men up and ready for the dawn attack. He placed his machine guns to provide support and deployed his mortars to the rear, where Guarnere began presetting the ranges.

At that moment German mortar shells began dropping on the Americans. "Take cover," Winters yelled and men dove for their foxholes as the explosions tore into the hedgerow. The ground vibrated from the blasts. Hot steel and wood splinters filled the air above the cowering men. The barrage was short. When it let up, Winters jumped up and began racing along his line.

"Get ready," he said. "They'll be coming now. Mark your targets."

Silently, solemnly, men removed ammo clips from their bandoliers and grenades from their belts. They placed these on the ground in front of their foxholes where they could be easily and quickly reached.

The German counterassault on the 101st was led by the 6th Fallschirmjager Regiment, angered by losing Carentan. All along the 506th's sector, toughened German paratroopers began pouring small arms fire on the GIs' line. The Americans fired back and slugs from both sides bit into the earth, thunked into tree trunks and clipped off branches. Spent brass casings tinkled melodically onto the ground. Men shouted and cursed in English and German, sometimes in anger, other times in pain or shock as a bullet found flesh. Cries of "Medic" and "*Zahnie*" emanated from both sides.

Above the roar of the battle Winters and his men soon heard a frightening new sound: Tanks. Panzer Mark Vs with their 75 mm guns, Mark IVs with the stubby, short-barreled cannons used mostly against infantry, and the turretless Jagdpanzer IIIs toting their deadly 88 mm guns arrived. Poking their deadly prows over the crest of the ridge, they fired into the American line, their shells tearing through the trees and bursting with a roar. The sudden and unexpected arrival of the tanks rattled Fox Company, which fell back in confusion. The retreat, justly or unjustly, would cost Captain Mulvey his job.

"Goddamn it," Winters muttered as he watched Fox pull out.

Its right flank now exposed, Dog Company also retreated. Like a row of dominoes, company after company, battalion after battalion gave ground until the 101st's left flank was pressed back into Carentan itself. Only Easy Company, on the far right, held fast in the teeth of the German firestorm.

Except for the loss of D and F companies, Winters was oblivious to his precarious situation. All he knew was that he had been ordered to hold. Moving in a crouch along his line, he scurried to the far left. There he found Welsh and first platoon trying to defend the gap vacated by Fox Company.

"Thank God, I'm glad to see you." Welsh sighed with relief. "The Krauts are trying to push through. I didn't know if I should pull back or what the hell to do."

"We're staying and holding, Harry," Winters said. "Keep pouring it on 'em. Don't let them flank us."

The men involuntarily ducked as a tank shell exploded nearby, wounding machine gunner Walter S. Gordon Jr., who had been spraying the German lines with .30 caliber slugs. The same explosion also wounded Private Roderick J. Strohl. A Jagdpanzer lumbered toward the gap where Fox Company had been. Welsh grabbed Private John McGrath and the two ran into the open. McGrath carried a bazooka while Welsh held a satchel containing several rockets. McGrath knelt as Welsh jammed a rocket into the rear of the bazooka. Once loaded, Welsh tapped McGrath on the head and the private fired. The rocket streaked at the tank, only to carom harmlessly off. Welsh hastily began reloading and Winters could hear McGrath shouting, "You're gonna get me killed, Lieutenant." The tank fired its main gun at the two men, but being on higher ground, the gunner couldn't depress the barrel enough and the shell passed overhead, slicing off some young saplings.

"Hold your fire until I tell you," Welsh said.

He waited as the tank climbed a small rise, then said, "Fire."

The rocket hit the tank's soft underbelly, pierced the thin armor and detonated. The tank exploded in a roar of smoke and flame. Carrying its dead crew, the tank rolled a few feet forward from its own momentum, then came to a smoldering stop. By that time, Welsh and McGrath were back in the cover of the hedgerow. The destruction of the tank had a sobering effect on the other armored crews, who halted their vehicles in place.

Strayer by now had managed to push Dog and Fox companies back on the line, although not quite to their original positions. Still, it was enough to secure Easy's flank and the hard fight continued through the day. Around 4:30 that afternoon Winters heard the bellowing roar of engines. Sherman tanks of the U.S. 2nd Armored Division rolled through the fields to Winters' left, machine guns and cannons blazing. One German tank blew up, then another, under the sudden onslaught of American armor. Pressed by the Shermans and taking casualties, the Nazis abandoned their attack. The surviving

German tanks shifted into reverse and retreated over the crest. Then the infantry began to fall back, ending what Winters called a very, very tough day.

Easy Company suffered nine men wounded, added to the ten Winters had lost the day before in Carentan. That night, he almost lost one more.

Relieved at 11 P.M., and still under harassing fire, Easy took to the road and trod back toward Carentan. Walking just ahead of Winters, Corporal Randleman was suddenly struck.

"Damn, I'm hit," he yelled.

Feeling moisture running down his back, Randleman dropped to the ground and, with Winters' help, began tearing off his equipment. The two were relieved to find that the bullet had punctured a spare canteen stowed in Randleman's pack.

"I couldn't afford to lose any more good men," Winters wrote in his journal that night. "And Bull is a good man."

Back in Carentan, Winters saw that his men were properly billeted in houses, then he and Welsh bedded down. With his injured leg stiffening up, Winters turned command over to Welsh to give the wound a chance to heal. The next day, Sink sought him out.

"Lieutenant, you did a hell of a job out there yesterday," Sink told him. "I want to thank you for holding down our flank. God knows what would have happened had you pulled back."

Sink also told Winters he was nominating him for the Congressional Medal of Honor for the fight at Brecourt on D-Day.

"It didn't mean a damned thing to me at the time," Winters said sixty years later. "All I knew is that it wasn't the Purple Heart." (Winters would get a Purple Heart for his leg wound.)

A few days later, Sink returned to Winter's CP, this time escorting General Taylor.

"Thank you for a fantastic job, Lieutenant," Taylor said. "If you hadn't held the line like you did, the whole division might have been dislodged and driven back into those goddamned swamps. You don't earn any medals for work like that, but I wanted to personally look you up and say well done."

"Thank you, sir," Winters replied, his heart welling over with pride in what his weary men had accomplished.

During the five days Easy spent in Carentan, Winters took time to catch up on letter writing, telling the folks back home that he was fine, even if military censorship forbade him from relating any details.

On June 17 he wrote DeEtta that he was okay and "making a tour of France," which was "all the rules and regulations permit me to say.

"If you read the newspapers (I haven't seen one for a long, long time) you'll get the big picture, which is more than I know. In fact, I am just dying to see a newspaper to find out what is going on in this war.

"Once you wrote and said, 'if you're ever in a tight spot, remember you must come back.' You'll never know how much that helped."

He also wrote to his parents, much to the relief of his anxious father, already suffering from bleeding ulcers, a condition he treated with lots of milk and a bland diet. Every evening the elder Winters turned to the radio, listening to the war news and consulting a map, hoping to pinpoint where his son might be that day.

★   ★   ★

While recuperating from his wound in Carentan, Winters got his first glimpse of one of the war's newest and more fearsome innovations. Looking up one night to spot the source of a noise in the sky, he noticed a small, bright light zooming overhead on a northward course toward England. "It looked like a falling star but it was going the wrong direction," Winters recalled. He'd seen one of the first of Hitler's new Vengeance weapons, the V-1: a pilotless bomb powered by a rocket engine.

June 20 found Easy back on the line south of Carentan. They had not seen more action, but there were plenty of outgoing and incoming artillery rounds sailing overhead.

Unfamiliar with German strength and positions, Strayer ordered a patrol to gather intelligence. Nixon relayed the order to Winters, who in turn told his friend to ask for volunteers. When no hands went up, Nixon picked Guarnere, Blithe and Private Joseph A. Lesniewski. Blithe, now fully recovered from his bout of hysterical blindness eight days earlier, was point man. Moving cautiously ahead, the young private spotted a German sniper but rather than fire his rifle, he inexplicably reverted to his training days and pointed at the German with his hand.

"Sniper, bang, bang," he yelled.

The German got off a round from his Mauser that struck Blithe in the neck.

"Let's get the hell out of here," Guarnere yelled as the men grabbed the downed Blithe and dragged him to the rear, where a medic tended his wound. Whether he reacted from instinct or fatigue from nearly a month in combat, Blithe's war was over. (Blithe would recover and remain in the army, serving in Korea in the 1950s.)

"He did exactly as he was taught in training," Winters later said. "Unfortunately, this wasn't training."

Malarkey led a second patrol that got into a brisk firefight. One German was killed.

That same day, Easy was pulled off the line and sent into reserve. Nine days later, the 101st was relieved by the 83rd Infantry Division, loaded onto trucks and sent to Cherbourg. Wandering the streets of the battered city a day later, Winters located a dry cleaning shop and had the uniforms of every man in the company cleaned. Out of appreciation, he footed the bill.

"I'm not going to spend it on booze, so what the hell," he told Nixon, who thought his friend was suffering from combat fatigue.

While in Cherbourg, Winters and some other company officers were called into regimental headquarters where, along with Colonel Sink, sat noted historian and author S. L. A. Marshall. After introductions, Winters was asked to take a seat. Sink began to question him while Marshall took notes.

"Okay, Lieutenant, tell us about the action at Brecourt," Sink said. "You took that battery of 88s."

"Yes, sir, that's right," Winters replied.

"Tell me how you did it."

"Well, sir, I put down a base of fire, we moved in under the fire and took the first gun. Then we put down another base of fire and we moved to the second gun and the third and the fourth."

"Okay," Sink said. "Anything else?"

"No, sir, that's basically it."

"Okay, thank you very much."

Winters was dismissed. Some time later he read Marshall's account of the action in which the author reported that Winters had led about two hundred men.

"Jesus Christ," he complained. "If I had had that many men, I could've taken Berlin."

Even if Marshall didn't appreciate Winters' solid leadership under fire, Sink did. In a June 25, 1944, interview with Walter McCallum of the *Washington Star*, Sink recounted the fight at Carentan on June 12–13. He said it was "Lieutenant Winters' personal leadership which held the crucial position in the line and tossed back the enemy with mortar and machine gun fire."

"He was a fine soldier out there," Sink told McCallum. "His personal bravery and battle knowledge held a crucial position when the going was really tough."

Though off the line, Winters did not let the men grow soft. Not knowing what the next move was, he set up a training program of tactics and maneuver. But the company was only a shadow of what it had been when it jumped into France. Of the 139 men who left England the night of June 5–6, Winters' June 30 roster showed just five lieutenants—Welsh, Compton, Rousch and his assistant platoon leader, Francis L. O'Brien, and himself—and sixty-nine men. He had three known dead: Privates Joseph M. Jordan, Everett J. Gray and William S. Metzler. The rest were wounded or missing.

Among the missing were the eighteen men of Stick 66, including Easy's commander, Lieutenant Thomas Meehan. Although officially listed as missing, Winters had received reports that witnesses saw Meehan's plane take an antiaircraft hit and roll to the right, losing altitude. The C-47 did a 180-degree turn and, it was said, the pilot appeared to have turned on his landing lights as if trying to find a place to set the crippled plane down. Then the aircraft struck a hedgerow and exploded.

Winters soon learned of another loss. Lieutenant George Lavenson, wounded in the behind at Carentan, was en route to a hospital in the United States when the plane he was on was lost over the Atlantic Ocean. Winters considered this the tragic loss of a fine officer and friend.

Winters now officially commanded Easy Company, and at a ceremony on July 1 he was promoted to captain. Medals were also handed out, including the ones earned by the men who accompanied Winters during the taking of the German artillery position at Brecourt. Winters received the Distinguished Service Cross for leading that attack, presented to him by General Omar Bradley. Winters also watched as the Congressional Medal of Honor, the one he had been nominated for by Colonel Sink, was presented by Bradley to Lieutenant Colonel Cole, for a bayonet charge he led in the assault on Carentan.

The next day, Winters wrote to DeEtta from "somewhere in France," telling her of his promotion and giving her some insight to conditions in that country; of how the French people were warming up to the Americans as the Germans were pushed back.

"They've all lost at least a little by our coming, yet they seem to take great pride in flying their flag once more. They wave at us as we go by and call 'Viva la France' or hold thumbs up or V for victory."

Winters told her he was listening to a sound-powered radio, and hearing "some of the first American music I've heard for two months" even though, he admitted, he was "not hep" musically. He also delighted over the fact that he was able to munch on his first piece of candy in weeks: a Hershey chocolate bar straight from the USA.

The 101st was trucked to Utah Beach on July 10, seeing from the land what they had last seen from the air the night of June 5: hundreds of ships sitting off shore as far as the eye could see. Smaller boats, LSTs, LCMs and other craft carrying men and supplies plied the waters between the ships and the sand. "It took your breath away," he recalled. Winters saw something else he had not seen for more than a month, a sight that literally brought tears to his eyes: the American flag. In 2003, the memory still left him choked up. "I didn't realize how much the American flag meant to me," he said.

As Winters watched the beach activity he spotted a German officer who was confined in one of two temporary holding pens on the beach. While most of his fellow POWs sat, heads hung low, morale completely gone, this "strutting, proud Prussian peacock" in full dress uniform stood hands behind his back, eyeing the massive unloading of supplies not in defeat, but in defiance.

"I wondered what he was thinking," Winters wrote. "The fact that he was a prisoner of war did not deflate his ego one bit. I never saw such arrogance."

The division camped just behind Utah Beach on July 11. The next day, as they prepared to board the boats that would ferry them across the English Channel to Southampton, the men turned in their weapons and equipment, which would be reissued to replacements coming ashore. For those going out, they took just their personal gear and souvenirs. For most this meant Nazi medals, flags, knives, pistols and so forth. But Private Alton M. More set his sites on bigger game: an American motorcycle and sidecar.

"Captain," he said to Winters. "I, ahh, found this bike. If I can get it on board the boat, is it okay if I take it back to England with us?"

Winters didn't care. The men had earned a little fun. "It's up to you," he replied. "I didn't see a thing."

Luckily, the navy men held the paratroopers in awe and were eager to please these combat veterans. "Whatever you want," was the rule of the day, Winters recalled, so the motorcycle and sidecar were rolled aboard with no questions asked.

On the LST an officer lent Winters his quarters so he might get a good night's sleep on a real bed with clean sheets. There was hot food and plenty of it; chicken, steak, soup, eggs and—Winters' eyes lit up at the sight—ice cream.

The LSTs struck out across the Channel and the men silently watched France fade into the distance. They reminisced about experiences they'd shared, and friends left behind. And they knew they'd be back.

CHAPTER 5

"I Just Knew You'd Do Well."

July 12–September 14, 1944

First Sergeant James "Punchy" Diel entered Dick Winters' office and handed him two sheets of paper.

"Here's that list you wanted, Captain," Diel said.

"Thanks, Punchy," Winters said, taking the papers. "By the way, Colonel Sink has asked all company commanders to recommend men for battlefield commissions. Seems the regiment lost a lot of junior officers in France. I've put you in for second lieutenant."

"Thank you, sir," Diel said. "But I'm not sure I want to be an officer."

"Too late." Winters smiled. "Besides, you're a damned fine soldier, Punchy. I think other men would benefit from your skills."

"Who'll take my place?"

"I haven't decided for sure," Winters said. "Probably Lipton when he gets back from the hospital. He's certainly the most qualified."

"Do you know what his first official action will be?" Diel asked. Winters shook his head. "He'll want to change his name on the roster from Clifford C. to C. Carwood. He's been after me to do that since we got back from France. He's even sending me notes from the hospital."

"Well, if that's what he wants, I guess rank has its privileges," Winters said.

"Yes, sir," Diel said, saluted and left.

Winters turned his attention to the papers in his hand. From the time Easy jumped into France on June 6 until they were relieved on June 30, the company suffered sixty-five casualties, or forty-seven percent of its strength. Some of those men had suffered minor wounds and were already back on duty. The papers Diel had given Winters told the rest of the story. The two handwritten sheets comprised the most depressing list Winters had ever seen. It held the names of forty men lost to Easy Company, along with their next of kin. Twenty-one of the men were in various hospitals, although some of those—Lipton, Boyle, Rod Strohl, and Popeye Wynn, for example—would be returning. Others had the million-dollar wound and would be heading Stateside.

A few of the men on the list were confirmed dead. Phyllis Jordan back in Muncie, Indiana, by now had the telegram telling her that her husband, Joseph M. Jordan, was not coming home. Daniel Gray in Keenesburg, Colorado, knew that his son, Everett J. Gray, had been killed at Carentan, as did Estaban Metzler, father of William S. Metzler, in Naco, Arizona.

The hardest part of the list for Winters to digest was the seventeen men of Stick 66, including Easy's commander, Thomas Meehan. The loss of this planeload of men had been confirmed, not just by Graves Registration, but by some of Winters' own soldiers. Sergeant Forrest Guth and others had come across the wreckage. Winters guessed that Royal Collins in Spencer, Massachusetts, and Jesus Moya of San Francisco now knew their sons, Herman F. Collins and medic Sergio G. Moya, were dead. He assumed that Nancy Murray knew that her husband, Elmer "Moe" Murray, would not be returning to Englewood, California, and that Helen Elliot of Cleveland, Ohio, and Nancy Roberts of Tampa, Florida, knew they were both widows.

In addition, Winters heard that Sergeant Terrence C. Harris, whom Sink had transferred out of Easy after the "Sobel Mutiny," had also been killed in Normandy.

Then there was Meehan. Among his personal effects was a letter to his wife, written just before taking off for Normandy.

"Dearest Anne, In a few hours I'm going to take the best company of men in the world into France. We'll give the bastards hell. Strangely, I'm not particularly scared but in my heart is a terrific longing to hold you in my arms. I love you Sweetheart, forever. Your Tom."

Damn! Winters thought. There were so many of them. Too many. And all he could do now for these grieving families was offer some tidbit of solace.

Opening a desk drawer, Winters took out a stack of writing paper and envelopes and began the hardest job he ever had to perform.

★   ★   ★

The return trip across the English Channel from France had been far less dramatic than the one going the other way on June 6. Arriving at Southampton at 8 A.M. on July 13, the division disembarked from the boats and was marched straight to a troop train. Winters and the 506th were "home" in Aldbourne by noon.

Easy Company's officers were assigned to a farmhouse while the men themselves settled into a large stable, the stalls serving as apartments. (This stable was shipped to Toccoa in 2004.) Winters, duffel bag slung over his shoulder, walked through the village to the Barneses' home. Stepping through the front door with the same ease he would have shown had it been 418 South West End Avenue in Lancaster, he was greeted by Mother Barnes, whose eyes lit up when she saw him enter.

"Richard," she said, and hugged him. "We're so frightfully glad to see you."

He shook hands with Mr. Barnes as Mother Barnes fiddled with a drawer. Extracting a newspaper clipping she proudly waved it in his face. It was an article about his company's action at Carentan and of his being awarded the DSC. (Unknown to Winters until later, papers back home in Lancaster added that he'd been wounded and hospitalized.)

"I'm so proud of you," she said. "I just knew you'd do well."

Elaine Stevens was elated to see her "big brother" return and Winters gave her a gift: the wristwatch he'd removed from the wrist of the dead Andrew Hill.

Once Easy Company was settled, the first thing on Winters' agenda was for the men to draw new uniforms, equipment and weapons. Winters picked out a new M1 Garand. Possibly recalling his boyhood love of cowboy movies, he took a pocketknife and carved five notches into the rifle stock; one for each German he'd slain.

The next day, July 14, Easy Company was granted seven-day leave. As the men prepared to hit London for a week of good times, Winters gathered them together.

"I know we've just come off a long, difficult time, but that doesn't mean you can go to London and act like fools," he told them. "Remember you are paratroopers and be proud of the uniform you are wearing. Keep your feet on the ground, stay out of trouble and don't embarrass yourselves or the company. You represent the best of the United States Army, so act like it."

When he had finished, Nixon said, "Do you really think that's going to do any good?"

"Probably not." Winters shrugged. "But I'm the company commander. It's like being a father. You have to say something to your kids. Maybe it'll sink in."

"Yeah," Nixon chortled. "Right."

By 9:15 A.M. Winters was the only Easy Company man left in camp. Still plagued by his leg wound, he remained a little longer in Aldbourne to nurse the soreness. Sitting in his room at the Barneses' home, leg propped up, he heard the bells of St. Michael's church echo through the village. The chiming reminded him of the clanging church bell at Ste. Mere-Eglise tolling the fire alarm the night he jumped into France.

Putting pen to paper, he wrote DeEtta, "Machine gun fire and rifle fire didn't scare me. But those bells, being all alone with only a knife, gave me the feeling of being hunted down by a pack of wolves." He told her he was glad to be back with his "adopted parents" and having "a seven day leave, all at one time, has really been wonderful." Still melancholy over his losses, he reflected on the isolation he felt as company commander.

"I've been a buck private, and when I was, I didn't want to fool around with the officers," Winters wrote. "All I wanted from them was good leadership. Now I am a captain and I find that buddy stuff is out. I am all in favor of knowing each and every man, getting in bull sessions with them, etc., knowing their background, likes, dislikes, capabilities and weak points. I want to be their friend and the guy they go to when they want a favor or they're in trouble. But I am not their buddy, I am their captain, and when I say something, that's it, you jump."

Winters wrote that he knew officers who went on picnics and other outings with their men and were well liked, but "in the end, their ideas and principles break down. You can't make a decision as quickly and thoroughly if your buddies are in a life or death situation."

On July 16 Winters arrived in London, taking a room on the third floor of a Red Cross-run hotel. Limping around the history-rich city he toured some of the sights, like Trafalgar Square, Buckingham Palace—heavily sandbagged against air raid damage—Big Ben and Tower Bridge. He took in a couple of USO shows. However, on a darker note, he saw buildings gutted by the Blitz and he was now on the receiving end of the Nazis' V-1 Buzz Bombs. He had seen these in France, of course, streaking mindlessly overhead on their way to create random destruction and death in England, but he had not been in any danger from them. In fact, in France he was told to report the V-1s when they had been spotted and to get the direction from which they came. This information could then be relayed to army intelligence in hopes of discovering the launch sites.

In London, he quickly understood that the V-1, or Doodle Bug as the Londoners called it, was harmless so long as one heard the distinct roar of its single rocket engine. It was when that engine quit that people ducked for cover. During the day, Winters ducked, too. But at night, dead tired and lying in a comfortable bed, he told himself that running and hiding was "for the birds."

Not a social animal, Winters grew bored with London after a couple of days and decided to leave. Adding to his desire to return to Aldbourne was that he had been forced to share his accommodation with an Army Air Forces officer who moaned and whimpered all night, sometimes while asleep, other times while awake, irritating the hell out of Winters.

"Jesus Christ," Winters complained to Welsh. "This guy goes out on a mission. Couple of hours later he's back and in his own sack with hot food. My God, we live it twenty-four hours a day, day in and day out. And he's laying there nursing his shattered nerves."

Back from leave, Winters now faced the daunting task of reorganizing his badly shattered company. Part of this meant promoting men he felt worthy and filling in officer and NCO gaps left by casualties. Winters elevated Harry Welsh to first lieutenant and named him company executive officer. Buck Compton, who would head 2nd Platoon, and Thomas A. Peacock of 3rd Platoon were also promoted to first lieutenant. Second Lieutenant Warren Rousch retained command of 1st Platoon.

New officers also came into the company. Second Lieutenant Robert B. Brewer became Rousch's assistant until Holland, when Rousch would be transferred to 1st Battalion to help make up for heavy losses. Second Lieutenant John G. Pisanchin joined Easy, as did Sergeant Charles Hudson, who had been promoted to second lieutenant and was transferred in from Able Company.

Second Lieutenant Raymond G. Schmitz, whom Winters had injured in the pre-D-Day wrestling match, also returned, but an uneasiness between the two men was evident and Winters transferred Schmitz to Fox Company. He would die in action at Bastogne.

Leo Boyle, back from his leg wound at Carentan, was elevated to staff sergeant and became Winters' "right-hand man." A few years older than the average paratrooper, Boyle had joined the army in 1934 for a three-year stint. He got out in 1937, the same year Winters graduated from high school, and went to work as a mechanic for Standard Oil in California. The army caught up to Boyle again in 1942 and he was drafted. Born and raised in the Pacific Northwest, Boyle was a natural outdoorsman, and had a tough, no-nonsense, strictly business air about him. Winters gave some of the credit for this to Wyn Hawkins, the Aldbourne girl Boyle had married in May. Winters felt the marriage had helped mature Boyle into a top-notch NCO and made him, in Winters' opinion, the ideal man to help train the replacements the company was soon to receive.

Sergeant Robert T. Smith was made a staff sergeant. Winters considered Smith a solid squad leader who showed leadership and self-discipline, and had the respect of the men.

Others deserving of promotion to sergeant were corporals Kenneth J. Mercier, "Bull" Randleman and Arthur C. Youman. A few men jumped from private to sergeant, these being Don Malarkey, Warren H. Muck, Paul C. Rogers and Myron N. Ranney, who had been a sergeant but was busted to private by Sink during the NCO mutiny.

Privates Burt Christenson, Walter Gordon, John Plesha, Darrell "Shifty" Powers and Lavon P. Reese were promoted to corporal.

Not all of Winters' promotions worked out as he'd hoped.

Winters boosted Sergeant Bill Guarnere to staff sergeant and put him in charge of the mortar platoon. Winters had been Guarnere's platoon leader at Toccoa, promoting him to corporal, then sergeant and squad leader. He considered Guarnere "a damned fine soldier" who did an "outstanding job" in Normandy, so much so that Winters nominated him for the Distinguished Service Cross after Brecourt. Guarnere had a great sense of close order drill, which combined with his abrasive, sandpaper rough "South Philadelphia attitude," made him stand out among the other men. On a personal level, however, Guarnere was a loose cannon, and shortly after his promotion, he "misused his rank," Winters later wrote, "by trying to make the army co-ed."

Pressed for accommodations in Aldbourne, several houses were made available for NCOs, putting them out from under direct supervision by the company officers. Following a leave in London, Guarnere and his housemates had, not surprisingly, picked up several women. Rather than kiss the girls good-bye at Swindon, as was generally done, they brought them back to Aldbourne and secreted them in the loft of the house.

The GIs might have gotten away with this breach of rules had it not been that Lieutenant Peacock picked the next day to do a routine inspection. As he moved about the first floor of the cottage he heard movement in the loft above. Suddenly a female foot, treading on a section of old flooring, came crashing through the ceiling. Peacock duly informed Winters of the infraction.

"You arrange to have those women taken back to London," Winters said, rising from his desk. "I'm going to find Sergeant Guarnere."

He discovered the sergeant walking along a village street. "Wild Bill," as he had come to be known from his legendary exploits in France, knew he was in trouble when he saw his commander stalk malevolently toward him.

"Goddammit, Bill, how could you do that?" Winters demanded, his face reddening. "How could you deliberately go against my direct order and bring those chippies here? What in the hell were you thinking?"

"No excuse, sir," Guarnere said, rigidly at attention.

"You've abused your rank and the privileges that come with it and as of right now, Bill, you're a private. I'm busting you," Winters said. "And furthermore, since you are so good at giving close order drill, you are to report to

Company HQ and give close order drill as loud and clear as you can to an imaginary company until I tell you to stop."

"Yes, sir. Yes, sir," Guarnere kept replying to the tirade.

Winters turned and stormed away.

As ordered, Guarnere arrived and began barking out drill commands to imaginary men, but the exercise soon proved too difficult for the feisty, now ex-NCO.

"I can't do it, sir," he told Winters. "I just can't. I can't drill men I can't see."

Winters, who had cooled down some by now, acquiesced.

"Okay, Bill," he said. "But you're still a private. Because I value you as a soldier and a leader, I'm keeping you in command of the mortar platoon. But you're taking a two-thirds cut in pay."

*   *   *

A few days later Diel's promotion to second lieutenant came through. Winters called him into his headquarters to present the new officer with his gold bars. He also informed Diel that, as required by regulations, he was to be transferred to Fox Company since the army did not permit enlisted men elevated to officer status to remain in the unit with which they had been serving. The army felt the new officer might not get due respect from the men, and that he would be hesitant to give an order that might get one of his friends killed or wounded. Winters gave some parting advice to Diel as he pinned on the new bars.

"Don't feel you have to prove anything, Punchy," he said. "A lot of new officers come in to a company and they feel they have to earn the respect of the men, so they take needless chances that often end up getting them on the casualty list. All you've got to remember is, you're in charge. You can be friendly with the men, but avoid getting too close. When it comes to giving orders in combat, your discipline won't tolerate that. You're a good man, Punchy. You've got nothing to prove to anybody. Lead from the front, that's what being a leader means, but don't get careless."

The two men shook hands and Diel left to pack his gear. Winters hated to lose Diel. He was not only a good NCO, but also a friend. He thought of Diel as a "self-starter, highly motivated, dependable" man with a "no-nonsense, low-key style of leadership that had the respect of the men." Winters knew he'd do well as an officer.

As expected, Lipton returned to Easy and Winters immediately elevated him to company first sergeant. Winters had no doubt that Lipton was the best man for the job. Two years younger than Winters, Lipton had been just ten years old when his father was killed in a car accident. His mother had been paralyzed in the same accident. Lipton's father, a successful contractor, had all his money in the business and none in insurance, so the company was now lost and Mrs. Lipton was forced to rent out the family home in Huntington, West Virginia, as a rooming house to help pay the mortgage.

Taking odd jobs where he could get them, Lipton, at age eighteen, was able to enroll as an engineering major at Marshall College, but he soon had to drop out due to his mother's deteriorating health.

In mid-1941 he took a job in a defense plant, International Nickel Company, and earned a whopping $52 per week. But despite a 3-C classification from the Selective Service Board, which meant he couldn't be drafted because he had an essential civilian job, Lipton enlisted in the army in 1942 after reading a *Life* magazine article on the paratroops. Lipton proved to be a smart, self-disciplined soldier, thoroughly dedicated to Easy Company. In past engagements Lipton proved he had the kind of leadership skills Winters admired. And it wasn't just Winters who felt that way. From his hospital bed, Ed Tipper wrote his captain to say that Lipton was "the best noncommissioned officer in the whole army."

Winters' promotions that July demonstrated a pattern he would show throughout the war of putting Toccoa men in positions of leadership. He felt they were thoroughly tested and hardened at Toccoa, at Benning and in combat. In fact, this pattern was reflected throughout the entire regiment, as the Toccoa men became the backbone of the 506th. Through them, Winters was able to restaff Company E with no loss of leadership or morale, despite the heavy losses in Normandy.

★　　★　　★

"Now, once again, it's back to work, getting a company ready for combat," Winters wrote DeEtta on July 22. "What a job, being papa to a hundred and sixty odd men and seven so-called officers. Also, what a headache at times.

"After three years, the romance sort of fades from army life. You've been around. In the navy, you're an 'old salt.' When you're in the army, you're an old—. Of course, things of a humorous nature happen every day as well as new problems and new ways of handling them. But you lost the schoolboy desire to write and tell everybody back home what a big boy you are. One thing about combat is that a lot of men you thought were men are just petrified mummies and when they aren't petrified, they're shaking like a bowl of jelly. Now you sort of just look right through them without even smiling."

New men began filtering in from replacement depots, or Repo Depos, and

Winters assigned them to various platoons to fill up the ranks. Overall, he was impressed with the quality of the replacements, but he did not envy their task of trying to fit in with the Toccoa vets, who were outwardly resentful of these kids moving in to take the place of their friends, men who had already proved themselves on the grueling runs up Currahee and among the bloody hedgerows of France.

"They had a tough job joining up with a group like us who had been together since Toccoa, and then been bloodied at Normandy," Winters said in August 1990. "We were just feeling pretty goddamn cocky. That's all there is to it. We didn't *think* we were good. We *knew* we were good. And you're a replacement coming into a bunch like this? That's a tough job. But as a whole, that bunch was good. You look back on them, they were good men."

Reequipped and with new weapons in hand, it was crucial that the men familiarize themselves with the rifles and get them zeroed in. Soon rifle ranges crackled to life. Winters next established a training schedule that included field exercises. These were mainly for the benefit of the replacements. The veterans were given easier tasks, but some of the men tried to shirk even these. On several mornings Winters had to check the barracks to roust men from hiding and get them out on the training field.

To give the exercises a depth of realism, Winters armed his machine guns with live ammunition he'd smuggled back from France and kept hidden. He knew he was taking a grave risk, for if anyone had gotten hurt, "it would have been my tail." But he felt the opportunity to let the men, especially the new ones, experience what it was like to advance under actual fire was worth the risk. Still, even though the guns were sandbagged down so they would fire safely over the heads of the men, the use of live ammunition unnerved recruits and veterans alike.

"The key to a successful attack is to lay down a good steady base of fire and advance under that fire," he told the men as he briefed them on the exercise. "If done correctly, it gets the job done and saves lives. You can talk about it, you can go through dry run exercises, but you only get the feel of it with actual experience."

Off duty the men spent time relaxing in camp or hoping for passes to London. One man who was especially adept at finagling passes was Joe Liebgott, a clever and highly talented soldier who doubled as the company's barber.

"You know, sir," Liebgott said as he trimmed Winters' hair, "between all the drills and the men wanting haircuts, it really wears me down."

"Joe, why is it this subject only comes up when you are halfway through my haircuts?" Winters asked.

"Ahh, Captain," Liebgott whined. "You make it sound like I'm deliberately maneuvering you. It's just that when I have you in the chair is when I think of it."

"Uh-huh," Winters said. "And if I want you to finish the job on me and make it look good, you need to be assured of a three-day pass."

"It sure would help my mental well-being," Liebgott said.

"Okay, Joe. If you don't cut my ear off, you got your pass."

Liebgott smiled. It worked every time.

*   *   *

In mid-July an increasingly worried DeEtta, who had joined the Navy in February as a Wave, wrote to Winters, wishing he was still a private and stationed back in the States. Winters wrote back on July 22 and quickly chided her on her errant thoughts, saying if he were a private and still in the States after three years, he'd "go nuts" and be "worse than sad sack."

"No responsibilities, no thinking to do for myself, no problems or excitement, no nothing but to feel 'well, if I don't die of old age before the war is over, I guess I'll get back home.' Then to have somebody else doing the fighting for me! No thanks! I'll just stay right here where I am and dodge bullets for a living."

On July 30 Winters found himself at the jump school at Chilton Foliat where, with a number of other men, he took part in what he termed a "Glory Jump," a jump made "just for the hell of it." Winters was number five man in the stick, making it the only jump he ever made where he was not jumpmaster.

As summer wore on, Winters reflected on his family back home. On August 6 he wrote DeEtta, complaining that his parents worried more about him than he did about himself. He wrote that he hoped his father was proud of his promotion to captain and that that, coupled with articles in the local newspaper, would leave the elder Winters thinking that his son is "a regular hero."

Winters downplayed his wounding at Carentan, equating his being "pinked in the leg" with cutting oneself while shaving. "The only difference is you get a Purple Heart."

Turning his thoughts to his "kid sister" Elaine, Winters anguished over her suffering and fretted about her future. "Just about five years now she's been away from home, parents, poor as hell. Education most likely to stop in another year and then what can a kid that age do? I get a kick out of taking her to the officers' mess once in a while and keeping her in spending money. Reminds me of my sister."

*   *   *

Even as the men of the 101st were safely enjoying their peaceful English summer, they kept close tabs on what was happening across the Channel. The fighting in France had left the beaches only to bog down inland among the thick tangle of the Norman hedgerow country, or *boscage*. There American and British forces suffered heavy losses in men and equipment in exchange for minimal gains against the firmly entrenched Germans.

Then General Bradley unleashed Operation Cobra on July 25. Preceded by intense bombings by over 1,500 B-17 and B-24 bombers, Allied troops at last broke the stalemate and rolled forward over the shattered German defenses.

In conjunction with Cobra, the newly activated U.S. 3rd Army under the flamboyant General George S. Patton hit the German left flank like a pile driver, and by July 29 the entire Nazi army in France, suddenly in danger of being cut off and annihilated, was retreating toward the Fatherland.

For the airborne troops waiting back in England, August was a tense period of one alert after another. But even as a return to combat drew nearer, Winters noted that there was no attempt by the battalion or regimental officers to sit down and discuss the lessons learned in Normandy and look for possible ways to improve their skills. They had let opportunity pass them by.

Winters intensified the training of his own company, especially the replacements, and his order to his NCOs was "Get them in shape because the next jump is near."

The next jump, in fact, was nearer than Winters suspected. In mid-August Winters and the other 2nd Battalion officers were briefed on Operation Transfigure. Set for August 17, it called for the airborne troops to be dropped south of Orleans. There they would block the route of the German 7th Army as it was pushed south by Patton's advancing columns.

Orders were written, maps memorized, drop zones laid out, equipment readied and the men briefed on the upcoming operation. Then, on August 16, the day before the jump, Patton's men, moving faster than anticipated, overran the 101st's drop zones and pushed on to Rambouillet. Operation Transfigure was canceled.

It was just as well, too, as far as Winters was concerned, because he was not in a condition to jump anywhere. He was in agony.

Some days earlier Winters had developed a skull-crushing toothache. The culprit was a lack of Vitamin C in his diet. Vitamin C was available to the men in the form of the lemonade powder that came in the K Ration, but the powder was universally hated and was often thrown away. Unfortunately the army failed to inform the men of the importance of Vitamin C, or that the lemonade powder was the K Ration's sole source of that important nutrient. Subsequently, many combat soldiers developed cavities.

Feeling like someone was working over his mouth with a jackhammer, Winters visited Captain Samuel "Shifty" Feiler, the regimental dentist. Since a jump was imminent, Feiler quickly drilled out the cavities in two teeth with a foot-powered drill and "slapped in a filling." Despite that "dental care," Winters remained in agony, possibly worse now than before. The night before Transfigure was canceled, Winters, wracked by pain, lay awake.

"Why don't you go on sick call, Dick?" Welsh asked. "Being in agony like that, you can't think straight and God knows you of all people need to keep your head."

"Dammit, I can't do that, Harry," Winters told his XO. "We're jumping into combat tomorrow. I'm the company commander. The men expect me to be there. I expect me to be there, and I will even if my head explodes."

Luckily it didn't come to that. Transfigure was off. Easy Company was trucked back from the marshaling area to Aldbourne, where Winters reported to the division hospital seeking a "real" dentist. Ironically, the captain he found was a professional dentist from Harrisburg, just forty miles from Winters' hometown. He drilled out the new fillings then poked around in the young officer's mouth.

"This is bad," he announced. "When Feiler drilled he cut the nerves in both those molars. They are perfectly good teeth, Captain, and if we were back in Harrisburg, I could save them. It's a time-consuming procedure and you'd be out of action for a few days. But here, under these circumstances, with you possibly going back into combat any day, the only thing I can do is pull them out."

"Then get to it, Doc," Winters said. "Anything's better than this."

Later Winters discovered that his case was not isolated. Problems with Feiler's dental work happened time and time again and soon no man in the regiment dared to see the dentist.

His dental emergency behind him, Winters was back to running the company. He kept up the rigorous training schedule of field exercises and combat scenarios in an effort to make the men as ready as he could when the jump order came.

Winters wanted to get back into the war and he related his anxiety to DeEtta on August 26.

"The sooner they put me back in the fight the better I'll like it, for it's no good letting the other guy do it for you," he told her. "It just doesn't feel right."

Five days later the regiment was trucked back to the marshaling area and ready to board the C-47s for Operation Linnet, which would drop them just behind the Maginot Line near the village of St. Maur. They would then move north to take the town of Tourneau and the bridge over the Escaut River. By September 2, the fast-moving front again caused the mission to be scrubbed.

Also canceled on September 4 was Linnet II, a hastily thrown together plan which called for the paratroops to land and seize bridgeheads over the Meuse River. The 506th headed back to Aldbourne again.

Preparing for the combat he knew was coming, Winters found he had to request replacement equipment through the regiment's new S-4 supply officer, Captain Herbert Sobel. To avoid any lingering personal problems between the two men, Winters did not deal with Sobel directly. On those rare occasions when he did see his former commander, Winters wondered if Sobel appreciated the fact that, had he not been relieved of command of Easy, it would have been him and not Thomas Meehan who died in the fiery plane crash on June 6.

While waiting for something to happen during those final days of summer, Winters had new photographs taken of himself in his dress uniform. The pictures showed a young man whom combat had aged beyond his twenty-six years. He was so shocked by his own appearance that he balked at sending a copy home to his family.

"I'm actually afraid to send them home to my mother for I know she'll worry and wonder what this army has done to her son," Winters wrote DeEtta on September 10. "Her son, who could never even get mad enough to raise his voice. However, I don't feel quite so hard inside as I did there for a while but I guess I still look the part. As for the twinkle in the eye, sometimes I think it must have been frozen to death, and there may be a day when it'll warm up, but never as long as there's a war on and I've got to push a company."

Winters addressed DeEtta's concern over future casualties, which he himself shared. However, he told her, "Victory is ours but the casualties that must be paid is the price that hurts."

On September 13, Winters and the other 2nd Battalion officers again sat down for a briefing. Before them was a large map of Holland with several towns circled in red. Major Oliver Horton, Strayer's executive officer, stood before the men, a pointer in his hand. Next to him was Captain Clarence Hester, regimental S1 and Nixon, the S2.

"Relax, gentlemen, smoke 'em if you got 'em," Horton said, then pointed to the map. "This is Operation Market Garden. It's a combined air/ground thrust intended to smash through the German lines and get us into Germany itself, and it's a monster. Four days from now, over one thousand five hundred C-47s and another four hundred fifty-plus gliders will be taking off from twenty-four different airfields. They will drop three entire airborne divisions behind Kraut lines. The British 1st Airborne, the guys who wear those red beanies . . ."

"Berets," someone chimed in.

"Whatever, gets the brass ring." Horton tapped the map with the pointer.

"Arnhem. There they will seize and hold the bridge over the Rhine. The 82nd is next in line. They will be dropped around Nijmegen and will take the town and hold the bridges over the Maas River, the Maas-Waal Canal and the Waal River. Our drop area will be here, between the Wilhelmina Canal, the Willems Canal and the Aar River. Our objectives are the six bridges in that area, the Son Bridge, the bridge at the Willems Canal and the four bridges around Veghel at the Aar. We will also liberate Eindhoven itself.

"Meanwhile, the British XXX Corps is going to throw everything it has up this road in a rapid dash toward the Rhine. Our job, besides the taking the bridges—intact I might add—is to hold this road open. That's a fifteen-mile stretch, and if Jerry cuts it anywhere, it screws up the entire operation. The idea is to get to Arnhem and relieve the Brit paratroopers in two days."

"What's the distance," Winters asked.

"It's sixty-five miles of two-lane, hard-surfaced road," Horton replied. "And if you're at all familiar with Holland, you know it's wide-open and flat as an ironing board. Like I said, this is a monster."

"What's the opposition?" another officer asked.

Horton gestured to Captain Nixon, the battalion's planning officer.

"We're assured by G-2 that the Germans have been seriously hurt by the setbacks of this past summer, and are unlikely to be able to put up any type of organized resistance," Nixon said. "Plus, the Brits tell us that the Germans in this area are poorly trained, second-rate troops, either kids fresh out of the Hitler Youth or older men not deemed fit for front-line duty. The consensus is they can be quickly pushed aside."

Some derisive snorts of laughter erupted.

"Whether you believe it or not," Horton said, "don't count on this one being canceled. This is the brainchild of Field Marshal Sir Bernard Law Montgomery, and you know how he likes to have his ass kissed. So brief your men, pack your gear and make sure you have adequate ammo and supplies. Tomorrow we leave for our marshaling area, which is the airfield at Membury. You'll brief your companies there."

*   *   *

By the next morning Winters had all his gear packed away. The items he was leaving behind had been sent off to storage to await his return. The rest was in his duffel bag by the front door of the Barneses' cottage. Now it was time to say good-bye to the family, particularly Mr. Barnes.

Plagued by heart problems, Francis Barnes' health had deteriorated with startling rapidity the past summer and it was plain to see that the downward trend would continue. Winters found his adopted father sitting up in bed.

Winters sat beside him. He hadn't told Father Barnes he was heading back to Europe, not wanting to put added strain on the weakened heart.

"You're leaving now, Richard?" Barnes asked.

"Yes, sir," Winters said. "But it's nothing for you to worry about. Just another of those extended training exercises the army is so fond of."

Barnes smiled sadly.

"You're a good lad, Richard," he said. "You're a fine soldier and you're every bit the man I think my own son would have become. But you're a god-awful liar. I've seen the preparations and heard the trucks rattling past. They're sending you back to the Continent."

Winters opened his mouth to speak but Barnes raised a hand. "It's all right. You didn't want to worry the old man. Just make sure you come back. And if I'm not here when you do, you be sure to stop in and see Mother and let her know you're well."

"I'll do that, sir," Winters said.

"Off with you, then," Barnes said. "And God be with you."

Winters shook the man's hand and left, both knowing they would not meet again this side of eternity. After a farewell hug for Elaine, Winters faced Mother Barnes.

"Let me know how he's doing?"

"I'll write," she promised.

"Thank you for everything," he said. "I'll be back."

"I know you will," Mrs. Barnes replied. "Good-bye and God bless you." She kissed his cheek.

A jeep idled in the street. Throwing his duffel in the back, Winters climbed into the passenger seat and took one last look at the house. Elaine and Mrs. Barnes were watching from the doorway. He waved, then slapped the dashboard with his hand.

"Let's go," he said to the driver. "Hitler's waiting."

CHAPTER 6

"We Took a Hell of a Licking."

September 17–September 28, 1944

As the C-47s carrying Easy Company crossed over the Dutch coastline and penetrated deeper into Holland, the paratroopers on board wondered what awaited them over the drop zone. The veterans recalled June 6, when the sky around them was a maelstrom of colored tracers, exploding antiaircraft shells and twisting, burning airplanes, and thus anticipated a violent welcome. The new men, knowing it was Sunday and that the drop zones were well behind enemy lines, hoped the Germans might be surprised and slow to respond.

But whether they anticipated a hot reception or a cold one, the last thing they expected, or even dared hope for, was no reception at all. Yet that's what they got.

The first intimation Dick Winters had that this jump might be easy was when he looked out of the plane's open doorway at the peaceful Dutch countryside flashing by below him. There seemed to be no alarm, no bustle of German trucks or troops. And when the red "ready" light came on, there was no booming of ack-ack guns, and his hopes soared still higher.

The drop zone for the 506th and 502nd regiments was in a field outside the village of St. Oedenrode and a half mile north of their objective, the highway bridge spanning the Wilhelmina Canal at the town of Son. The 502nd was to head north and seize St. Oedenrode, while also sending a detachment to capture the mile-long bridge at Best, four miles west of Son, in case the former was destroyed. The 506th was to prevent that by taking the Son bridge intact, along with the town itself, and then capturing Eindhoven.

All this was on Winters' mind when the green light by his side flashed on.

Without hesitation, he launched himself out of the plane, rapidly falling fifty feet before he felt the jolt of the opening parachute. All around him the sky was filled with blossoming chutes. It was one of the easiest jumps he had ever experienced, as easy as any training jump and better than some.

Immediately after touching down Winters regained his feet and collapsed his canopy. Smacking open the snap release, he shucked his harness and began jogging east toward the highway and the rally point. His biggest fear in crossing the field was not the Germans, as he initially expected, but of being struck by the men who were still coming down or by heavy equipment bundles, as well as helmets, weapons and musette bags jarred loose by the opening of the parachutes.

"Easy Company, on me!" Winters yelled above the roar of the planes still overhead, disgorging their human cargo.

Despite the ease of the daylight jump, assembly took longer than Winters thought it should have, and they now embarked on the long, dusty march to the bridge. Second Battalion led the way and Colonel Strayer put D Company out in front, followed by Easy, then Headquarters Company and Fox. The troops followed the road, the formation strung out along both shoulders. Initially it was like a lazy field exercise back in England. No shots had been fired by either friend or foe.

That peacetime maneuver-like attitude changed as the bridge loomed into sight. Entering the outskirts of the village, the GIs ducked reflexively as a shell from a German 88 mm gun whistled overhead and burst nearby. An MG-42 machine gun began to rattle its own deadly welcome to Holland. Strayer deployed his battalion astride the road with Easy on the left and Dog on the right. The two companies probed forward cautiously, hugging the houses for cover. The 88 fired again. A bazooka team from Dog inched its way forward and fired a rocket at the gun emplacement, which erupted in a roar of smoke and flame. Picking their way past the smoldering 88 and its dead crew, the GIs continued to take small arms fire from Germans hidden in the village or beyond the canal. Laying down covering fire with machine guns and mortars, Winters urged his men forward. With the Americans still about fifty yards from the bridge, an explosion lifted the span, throwing wood and stone high into the air. The GIs sought shelter as the debris rained down on them. Rising slightly and brushing himself off, Winters turned to his left and said to Nixon, "What a hell of a way to die in combat."

Colonel Sink, who had also come up, said it more concisely. "Goddamn it," he muttered. The loss of the bridge was a bitter blow to the hardened soldier.

As soon as the hail of falling bridge remnants ceased, Winters brought his machine guns up to the edge of the canal and opened fire on the German rear guard. His gunners were soon sending a stream of lead across the canal. Winters felt a presence beside him. It was Hester.

"Sink's sending 1st Battalion across to get a foothold on the other side," he said. "He wants you to give them covering fire."

As Winters watched, 1st Battalion made its way to the canal bank. He saw its commander, Major James La Prade, out in front, tiptoeing from rock to timber to rock as he picked his way across on the rubble of the bridge. In his hand, La Prade was carrying a .45 caliber pistol, which Winters thought, under the present situation, to be ludicrous.

"For God's sake, man," he said to himself. "Carry an M1 rifle if you're expecting trouble. It'll give you a little firepower and won't advertise that you're an officer."

Gaining the far bank, La Prade and 1st Battalion quickly secured the ground. The central span of the bridge remained intact and within two hours engineers, using black-market timber that had been hidden in a nearby barn but was turned in by grateful Dutch residents, had constructed a temporary span. Sink pronounced this makeshift bridge "unsatisfactory from every point of view," but it allowed him to cross the rest of the 506th with dry feet. By dark, Easy was over the canal. Rain began to fall and Winters bedded down in the shelter of a woodshed.

Next morning the 506th advanced on Eindhoven. Sink put 3rd Battalion in the lead, followed by 2nd. First Battalion remained in the rear to help hold Son and the road, while engineers replaced the destroyed span with a British mobile Bailey Bridge. In 2nd Battalion, Strayer had F Company take the point. The paratroopers covered the ground rapidly and almost resistance-free until they reached the outskirts of Eindhoven. There the regiment stopped and deployed in preparation to move on the town. Second Battalion led the way, with Easy on the right and Fox on the left.

As Winters' men moved forward an 88 mm gun opened fire. Relaying orders from Strayer, Captain Hester told Winters to swing Easy Company to the left and approach the town from the north. Winters directed Lieutenant Brewer to take the point with his 1st Platoon. The flat fields approaching Eindhoven were devoid of cover. The twenty-year-old Californian, who had joined the airborne under the mistaken impression that they would be used as ski troops, expertly deployed his men in perfect formation with a thin skirmish line out in front. Ahead lay an orchard where Brewer had heard Germans were lying in wait. Setting up a machine gun to provide covering fire, Brewer ordered the platoon forward, but his greenness in battle now became evident. Instead of staying with the platoon, the gangly six-foot four-inch officer moved with the skirmishers. Worse, he stood tall and waved his arms in obvious gestures of command, his map case and binoculars in plain sight. Winters watched in horror as his platoon leader made himself a target. "Everyone knew what was coming," he said years later. "I had told him a hundred times in training, don't walk around out in front like that, you'll get it sure as hell."

Winters turned to Joe Liebgott who was toting a handheld SCR-536 radio.

"Get 1st Platoon," Winters ordered Liebgott.

The so-called "Handy-Talkie" was a piece of crap in hilly or wooded areas, but here on the flatlands of Holland, it was the ideal radio, light and easy to use. Leibgott raised 1st Platoon and handed the set to Winters, who yelled over and over into the mouthpiece, "Get back. Drop back. Drop back."

A shot rang out and Brewer, struck in the throat, went down like "a tree that's been felled by an expert lumberman."

"Goddamn it," Winters cursed. He was convinced Brewer was dead, but there was no time for pity. Even as Smoky Gordon and several other men, against orders, ran to the side of the stricken officer (Brewer would survive), Winters took over the platoon and pushed it across the field as fast as he could. Sporadic fire harassed the advance, but Easy suffered no further loss. A pair of 88s opened an ineffectual fire but they were quickly silenced by mortars and bazookas. Some fifty prisoners were rounded up.

Easy Company cautiously entered Eindhoven, picking its way along Woenselsche Straat. There they encountered a new problem: jubilant Dutchmen. From almost every building men, women and children swarmed out to meet the Americans. Kids waved orange flags; men shook hands and offered drinks. Women passed the soldiers food and kissed them in joyous celebration.

"Quite a different reception here than in France, huh?" Harry Welsh said. "There I suspected everyone of being a sniper."

"Yeah, but we've got to keep the men moving," Winters said.

He gestured for First Sergeant Lipton to join him. Lipton hurried to his commander's side.

"Lip, we've got to get through town and take the Dommel River bridge," he told Lipton. "Pass the word to the platoon leaders. Keep the men moving."

As Lipton went about his errand, Winters saw an elderly man drag a pair of chairs out of his house and invite soldiers to take a load off their feet. Two did, stretching out their legs. Winters ran over to them.

"Get goin'," he said angrily, waving them forward. "This is no time for goofing off. Move it."

Chagrined, the men hurried away. As they left, Brewer's image flashed in

Winters' mind, so to avoid tempting any lingering snipers, he tucked his map case and binoculars inside his field jacket and pulled up his collar to hide his silver bars. Carrying just his M1, Winters figured he now looked like any other GI.

Working his way through the sea of celebrating citizens, Winters stopped briefly by a crowd chanting something in Dutch while men roughly shaved the heads of several women. The women's offense, Winters learned, was that they had engaged in sex with German soldiers. He understood the people's anger. Still, his own mother had raised her son to have an abiding respect for women and this spectacle offended him. He walked away very much disturbed.

The 506th managed to get through Eindhoven in good order and the bridge over the Dommel was secured intact. But the loss of the Son bridge cast a pall of guilt over the men. That guilt was short-lived, however, as lead elements of the British XXX Corps arrived at Eindhoven by midafternoon and halted, the men stepping down from their tanks. Nixon and Winters watched a group of Tommies gather around a hastily built fire and heat water.

"What the hell are they doing? Nixon asked.

"What's it look like?" Winters replied bitterly. "A full day behind schedule and they're brewing tea. So much for this critical timetable we had to maintain."

That evening Winters took out his ledger (men weren't allowed to keep diaries) and wrote, "This total lack of urgency for the need to push on to the Dommel, the 82nd at Nijmegen and the British at Arnhem leaves us feeling bewildered. I can't understand this lack of concern for their fellow countrymen and the absence of a sense of duty toward the mission."

*   *   *

The next day, Easy Company was out in front again as the battalion moved out.

"We're heading for Helmond, about eight miles east of here," Hester said during the briefing. "The Dutch underground tells us it's a major German staging area. We're going to find out. Dick, you're point again. You'll have Brit tanks to keep you company."

The tanks were six ungainly Cromwells. Winters and his men climbed aboard the twenty-seven-ton vehicles and made themselves comfortable. Rolling along the flat Dutch countryside, the men made small talk while watching ahead for signs of trouble. Winters glanced to his right, where Popeye Wynn was leaning uncomfortably against the turret, one hand on the 75 mm gun.

"How are you holding up, Popeye?" Winters shouted above the deep rumble of the six-hundred-horsepower Rolls Royce Meteor engine.

"Well, sir," Wynn drawled. "I'm still a bit weak and my butt hurts, but I'll be fine."

"Still wish you were back in that hospital, being waited on by those pretty nurses?" Winters joked.

"No, sir," Wynn said.

After a brief silence, Winters asked, "What got you into the paratroops, Popeye?"

"Shifty did," he replied, referring to Darrell "Shifty" Powers. "At the recruitin' station we saw these posters tellin' about how glamorous the paratroopers were, sayin' things like, 'Don't walk into battle, jump.' Shifty bet me five bucks I was too chicken to join up. But I did, and then he had to, too."

Winters chuckled. He was glad to see Wynn back after he'd been hit in the buttocks at Brecourt. When he heard the company was moving out, Wynn released himself from the hospital and made his way to the marshaling area, still weak, but ready to go back into action with his buddies. Also making it back in time was Private Rod Strohl, who'd been hit outside Carentan. When Strohl heard Easy was leaving, he slipped out of the hospital and headed for Membury. Winters was amazed when he saw Strohl climb out of a jeep that contained Captain Herbert Sobel.

Winters was among the first to greet Strohl.

"That your new friend?" he asked Strohl as the jeep pulled away.

"No, sir," Strohl said with a grin. "He picked me up along the road and asked me where I was going, so I told him. He knew I didn't have a pass or anything, but he didn't give me hell. He just said, 'You know, Strohl, you don't have to make this jump.' I told him I wanted to, so he brought me here."

"He must be getting soft." Winters shrugged.

★   ★   ★

About three miles east of Eindhoven the Cromwells clanked through the small hamlet of Nuenen. Just beyond the town Winters heard someone—he thought it sounded like Private Jack F. Matthews—shout, "Kraut tanks." Winters jerked his head up and gazed down the road. The dark, squat hulls of German armor began to materialize from a distant tree line, moving toward Nuenen. The vehicles belonged to the 107th Panzer Brigade, which was counterattacking from Helmond against the advancing Allied troops. Winters estimated the number of enemy vehicles at about fifty, certainly more than he had ever seen in his life. As they spotted the oncoming American column, the Panzers began fanning out across the field ahead, infantry moving up from behind them.

"Take cover! Take cover!" Winters yelled, jumping down from the tank and into an adjacent field crisscrossed with irrigation ditches. The company rapidly dispersed into the field, hugging the ditches, and began laying down a fusilade of small arms fire. The company's .30 caliber machine guns joined the fray.

"Guarnere! Get those mortars working!" Winters yelled.

The Cromwells began spreading out, but not quickly enough. A German Panzer tank fired, its shell ripping into a Cromwell. The crew fled the crippled machine, abandoning one man who had lost his legs. A second tank exploded in flame, shards of hot metal streaking across the fields. Winters saw a German half track erupt in a ball of fire, men pouring out of it, some with their clothes aflame. A German tank took a glancing shot that severed one of its heavy treads, which snaked out onto the ground, bringing the wounded beast to a halt.

All around the men of Easy, bullets whined and tank shells split the air. The roar was incredible and the firepower coming at the GIs was intense. Winters knew there was only one direction his men could go.

"Back!" he yelled. "Pull back."

The men withdrew into the village, firing as they went. Private Robert Van Klinken was reaching for a dropped bazooka when he was hit and thrown to the ground. Winters knelt over the fallen Toccoa man, but Van Klinken was dead. Another body lay nearby. It was James W. Miller, a new replacement. Lieutenant Buck Compton fell, hit in the buttocks. Winters saw three men, Guarnere, Malarkey and Toye, rip a door off a nearby barn, load Compton on it, then drag the wounded officer rearward. They hoisted Compton up on the rear of one of the two surviving British tanks before the vehicles pulled back.

The GIs began taking shelter by the houses of Nuenen, firing at the advancing armored vehicles and accompanying German infantry. A Nazi half track was hit and its crew shot down as they fled the smoldering wreckage. Incoming machine gun and rifle slugs pinged off the stone walls of the houses. A tank shell tore through the wall of one house and the building blew apart, the concussion flinging GIs to the ground under a shower of wood and masonry. Men were cut by flying glass.

Though tightly squeezed and under heavy fire, Easy held its ground. The Germans did not enter Nuenen. As the sky drew dark, Winters, badly outnumbered, finally ordered his men to withdraw. A short distance west of the village, a line of American deuce-and-a-half trucks waited for them, as did Lewis Nixon. He had been with Easy when it ran into the Germans. Knowing Winters would need help, he made his way back to battalion and ordered up the trucks.

"Thought maybe you could use a ride," Nixon said to Winters as his friend approached.

Exhausted, Winters could only smile and nod. The wounded were loaded on the trucks and Winters led the rest back to Eindhoven on foot. Approaching the town at about 8:30 P.M., the drone of engines sounded overhead, growing louder every second.

"Theirs?" Welsh asked.

By way of answer, searchlights blinked on ahead and scanned the night. Then British ack-ack bursts speckled the sky. Stuka dive bombers, each capable of carrying a four-thousand-pound bomb, came screaming out of the darkness, releasing their loads of high explosives. From a distance Winters and his men watched huge orange-and-red explosions rend the night. After the Stukas had finished came the heavier sound of two-engine Heinkels. More antiaircraft fire arced skyward to meet these bombers as their bomb bay doors swung open and they released their payloads on the hapless town. A bomber was struck. It flamed brightly, then carved a fiery streak in the night as it plummeted downward. The rumble of the detonations reached the ears of the men of Easy. They felt the concussions sweep through the air and the ground vibrated beneath their feet. Raging fires created a bright orange glow that silhouetted the nearest buildings and Winters could not help but think about the joyous crowds that had met them in Eindhoven a few days earlier. The Germans now levied a heavy price on the citizenry, killing 227 and injuring another 800. The next day, there would be no happy Dutch faces or orange flags, just sad expressions that expressed disappointment and betrayal.

Easy Company reached Tongelre, a suburb of Eindhoven. There Winters bedded down his men before reporting to battalion headquarters. For some reason, the headquarters atmosphere was jovial as Strayer and his staff enjoyed a pleasant dinner. As Winters entered the house Strayer was using for his HQ, the colonel turned and flashed a big smile in his direction.

"There he is," Strayer said. "How did it go today, Winters?"

Winters stood quietly for a moment, gulping down the resentment he felt at the spectacle laid out before him.

"We ran smack into an advancing armored column," Winters said without preamble. "I had fifteen casualties today, lost four tanks, and I took a hell of a licking."

Conversation stopped in midsentence and the party mood evaporated as Winters departed.

The excursion to Nuenen had cost Winters four dead: Robert Van Klinken, James Miller, William T. Miller (no relation) and Vernon J. Menze. Plus he had ten men wounded and one missing, but that one was Corporal Bull Randleman. No one seemed to know what had happened to Bull, only that he had been hit and somehow separated from the company. Winters fretted over this. Bull was a valuable man and a good platoon leader, both of which Winters held in high esteem. But that wasn't the end of Winters' lousy night. Entering the small house he was using as a temporary HQ, Winters took off his equipment and helmet and sat down in a chair to relax as Nixon walked through the door.

"We can't find Bull," Winters said.

"Yeah, well I got some more bad news for you," Nixon responded. "Punchy Diel's dead."

Winters felt an emptiness in his soul as he absorbed this latest blow.

"What happened?" he asked.

"According to Doc Neavles, the company was attacked by some armor. Punchy tried to take out a tank with a bazooka but the tank fired first. Direct hit. I'm told there wasn't much left."

Winters was silent.

"Sorry to be the one . . ." Winters held up a hand to quiet his friend, and Nixon left. Alone, Winters reflected on the smiling face of Diel and remembered the "Don't take unnecessary chances" speech he'd given Punchy when he pinned on those new lieutenant's bars back in Aldbourne. Winters closed his eyes and tried to sleep.

★   ★   ★

The grim cloud over Winters was lifted considerably next day when Randleman showed up, wounded but alive. Injured by flying shards from an exploding tank, he had hidden in a barn. There, he killed a German in a bayonet fight and covered the body, and himself, with hay until daylight. The next morning, companies A and D made their way back into Nuenen without a fight and found Randleman holding the town single-handedly.

On September 22 Winters and his battle-weary men hauled themselves back onto the trucks, this time headed for Uden, a small hamlet about four miles beyond Veghel. There, according to the Dutch underground, a large enemy force was moving in their direction. Sink dispatched 2nd and 3rd Battalions under the command of his executive officer, Lieutenant Colonel Chase. This portion of the road, which featured four bridges, was the most vulnerable stretch along the entire sixty-five miles of what the Americans were now calling Hell's Highway. It needed to be kept open at all costs.

"Second Battalion has the lead," Chase told Winters. "But we're short of trucks. We can take about one platoon from each company. Load up your first platoon. When more transport gets here, the rest can follow."

Winters didn't like this plan very much, but orders were orders. He got the men loaded, then he, Welsh and Nixon climbed into a jeep with Chase. The small convoy, accompanied by a trio of British-driven Sherman tanks, nicknamed the Firefly by the Brits and toting a seventeen-pounder gun in place of the normal 76 mm, passed through Veghel without incident, rolling into Uden a short time later. Halting in the empty street, Winters climbed out of the jeep. Standing by a church, he looked up at the belfry.

"Shall we?" Nixon said, and the two men went inside and quickly ascended the narrow stairway. The church tower gave them a perfect view of the surrounding terrain and a clear view of their rapidly deteriorating situation.

"I'll be damned," Nixon muttered.

Like Winters, he was watching a column of German armor roll in from the west and cut the highway the paratroopers had just traveled. Winters tapped his friend on the shoulder and pointed. About forty German infantry were scurrying over the fields, headed straight for Uden. Winters and Nixon ran down the steps to where 1st Platoon waited.

"The Krauts have cut the highway behind us, so there's nothing to get excited about," Winters said. "The situation is normal. We're surrounded. Not only that, there's an enemy patrol heading this way. Follow me."

Winters led his men to the edge of the village and deployed them.

"Hold your fire until I give the word," Winters said as they watched the German approach. Then, "Fire."

The weapons of 1st Platoon blazed to life, toppling several of the enemy. The rest hit the ground and, obviously stunned, returned a feeble fire. After about twenty minutes of this one-sided fight, the Germans slowly pulled back, dragging their wounded with them. A few silent forms remained.

Following the skirmish with the German patrol, Chase found Winters and directed him to set up a defensive perimeter around the town.

"That's all he said?" Lipton asked when Winters relayed the instructions.

"Yep," Winters replied. "Guess he figured he'd done his job, then he went back to his CP, wherever the hell that might be. Anyway, Lip, set up roadblocks at either end of the town. Place the machine guns and mortars to cover the most likely approaches. Put every man you can on the line, including the Brits, but keep a squad in reserve for use wherever we might need them. Get some men to work on Molotov cocktails. Round up some bottles and get some gas or kerosene. Get some Composition C charges ready too. If the Germans break through and get into the town with tanks or armored cars, we can drop those things on them from second-floor windows. We're holding here, Lip. Retreat is not an option."

The ever-competent Lipton did as instructed. He had no trouble setting up the defense where the GIs were concerned, but getting the cooperation of the British was a different matter. The three tanks sat idly in the center of town, their crews indifferent to the danger. Informed of this, Winters stomped up to the tankers.

"I want you men to get off your asses and get those tanks into position at the roadblocks," he said. "I want two at the southern roadblock and the other one at the north roadblock." The British soldiers stared at him. "Move it! Now!" he ordered. The drivers kicked over their engines and the tanks headed for their assigned places.

Winters took some time to establish his command post in the home of a family named Van Oer. They were more than accommodating and moved, without argument, to the cellar. Nor did they complain as Winters' men repositioned rugs and furniture, converting the house into a defensive strongpoint. Winters liked the family and the Van Oers were appreciative of Winters' concern for them and their safety. (The Van Oers' daughter, Nel, became a longtime pen pal of Winters' sister, Ann.)

The rumble of the battle now going on behind them began to reach the ears of the men in Uden as the attacking Germans ran into the advancing Americans. Winters feared for the fate of the bulk of Easy Company. (Although he didn't know it until later, the rest of Easy Company also feared for the safety of Winters and the men with him. Each thought the other might have been annihilated.)

Winters and Nixon returned to the church belfry and looked to the south. Although Holland is basically flat, Uden is about twenty feet higher than Veghel in elevation, and the two men had a grandstand seat for the battle. Winters gazed in fascination at the desperate struggle raging just a few miles away. He watched German tanks roll forward in battle formation while Luftwaffe planes strafed the ground ahead of them. The roar of artillery and the incessant rattle of small arms fire echoed across the fields while tracers blazed through the sky.

Moments later the observers became the observed as an artillery shell whooshed by the bell tower. Winters and Nixon raced down the stairway. "I don't think our feet touched the steps more than two or three times," Winters later reflected. Back on the street, Winters prepared the men for a possible attack, but Uden remained unmolested.

Nighttime found Winters sitting at a table in the Van Oer home, maps laid out in front of him. Across from Winters sat First Sergeant Lipton, and next to

him, Lewis Nixon, who was enjoying his favorite beverage, Vat 69, which
Winters felt his friend consumed far too liberally. Ever since they had know
each other, Nixon had been a hard drinker, and he had taken to hiding his
stash in Winters' baggage during moves, knowing that it would remain undetected there.

"That stuff's going to kill you one day, Nix," Winters commented.

Nixon held up his flask in mock toast. "Here's to that day," he said and
took a slug. He offered it to Lipton, who shook his head.

The Van Oers had a radio that Nixon had turned on and was now belting
out a Benny Goodman tune.

"That was 'Let's Dance,'" cooed the female voice on the radio, known to
the men as Arnhem Annie. "Wouldn't you just love to be home dancing with
your girl right now? I hope you lonely GIs don't miss home too much. After
all, here you are, suffering and dying here in Holland while Eisenhower sits
back in London dining on all the luscious foods you may never get to taste
again. And speaking of food, some of your comrades are right now enjoying
hot meals being served to them by our excellent German army cooks. I will
now read to you a list of the Americans we have captured today." She read a
list of names. "How fortunate they are. Their war is over. They now have hot
food and shelter from the rain, thanks to the victorious forces of our Führer.
Perhaps you'd wish to join them and end the risk of dying in a cause that no
one back in your homeland cares about. Especially your president, the Jew
Roosevelt, whose family now runs your entire nation."

Always considerate, Annie told the men what to bring in the way of personal gear if they cared to surrender.

"Think about that, boys, as you listen to 'Humoresque' by Glenn Miller,"
Annie said. "And remember, you can listen to our music, but you can't dance
in our streets."

"Maybe we should get our personal gear together," Nixon said in jest.
"Sounds like the Krauts'll be here for us soon."

"Why should they?" Lipton said. "We're not going anywhere."

"Lip's right," Winters said. "Right now they're focusing on the main body
behind us, and in cutting the road. They can mop us up anytime they
choose." He glanced at his watch, then rose, placed his helmet on his head
and picked up his M1. "It's 2200. I need to check on the roadblocks. Care to
go along, Nix?"

"Why not?" Nixon said and got up.

Leaving Lipton in charge at the CP, the two men went out into the darkened village. "You take the roadblock to the south; I'll check the other one,"
Winters said.

The roadblock at the northwestern end of Uden was manned by one British tank and a squad of Easy Company men under Harry Welsh. A large house stood near this roadblock, off to the left, and served as the command post. Across the street was a tavern. As Winters approached, he saw the Firefly tank on guard but, drawing closer, he saw no men except for three members of the tank crew. They looked bored and not one was watching the road ahead. Anger flared through Winters.

"Where's your officer?" Winters said tersely, barely able to contain himself. A man pointed to the large house. Winters strode up to the house and hammered on the door. A young maid answered.

"I want to see the soldier," Winters said, but the blank look on her face showed she had not understood a word he said. "*Soldat. Soldat,*" he said, pointing to his uniform and then into the house. "*Soldat.*"

Comprehension swept over her. "*Die Soldaat,*" she said, waving him inside. "*Binnenkom.*" The maid escorted him through an ornate foyer. "*Volg mij,*" she said, motioning him forward.

The maid led Winters along a mahogany hallway to a set of large, ornate doors. Opening them, he entered a lavishly furnished living room where he found a lovely young Dutch girl sharing a meal that included fresh eggs with the British tank commander. The two sat on the floor in front of a huge fireplace with a blazing fire to help fend off the dampness outside. The British lieutenant looked up as Winters came in.

"Are my tanks outside yet, old chap?" he asked.

Risking a serious setback in British-American relations, Winters blew up.

"What the hell's the matter with you?" he fumed. "In case it has escaped your notice, we're surrounded. The damned Germans could walk into this town at any time. What would you have done if I'd been a Kraut? Get the hell out there where you belong."

The lieutenant jumped to his feet, saluted quickly and ran from the room. Winters looked at the shocked girl, now suddenly alone. He smiled, nodded his head and left. Outside he saw the tank crew now on alert. Okay, he thought. So where's Harry?

The tavern was the only logical choice, so Winters crossed the street and opened the door. Inside he found GIs sleeping or lounging around. Welsh and a few other men were sacked out on the bar. Winters' entrance roused Welsh, who sat up. Winters gestured for Welsh to follow, then stepped back outside. His executive officer soon followed, the sheepish look on his face making it plain he knew he had screwed up.

Jerking his head in the direction of the tavern, Winters said, "Do you think this is a good idea, Harry?"

"No, sir," Welsh said. "I'm sorry, Captain."

"Get half the men on line and rotate them," Winters ordered. "Then get some rest yourself. If the Germans come, I need you thinking straight."

Welsh saluted as Winters left. Winters hated to chide Welsh. Harry was a good man and a friend, but he suffered occasional lapses in judgment.

★ ★ ★

The battle for Veghel continued the next day with Winters and his men again in the role of spectators. Now, besides the artillery and tank fire, American P-47 Thunderbolts and British Typhoons, all carrying bombs or air-to-ground rockets, screamed in out of the sky to pummel the German attackers. The Americans had been reinforced by the 32nd Guards Brigade, and after a day of heavy fighting the road was finally reopened, but not before the critical Allied timetable for reaching Arnhem had suffered another twenty-four-hour delay. On September 24 Winters watched as U.S. soldiers entered Uden, led by the balance of Easy Company. It made for a joyous reunion. Heading up the welcoming committee was Lieutenant Colonel Chase, whom Winters had not seen since the day they were surrounded. Winters wondered where he'd been hiding.

Early the next morning, Winters and the other officers of the 2nd Battalion were roused and ordered to the building where Strayer had set up his CP. Winters looked at his watch. It was 3 A.M. Jesus. Stepping out of the Van Oer house, Winters was greeted by a cold, pouring rain that drummed relentlessly on their helmets before running off in steady rivulets. Strayer and Horton were waiting for the officers at Battalion HQ. Horton began.

"The Krauts have cut the highway again," the battalion XO said. A moan rippled across the room. "This time south of Veghel. We're attacking at 0830 with 1st Battalion on the right and 3rd on the left. We're regimental reserve. Get your men up and make sure they've drawn more ammo. We're leaving here at 0445."

The rain had let up in time for the morning attack, but by 1 P.M., 1st and 3rd Battalions had been halted by stiff resistance. Captain Hester called a meeting of 2nd Battalion officers.

"We're being sent around the left flank," he said, holding up a map. "The Brits are giving us a trio of tanks. Dick, Easy has the point. Two of those tanks will be assigned to you."

"Fine," Winters said. "But I'd like to poke ahead on my own and pick out the most tank-friendly terrain."

Accompanied by Nixon, Winters performed another of his personal reconnaissances, choosing ground he felt would be most advantageous for his men, and best suited for tank support. What Winters saw wasn't encouraging. He found a wood line that would provide a good approach for the men and tanks. The problem was that the woods ended about 350 yards from the highway, with nothing but open field the rest of the way. Winters quickly brought his company through the woods to the edge of the field. There he deployed them much the way Brewer had at Eindhoven, spread out with no bunching, a thin skirmish line out in front. Walking with weapons held at the ready, they made it about halfway across the open, rain-softened ground when German machine guns opened fire. With nowhere to go but down, the men dropped and hugged the earth. Effectively pinned down, Winters turned to his left rear and yelled, "Guarnere, put that 60 mm on those machine guns." But Wild Bill was one step ahead of Winters. He had already been giving coordinates to Malarkey, who was now the only man in the field not lying down as he worked his mortar. Within moments, Winters heard the dull *thunk* as a mortar round left the tube, headed for the highway. The shell erupted on target.

"God, they're good," Winters thought, reflecting on his mortar men.

Looking through his binoculars, Winters spotted a new threat: the massive bulk of a Tiger tank, positioned in such a way that only its turret was visible above the road embankment. Winters knew that all soldiers up against a German tank assumed it was a Tiger, but this, he felt, was one. It was the "biggest damned tank I'd ever seen," he later noted. It was also in full hull defilade, and impossible to hit from where he and his men were, even if they had something that could penetrate its thick four-inch frontal armor, which they did not. Even the Fireflies, back in the woods, couldn't knock out a Tiger in a head-on attack.

A dull clang to Winters' left drew his attention. Nixon, a stunned look on his face, removed his helmet. A machine gun bullet had pierced the metal shell near the front, deflected, and exited at the side. It had left a burn mark on the left side of his forehead, but did not break the skin. Nixon would be one of the few Easy Company men to go through the entire war and never get the Purple Heart.

"Are you okay, Nix?" Winters asked urgently.

"Yeah, I think so," he said, mildly dazed and feeling his forehead for blood. Finding none, he put the damaged helmet back on his head. Winters knew he had to get his men out of this field. The nearest officer was First Lieutenant Benjamin W. Perkins, who had replaced the wounded Compton as leader of 2nd Platoon.

"We're leaving," he told Perkins. "Tell the machine guns to give us covering fire. Then we'll pull back the riflemen."

Perkins nodded and passed the word.

"Okay," Winters shouted. "Back. Pull back!"

Slithering across the field, the men made their way to the wood line. Reaching the trees, Winters looked back and saw that some of his men crawled on all fours while others, the married men he assumed, were on their bellies "like babies." One of these latter was Lipton who, head down, bumped into Winters' foot. He glanced up, an embarrassed look on his face. Winters smiled. It was a moment that would make Lipton blush for the rest of his life.

"Lip," Winters said, "take Talbert and go back and get more ammo for the machine guns. They'll need it when they get back." Lipton left, and Winters now turned to the rest of Easy. "Covering fire!" he ordered, and the men sent volley after volley at the road as the machine gunners dragged their weapons to the rear. With everyone now safely back and no one hit except the rattled Nixon, Winters set about trying to do something about the Tiger tank. Retreating through the underbrush he hurried back to where the two British Fireflies sat waiting. Grasping the seventeen-pounder cannon barrel, he hauled himself up onto the lead tank and hammered on the hull with his rifle butt. A young British officer popped up.

"Sir?" he asked.

"There's a Tiger tank out in front of us just beyond the highway, but he's in hull defilade. You can't get at him from this direction," Winters said. "Do not pull out into the open. If you can, work your way around to the left and get behind the bank on the edge of the woods, and maybe you can get a shot at him."

Winters hopped down off the tank as the engine roared to life. Satisfaction turned to disbelief as the tank, in complete contrast to his advice, pulled straight ahead, knocking down several small trees, and burst out into the field. The second Firefly followed.

"My God," Winters muttered aloud.

The lead tank rolled into the open, spotted the Tiger, and turned slightly to the left, stopping to line up the shot. The German wasn't waiting. He swiveled his turrent and the Tiger's 88 belched smoke as the first shell screamed toward the British tank. It caromed off the seventeen-pounder gun, then ricocheted off the turret. The Firefly driver slammed his tank into reverse in an attempt to get the hell out of the field, but the Tiger fired a second round that plowed straight through the steel hull and exploded. The young commander Winters had spoken to just moments earlier was blown out of the turret like a champagne cork, dead before he hit the ground. The second Firefly had pulled up beside the first, its turret rotating for a shot when the Tiger's third round struck it. The tank seemed to lift off the ground as it exploded. Both British tanks were now engulfed in flames as ammunition stored within began to go off. Pillars of thick black smoke billowed skyward and the air took on the sticky-sweet aroma of burning flesh and hair as the armored vehicles became crematoriums for their dead crews.

"Goddamn it," Winters said. "Put machine gun fire on that road. Malarkey, crank up that mortar."

From his position at the edge of the woods, Winters and his men raked the road with everything they had. Nixon arrived bringing along a heavy 81 mm mortar and a crew from headquarters company which added its weight to the barrage.

As night descended, the two tanks continued to burn, the roar of the flames punctuated by the occasional crack of an exploding machine gun bullet. A heavy rain began to fall again on Winters and his men, huddled miserably among the trees. Winters had stopped firing with the darkness, not wanting to give away his position through muzzle flashes. Sometime around midnight, Winters heard engine noises on the road ahead and the distinct clank of tank treads. He hoped the Germans were pulling out, but he held his line, waiting for daylight. As he listened to the noises, he looked at Nixon, who was huddled next to him. Somehow his friend had procured a bottle of schnapps and was in the process of finishing it off.

"Where the hell do you find this stuff?" Winters asked in a low tone.

Nixon waved the bottle at him drunkenly and said, "Never underestimate the resources of a man in need."

Winters shook his head in disapproval. He would not take this kind of behavior from any other man and was not sure why he tolerated it from Nixon. But he knew Nixon would be there doing his job when needed.

Next morning, with a rainy mist obscuring the dawn, Winters sent a combat patrol on a flanking move around the German left. Giving the burning tanks a wide berth to avoid being spotted in their glow, the patrol crept across the field, jump boots squishing on the soggy earth, and made its way to the road. As Winters had hoped, when the patrol reached the road, it found the Germans had gone. They signaled Winters, who brought the rest of the company forward. There, standing again on Hell's Highway, the men saw firsthand the accuracy of their own machine gun and mortar fire. Several bodies lay abandoned on the road. Winters spotted a machine gun emplacement, its MG-42 ruined, with three dead German paratroopers sprawled around it. He turned to Malarkey, who was lugging the 60 mm mortar.

"Don," Winters said, pointing to the machine gun nest. "Good shooting."

Then he noticed that one of the dead paratroopers was wearing new jump boots. Winters gazed at his own well-worn boots, the left one still bearing the hole where a ricochet had hit him at Carentan, and decided on a swap. Sitting down on the roadway by the dead man, he lifted the German's foot and put it up against his own. Then he scowled. Damn, just a tad too small.

Winters got his men together and they walked through the drizzle back to Uden. Hell's Highway was open again, and the British relief force for Arnhem was moving forward: trucks and tanks as far as Winters could see. But the timetable had been thrown off another forty hours.

As Easy Company trudged along the rain-splattered road, Winters took mental stock of his plight. The company had lost three officers wounded—Brewer, Compton and Charles A. Hudson, a replacement lieutenant from Able Company—four enlisted men were dead and fifteen wounded.

And they'd only been in combat for ten days.

CHAPTER 7

"My Luck Is Still Holding . . ."

October 2–November 25, 1944

The area of Holland known as the Island is a long, narrow, low-lying stretch of land north of Nijmegen and sandwiched between the Lower Rhine and Waal rivers. The ground is mostly flat farmland sprinkled with a few small towns and villages. The roads, averaging ten to twelve feet in width, run along the tops of dikes elevated twenty feet or so above the fields. The dikes serve the dual purpose of holding back the rivers and dividing the fields. The steep banks of the dikes are blanketed with heavy vegetation to avoid erosion, while down on the flat fields, crisscrossed with irrigation ditches, farmers raise carrots, beets and cabbages as well as apple and pear trees.

The 506th, temporarily attached to the British XII Corps, had been trucked to the Island on October 2 following reports by the British that the German 363rd Volksgrenadier Division, which had been badly cut up in Normandy in June and July, had been reinforced and was now in the vicinity and awaiting redeployment.

The weather remained dreary with a mizzling of rain that coated everything and everyone with a wet sheen, guaranteeing that the ground remained soggy, the air misty and the men stuck in the foxholes miserable. The GIs made the best of life under those drab conditions. Easy's cook, Joseph P. Dominguez, tried to get meals to his fellow troopers before the food got cold, while the men comforted themselves by cursing the war, the Germans, the weather, their draft boards and anything or anyone else they could think of. Winters recalled keeping up his spiritual morale by attending church services held in a barn where, along with the worshippers, cows and horses stood nearby, munching on hay and adding their own special aroma to the worship.

Second Battalion of the 506th had been ordered to take up position at the village of Zetten, and the next day, October 3, hiked to the front to relieve the British 43rd Division.

A few days before the regiment had moved into Zetten, Winters and some other officers were sent ahead to get the lay of the land. While they were there the British launched a major attack on the German position. Standing back from the fight, Winters observed the action with horrified fascination. A carpet of British troops in their soup bowl helmets spread across the field casually, almost carelessly. The soldiers lugged their Lee Enfield rifles loosely in their hands; the officers kept their arms holstered. When the expected German fire opened up, no evasive action was taken, nor did anyone look for cover. They just plodded on. "What in the hell are they doing?" Winters thought. The spectacle reminded Winters of a Civil War battle, when lines of men moved across open ground under withering enemy fire despite appalling casualties. It was very noble, but very foolish. Winters shook his head in disbelief at the lack of tactical thought and seeming indifference to losses displayed by the British commanders, especially in light of Britain's dwindling manpower reserves.

"I never saw anything like it," Winters later told Nixon. "The Krauts just cut them to pieces. The whole thing made no damned sense."

Expected to cover a six-mile front, now vacated by the British division, with a single regiment, Sink spread the men out, with 3rd Battalion anchored on the Waal River with its line stretching east three miles through Opheusden to Randwijk. There 2nd Battalion took over, extending its line east two and a half miles, ending near the village of Heteren. First Battalion was held in reserve near Sink's headquarters at Hemmen.

All of the battalions were at half strength or less following the hard fighting along Hell's Highway, so the line was stretched dangerously taut. Strayer deployed 2nd Battalion with Easy on the right, Fox on the left and Dog in reserve, forcing Winters to cover about a mile and a half of front with a hundred thirty men. To do that, he established a series of outposts rather than a continuous line, even though he was keenly aware that this arrangement left his front susceptible to enemy infiltration. After personally looking over the ground, Winters ordered 2nd and 3rd Platoons to man the outposts, with 1st Platoon in reserve. He maintained contact using field telephones and radios, and sent out regular contact patrols to watch for the enemy. It wasn't long before one of these made contact.

During one of their first nights on the line, Sergeant Don Malarkey and Privates Roderick G. Bain and Eugene E. Jackson were manning an outpost along the bank of the Rhine when they heard a sound out in the predawn gloom. Moments later a German shepherd dog materialized out of the mist, trotted up to them and began sniffing the ground. There quickly followed another noise and the dim forms of seven German soldiers appeared, hands raised.

"*Kamerad,*" one said.

"*Kommen Sie hier,*" Malarkey ordered, and the men, eager to get out of the war, meekly entered the OP. Malarkey patted them down for concealed weapons and any papers while the other two kept them covered.

"What the hell are we going to do now?" Bain asked. "We got a quarter mile of open ground to cover with seven POWs, and the sun'll be up before we get halfway across. And you know the Krauts. If they see any movement at all, they'll toss in an 88."

"Well, we can't keep them here," Malarkey said to Bain. "Get on your radio. Tell Captain Winters what we got and ask him to alert the sentries that we're coming in."

Bain was soon talking to company HQ.

"We'll be watching for you," Winters said. "But don't goof off. Get back here on the double quick."

The men herded their prisoners back without incident.

★   ★   ★

In the dark, early-morning hours of October 5, Private First Class Roderick Strohl led out a three-man patrol. The enemy had been spotted near Randwijk, and his mission was to see what they were up to and discourage them, if possible, by calling in artillery fire. They never got to Randwijk. Bursting into company HQ lugging a wounded Private James H. Alley Jr., Strohl had some serious news for Winters.

"We ran into a large Kraut patrol less than a mile from here," he said.

"Show me," Winters ordered, indicating his map. Strohl looked at it briefly, then pointed to a crossroad.

"Here," he said. "The Krauts tossed grenades at us and we threw a bunch back."

"Jesus, that puts them halfway between the company CP and 1st Battalion," Winters said anxiously. He turned to First Sergeant Lipton. "Stay by the radio, Lip." He next turned to Sergeant Leo Boyle. "Boyle! Grab the Handie-Talkie and follow me."

Outside the HQ, 1st Platoon sat in reserve.

"First squad," Winters yelled. "On me. Let's go."

As a medic arrived to tend Alley, who'd been hit by grenade shrapnel, Winters' patrol departed. Hunched forward at the waist, the men ran through the darkened field by the base of the dike. As the crossroad loomed ahead, a machine gun suddenly chattered in the night. Instinctively the paratroopers dropped to the ground, but the gun continued firing and Winters realized it was not shooting at them. Advancing the patrol to within eight hundred yards of the sound, he silently held them up. There was supposed to be a Canadian forward artillery observer, whom Winters had hoped to contact in order to call in some fire, but the man was nowhere to be seen. Winters turned to Boyle and told him to hold the patrol in place. Scaling the dike alone, Winters scurried across the road and partway down the reverse slope. Below he saw a field with a ditch about thirty inches deep running parallel to the road.

He nodded to himself, then rejoined the patrol. At Winters' command, the men crossed the dike. After halting to place a two-man rear guard, he led the others down the reverse slope and into the ditch. Still hunched over, they scurried forward along the ditch until they came to another, perpendicular to the first. Still about 250 yards from the crossroad, Winters halted the patrol and moved on ahead, alone. Feeling, he later said, like he was living a scene from the movie *All Quiet on the Western Front,* he reached the point where the roads intersected and crawled silently up the dike for a peek. A cluster of Germans, several in long greatcoats, stood in a knot by the gun, which continued firing into the darkness. It made no sense to Winters. Battalion HQ was in that direction, but was much too far for the Germans to either see or hit with an MG-42.

Winters returned to the patrol and filled them in. "There's a bunch of Krauts up ahead," he told them. "They have no idea we're here. Follow me. No noise, and keep low."

Aware that he was losing the cover of night, Winters swiftly moved the patrol to within forty yards of the crossroad. He halted the men and turned to Sergeant Warren H. "Skip" Muck and his buddy, Private First Class Alex M. Penkala Jr., who were lugging a 60 mm mortar and ammo.

"Muck. Penkala," Winters whispered. "Mortar here."

He continued forward. The patrol scaled the dike and was now within sight of the Germans. Winters whispered to Sergeant William H. Dukeman Jr. and Corporal Burt Christenson to set up the .30 caliber machine gun and to fire on the MG-42. He then assigned each of his riflemen a particular human target.

Stepping back, he said softly, "On my command. Ready."

The men sighted their weapons.

"Aim."

Corporal George R. Higgens, a former battalion mess cook who got bored with preparing meals for officers and asked to be transferred to a combat unit despite his lack of infantry training, got nervous. "Don't talk so loud," he whispered.

Winters ignored him.

"Fire!"

The machine gun fired high but the riflemen's aim was true. Seven Germans fell. Three ran. Winters and his men opened up on them. Then Winters said, "Fall back!"

The patrol raced back along the trench. Unseen Germans fired at them, their tracer bullets streaking by overhead. Muck and Penkala's mortar fire, which they were dropping with fine precision, helped spoil the Germans' aim as Winters and his men took cover in the east-west ditch, two hundred yards from the crossroad.

"Get on the radio, Boyle," Winters said. "Tell Welsh to bring up the rest of 1st Platoon, and to grab Lieutenant Reese and have him bring up a section of machine guns from headquarters company."

As they waited in the growing dawn, a German rifle grenade burst nearby. A shard of shrapnel struck Dukeman in the shoulder, knifing through his body and piercing his heart. He fell dead. Paratroopers returned fire and killed three Germans hidden in a nearby culvert.

With the arrival of his reinforcements, Winters crawled some fifty yards away from the men, needing solitude to ponder his next move. None of his choices were good ones. As he saw the situation, he was stranded in an open field with about forty men, with an unknown number of the enemy beyond the dike road in front of him. To pull out now meant doing so without the cover of darkness. Worse, once the Germans realized that they had the upper hand, they could easily advance along the top of the dike and put down a killing fire on his vulnerable right flank. On the other hand, even if he could retreat, he wouldn't. If this incursion was the prelude to a German attack, the enemy could roll straight down the road and hit battalion HQ at Hemmen from the rear.

"God give me strength," Winters prayed softly, and rejoined the men where Welsh, Lieutenant Peacock, First Lieutenant Frank Reese and Sergeant Talbert awaited his instructions. Winters laid out the situation as he saw it, then told them he planned to attack.

"Talbert, I want you to take 3rd Squad to the right," he ordered. "Peacock, you and 1st Squad will be on the left. I'll take 2nd Squad up the middle. Reese, place your machine guns between the columns to provide a good covering fire until we reach the roadway, then lift your fire and move up to join us. Any questions? Okay. Get your men in line quickly and fix bayonets. Peacock, when everybody is in position I'll give you a hand signal and you drop a smoke grenade to signal the jump-off."

As they left to carry out their assignments, Winters gathered 2nd Squad.

"All right, fix bayonets," Winters said. As the men slid the bayonets from their scabbards and snapped them in place on the business ends of their Garands, Winters saw Private First Class Donald B. Hoobler, adrenaline flowing, swallow hard, his Adam's apple "making the difficult trip up and down his throat." Winters smiled. His adrenaline was flowing hard, too. He nodded to Peacock, who tossed the smoke grenade. The machine guns blazed.

"Follow me," Winters said.

The men wordlessly rose to their feet and raced forward. Winters later reflected that he had never run so fast in his entire life. Blood pounding in his ears as he ran, his sole focus was on the dike road ahead and he unknowingly pulled away from the men behind him. Even the occasional strands of barbed wire, strung at shoe-top height, didn't slow him. Although he tripped a few times, Winters kept his feet and sprinted ahead.

Feet pounding, the men ran hard, each fully expecting to be fired on at any time. Yet amazingly, the Americans crossed the two hundred yards of open ground unmolested. The road ahead, running east toward the Rhine, lost height the farther it got from the intersection, so that where Winters was about to hit it, the bank was just a few feet high. Reaching the embankment, Winters leaped up on the road and was suddenly confronted with a German sentry directly in front of him. The man was hunched down below the level of the roadway to avoid Reese's machine gun fire. In that same fraction of a second, Winters also noticed a mass of Germans just to his right, many in greatcoats and wearing backpacks, also ducked down below the embankment for cover.

Jumping back down to his side of the road, Winters slipped a grenade from his belt, yanked out the pin and heaved it at the sentry. The German replied by tossing a potato masher grenade in Winters' direction. As soon as he'd thrown the pineapple, Winters knew he'd goofed. Wary of accidental explosion, he had gotten into the habit of taping down the arming lever, so merely pulling the pin was not going to activate the grenade. Knowing the German hadn't made the same mistake with his grenade, which he had overthrown so that it landed twenty yards away, Winters leaped back up onto the road as the potato masher harmlessly went off. Awaiting the detonation of the American grenade, which he didn't know would never come, the sentry had his head down again. Suddenly aware of Winters' presence above him, the man quickly tried to straighten but Winters, his M1 leveled, fired from the hip. At that distance there was no way he could miss. The German, struck square in the chest, was bowled over backward and fell heavily onto the grassy field. But before he had hit the ground, Winters swiveled toward the mass of Germans to his right and, still holding the weapon at his hip, opened fire.

As Winters recalled years later, now everything and everyone except himself seemed to move in slow motion. "I was the only one moving at normal speed," he recalled. "It was so unreal." His men, racing up from the rear, seemed to take forever to arrive. The Germans, being fired on from their unprotected rear and following basic human survival instincts, began to flee as Winters emptied an entire eight-round clip in their direction.

Ker-ching, the spent clip sounded as it flew from the breach. Winters slid in a second clip and fired off eight more rounds. This second clip ejected and Winters slammed in a third and resumed firing.

A few Germans had regained their composure and sent a smattering of fire at the lone American rifleman standing on the roadway, but their aim was thrown off as they were jostled by their comrades hurrying away. Then the American was no longer alone. Talbert, with his squad, suddenly crested the hill smack on the German flank. It was, as Winters later expressed it, a "duck shoot," as Germans spun and dropped. The GIs could hardly miss.

Confused and being raked by a withering fire, the Germans turned and fled across the open field toward a distant clump of trees near an old windmill that stood forlornly on the dike. As the GIs continued to pour a stream of lead into the backs of the retreating Germans, a shout of warning sounded from one of Winters' men. Another entire company of the enemy, which had evidently been on the other side of the crossroad, now poured over the dike on the American right flank and straight into the blazing muzzles of the GIs. Without hesitation, the Americans turned their fire on these new targets. More enemy soldiers fell while the rest joined their comrades in a confused sprint for the distant woods. They were sped along by Private Roy Cobb, who set up a light machine gun and sent a hail of .30 caliber bullets into the German rear.

To Winters' left, Peacock and his men tangled with a German rear guard, killing six and wounding nine before the rest fled.

As the enemy pulled back toward another dike road about a mile to the north, Winters hastily consulted his map. Taking the radio from Boyle he called for artillery fire, shouting the coordinates into the mouthpiece. He also requested reinforcements, saying he was up against two German companies with just one platoon. Within minutes the air overhead heralded the arrival of the "incoming mail." The bursting shells blossomed among the mass of running men, the concussion of each detonation sweeping across the field. Veteran German soldiers had a deep respect for the accuracy of American artillery and the pace of the retreat quickened to avoid this new, deadly menace.

As the bursting shells "walked" along the field after the Germans, Winters lifted his binoculars. The Germans, he noted, seemed to be rallying along the next road, which ran parallel to the one he and his men now firmly held. He looked again at his map and realized the Germans were trapped between the Rhine and Waal rivers. Their only escape was to cross the Rhine at a ferry crossing. That ferry, however, was at the end of the road Winters now occupied, putting him closer to it than the enemy. He looked at Boyle.

"Once those reinforcements get here, we're going to push down this road to the ferry crossing," he said. "If we take that and hold it, they won't be able to recross the river and we'll have them cut off."

A platoon from Fox Company, which had been in battalion reserve, soon arrived. Before striking out for the ferry, Winters decided to send his POWs to the rear. He saw T/5 Joseph D. Liebgott sitting at the base of the embankment. Liebgott, a capable soldier whose being Jewish left him with a pronounced dislike for the Germans, had been slightly wounded in the fight. "Liebgott," Winters said. "Get those prisoners back to battalion. Then get Doc Neavles to look at that wound."

Liebgott rose, clutching his weapon firmly, and muttered, "Oh, boy. I'll take care of them." He began walking toward the prisoners. Winters knew Liebgott had mistreated prisoners in the past, an action he personally disapproved of, and suddenly he worried that this group might not survive the three-and-a-half-mile trip back to battalion.

Intercepting Liebgott, Winters said, "There are eleven prisoners, and I want eleven prisoners handed over to battalion. Empty your rifle."

Liebgott's face reddened with anger. Winters dropped his M1 to his hip and threw off the safety. Liebgott was a volatile man and Winters did not know how he would react to the order.

"Joe, drop your ammo clip and empty your rifle," he ordered. Liebgott swore bitterly but did as he was ordered. "Now, you can put in one round. If you shoot a prisoner, the rest will jump you."

As Liebgott did as he was told, Winters noticed one of the prisoners, an officer, who had been pacing nervously throughout the exchange. Winters assumed the man could understand English, for when Winters allowed Liebgott just one round, the officer's expression changed to relief and he sat down. Winters checked with Nixon the next day. Battalion had received eleven prisoners.

*   *   *

With the arrival of F Company came more ammunition. Now reinforced, resupplied and rested, Winters began advancing on the ferry crossing just six hundred yards away. To cover the move, Winters set up a base of fire with his machine guns, then sent one platoon forward a hundred yards. There the men knelt, weapons at the ready as the 2nd Platoon advanced through them to take up position another hundred yards out in front. In this way, the paratroopers leapfrogged along the road. As he closed the distance on the Rhine, Winters could look across the river and see the rooftops of the village of Renkum. Another two hundred yards and they'd have both the factory and the ferry crossing.

Without warning, the air above them whooshed with the sound of incoming shells that burst around the advancing men. The GIs dropped and hugged the ground to avoid the jagged shrapnel. Winters lifted his binoculars. Unseen until they had made their deadly presence known, Winters now spotted German artillery and mortar men working their pieces on the high ground beyond the river. He had not seen them, but they had been, in Winters' words, "watching this whole cockeyed thing" from the time he'd driven the enemy from the crossroad, until he advanced on the ferry. Not only that, the German infantry Winters had hoped to trap was now moving up on his right flank. In a reversal of fortunes, Winters discovered that he was the one now in danger of being cut off. It was time to get out.

Reversing his strategy, Winters leapfrogged his men back along the road the way they had come. All went smoothly until the GIs regained the crossroad, where the German fire suddenly intensified.

"Take cover," Winters yelled. "They have us zeroed in!"

Amid the hail of shells, Winters realized the enemy gunners had the exact coordinates of this intersection. The only reason they had not fired earlier was out of fear of hitting their own men. Winters took the radio from Boyle and made two frantic calls. The first was for artillery support, and soon 105 mm shells from a Canadian battery streaked overhead, on their way to the far side of the Rhine. The next call was to Doc Neavles, requesting ambulances and medics.

"How many wounded do you have, Dick?" Neavles asked.

"About two baseball teams' worth," he replied.

"How many is that?" Neavles asked by way of clarification.

"Get the hell off the radio, Doc, so I can get more artillery support, or we'll need enough for three baseball teams," Winters said, and rang off.

A mortar round erupted close behind Winters and he heard a *twang*. Recalling Nixon's brush with death, he took off his helmet and inspected it. Nothing. As he replaced his steel pot he noticed that shrapnel had neatly clipped off the radio antenna at the base. Worse, Boyle had been hit. Winters yelled for a medic while doing what he could for the injured man. Boyle would recover, but his war was over and Winters had lost the ability and experience of "a very good and loyal friend."

The barrage was brief but intense, leaving Winters with eighteen men wounded. After the ambulances arrived and began evacuating the injured, Winters deployed his remaining men into several defensive strongpoints, careful to avoid placing anyone at the crossroad itself. That done, he drifted off by himself and sat down in a secluded spot, deep in thought. That's where Nixon later found him.

"How's everything going?" he asked.

Winters turned to his friend and replied, "Gimme a drink, Nix. Of water, please."

Nixon handed over his canteen. As Winters drank he noticed his hand was shaking uncontrollably. It was something he had never experienced before.

For the rest of his life, he would consider October 5, 1944, the best single day in Easy Company's history.

"This action by E Company is, in my estimation, the highlight of all E Company accounts for the entire war," he wrote a few years later. "This action on 5 October demonstrated E Company's overall superiority of every man, of every phase of infantry tactics: patrol, defense, attack under a base of fire, withdrawal and, above all, superior marksmanship with rifles, machine gun and mortar fire. All this was done against superior forces, who had an advantage of ten to one in manpower, plus the enemy had excellent observation for artillery and mortar support."

With just thirty-five men, Winters had routed two companies of SS infantry, about three hundred men. Through skilled use of tactics, he had pinned the enemy down with two machine guns while he attacked across two hundred yards of open ground. Reinforced by another platoon, Winters then came close to cutting off the enemy and capturing the lot.

Winters now took a head count of his men. Easy and Fox companies had suffered twenty-two wounded but none killed in the fight at the crossroad. On the other side of the sheet, the enemy had lost an estimated fifty killed, an unknown number wounded and eleven who were now prisoners. Earlier in the day, however, Winters had lost Dukeman, a man he had known since Toccoa. Dukeman had been well respected by his comrades.

"He was a prince of a man," Winters later wrote.

Corporal Christenson told Winters he estimated that he had fired 57 clips, or 456 rounds of ammunition, that day. Overnight, after the tension of the fight had been released and while on outpost duty, Christenson guessed that he had pissed thirty-six times.

"I'll take his word for the accuracy on both counts," Winters noted.

Later that same day Colonel Sink arrived. He looked over the scene of the battle, German bodies strewn in the field where they fell, as Winters briefed him on events.

"What you did here was very impressive, Dick," Sink said. "Very impressive."

"We were very lucky, sir," Winters told his CO. "They were poorly led; there's no other reason that they would've allowed us to lie out there in that ditch, almost totally unmolested, for about an hour, then attack and take them under fire from the rear. With the firepower they had, they could have come along the road on top of the dike and taken us on the flank, and we'd have been sitting ducks. They could have swept us away. They never should have allowed me to get out of that ditch."

"But they did," Sink said. "And you made them regret it. By the way, these fellas are with the 363rd Volksgrenadiers, and while you were taking them on, their buddies launched an attack on our main line. They hit 2nd Battalion pretty hard. Ollie Horton was killed."

The news startled Winters. "I'm very sorry to hear that," Winters said. "He was a good man." He was also a helluva lot smarter than Colonel Strayer, Winters thought, but wisely did not add.

Sink nodded. "G2 thinks these two companies were intended to cut off our retreat if the main attack had been successful," he continued. "Good job, Captain."

Sink left. That evening, thinking of the German sentry he had shot, Winters took out his pocketknife and carved a seventh and, though he did not then know it, final notch in the stock of his Garand.

Winters would forever be proud of the accomplishments of that day, but refused to ever take any credit for himself. In his October 17 after-action report, Winters deliberately omitted the word "I" in order to highlight the contributions of each man.

On October 27 Sink issued a citation to Easy Company, commending them "for their daring and aggressive spirit and sound tactical ability."

* * *

Actual nose-to-nose combat on the Island subsided after October 5, but not the danger. German artillery spotters across the Rhine had no qualms about calling down fire on any target that might present itself, even if it was just one man. The only defense was to lay low and remain still.

On October 9, four days after the crossroad fight, Sink arrived at Winters' company command post. As usual, the colonel was direct. "Dick, I'd like you to take over for Major Horton as battalion XO," he said. "Do you think you could handle the battalion?"

Winters had never given anything like that a thought, but said immediately, "Yes, sir. I think I could lead the battalion in the field. I'm confident that I can direct tactics and men, but the administrative end of it? No, I don't have a handle on that at all. I'm not an administrator. I've been a field soldier the whole time."

Sink nodded. "Don't worry, I'll take care of that. My main concern is that 2nd Battalion be run on a sound tactical basis, and there you are more than qualified."

What about Colonel Strayer? Winters thought. He's the commander. But he held his tongue. Then another thought hit him. He'd be leaving Easy Company.

"Who will take my place, sir?"

"Moose Heyliger is next in line in seniority," Sink said.

Winters liked Heyliger and knew he'd do well. A former E Company man, he now led the headquarters mortar platoon.

The days that followed the promotion were long and dreary. Rain fell much of the time, saturating the ground and the men. Temperatures began dropping drastically as October neared its end. Despite what Sink had told him, Winters spent much of this period bogged down in clerical and administrative duties. He was ably assisted by the recalcitrant Nixon who, though competent, was seriously hindered by his drinking. He seemed to have an endless supply of liquor, which he consumed freely. Winters overlooked much of this because of their friendship and Nixon's ability to do the job when real work was needed.

One main difference between the two was the hours they kept. Winters was an early riser. He loved getting up early and getting a start on the day. Nixon was a night owl. He did his best work in the afternoon and at night. When they were out on the line, this proved an ideal arrangement. Winters kept tabs on the men during the day; Nixon made the rounds at night. This kept company commanders on their toes because they never knew when one or the other would show up and expect a status report.

Nixon hated getting up in the morning, however, even when it was necessary. On one particular morning Winters needed Nixon to accompany him on a battalion inspection tour and sent a man to fetch him. The man returned empty-handed.

"I couldn't get him up, sir," the man said. "I tried."

Winters sent the man again, and again he came back empty-handed. Winters decided to go in person. Inside Nixon's darkened bedroom he found his friend sound asleep.

"Come on, Nix," Winters said, tapping his friend on the shoulder. "Time to get up. I need you."

"Go away," was the muffled response.

Winters grabbed Nixon's feet, still encased in the sleeping bag, and hoisted them up on his shoulders.

"Are you going to get up?" he asked again.

Nixon's mumbled response was unintelligible. Spotting a pitcher on the bureau, Winters reached for it and held it over his friend. "Get up now, or I'm going to let you have it," Winters said and tipped the pitcher.

Nixon's eyes shot open in horror. "No, no!" he yelled, but it was too late.

It was too late for Winters, too. The liquid was on its way down when he realized the pitcher contained not water, as he'd assumed, but Nixon's own urine. Nixon, swearing and laughing at the same time, burst out of his sack. Both men had been splattered, and Winters, always good at thinking on his feet, suggested a change of plans. Instead of inspecting the troops in search of any military infractions, they drove into Nijmegen in search of the hot showers.

★   ★   ★

On the night of October 23–24 Easy Company went on its first mission without Winters at its head. Heyliger had been tapped to lead twenty-three men across the Rhine to rescue members of the British 1st Airborne Division, stranded on the far bank since the failure of the Market Garden operation. Winters attended the briefing at battalion headquarters when British Lieutenant Colonel David Doby went over the plans with Heyliger, but aside from a few suggestions, Winters was excluded from any direct role. Stuck in his office while his friends crossed the river in rubber dinghies, Winters paced like a nervous father in the delivery room until he heard the men had returned with 125 grateful Tommies.

Four days later the regiment's defensive line was enlarged to include the area south of Arnhem near Driel, formerly held by the 501st. Colonel Strayer established 2nd Battalion headquarters in the imposing stone gatehouse of a farm at Schoonderlogt, west of the village of Elst. A railroad track ran along the Allied side of the Rhine and both sides reconnoitered the area by sending out contact patrols. German artillery held the high ground beyond the river, and freely dropped shells on anything that moved.

Being battalion executive officer became increasingly frustrating for Winters, who craved the decision-making responsibility of company command. Now he was making no decisions, just recommendations, and he was unable to use the skills and instincts he had honed to a razor-sharp edge as a combat leader. Restless to do something—anything—other than sit on his behind at battalion headquarters, on the afternoon of October 31 he called Heyliger.

"Hey, Moose," he said. "I'm concerned about the enemy activity in your area. Besides that, I need to get away from this desk and do something. What say we check the outposts together tonight? Say, around twenty-one hundred?"

"Sure," Moose agreed. "Come on down. I'll alert the platoon leaders."

At 2100 promptly, Winters arrived at Easy's command post and the two men struck out along the line. Their first stop was to be 1st Platoon. Harry Welsh had set up his CP in a barn fifty yards west of the railroad tracks, along which the Germans had established outposts. Winters and Heyliger walked along a dirt lane lined, as so many Dutch roads are, by three-foot-deep irrigation ditches on each side. Instinct told Winters they were nearing 1st Platoon's area when a voice in the night called, "Halt."

Winters glanced at Heyliger and saw him open his mouth to respond, then stop.

"My God," Winters thought. "He's forgotten the password."

Heyliger, generally easygoing and tough to get flustered, had indeed forgotten the password, so he started to say his name.

"It's Moo . . ." he began, but before the word left his lips, the sentry's rifle cracked three times. Winters saw the winking of the muzzle flashes not fifteen yards away and out of sheer instinct he hit the ground and rolled to his left, into the irrigation ditch. Heyliger never had the chance. Hit twice, once in the right shoulder and again in the left calf, he moaned and dropped heavily. The sentry came forward, saw what he had done, then turned and ran toward the platoon HQ. At first Winters thought they'd run into a German patrol, until he heard the receding footsteps of the panicked sentry. Crawling from the ditch, he rose and made his way to the wounded Heyliger. Ripping the first aid kit from where it had been attached to the webbing of his helmet, Winters removed a bandage and applied pressure to the leg wound, by far the worst of Heyliger's injuries. Moose was conscious but stunned as Winters tried to stem the blood flow. A voice in the night whispered, "Dick? Moose?" It was Welsh.

"Over here, Harry," Winters said. "Moose is hit."

Welsh and several men arrived.

"Shit," Welsh cursed, then turned to one of his men. "Get back to the CP and order up an ambulance. Quickly."

They bandaged Heyliger as fast as they could and jabbed him with a couple of morphine syrettes—how many no one remembered. Then they hauled him to the CP, where the ambulance was just arriving. Suffering from shock and loss of blood, Moose's skin had a white, waxy pallor and his breath came out in a wheeze.

"God, I hope he makes it," Winters said as the ambulance raced off.

Heyliger did survive his wounds, but would not return to Easy.

On November 7, Winters received a letter from his friend.

"Here I am lying flat on my back taking it easy," Heyliger wrote from the hospital. "I want to thank you for taking care of me that night. It sure is a stupid way of getting knocked off."

Moose said he had lost so much blood that he needed six transfusions. He also took time to complain about the treatment he'd gotten in the hospital. "Jesus, Dick," he wrote. "They put the casts right over my wounds and it smells as if a cat shit in my bed. I can't get away from it."

Winters never got over the Heyliger incident, not just because of the loss of his friend and a competent officer, but because of how close he himself had come to death. "But for the grace of God that could have been me," he said years later. "We were side by side."

Winters did not blame the sentry for what happened to Heyliger, and has even forgotten who fired those three shots. Or at least says he has. "I tried to forget it," he said in 2004. "And I've done so convincingly."

He did hold Harry Welsh responsible, although never outwardly. Inside, though, he felt Welsh had failed in his job of alerting the sentries of the inspection.

Heyliger's replacement was First Lieutenant Norman S. Dike, who was "blessed" on Winters by General Taylor and transferred from Regimental HQ. As was his custom, Winters interviewed all incoming officers—and enlisted men when time allowed—taking the measure of each man in order to get a feel for his strengths and weaknesses. A Yale graduate, Dike came from the well-to-do family of a New York attorney. He was, Winters recalled, "very well spoken" with a "military bearing that was deceiving." This, Winters felt, gave Dike the air of a man who believed he had leadership skills far beyond what he actually possessed. Dike did not impress Winters as a combat commander, capable of making quick decisions, but he was stuck with him.

Winters would institute two other changes a few weeks later, both on battalion level. Clarence Hester, Strayer's S2, had been promoted to major and moved up to regimental G2. Winters, with Strayer's aquiesence, moved Nixon from S3 to S2 and plucked Welsh out of 1st Platoon of Easy to fill Nixon's spot. Peacock assumed command of 1st Platoon.

*   *   *

As November deepened, so did the misery suffered by the men on the line. Aside from the Germans lobbing random shells, plus intermittent patrol actions, every day seemed to bring a cold rain. The ground grew saturated and foxholes became wading pools. Leaves had fallen from the trees with the result that natural camouflage was gone. Trucks, jeeps and tanks moving along rain-swamped roads pushed up waves of mud like the curl of a ship's wake.

The Dutch countryside, once a scene of pastoral tranquility, was desolate. The people were gone and most of their houses had sustained some degree of damage. Walls had been knocked down and roofs blown off. In the meadows, dead horses and cows lay bloating, their legs often sticking stiffly up in the air, which itself was permeated by the sickly odor of decaying flesh.

Winters used this period of inactivity to catch up on his letters home. He sent his sister Ann a package containing German and British military insignias to "stick on her junk coat." This was a jacket she had festooned with items, captured or traded for, and sent home by her big brother.

He wrote to Mrs. Barnes, whose husband by that time had died, and he reflected on his own good fortune at having come so far relatively unscathed in a November 14 letter to DeEtta.

"My luck is still holding," he wrote, "and by now I am just a little superstitious that it's your dog tags that hold the charm. I lost my own dog tags the first day and since receiving yours I've been wearing it. Hope your folks aren't informed some day that you're missing in action."

As the days and weeks dragged on, looting by bored, miserable GIs increased. In his job as battalion XO, Winters' duties included presiding over the courts-martial of men who had been caught stealing. He hated the job. He knew most of them and respected them as soldiers and friends, yet he had his orders from on high.

"This looting must stop," Strayer told him. "Lower the boom on them. If they're caught, sentence them to six months in a stockade and deduct two-thirds pay."

On November 25, the 101st Airborne was finally relieved after seventy-two straight days on the line. The stay in Holland cost the 506th 804 casualties, including 176 killed, 565 wounded and 63 missing out of 181 officers and 2,429 enlisted men.

The division was loaded onto trucks headed for a rest area at Mourmelon-Le-Grand, France, and men began to compute how much leave time they had accumulated. Winters guessed he had forty-five days coming. He was looking forward to a long, well-earned period of rest.

CHAPTER 8

"Here We Go Again."

November 25–December 31, 1944

Arriving at Mourmelon, just twenty miles from the famous champagne town of Reims, wasn't as good as checking into a five-star hotel, but it was still heavenly for men straight off the line who'd spent weeks living in waterlogged foxholes. The former French army post featured low stucco barracks which, although in need of repair, were at least warm and dry. Each barracks contained individual rooms that once housed twelve French soldiers. Predictably, the ever space-thrifty Americans used double bunks to cram twenty-four men into each room. Perhaps best of all were the indoor toilet facilities, meaning the men no longer had to brave the cold outside to answer the call of nature.

Weapons and equipment were turned in for repair and maintenance and the weary men rejoiced at the news that training would be limited to close-order drill and calisthenics.

Kitchens served up hot food and plenty of it, and gripe as they might about army chow, it was still better than living out of the can as the men had done for more than two months.

Field rations during World War II, the diet for men in the field, came in several different varieties, none of which were favorites.

The D Ration came in a small box and was to be carried in case the men were cut off and resupply was not possible. Totaling six hundred calories, it consisted of a four-ounce chocolate bar made from sugar, skim milk powder, cocoa fat, oat flour, vanillin and artificial flavoring. This bar could also be dissolved in hot water and used as a beverage.

The C Ration was packaged in twelve-ounce, smooth, gold-toned lacquered cans. The M-Unit cans consisted of meat and beans; meat and vegetable hash; meat and vegetable stew; spaghetti and meat; ham, eggs and potatoes; meat and noodles; meat and rice; pork and beans; franks and beans; ham and lima beans; or chicken and vegetables. The accessories, or B-Unit cans, held potatoes, dry onions, carrots, white beans, tomato juice and spices, five concentrated biscuits, five pieces of assorted flavors of hard candy, three sugar cubes, a container of soluble coffee, jam, crackers, powdered drinks and cereals. Six cans, three M-Units and three B-Units, constituted one day's ration.

The one most remembered by the men was the K Ration, which came in three varieties—breakfast, dinner and supper. Each was packaged in a waxed six-and-a-half-inch-long box. The breakfast ration contained biscuits, ham and eggs, a fruit bar, soluble Nescafé, pressed sugar tablets and Wrigley's chewing gum. The dinner ration consisted of biscuits, pork luncheon meat, processed American cheese, malted milk, dextrose tablets, concentrated bouillon, lemon juice powder, a D Ration bar and Wrigley's gum. The supper ration contained biscuits, veal luncheon meat, a can of cheese or potted meat or, more commonly, a two-ounce ration D bar, sugar, orange or lemonade powder, and gum. To heat their meals in the field, soldiers carried pocket paraffin heaters or candles. Each meal included four cigarettes, usually Camels, Chelsea or Old Gold, and a book of matches.

On occasion the food prepared in camp was worse than what came from a ration tin. In late November the men of the 506th were served a belated Thanksgiving dinner that not only tasted bad, but was evidently prepared under questionable sanitary conditions. Consequently, men suffered from what Easy Company's Sergeant Robert Rader called "the Aztec Two-Step." Medics treated sufferers with codeine paragoric to stop the bowel spasms.

Yet more than hot food, real beds, indoor crappers and occasional bouts of diarrhea, Mourmelon offered the war-weary troopers recreation and a chance to unwind. Red Cross clubs were established and athletic equipment was issued. Regiments formed football teams and set up game schedules. The men of the "Five-Oh-Sinks" and the paratroopers of the 502nd scheduled a Champagne Bowl to be played in Reims on Christmas Day, and bets were already being laid down.

The USO visited Mourmelon and surrounding camps, and men flocked to the shows to see stars like Marlene Dietrich and Mickey Rooney, or to talk baseball with Mel Ott.

Lastly, between football games and USO shows there was plenty of gambling, with men exchanging money over poker and craps.

With the 101st encamped for the foreseeable future, its commander, General Maxwell Taylor, was ordered to Washington, D.C., by General George C.

Marshall, Roosevelt's chief of staff, to discuss airborne operations and their effect in battle. Brigadier General Gerald J. Higgins, Taylor's executive officer, was in London lecturing new troops on the lessons learned in combat. In the absence of both, Taylor turned command of the division over to his chief of artillery, Brigadier General Anthony C. McAuliffe.

Men with far lesser rank than Taylor and Higgins also began thinking about passes. In early December, Winters was one of several officers packed off for three days in Paris. Ever cost-conscious, he checked into a Red Cross hotel to insure he got the cheapest rate, then posed for a group photo near the Arc de Triomphe before going out on the town.

"The last time I saw Paris, her heart was young and gay," he wrote DeEtta. "What a town that is. Boy, it really is all they say about it. Even after taking into consideration the fact that I hadn't been around civilization for some time, it's still some town. Went on a tour and found about how many people were beheaded here and how many nuts and bolts in the Eiffel Tower and all the rest of the worthless information. Took in a couple of good shows, bought some clothes, and best of all, got to sleep between two sheets on a bed with springs. Yep, and I even had a hot bath. Boy, what a time!"

Curiosity lured Winters into the Paris Follies. The smoke-filled, raucous club was packed, he recalled, and he had difficulty getting a seat, but admittedly enjoyed the show.

On his second day of playing an American in Paris, Winters heard a voice call his name.

"Captain Winters?" the man said.

Winters turned to find Private Alley, who had been wounded by seventeen pieces of grenade shrapnel at the Island on October 5.

"Alley," Winters said, amazed at finding one of his own men in the crowded city. "How are you feeling?"

"I'm fine, sir," Alley said. "I got thirty-four holes in me, but I'm ready for duty."

"Were you looking for someone?" Winters asked.

"Yeah, you, sir," Alley joked. "In truth, I don't know where the division is. I was wandering around, hoping to find someone to point me in the right direction. I certainly never expected to find you."

Winters laughed and told Alley where the regiment was encamped and helped him arrange transportation.

Eventually, though, even the City of Lights bored the socially reserved Winters. Deciding to spend his last night of leave alone, he boarded the Paris Metro in the center of the city, intending to ride it to the end of the line and back. Unfortunately, when the train reached the outskirts of Paris and he was asked to step off, Winters realized he'd taken the last train of the night. He would have to walk back to his hotel.

Lost in thought, Winters strolled pensively through the city, along the famed West Bank, past Notre Dame Cathedral and along the Seine. Traffic, much of it military, moved around the Arc de Triomphe and lights winked on the steel framework of the Eiffel Tower.

"I spent the rest of the night walking through Paris," Winters recalled sixty years later. "It was the best medicine that I could have had. I could relax and it gave me a chance to reflect and be alone."

*   *   *

Back in camp after his Paris excursion, Winters was informed by Colonel Strayer that he was temporarily being placed in command of 2nd Battalion.

"I'm returning to England to attend Colonel Doby's wedding," Strayer said. He had befriended the British paratroop officer following Easy Company's rescue of Doby's men from across the Rhine in October. "Word is we're to be here until spring at least, so there shouldn't be too much to do."

Strayer's departure meant Winters and Nixon were the sole battalion officers remaining in camp. Nixon spent much of this time quenching his thirst for Vat 69, his beverage of preference, of which he had a never-ending supply, while Winters caught up on letter writing. On December 13 he wrote DeEtta that he had a piece of white parachute silk he planned to send her as a Christmas present to be used as a scarf. Apologizing that it would be late, he added, "Next year, it'll be a grass skirt so don't complain."

He ended by saying he was going to spend some time reading his Bible.

"Nothing like a war to make a believer out of me."

*   *   *

On Sunday, December 17, a messenger entered 2nd Battalion HQ. He handed Winters a memo, saluted and left. Winters looked at the paper.

"What's it say?" Nixon asked, sitting in a chair, feet propped on Winters' desk.

"The Germans have broken through in the Ardennes," Winters told his friend. "We're being put on alert and are to get ready to move out."

"Jesus Christ, Dick, nobody's here," Nixon complained, sitting bolt upright.

"That's not the problem," Winters replied. "Our problem is that most of the equipment sent for repair hasn't come back yet. Plus the men have no winter clothes, and there's little ammo in camp. But we've no choice, Nix.

Cancel all leaves and get back any men who are gone. Alert the company commanders, especially Dike, to get ready to move. Have them grab all the clothes and equipment they can find. I don't care how. And ammo! Whatever they can get. Oh, and tell the men to remove their shoulder patches. For some reason G2 is worried about the Germans finding out what unit is coming in, as if it matters."

The two men exchanged long looks.

"Here we go again," Winters said.

The order to move came the next day, December 18, and 380 trucks were hastily assembled. Lugging their weapons and personal gear, men were shoehorned into the trucks, consuming every inch of available space. The convoy stretched for ten miles as it relentlessly rolled northeastward all that day. In many of the jam-packed trucks, the air took on the stench of vomit as men in the bouncing, seemingly springless vehicles succumbed to motion sickness and puked into their steel helmets. Periodically, the helmets were passed to the rear and the contents dumped out over the tailgate. Sick, scared and concerned for the future, few men failed to appreciate that, as they hastened toward a new battlefield in this war, they were passing the blood-soaked fields from a generation earlier: the Marne, Verdun and Sedan, whose trenches now yawned vacant.

Winters, riding in a jeep with Nixon, had no idea where they were headed, but as darkness fell, he got a sense of the urgency. Vehicles rolled through the night with their headlights beaming brightly, many without the benefit of cat's-eye blackout slits, exchanging the cover of darkness for speed of deployment.

The closer the convoy moved toward the front, the slower the progress became as increased traffic clogged the often unpaved roads, some heading east, but more—too much more, Winters thought—heading west. These latter were refugees from the previous three days' fighting, units battered under the unexpected and vicious German onslaught.

Periodically during the trip, the convoy stopped to allow the men to jump out, stretch their legs and take a much-needed piss. Bill Guarnere took advantage of one long break to leave the truck and find a nice soft spot near a farm to lie down. It wasn't until the orders came to get back on the trucks that he realized he'd been lying in cow manure.

"Goddammit," Guarnere cursed as he tried to brush the steaming crap off his clothes.

Winters laughed and thought, "City boy."

Each time the convoy halted Winters jumped from the jeep and walked the line of trucks hauling the battalion, checking on the men. On one stop Second

Lieutenant Barnard F. "Ben" Staplefeld, a young replacement officer assigned to Fox Company, ran up to Winters.

"Sir, is there anything I should be doing?" he asked.

Winters was taken aback. Unaccustomed to someone being that conscientious, he gazed at Staplefeld and said, "Do you see what the men are doing?"

Staplefeld looked around. "Yes, sir. They're sleeping."

"You do the same," Winters told him. "When I need you, I'll let you know."

That encounter left Winters with a good impression of Staplefeld, whom he ever after considered a "damned good man." Had he known him better at the time, Winters later said, he would have moved the youngster up to battalion HQ.

At 0400 on December 19, the convoy again halted, this time outside the small village of Mande St. Etienne, and the order came, "Everybody out." After a brief rest to recover from the grueling trip, the troops were ordered to their feet to begin the two-mile hike toward the crossroad town of Bastogne.

As they tramped through the night the eastern sky glowed a dull red and the crumping of artillery began to reach their ears. What reached their eyes was even more disconcerting. Between the advancing columns of paratroopers, hundreds of GIs, many without equipment, overcoats or weapons, shuffled along the road, heading away from the fighting. Some wore dazed expressions, others seemed to evoke terror, telling the incoming paratroopers to run, that the Germans had tanks and artillery and massive numbers of troops, all heading that way.

"They'll kill you," men said. "They'll murder you. Get out while you can."

None of Winters' men acknowledged the panicked chatter.

"I was proud of them for that," he said later. "We gave them no recognition. We just went about doing what we'd been sent there to do."

These refugees were men of the 106th Division, a recently arrived unit sent to the "quiet area" east of Bastogne along a ridge called Skyline Drive just days earlier. The intent was for the Golden Lions to relieve the veteran 2nd Division as it moved north to capture intact the Rohr River dams before the Germans could blow them and flood the land, impeding the eventual American advance. In this backwater of the war, it was also thought the green troops of the 106th could gradually get their feet wet before the battles sure to come with the spring thaw.

Instead, the German assault had rolled over the 106th, as well as the 99th, another recent arrival, and the veteran 28th Division. Two of the 106th's three infantry regiments had been encircled and captured, the war's largest single American surrender since Bataan and Corregidor two and a half years earlier.

Winters, of course, knew none of this. All he and his men saw was a herd of Americans fleeing the front in a state of panic, and he felt ashamed for them as well as himself.

Some of the paratroopers used this opportunity to better their own predicament, taking ammo off the fleeing men, who willingly gave it up, thus lightening their own load as they retreated.

As he walked through the predawn darkness, the symphony of the battle reached more ominous notes as machine gun and rifle fire echoed through the dark hills. Winters spotted a road marker that read BASTOGNE.

"Well, at least we now know the name of the town we're going to," he said to Nixon.

"Yeah," Nixon replied. "But where the hell's Bastogne? Belgium? Luxembourg?"

"Does it make any difference?" Winters asked

Entering Bastogne, the 506th tramped along Rue de la Roche, turning left onto the Rue Pierre Thomas. The town was dark, silent, brooding. Germans had marched through Bastogne in 1914 and again in 1940. They had retreated through it two months earlier, and now they were coming back again.

Very few citizens were visible on the streets as the 101st slogged along, although some who were offered the GIs coffee. The strong, hot joe was gratefully accepted as the men, chilled by the night, headed for their defensive position to the northeast, in the direction of the towns of Foy and Noville some five miles ahead. During the march, Colonel Strayer, still in the Class A uniform that he had worn to the London wedding, caught up to the battalion.

As the rumble of battle droned ever louder, the regiment ran into Second Lieutenant George C. Rice, supply officer for Combat Command B, 10th Armored Division. Rice was attached to Team Desobry, named for the group's leader, Major William Desobry. Like the 101st, this contingent of men and tanks had been sent forward to help stem the German tide. Hearing the advancing paratroopers were ill-supplied, Rice raced ahead to an ammo dump in the village of Foy and, piling all the ammo boxes he could carry into a borrowed jeep and a deuce-and-a-half truck, drove to meet the incoming Screaming Eagles. Stopping along their line of march, he tossed boxes out to the men. Soldiers scrambled, some on hands and knees, to retrieve the precious M1 clips and grenades as if they were golden nuggets.

*　　*　　*

Second Battalion's new home was a heavily wooded area between Bastogne and Foy called the Bois Jacques. Looking the ground over, Winters instantly hated the position, which offered lousy fields of fire. Yet he knew falling back to look for a better position was not an option. He had to make do with what was available. Nor would he be the first to fight over this ground. Frozen American and German bodies lying in grotesque poses provided grisly evidence that bullets had flown here earlier.

Beneath a canopy of tall evergreens, whose interlocking branches meant that little sunlight—had there been any—could reach the ground, Winters and his men labored to hack foxholes into the frozen earth with their entrenching tools; small shovels whose blades could be cocked at a forty-five-degree angle to double as a pickaxe. Branches were cut from trees to form protective roofs over the holes, although a lack of good cutting tools made this task difficult. Winters watched one battalion officer, Second Lieutenant Ed Thomas, solve the problem by fashioning his roof from a trio of stiff German corpses.

The regiment's position straddled the Bastogne/Foy/Noville road, with 2nd Battalion dug in to the right, along a five hundred-yard front. This stretched the battalion thin. Strayer left most of the tactical handling to Winters, who placed Easy Company on the left and Fox on the right, with Dog in reserve. Battalion HQ was roughly centered behind the two companies in the line, although slightly shaded in Easy's direction.

The 101st's defense of Bastogne began almost immediately, with 1st Battalion of the 506th and Team Desobry moving through Foy to attack Germans advancing from Noville. Through binoculars Winters could see the battle rage throughout December 19 and 20. Although Winters didn't know it until later, 1st Battalion's commander, Lieutenant Colonel James LaPrade, whom he had criticized for crossing the wrecked Son Bridge in Holland back in September while carrying only a pistol, was killed in this action. On December 20 the Germans flanked the American forces, slipping behind them and occupying Foy. Ordered by Sink to pull back, the cut-off Americans had to fight their way through enemy lines. Gunfire rattled all that day and plumes of oily black smoke from destroyed vehicles smudged the sky. Sink ordered 3rd Battalion forward to ease pressure on 1st Battalion and Team Desobry. The fighting was intense, but the Americans managed to return to their lines while halting the 2nd Panzer Division and buying time for McAuliffe to solidify his defensive ring around Bastogne.

Meanwhile, Winters had his own problems. The battalion's right ended at a railroad track by a small station which, despite its commanding name of Halte, was little more than a stone house and a platform. Beyond the tracks, the 501st Regiment was supposed to be in position. Trouble was, contact with them was spotty at best. First they were there, then they weren't, then they were again. Winters worried that his right flank was wide open, an assessment that soon proved accurate. A day after the regiment's arrival, two companies of Germans slipped unnoticed through the gap and dug in behind 2nd Battalion. Winters discovered this one brutally cold morning. Lathering up his face to shave (Colonel Sink had ordered that officers shave every day, Winters later recounted. "He told us, 'You shave every night for the ladies and you shave every morning for the men.'"), he had just begun skimming the growth of whiskers off his cheeks, trying not to cut himself as his teeth chattered, when he spotted a lone German soldier approaching through the ever-present fog. Several other men near Winters raised their rifles but Winters stopped them.

"Hold up," he whispered.

The German, evidently lost in the mist, approached the battalion slit trenches. He removed his greatcoat, hiked down his trousers and squatted over the trench. Winters politely waited until the man had finished the job he'd come for, then raised his M1.

"*Kommen Sie hier*," he ordered. Startled, the German looked up like a deer caught in headlights.

"*Kommen Sie hier*," Winters repeated, trying to sound malevolent.

The German raised his hands and stumbled forward. A search of his prisoner turned up some family photographs, a few trinkets and the heel of a loaf of dense, black bread, but nothing of any value. Winters sent the frightened man to the rear.

As he watched the young German being led away, Winters muttered to the soldier next to him, "I wonder how his first sergeant is going to report his disappearance on his morning report?"

The presence of Germans behind 2nd Battalion was a serious concern, so next day, after conferring with Strayer, Winters ordered Easy and Fox companies to eliminate the pocket. Captain Joe McMillen, Winters' favorite company commander, sent the 1st and 3rd Platoons of D Company forward. Gunfire echoed through the woods the rest of the day as the paratroopers clashed with German outposts. First Platoon lost two men killed, Sergeant Gordon Mather and Corporal George Lovell, both of whom had been advance scouts and were cut down in the initial fusilade, but the Germans were soon forced to withdraw under pressure, thus preserving the future sanctity of the battalion's slit trenches.

The young German Winters captured wasn't the only one confused. Officers on the line were often uncertain about their responsibilities and instructions. Not the least of these befuddled men was Strayer himself. After attending briefings at regimental or division HQ, Strayer would gather his battalion staff around him and fill them in. Unfortunately, Winters often found Strayer's information vague and confusing. He cast questioning glances at

Nixon, who would respond by rolling his eyes. After these briefings, Nixon would walk back to regiment to meet with Major Hester for clarification.

"Strayer had no goddamn idea what he was supposed to do," Winters said sixty years later. "But there's more than one way of skinning a cat, and the system Nixon and I had worked. Nixon did a good job. He kept 2nd Battalion out of a lot of trouble."

Hester had recently been promoted to regimental S3 by Sink. Now Winters, as battalion XO, replaced him as battalion S2 by bringing Harry Welsh up from 1st Platoon of Easy. Ordinarily, this appointment would have been Strayer's responsibility, but Winters saw little of his commander as the siege of Bastogne deepened. Strayer had "a warm sleeping bag and a deep foxhole," Winters derisively recalled, and seemed loath to leave them. For all intents and purposes, Winters was running the day-to-day chores of the battalion, which suited him fine.

Winters' philosophy of command called for constant contact with the men under him, so he moved freely between the company CPs, talking to the officers and chatting with the GIs. (He walked the line so often that fifty years later he was still able to pace it off.) Winters' toughest job was keeping up the morale of men who had to live day to day with freezing cold, no hot food and frequent enemy shellings. One of Winters' methods to maintain the men's spirits was to do "goofy things," like obeying Sink's ridiculous order of shaving each morning, even when he had to break the icy layer off his water basin—often an empty ammo box—to do so. Another method was to take a "French bath" by stripping to the waist and washing in ice-cold water. All of this was intentionally designed to let the men know he was sharing their hardships and deprivations.

Snow arrived on December 22, blanketing the trees and the forest floor with several inches of cold, white powder. Still, Winters made his rounds of the line. Stopping by the foxhole occupied by Bill Guarnere and Edward "Babe" Heffron, a shivering Winters asked, "How's it going, guys?"

"Just peachy, sir," the always flippant Guarnere replied. "Except we're freezing our asses off."

"You and a hundred other guys in this company, Bill," Winters replied. "Wish you were back in Philly?"

"Prob'ly a helluva a lot warmer there, sir," Guarnere replied. "Prob'ly warmer in Lancaster, too."

Winters smiled at the well-intentioned jibe. "Have you seen anything out there?" he said, indicating the distant tree line.

"Nope. It's all quiet, just the way I like it. They're probably as cold as we are." Then Guarnere asked, "Any news on what's happening?"

Winters shook his head. "They don't tell me jack, Bill, you know that. All I know is we're to sit here and hold this line until the weather clears and the airplane jockeys can win the war."

Winters looked at Heffron, who was hugging himself for warmth. He liked Heffron who, like Guarnere, was a South Philly boy. In fact, the two had almost been neighbors. Heffron had arrived with the replacements after Normandy and he and Guarnere had formed an instant bond.

"Heffron? You okay?"

"My feet are like Popsicles, sir," Heffron said.

Winters nodded. This was a common complaint. The men had been sent out with improper winter clothes and footwear, and there was no chance of them getting those items anytime soon.

"Just wiggle your toes," Winters advised. "Keep wiggling them. Don't let them freeze up on you. And keep dry socks on. The last thing you want is frostbite." He rose. "Stay alert, guys," he said, and moved on to the next foxhole, where he would ask the same questions and likely get the same responses.

Winters also used these times to chat with his company commanders and platoon leaders. Winters' main concern with them was not so much that they kept up the morale of their men, but that their own morale didn't sag. Of these leaders, it was Easy's commander, Norman Dike, who was a major concern for Winters. He seemed indifferent to the men and often vanished for long periods of time.

Trying in vain to make himself comfortable in his foxhole one brutally cold night, Winters glanced up as Nixon slid in beside him.

"How is everything?" Winters asked Nixon, who'd been making his own nocturnal rounds of the battalion.

"Fine, except that it's cold as hell," Nixon said. "Oh, and Dike's gone again. I can't find him anywhere. He's probably crapping out back in regiment again."

"More likely he's back in Bastogne with division. That's where all his buddies are," Winters said sarcastically. "I quit worrying about where he is anymore. My wonder is how the man can expect to be a leader when he's never around to lead. You talked to Peacock, Compton and Shames?"

Thomas Peacock, Buck Compton and Ed Shames commanded the three platoons.

"Yeah," Nixon said. "Compton'll take over till the happy wanderer returns."

"Between him and Carwood, I'm not concerned for Easy," Winters said. "The company's much better off in their hands than in Dike's."

In the bitter cold men did everything they could to keep warm. As a means of fending off frostbitten feet, men wore one or two pairs of socks, while keeping another pair dry by wrapping them around their necks. Medics prevented morphine ampules from freezing by placing them under their shirts, next to their bodies. Winters watched Don Malarkey shuffle around through the snow, his feet wrapped in blankets.

Some men were not above petty thievery to make sure they had the items needed for their personal comfort and safety. Unwatched weapons, ammo and personal gear were all fair game. And no one was immune from theft. Returning to his foxhole one afternoon, Winters found his M1 Garand missing. Armed now with just a .45 caliber automatic pistol and a few grenades, he searched for the missing rifle for several days without success. Then he unexpectedly found it, identifying it by the telltale seven notches, in the foxhole of Sergeant Frank Perconte, who had evidently lost his, either to thieves or one of the German shellings. Winters leaned down and snatched up the weapon.

"This is mine, Frank," he said. "You go find one somewhere else."

The bitter cold took its toll on the men. Joe Toye was among many of Winters' friends who suffered severe frostbite, and like most, he refused to leave the line and abandon his buddies. Winters recalled one unidentified man in 3rd Battalion whom he could hear coughing and hacking through the night, even though the man was a hundred fifty or more yards away.

"That keeps up," he said to Nixon, "he's going to give our position away."

The coughing persisted for three days, then stopped. Either the man was shipped back to Bastogne, Winters thought, or he died. He never discovered which.

Even had the man gone back to Bastogne, there was little there in the way of good medical help. Shortly after the 101st arrived at the crossroad town, the 326th Medical Company had been captured, along with its patients, doctors and supplies.

Food was scarce and always cold, for a fire was certain to bring German artillery shells zooming in. Shellfire in the Bois Jacques was especially horrific. Tree bursts, the result of shells set to explode on contact with the tall trees of the forest, sent both metal shrapnel and huge, sharp splinters of wood knifing through the air in all directions. Large branches or whole trees, split and torn, came tumbling down on the men. As a result, after a few weeks many of the trees, which had stood in neatly planted rows, had been smashed into kindling.

Walking the battalion line on December 22, Winters heard the whine of artillery shells whistling in from the direction of Foy.

"Incoming!" he yelled. "Take cover!"

Everywhere men took up the cry and frantically sought the nearest foxhole or any sort of depression in the earth, so matter how slight. Men with nowhere to go hugged a tree, wrapping their arms around the trunk and trying to pull their entire bodies up under their helmets. Winters dove into a convenient foxhole as the first shell splintered a nearby tree. He curled up into a defensive ball, making his body as small as possible as shards of hot steel and jagged chunks of wood skimmed by overhead.

"Tree bursts were the worst," Winters recalled years later. "You just tried to keep as low as you could until it ended. And you could tell when it ended. After you've been shelled enough times, you got a sense or feeling that that was the last round."

Sensing that the last shell had landed, Winters leaped to his feet. He knew that the calm after a barrage often left men sitting dazed, as if in a stupor, unsure of what to do next or even unsure of where they were. It was crucial, as an officer, to talk to them, give them direction and "get their heads working again."

"Stay alert! Stay alert," he said, running along the line of foxholes. "They might be coming. Keep an eye peeled out in front. Get those machine guns ready."

As he ran back and forth, Winters was also aware to keep his own ears open. Sometimes artillery barrages heralded an attack, but more often the enemy waited a few minutes, hoping that their enemies would leave the protection of their foxholes to tend wounded buddies; then the guns would open fire again.

As Christmas approached, the scarcity of ammunition and supplies among the men rose alarmingly.

"When I was back in Bastogne after Strayer's briefing this morning," Nixon told Winters, "Sink told me our artillery is critically low on ammo."

"I know," Winters replied. "Yesterday I helped site a piece that had only three rounds. They were told to use them only for antitank fire. Some of our mortars are down to six rounds and most men have only one bandolier of ammo. This keeps up, we can challenge the Germans to a Christmas Day snowball fight. That's all we'll have."

A supply drop on December 23 helped. Some 260 C-47s dropped 334 tons of supplies, but it wasn't enough to fend off the growing feeling of despair among the men of the encircled division. Winters tried to bolster sagging morale by getting men off the line, however briefly. He later wrote, "Just being back fifty yards off the front line made a tremendous difference in tension."

Sometimes a day or two, or just a few hours, off the line helped. Other times it didn't. Winters considered T/5 Joseph D. Liebgott an excellent combat soldier, who had proven his worth in Holland. But in the woods outside

Bastogne, Winters saw a change in the man; a serious moroseness brought on by unrelenting stress.

Kneeling by Liebgott's foxhole, Winters said, "Joe. I need a runner for a few days. I'd like you to take the job."

Liebgott looked up at his captain, then nodded. "Yes, sir. Thank you."

After a few days, Liebgott requested permission to return to Easy. It was granted, but once back on the line his problems returned. Strayer intervened and temporarily reassigned Liebgott to division G2 intelligence, where his ability to speak German could be used to interrogate prisoners. Winters opposed this transfer. Liebgott was Jewish and had an undisguised hatred for the Germans. But the transfer went through.

Between the depression and the relentless cold, Winters knew well the suffering of the men under him. Yet he felt great pride in the way they endured it. Naturally they bitched and moaned, but they stuck it out, refusing, in most cases, to leave their friends. Winters appreciated the importance of this. If all the men who had a truly legitimate reason to leave their unit and go back to the aid station at Bastogne had done so, he'd have had no front line, just a row of outposts.

Winters, however, did not personally practice what he preached. Not once during the siege of Bastogne did he leave the battalion.

Some men endured the hardship better than others. Making his rounds just before Christmas, Winters passed a soldier sitting on the edge of his foxhole, a towel wrapped turban-style around his head, with his helmet placed on top of the towel. The man was staring intently ahead over his light machine gun. Winters strode past without recognizing twenty-three-year-old Walter Gordon. Then he stopped, turned and did a double take.

"Damn, Gordon," Winters thought. "You're maturing. You're becoming a man."

Winters liked Gordon even though the two had little in common. Unathletic and unambitious as a youth, the Mississippi boy had spent more time on girls than on his studies. He managed to gain admission to Millsaps College in Jackson, Mississippi, where, over a three-year period, he made mostly Ds and Fs—including one term paper that had no grade at all, just the professor's scrawl in red pencil that read "Revolting."

Rejected by the army after Pearl Harbor because he was color blind, a sympathetic old sergeant overlooked that flaw when Gordon told him he wanted to go into the airborne. He had since evolved into a fine soldier whom Winters had grown to admire. Winters also ignored the color blindness.

The morning Winters watched Smoky Gordon man his foxhole was the last time he'd see his friend unharmed. A day later, December 24, a German attack exploded on Easy Company's front. Infantry supported by half-tracks rolled out of the opposing tree line. The quiet forest erupted in a cacophony of gunfire. The concussions from mortar and bazooka blasts jarred small avalanches of snow down from the tree boughs overhead. Gordon was brewing coffee over a small paraffin heater when the assault began, and one of the very first rounds, fired by a sniper who was later killed by Gordon's buddies, struck him in the shoulder, passed through his body and nicked his spinal cord. Amid the whizzing of bullets, Lipton, Alley and Paul Rogers pulled Gordon from his foxhole and dragged him to the rear out of the range of further harm. Medic Eugene Roe hurried up to him and began treatment.

"Lip?" Gordon weakly croaked while Roe worked on him.

"Yeah, Smoky?" Lipton said, leaning close to catch the words from his injured buddy.

"You're standing on my hand," Gordon said.

Apologizing, Lipton quickly moved his foot. A jeep rolled up and Gordon was loaded onto a stretcher for the ride to Bastogne, the first stop on his journey home.

Winters raced to the sound of the fight, shouting orders and moving among the men. Machine gun and antitank fire forced the half-tracks to retire, and without their support, the Kraut infantry soon followed. As quiet settled on the front, several ruined vehicles and thirty-eight German soldiers lay sprawled in front of Easy. Three had been taken prisoner.

"How's Gordon?" Winters asked Roe that afternoon.

"He'll survive, but he's paralyzed," Roe said. "I don't know if it's permanent."

Winters received the news with mixed emotions. He had lost from the line a good man and a friend, yet he felt happy that Gordon's war was over.

Gordon's loss wasn't the only one Winters would experience that Christmas Eve. Sitting in his foxhole alone that night—Nixon was out making his rounds of the battalion—Winters was calmly listening to German soldiers across the morning's still-smoking battlefield singing Christmas carols, particularly "Silent Night," or "Stille Nacht," a favorite whether one wore olive drab or field gray. Hearing low voices nearby, he popped his head above the edge of his foxhole and spotted a dim glow. Several of the men of 2nd Battalion HQ had built a small fire and were clustered around its feeble flame, warming their hands. Winters hurried over, not sure whether to curse them or join them. The fire looked so inviting.

"Are you men nuts?" he said, reaching in with his hands to snatch the first moment of genuine warmth he'd felt in a week. "The Krauts are going to throw an 88 in here and really cook your goose."

"It's okay," said Welsh, who was just to the right of Winters. "We're sheltered here. They can't see us."

"I'll take your word for it," Winters replied, rubbing his hands together briskly.

After a few moments Welsh snorted and said, "Dick, did I ever tell you how I cheated on the eye exam to get into the paratroopers?"

"No," Winters said. He had seen Welsh straining to read maps and reports, but never inquired.

"I wanted to get in badly, so when we were in line for the exams I kept asking the guy ahead to read me the 20/20 line," Welsh said. "When I'd get too close to the front of the line, I'd duck back a few places, then ask someone else to read me the 20/20 line. I kept doing that until I had it memorized."

Before Winters could respond, there was a jostling of the men and Colonel Strayer burst in through the small circle, shouldering men aside.

"Let me in there," Strayer said.

Reaching the fire, the colonel turned his back to it and bent forward, poking his butt out over the small flame. After a few moments, he turned and bent forward over the fire to warm his face and hands. The smoke, using his body as a chimney, curled up his legs and billowed freely into his face. Coughing and sputtering, his eyes burning, Strayer bounced back from the fire.

"Goddammit," he cursed, then pushed around to the other side of the fire, away from the troublesome smoke. Strayer again leaned out over the fire, but again the remorseless smoke followed the curve of his body and streamed up into his face.

"Jesus," he swore again, backing from the fire.

Around him, his officers shook their heads and exchanged smirks.

The smirks vanished with the whoosh of an incoming mortar round. Men dove for the snow in all directions as the shell burst. Welsh yelped in pain. Winters was the first to reach the stricken man. Welsh's trousers were bloody and Winters saw the look of terror on his friend's face as he gazed down at his bloody crotch. Winters tore open Welsh's trousers and took a peek. It was close, but Welsh could still be a father.

"You're okay, Harry," Winters said, then ripped open his first aid kit.

A medic arrived. Welsh was jabbed with an ampule of morphine, loaded onto a hastily summoned jeep and hustled back to Bastogne.

Christmas Day 1944 was the dreariest Winters had ever experienced. He attended church services presided over by a regimental chaplain, standing amid a curtain of fog and praying beneath the snowy cathedral of the Bois Jacques. Easy Company's cook, Joseph Dominguez, whipped up a vat of bean soup that would serve as a meager Christmas meal. Winters joined the company and, as was his policy, and one that was popular with the enlisted men, officers ate last. Some of the men took harsh advantage of this policy and sneaked back into line for refills, so that by the time Winters reached the cook pots, all Dominguez had to ladle out was half a canteen cupful of beans and broth from the bottom. Winters looked down at the food and shook his head dismally, thinking, "Oh my God." He ate his pitiful meal in silence.

★   ★   ★

The one bright spot that drab Christmas Day happened when Colonel Sink's well-used jeep rattled to a halt at Easy's CP. Sink had been moving between companies on a special Christmas mission.

"Dick," Sink said to Winters as climbed from the jeep. "General McAuliffe received a surrender demand from the Hostile Boys."

Winters nodded. Hostile Boys was one of Sink's pet phrases for the Germans. The colonel continued. "I'd like to read his response to the men."

"Please, sir. Go ahead."

Sink ordered Easy to gather around and told them of the demand that had come in through the lines under a flag of truce three days earlier. He then read McAuliffe's reply.

"Merry Christmas," he read. "What's merry about all of this? We're fighting—it's cold—we aren't home. All true, but what had the proud Eagle Division accomplished with its worthy comrades of the 10th Armored Division, the 705th Tank Destroyer Battalion and all the rest? Just this: We have stopped cold everything that has been thrown at us from the north, east, south and west. We have identification from four German panzer divisions, two German infantry divisions and one German parachute division. These units, spearheading the last desperate German lunge, were headed straight west for key points when the Eagle Division was hurriedly ordered to stem the advance. How effectively this was done will be written in history; not alone in our division's glorious history, but in world history. The Germans actually did surround us, their radios blared our doom. Their commander demanded our surrender in the following impudent arrogance:

December 22, 1944

To the U.S.A. commander of the encircled town of Bastogne:

The fortune of war is changing. This time the U.S.A. forces in and near Bastogne have been encircled by strong German armored units. More German armored units have crossed the river Ourthe near Ourtheuville, have taken Marche and reached St. Hubert by passing through Hompré-Sibret-Tillet. Libramont is in German hands.

There is only one possibility to save the encircled U.S.A. troops from total annihilation: this is the honorable surrender of the encircled town. In order to think it over, a term of two hours will be granted with the presentation of this note.

If this proposal should be rejected, one German Artillery Corps and six heavy A.A. battalions are ready to annihilate the U.S.A. troops in and near Bastogne. The order to fire will be given immediately after this two hours' term.

All the serious civilian losses caused by this artillery fire would not correspond with the well-known American humanity.

The German commander

"The German commander received the following reply:

22 December 1944

To the German commander:

NUTS!

The American commander

"Allied troops are counterattacking in force. We continue to hold Bastogne. By holding Bastogne, we assure the success of the Allied armies. We know that our division commander, General Taylor, will say: 'Well done!'

"We are giving our country and our loved ones at home a worthy Christmas present and being privileged to take part in this gallant feat of arms and are truly making for ourselves a Merry Christmas.

"A. C. McAuliffe, Commanding.

"Well done, Easy Company," Sink concluded. "Well done."

He saluted them, got back into his jeep and sped off to the next stop.

Sink's reading of McAuliffe's message gave the men a much-needed boost in pride and spirit, but the everyday drudgery of life in a freezing foxhole, of severe shellings and probing attacks, continued. On Christmas night, Winters and his men listened in silence as German bombers and artillery plastered Bastogne. The rumble of detonations rolled across the land and flames from the ruined town lit the distant sky. The next day the Germans launched a major assault on the far left of the 502nd and, depending on wind direction, the sound of this desperate fight reached the anxious ears of Winters and his men. What Winters did not know until later was that even as this fight raged to the west, on the southern end of the encirclement, leading elements of the 37th Armored Tank Battalion, attached to General George Patton's 3rd Army, had made contact with Company C, 326th Engineers, opening a tenuous corridor. The siege of Bastogne was broken. An airdrop of supplies from an armada of C-47s also helped relieve, to some extent, the misery of the men who had held the Germans off for eight days.

Still, the troops defending Bastogne were far from saved. On 2nd Battalion's front, soldiers continued to keep their vigil. Winters ordered patrols each night, although finding volunteers among the bone-weary men proved increasingly difficult. One exception was battalion staff sergeant Steve Mihok, who volunteered every night.

"You don't have to do this, Mihok," Winters told him when the call went out for another patrol. The dark circles under the man's eyes were stark proof of his fatigue. "You've done your part. Take a break tonight."

The little sergeant with the Tommy gun slung over his shoulder eyed his captain and said, "I'll go, sir. I want to."

Winters relented. He eventually put Mihok in for two Bronze Stars, saying later it should have been a dozen.

*　*　*

American soldiers are probably unique in that, when conditions got roughest, they endure, in part, by their ability to laugh at their own miserable situation. The paratroopers were no exception. On Christmas Day, the *Para-dice Minor*, a homemade, tongue-in-cheek newspaper that circulated among the men, carried an article by its society editor, Miss Champagne Belch, on locations in Bastogne, offering fine dining and atmosphere. One suggestion was the Bastogne Bar and Grill, where the menu featured "Ratione de Kay avec Café GI." Music was provided by Gerald Kraut and his 88-piece band with after-dark visits by Mr. Looft Waffe performing his famous Flare Dance.

Another fictitious eatery was the Blue Boche, where performers danced the German War Waltz, in which they held their hands over their heads while singing "I'm Forever Shouting *Kamerad*."

New Year's Eve was intensely cold. Additional snow meant that the white stuff measured as much as twelve inches in most places. Sitting alone in his foxhole, smothered in blankets for warmth, Winters was thinking of his home and family on this festive night, and he was certain they were thinking of him. His reverie was broken as Nixon, just back from making his rounds of the battalion, came sliding into the foxhole. Nixon extended his hand toward Winters.

"It's midnight," he said. "Happy New Year, Dick."

Winters reached out and shook Nixon's hand. "Happy New Year, Nix," he said. "Helluva place to spend it, huh?"

"At least we're alive," Nixon said.

"We have to be," Winters replied. "Otherwise we wouldn't be feeling this miserable."

All around the darkened forest, men began to quietly shake hands and pat each other on the shoulder. A whispered "Auld Lang Syne" was sung. Winters and Nixon listened until the song was finished, then the silence of the night resumed.

"I wonder where we'll be next year at this time," Nixon mused.

"Or how many of us will be left," Winters added.

CHAPTER 9

"You Can't Leave Us, Sir."

January 1–January 17, 1945

As 1944 dissolved into 1945, the Germans sent the besieged Americans defending Bastogne their own special New Year's gift: high-level bombers. On New Year's night lethal flocks of Heinkel HE-111 bombers droned unseen in the darkness above. Each capable of carrying nearly two and a half tons of explosives, the twin-engine bombers dumped their loads on the GIs' heads. Like everyone else, Dick Winters was curled up in his foxhole as the bombs whistled down through the perpetual fog, bursting in the woods, shrapnel singing overhead.

This was the end of a bad day that had gotten the new year off to an ominous start for Winters and the men of 2nd Battalion. That morning he had ordered Easy Company to send out a contact patrol to probe the gloomy forest for the German line. They had found it, leaving a dying Private John T. Julian in the woods, unable to recover him.

Julian had been the first man in the battalion to die in 1945, but the last two weeks of 1944 had also been tough on flesh and bone. In Easy Company, bullets or shrapnel had killed five men: A. P. Herron, Francis J. Mellet, Carl C. Sawosko, John E. Shindell and Harold B. Webb. Fox and Dog companies had also each lost five men killed. In D Company, Captain Joe McMillen had lost Private First Class George E. Lovell, Private First Class Salvador G. Ceniceros, Sergeant Gordon E. Mather, Sergeant Willie A. Morris and Private Earl V. Shade. In F Company, enemy action killed Private Ulysses E. Austill, Private Victor C. Churinski, Private Raymond E. Cronin, Sergeant Thomas W. Manry and Private First Class Don G. Hackman.

Wounds and sickness had plucked even more men from the line, making for grim reading on Winters' morning reports. And now the air raid.

Even before the bombs ceased bursting, a cry went out for a medic. Winters recognized the shouting voice as belonging to Joe Toye. Luckily, the injury was minor, yet serious enough that medics sent Toye to the aid station in Bastogne. D Company wasn't as fortunate. Sergeant Chester Hickman was killed by falling bombs.

In a perverse way, the men suffering on the line envied men like Toye and Hickman, for war turns the world upside down for soldiers in combat, as the illogical somehow becomes logical, the horrific becomes commonplace and mourning is put off until a more convenient time. Men raised from childhood to believe in the value of human life now find that life has almost no value. They can kill an enemy without emotion or remorse. Worse, when a friend is killed or wounded, it is viewed not so much as a loss, but as an escape. For the dead, grief is mixed with envy as his buddies realize that his suffering is at an end, and he is at peace. When a friend is wounded, his comrades understand that he will be sent to the rear and get a break from the day-to-day tensions of the line and, if it's the million-dollar wound, a trip back to the States. The wound itself becomes secondary to the feeling of elation for their buddy. "He made it," is the general thought. "The lucky bastard's going home."

As a commander, Winters tried not to let his personal feelings of loss interfere with the job he had to do. He would miss men like Toye and Hickman, but he still had to assist Strayer in running 2nd Battalion, which in effect meant he had a battalion to run.

"You look around and you see men hit every day, or getting frostbite or combat fatigue," Winters said in 2002. "Each day the line gets thinner and thinner. Every morning my present for duty roster kept going down. I couldn't focus on each man's loss. I had the rest to worry about."

Yet those losses were a source of concern for Winters, especially when they were men he considered the backbone of the battalion: Toccoa men, bonded by over two years of shared experience, training and hardships. These proved irreplaceable.

The new year was just three days old when Winters lost three highly valued Toccoa men.

Late in the afternoon of January 2, twelve hours after the air raid, Winters stood, binoculars in hand, surveying the fields to the battalion's front. Several hundred yards ahead lay the village of Foy. Winters could see Germans moving about the ruined houses. Lowering the glasses, he was slipping them back into his case when he spotted movement off to his left. It was Joe Toye, his right arm in a sling, walking back from Bastogne. Winters intercepted him.

"Joe," Winters said. "What are you doing back here? You're no good to me with one arm."

"I'm fine, sir," Toye replied. "I hardly notice it."

"Joe," Winters tried again. "You've been hit three times since Normandy. You don't have to come back on the line right now. You deserve a couple of days off. Go back to Bastogne. Sleep. Eat some hot food."

"If it's all the same to you, sir, I'd just as soon be up here with the fellas," Toye said.

Winters saw no point in continuing the discussion, nor did he see any benefit from ordering Toye to go to the rear. He appreciated Toye's dedication to the company, going back as far as he had known him. Originally Toye had been assigned to what he called a "parade outfit" that guarded government buildings in Washington, D.C., with unloaded weapons. The only way out of that boring duty was to volunteer for the airborne, so he did, and had grown to become one of Winters' most dependable soldiers. Winters grudgingly let his friend pass.

Less than twenty-four hours later German shells fell on Easy Company like a January snowstorm, shattering trees and spewing hot shrapnel. Toye was caught in the open. Racing for cover, an exploding shell ripped off his right leg. During the lull that followed, his pleas for help were heard echoing through the woods. Bill Guarnere, recognizing Toye's voice, leaped to his feet and ran toward the cries. Grabbing his severely wounded friend, he began dragging Toye to shelter, leaving a bloody trail behind. Neither man made it. The Germans resumed firing and an 88 round burst near Guarnere, who fell alongside his friend, his right leg mangled beyond salvage.

The loss of two key veterans stung not just Easy Company, but Winters as well. Both men were top-notch leaders. As he watched medics work on Toye, tying off the bloody stump, Winters recalled the day Easy was pinned down outside Nuenen, scurrying for cover in roadside ditches while their British tank support was being converted into scrap metal under withering fire. It was vital that Winters know who and what he was up against. Looking around, he had spotted Toye.

"Joe! I need a live prisoner," he said.

Wordlessly, Toye left his squad behind and crept out alone into no-man's-land. A short time later he returned with a frightened young German who proved to be from the 107th Panzer Brigade.

Guarnere was also highly prized by Winters, even if he was something of a problem child. Winters recalled the early hours of D-Day when he, Lipton and Guarnere, all having lost their weapons in the jump, joined up with Colonel Cole and his men. The group had attacked a German supply train, and in the melee that followed, the three had managed to pick up German pistols. Preparing to move out after the fight, two shots rang out in the darkness. He found Guarnere standing over the bodies of the two POWs he'd been told to watch, the pistol in his hand still smoking. Winters blew his top and chastised the Philadelphia boy severely for gunning down the prisoners.

But Winters had a deep respect for Guarnere's abilities, both as a mortar platoon leader and as a man. Putting Guarnere in for the Distinguished Service Cross after Brecourt would be the highest nomination for valor Winters would make during the entire war.

On top of these two crippling losses came a third; not from shellfire, but rather as a direct result of the wounding of Toye and Guarnere.

Winters had not had to contend with combat fatigue in Normandy, where the closest any man came to breaking down under fire had been Private Blithe's brief bout of hysterical blindness. Prolonged fighting and the miserable living conditions in Holland resulted in a few cases. But at Bastogne, the emotional strain of being in daily contact with the enemy, the freezing temperatures, the growing hopelessness that things would ever change and the lack of hot food wore the men down physically and mentally. Combat fatigue rapidly became an enemy as potent as the Germans.

Sometimes a man gave a warning that he was on the edge. He'd become listless and detached from his surroundings, and when the fatigue finally hit, he'd drop his weapon, throw down his helmet and run his hands through his hair. Buck Compton gave Winters no warning that he was on the verge, or Winters would have intervened and gotten him off the line for a rest.

The break came after Compton saw Guarnere and Toye lying mangled in the scarlet-splattered snow, medics working to stem the flow of blood and get the two to the rear. It was more than Compton could bear.

George Luz saw it first. Compton, weaponless and helmetless, shuffling toward the rear as if mesmerized. He ran to the lieutenant.

"You can't leave us, sir," Luz said.

But Compton brushed on by as if Luz was merely a specter in the swirling mist. Luz grabbed Compton and tackled him to the ground.

"You can't leave us," he said again. But one look into the lieutenant's vacant eyes convinced the sergeant that his pleas had gone unheard. Compton rose to his feet and continued walking away, leaving Luz kneeling helplessly in the snow.

Winters saw him next, still trekking rearward through the forest.

"Buck!" he called, jogging toward the dazed man. Winters recognized the symptoms right away. "Buck. Where do you think you're going?"

Compton stopped and looked at him but did not answer.

"Get back to your platoon, Buck," Winters said. "Think of your men. They need you. I need you."

Still no response.

Winters fretted over this breakdown, not just for Compton's sake, but also for the impact this could have on the morale of the men.

"Buck, you're an officer; you've got to get a hold of yourself. I can't excuse you for this. If I excuse it for the officers, then what reason do I have to expect the men to put up with the same conditions?"

"I can't take it anymore," Compton said finally. "I just can't take it anymore. I'm sorry."

Winters saw the futility of further argument and let him go, and though the two men remained lifelong friends, Compton's breakdown remained a sore on Winters' soul that never healed. As an officer, Winters felt one had to share the men's hardships. Compton failed that, having lost what Winters called his "mental discipline." Compton was also paying a price for something Winters had always preached against: getting too close to the men. The loss of both Guarnere and Toye pushed Compton over that thin line of stability combat soldiers walk.

Compton's leaving coupled with the loss of the two veteran sergeants came as a severe blow to Easy Company, but there was more to come. On January 10, Winters was standing near his foxhole at the battalion CP when he saw First Sergeant Lipton approaching, looking ashen-faced.

"Carwood," he said. "What's up?"

"It's Private Hoobler, sir," Lipton said. "He's dead."

The news was a shock. Winters had heard of no enemy action, so he asked what happened.

"It was the Kraut pistol he picked up off that officer the other day," Lipton began. "You know what I mean?"

"Yes, he was brandishing it all around the company," Winters said. "He showed me twice."

A few days earlier, the battalion had taken part in a brief but bewildering attack along the Foy-Bizory road. Deployed in dense woods, contact between companies, platoons and even squads was often lost. At one point Hoobler and some others confronted a Nazi officer mounted on horseback. The man spun the horse around and tried to flee. Hoobler leveled his rifle and dropped the officer. The pistol, a Belgian-made .32 caliber automatic, was his trophy.

"Well, he had the gun in his pocket," Lipton said. "It went off while he was shaking snow off his shelter half. The bullet hit him in the right leg. Doc Holland did what he could for Hoob but the bullet must've cut the artery. He bled to death. Heffron was one of the first ones to him. Babe said Hoob seemed to know he was done for, that you could see the life running out of him."

Winters nodded slowly, thoughtfully. Hoobler was a likable kid from Manchester, Ohio. His father had died when he was a boy and his mother took on odd jobs to put bread on the table for herself and her son. She became an enthusiastic fundamentalist and began preaching to her friends and neighbors to the point of being overbearing. It quickly made her, and by extension her son, unpopular and misunderstood.

Hoobler made up for that in the army. He was an energetic soldier and outgoing. He liked everyone, and the men exchanged the sentiment. Winters found Hoobler to be a capable, dependable soldier, always ready to do what was asked of him. He recalled the young man choking down his fear as he fixed his bayonet just prior to the desperate charge at the crossroad in Holland a little more than two months ago.

What a goddamned shame.

Then another thought hit Winters.

"Why am I not hearing this from Dike?" he asked.

"I thought I'd deliver the news, since I've known Don since Toccoa," Lipton replied quickly.

Winters knew Lipton was just being a good company sergeant and covering his commander's ass, but he saw no point in pursuing it. "Thank you, Sergeant," he said and Lipton left.

Hoobler's death was the first of two tragedies to befall the men that day. Later in the afternoon a hail of German artillery shells rained down on the company. As men hit the ground and tried to pull the earth up over their heads, an 88 round plunged straight into the foxhole of Skip Muck and Alex Penkala. The two friends died together in a blinding flash. Their deaths sent Don Malarkey into a state of despair. Winters found Malarkey sitting quietly on the lip of his foxhole.

"Don," Winters said. "I need a runner for a few days at battalion. I'd like you to take it. You might even get a chance to get back to Bastogne and find a hot meal."

Malarkey looked up at the captain. "Thank you, sir," he said. "But I don't want to leave the fellas. I'm fine. Really."

Winters looked at Malarkey awhile, then nodded.

"Okay. Let me know if you change your mind."

Winters was proud of Malarkey. He knew the man wanted to quit—hell, all of them wanted to quit—but his pride would not let him. So he endured like the rest.

★   ★   ★

Four days before Hoobler, Muck and Penkala died, Winters had some quiet moments to write his first letter since arriving in Bastogne three weeks earlier. It was short and addressed to "My favorite Wave."

"Just a note to let you know that mysterious feelings you've been having about me being wounded, back in the States, and all that is just a point to prove how far wrong a woman's intuition can be," he wrote. "Read the papers and keep an eye on the 101st and you'll know generally where your paratrooper is spending his time."

Where he would be spending his time, he soon discovered, was in Foy. Less than a week after writing to DeEtta, the battalion was informed that the nearly one-month siege was ended and they would be going on the attack. The objective, to no one's surprise, was Foy.

"We'll jump off at first light tomorrow," Strayer told his officers on January 12. "I Company will be making the assault, along with one company from 2nd Battalion."

After the briefing, Strayer pulled Winters aside.

"Dick, we'll use Easy as the assault company. Keep Fox and Dog in reserve. Why don't you take over the attack? It'll give you good practice."

"Practice for what?" Winters thought, but remained silent.

*　　*　　*

That night, by the dim light of a candle, Winters sat in his foxhole pouring over infantry assault tactics in his copy of the army manual. Nixon watched him, then said, "You telling me you lugged that damned book all across Europe?"

"Yeah," Winters said disgustedly, closing the manual. "And I'd just as soon it had been a Hershey bar. This stuff is too elementary for what I need tomorrow."

Then Winters noticed something strange.

"Is it my imagination, or is this foxhole getting smaller?" he asked.

Looking about, he discovered that the frost created by the freezing fog was building up on the sides of the foxhole. Stiffening his shoulders, Winters rubbed them back and forth, using friction to melt away the icy layers. He then glanced upward as a figure approached. It was First Sergeant Lipton. He knelt by his captain's foxhole. Winters always kept his door open for Lipton whenever his highly regarded first sergeant had something on his mind.

"Everything okay, Lip?" Winters asked cautiously, recalling the last time Lipton visited him, with news about Hoobler.

"The men are fine, sir. They're bedded down, trying to get what sleep they can," Lipton replied. Then he was quiet.

"Anything else, Sergeant?"

"It's Lieutenant Dike, sir."

"Is he missing again?" Winters asked disgustedly.

"No, he's in his foxhole, sir," Lipton said. Then he hesitated. "It's just that, well, the men are concerned about him leading this attack tomorrow. They don't feel he can cut it, and to be quite honest, I agree. I don't think he knows what he's doing."

"He'll be fully briefed tomorrow," Winters replied. "I'll be doing it personally. Anything else, Sergeant?"

"No, sir," Lipton said, then saluted and left.

Nixon looked at Winters.

"He's right, you know," Nixon said. "Dike's a bean counter. He's not cut out for this."

"I'm aware of that, Nix, but what can I do? I can't relieve Dike because I think he's incompetent and I don't like him. No, I have to go with the hand the army dealt me and it doesn't matter how I feel."

At dawn, 2nd Battalion was ready and Easy Company was in its assault position at the edge of the Bois Jacques. Winters met with Dike and gave him his final instructions.

"You've got two hundred fifty yards of open ground to cover, so you can't hesitate," Winters told his lieutenant. "You've got to get the company across fast. Push them, kick them, shove them, whatever, but keep moving and don't bunch up. Lieutenant Reese has two sections of machine guns set up to cover you. But most importantly, you have to keep moving. Get into the town, secure the area and link up with I Company."

Winters had done all he could. The rest was in Dike's hands, a realization that left Winters extremely uneasy. That uneasiness proved well-founded. The attack got under way in good form, with the machine guns blazing away at the village and the men of Easy dashing across the snowy plain. Sporadic fire came from Foy's defenders, but nothing severe enough to stop the charging men. Still, every time a machine gun stopped firing so the crew could change belts, Winters held his breath, thinking, "Come on. Come on. Reload."

Seventy-five yards from the town, the company inexplicably halted, men squatting in the open where they stopped. Winters couldn't believe his eyes. He yelled, "Get moving, get moving," then realized he couldn't be heard. Snatching up the radio, he made contact with George Luz, who was carrying the company's set.

"Keep moving," he ordered. "For God's sake, George, move."

"Lieutenant Dike ordered a halt, sir," Luz replied.

"Get Dike on the radio."

Dike, frozen by panic and indecision, did not take the radio from Luz, and no amount of coaxing or yelling could budge him. Colonel Sink, who had come up just as the attack commenced, stood behind Winters, watching the scene unfold.

"Dick, why are you running this attack?" he asked. "Where's Colonel Strayer?"

"Back in the CP, Colonel," Winters replied crisply, his mind distracted by the events out in the field.

Sink nodded and pointed at the fight. "You take care of that," he said, and went in search of Strayer.

Angered almost beyond reason, Winters unslung his rifle and took several steps toward the action. Then he stopped himself.

"I'm the commander," he thought. "I can't do this. If I commit myself, who's going to make the decisions and run this thing?" He glanced around quickly, looking for an officer, any officer, he could send out to take charge. The nearest was Lieutenant Ronald Speirs, a D Company platoon leader.

"Speirs, get over here!" Winters shouted. Speirs hustled as ordered.

"Sir?"

"Go out there, relieve Dike and get that attack moving."

Wordlessly Speirs, an almost fearless man, ran forward through enemy fire. Moments after he reached Easy, the men rose up and finished their interrupted charge into Foy. Even as gunfire echoed from the town, Winters breathed a sigh of relief. Dike, out of a job, trudged rearward with the aid of a medic. Winters ignored the man.

The attack on Foy cost Easy Company two men killed, Patrick Neill and Kenneth J. Webb, plus several wounded, but had Speirs not gotten them moving after Dike froze, Winters knew the cost would have been much higher.

"Speirs did a wonderful job," Winters said years later.

While Speirs and the rest of the company were in town rooting out German snipers, two war correspondents arrived on the scene. At first the pair began taking photos of the action, mostly of medics carting back wounded men. That was part of the newsmen's job and, while Winters didn't like it, he tried to ignore it. The two stayed back, never going more than twenty or twenty-five yards from the woods, thus staying well away from any flying lead. Then one of the men, acting on an inspiration of false bravado, grabbed the end of a stretcher bearing a wounded soldier. After making sure he got some of the injured man's blood on the sleeve of his heavily fleeced jacket, the war correspondent took on a facial expression of being utterly fatigued. His buddy sighted through his camera and fired off several frames, capturing this "heroic" act on film. Winters shook his head in disgust at the charade.

That evening, the fight over and Foy secured, Sink held a regimental debriefing at his headquarters to go over the day's events. Turning to Winters, Sink said, "Dick, what do you plan to do about Easy Company's situation?"

Winters wondered why Sink asked him and not Strayer, who was sitting close by, but he replied instantly. "I'm relieving Lieutenant Dike from command and replacing him with Lieutenant Speirs."

Sink nodded. "Very well."

With that, Speirs became Easy's newest and, as it turned out, last wartime commander. Winters' appointment of Speirs was not without some reservations. He knew the tough officer had executed six German POWs on D-Day, and on D-plus 2 he had shot one of his own sergeants through the forehead for twice refusing a direct order under fire. The men under Speirs didn't necessarily like the man, but they respected him and feared him. Winters did not approve of using fear as a leadership tool, but there was no denying the fact the Speirs was a fine officer who got the job done, and his handling of the company under fire earlier in the day had impressed Winters. Dike was shipped back to division, where he became an aide to General Taylor. Winters never saw him again.

"I didn't want to," he said sixty years later.

Asked if he knew how Dike fared at division, Winters tersely replied, "I hope to hell they found something he could do."

Sink's inquiry to Winters about his plans for Easy's command heralded another change in leadership. While Winters was still officially the 2nd Battalion's executive officer, after Foy he became, in fact, its commander. Strayer was attached to Sink's staff and exerted no further direct influence on the operation of the battalion. While Winters welcomed the opportunity to command, it made for an uncomfortable situation. Winters still wore captain's bars, whereas battalion commanders usually wore the silver oak leaves of a lieutenant colonel. Plus, within the regiment there were men of higher rank and with more seniority than Winters who, by the army's way of doing things, should have been placed in command. Instead, by this appointment, Sink showed his confidence in Winters' leadership skills and tactical abilities.

★   ★   ★

It was Winters' hope that his men would be given a breather after Foy. Instead he was put on the alert for a move on the hamlets of Recogne and Cobru and the larger town of Noville. Like the men themselves, Winters now began to wonder if the fighting would ever end. The men, he knew, were being pushed to the limits of their endurance. About the only thing that kept them moving was their devotion to the unit and their own fierce pride.

"You know what this is, don't you," Winters told Nixon after receiving the orders. "Taylor's finally back and now he has to show off for Eisenhower."

"Yeah," Nixon replied. "He probably figures we've just been sitting on our asses back there in Bastogne, and now he expects us to go out and kick German butt."

Winters' awareness of Taylor's return was based on firsthand experience. Shortly after the commanding general's arrival, after the siege of Bastogne had been broken, Taylor had visited his men in the field. While inspecting 2nd Battalion's front, he strode briskly along the line with Winters and the other officers trailing along behind. Finishing, he turned to Winters and said, "Watch those woods in front of you." Then he left. Winters' jaw dropped, then he turned to Nixon.

"'Watch those woods in front of you'?" he said. "What the hell did he think we've been doing while he was back in Washington?"

Winters' growing anger was not lessened when the marching orders for Noville came through.

"They want us to move out at noon?" he said, posing a rhetorical question to his staff. "It's a mile and a half of open field to Noville, all uphill and through knee-deep snow with no cover whatsoever. The Germans are sitting atop that high ground, warming their hands over their tank engines and licking their lips. And we're to move on them in broad daylight? Taylor's got to be out of his mind. Why not wait until dark?"

Winters' staff had no response to these questions, nor did he expect any. He had his orders and knew he had no choice but to obey.

* * *

"We finally got a break," Winters said as he scanned Noville through his binoculars. He lowered the glasses, slipped them back in their case and turned to the bevy of officers with him. "The ground in front of us forms a steep shoulder as it nears the town. We're going to head for that. The closer we get to Noville, the more protection it'll give us." He paused before saying what was next on his mind. "The battalion will move across this field at single file."

Men's heads jolted up.

"Begging your pardon, sir," Lieutenant Joe McMillen said. "But why single file?"

"That's deep snow out there," Winters explained. "If we spread out the whole damned battalion will be exhausted by the time we get across. By going single file, it'll be tough on the men in front, but the rest will be able to walk across trodden-down snow and get to that shoulder without being worn out."

"And if the Krauts have machine guns trained atop that rise?" McMillen asked.

"Then I'm making the biggest mistake of my life," Winters said. "Speirs, you lead off with Easy, then Fox, then headquarters. Joe, you bring up the rear with Dog."

The attack began at noon as scheduled, and just as Winters had feared, the Germans had clear fields of fire, which they used to cruel advantage. As 2nd Battalion advanced across the snowy plain, Winters could see 1st Battalion, about four hundred yards to his left, come under heavy fire. Machine gun bullets cut men down in their tracks and explosions from 88 mm shells fired by tanks blossomed up from the snow, hurling men into the air. Years later Winters read *Dr. Zhivago* and it reminded him of Noville, with troops foolishly charging across snow-covered steppes.

But the deadly fire was not coming at 2nd Battalion. Plodding through the snow, the highly vulnerable battalion received no hostile fire, and with every step the head of the column took toward the protective slope, the higher Winters' confidence soared.

By midafternoon the entire 2nd Battalion was safe in the embrace of this quirk of geography. Winters held the men in place until the short winter day had ended and darkness began to descend. Reconnoitering the ground alone, Winters crawled to his right. He came upon an exposed draw created by a stream at the southeast corner of the town, and guarded by machine gun emplacements. To get to his attack position, Winters' men would have to cross this gap, briefly exposing themselves to enemy fire. Winters brought up his own machine guns to provide support, then sent men across the open ground, eight or ten at a time, while his gunners forced the Germans to keep their heads down. It took patience, but the battalion made it across unscathed.

Winters was now in position to attack Noville and he had not lost a single man.

"I earned my pay that day," he later recalled.

That night was the coldest Winters and his men had yet experienced. As the sun vanished and the temperatures began their inevitable downward plummet, the sweat from the day's exertions froze on the men's bodies, chilling them to the bone. The chattering of teeth accented the night. Winters' new S4, Lieutenant Alfred Winter, muttered that he could no longer stand it, and headed for the rear. He would never return to the battalion.

Hoping to catch a few hours' sleep, Winters curled up on the protective slope of a small knoll, but his violent shivering caused him to keep sliding down, so he gave up on the sleep idea.

Around 9 P.M., the roar of tank engines was heard from Noville: German diesel engines. Winters wondered if the enemy was pulling out or just repositioning their armor for the attack all knew would come with the dawn. Briefly, Winters considering launching his own night attack, which he felt was preferable to freezing to death in the dark. He soon put the idea out of his head, fearing the only men who'd end up getting shot in the darkness would be his own.

As light from the approaching day streaked the sky, Winters sent Easy into Noville with Fox Company supporting its right flank. Moving cautiously through the streets, house to house, doorway to doorway, the GIs met sporadic fire from enemy rear guard units. The main bulk of the Germans had pulled out under cover of the night. Winters and his men picked their way through the shattered town. The unfeeling, uncaring hand of war had touched nearly every building in the ruined village. Some had sustained light to moderate damage, with outer walls pockmarked by bullets or shrapnel. Other houses had been reduced to piles of shattered masonry, or stood partially or totally collapsed as roofless shells. Standing along the main street, the huge two-story town hall had taken a severe pounding. Oddly, half of it stood almost intact while the other half was a rubble heap. Squatting in front, as if on guard, a turretless Sturmgeschutz lay tilted inside a large crater, its 88 mm gun silently aimed at the approaching Americans.

On one street, Easy's 3rd Platoon commander, Lieutenant Ed Shames, accompanied by Private Alley, hailed what they thought was an American tank. "This way," Alley shouted, only to realize the tank was bearing an Iron Cross. The commander spotted them and swiveled his turret. The two men didn't wait for him to draw a bead, but raced around a street corner and ducked into a burned-out building. The tank clattered after them. Rounding the same corner, it hit the building and brought half of it tumbling down. The tank kept going as Alley and Shames climbed out of the building, shaken but unhurt.

First Sergeant Lipton, leading 2nd Platoon since Compton's breakdown, had a run-in with the same tank. Ducking for cover, he and several other men slid under a pair of dead Sherman tanks that had been knocked out in the fighting on December 20. The enemy tank stopped. Although the Shermans were useless, the German commander feared their guns might still be operational. Taking no chances on being attacked from the rear as he passed, the German put a round into each Sherman, jarring the teeth and eardrums of the men huddled underneath, but leaving them otherwise unharmed. The tank rolled past the hulks and made its way out of town. If the commander thought finishing off the two Shermans was going to save him, he was mistaken. His presence had been radioed to planes circling overhead and, as GIs watched and cheered, a P-47 Thunderbolt roared in from the sky. The Jug's pilot unleashed a five-hundred-pound bomb that hit the fleeing tank squarely. The smoldering wreck coasted to a halt.

Noville was now securely in American hands. The battalion had picked up a few prisoners, including two junior officers. Winters watched them standing in the street, hands on their heads, swastika-emblazoned decorations on their tunics. He turned to Lieutenant Ed Thomas, his S2 in place of the wounded Harry Welsh, and said, "Get what you can from them."

As they were junior officers, Winters did not expect too much from the interrogation. Like all armies, he surmised, these two probably only knew what their superiors deemed necessary. He was correct. The men had no useful information and Winters turned them over to MPs.

By now the men of the 2nd Battalion, along with the entire division, were exhausted after a month of combat in the hilly, forested land around Bastogne, but they had one more job to do; taking the town of Rachamps. Luckily, this proved to be a cakewalk. Winters' battalion attacked on a wide front, minimizing the effects of German artillery with its dreaded white phosphorous shells, whose foamy chemical floated on the air like a feather, but whose merest touch burned its way into a man's flesh. In his report, Winters listed only one man, a Private Martinson from F Company, as being wounded in the attack. He had been hit by shell fragments.

The 101st Airborne was relieved on January 17 by the 11th Armored Division and sent into Corps reserve. It had been exactly one month less a day since they had been herded onto trucks at Mourmelon-Le-Grande and ferried to Bastogne. During that time the 506th had suffered 762 casualties, or thirty-seven percent of its strength, including 102 men killed, 601 wounded and 59 missing.

On January 22 Winters finally had a chance to write to DeEtta. He told her he had gotten one letter from his father, but that it had been so long since he himself had written anyone that he was uncertain how to respond. All he could think of, he wrote, was "Thanks for writing, don't worry, I'm still okay, still ducking at the right times." On a more personal note, possibly hinting at inner feelings he didn't want to acknowledge in ink, Winters told her that military censorship of mail "stops a fellow cold."

"As for writing about love and all that, well I am about as brilliant as Li'l Abner along those lines. I just ain't got it."

DeEtta had written him in an earlier letter about Christmas and New Years back home, about the church service, carols being sung by the choir, and the holiday dinner. Winters' cryptic reply was, "I, too, will never forget this last Xmas and New Year's Day."

In the quiet moments, when he found some, Winters had taken to Bible reading and had become something of an authority on the Good Book even though, he hastily added, he had never intended to. Instead he told DeEtta that he read the Bible not to impress anyone but for relaxation and atmosphere. Often he read passages from wherever the book happened to open, and sometimes, he said, it opened at just the right spot that he needed for inspiration.

Winters had other, less holy thoughts as well. He told DeEtta he dreamed "about fights, fighting Jerries, out-maneuvering, out-thinking, out-shooting and out-fighting them." Fighting constituted eighty percent of his dreams, he said, but helped him devise solutions that, "in the cold morning light, it usually works. In fact, to date, they've always worked."

Of the remaining twenty percent of his dreams, he told her, "ten percent are about the happiness and pleasure of a nice, warm, comfortable home, good chow, and all the pleasures of a kid. The other ten percent are of future operations and plans for happiness. Believe me, I intend and hope to see the day when I can enjoy life a little bit and relax."

CHAPTER 10

"Their Guys Are Probably Dumber Than Ours."

January 20–March 31, 1945

Dick Winters was thoroughly pissed off. After thirty-six days of almost constant contact with the enemy in the snow-shrouded forests of Belgium, the 101st Airborne Division had been told it was going into corps reserve for a break. Instead, the battle-weary men now found themselves jostling their way to Alsace to help defend against what was rumored to be another German attack.

"My God," Winters complained, foreseeing another Bastogne. "Doesn't the army have any other troops who can plug those gaps?"

Lugging their weapons and equipment, the men of the division clambered aboard 112 10-ton and 98 2½-ton trucks for the 160-mile trek to the town of Drulingen. Heavy layers of snow covered the ground, in many places blocking roads and slowing the convoy to a crawl. In all, the trip took a bone-jarring, butt-numbing thirty-six hours, a seemingly unending time for the men riding in trucks built for functionality, not physical comfort.

Arriving in Drulingen on January 26, one day after the Battle of the Bulge was declared over, the men were no sooner out of the trucks and stomping their feet to restart their blood circulation than they were ordered to climb back in.

"The division is being attached to VI Corps at a place called Hochfelden, Dick," Sink told him when he issued the orders to remount the trucks. "It's supposed to be a quiet sector. We'll be in reserve at a town called Wikersheim on a little stream called the Moder River."

The "little stream called the Moder River," normally thirty to forty feet wide, was presently swollen by snow melt so that in many places it was now a football field in width. Swiftly flowing muddy brown water frothed and

swirled, and treacherous currents produced by the flooding would make sending out contact patrols a difficult and dangerous venture. The Five-Oh-Sinks
were positioned on the division's left along a thirty-five-hundred-yard length
of the Moder stretching from Wikersheim to Pfaffenhoffen. To Sink's right was
the 501st, the center of Taylor's line, with the 327th Glider on the 501st's
right. The 502nd was put in reserve.

Life in Alsace wasn't as cozy as it had been in Mourmelon, but it was infi-
nitely better than anything the men had experienced since December 18. The
most welcome change was that, except for some outposts and machine gun
and mortar positions, foxhole living was just an unpleasant memory. Now the
men had roofs over their heads and floors beneath their feet. And even if
those rooms were not heated—a smoking chimney would surely bring an 88
mm shell homing in, or worse, a shot from Alsace Annie, a fifteen-inch railroad gun whose incoming shell sounded like an approaching freight train—it
still beat the hell out of sleeping on the cold, wet ground.

The army set up portable showers that could cleanse 215 men an hour, and
entire companies lined up and passed through. The invigorating water
washed away weeks of grime and weariness. The men had access to news
from the outside, another rarity. *Yank, Stars and Stripes* and the division's own
newspaper, the *Kangaroo Khronicle*—Kangaroo being the division's code
name—were widely distributed.

Seven of Hollywood's most recent movies circulated the camps, including
Buffalo Bill, starring Joel McCrea, Maureen O'Hara and Linda Darnell, *Mrs.
Parkington*, with Greer Garson and Walter Pidgeon, and the Alfred Hitch-
cock suspense film *Saboteur*, with its hair-raising climax atop the Statue of
Liberty, although this latter brought about a bit of homesickness to men who
had not seen Lady Liberty in over two years. A Red Cross club arrived, giving
the men a chance to mingle, drink coffee, eat doughnuts, listen to the latest
big band music and maybe, if they were lucky, dance with a Red Cross girl
under a silky canopy of draped parachutes.

But, perhaps best of all, the Screaming Eagle shoulder patches they were
ordered to remove as they approached Bastogne could now be sewn back on.
The division had resumed its identity.

Not surprisingly, cases of frostbite and combat fatigue dropped dramatically.

Despite these luxuries, unimagined in previous fights, the men were still
on the line, and the danger of sudden death or injury remained. Both sides
sent out contact patrols to find and harass their enemies, and the air rippled
with incoming or outgoing artillery shells. Yet a new sensation was in the air.
The war was winding down. The Battle of the Bulge had been the Germans'

last gasp. The ferocious fighting like what the men had seen at Bastogne, Foy and Noville could well be at an end.

"There was just a feeling, and you began to tell yourself 'I might just make it after all,'" Winters said years later. "So you start to walk easy, watch where you step."

Unfortunately, one could not always walk easy or watch each step.

On February 4 Winters directed Lieutenant Lloyd Cox, commander of Fox Company, to send a patrol across the river between the villages of La Walck and Bischofen. Cox gave the job to young Lieutenant Staplefeld, who expertly moved his platoon across the formidable river. There the patrol ran smack into a German strongpoint. Machine guns and mortars blazed away at the intruders. Sergeant William Green died in the fight, but Staplefeld got the rest, including six wounded, back to safety.

The patrol had been repelled, and in reviewing the after-action report, Winters knew Staplefeld's actions had prevented heavier losses. The young officer went up one more notch in Winters' esteem.

Even as medics sprinkled sulfa powder on Staplefeld's wounded men and wrapped their injuries in gauze bandages, new supplies arrived at 506th HQ. Of course, now that the men were no longer living outside in the ice and snow, the army saw fit to ship them sixty-one hundred pairs of winter shoepacs, arctic socks, felt insoles and six thousand yards of white cloth, enough to make two thousand snowsuits.

"Oh my, how we could have used them six weeks ago at Bastogne," Winters said to Nixon as he looked at the stacks of cold-weather gear his men no longer needed.

"Guess we should be glad we got them at all," Nixon said wryly. "They could have shipped them to the Pacific."

Sink sent new orders the next day, February 5. The regiment was being relieved by the 409th Regiment of the 103rd Division and was being shifted to the town of Hagenau. There they would replace a regiment of the 79th Division. Opposite them was the German 25th Panzer Grenadier Division, which the 79th had been fighting since January 8 a few miles to the north of Hagenau at a town called Hatten. On January 21, the 79th broke off the fight and retired to Hagenau. As they left, they heard the German commander, Lieutenant Colonel Hans von Luck, celebrate their departure by slipping into a church, firing up the organ and playing the Johann Sebastian Bach chorale "Nun danket alle Gott" (Now Thank We All Our God).

Winters deployed his men on the south bank of the Moder, the river that still marked the front. Behind him, a one-mile stretch of open field ended at the heavily-wooded Foret de Hagenau.

Administratively, this was a troubling time for Winters. Classified as the acting battalion commander, he was technically still the XO. Worse, he was still a captain, so that when he had to deal with other battalion commanders and XOs, he was working with higher ranking officers. This put Winters at a "definite disadvantage."

In addition, he had no staff to speak of. Winters' S1 was Lieutenant Charles W. Bonning. His S2, Harry Welsh, had not yet returned from his Christmas Eve injury. His S3 was also gone. Sink had plucked Nixon away from Winters to be his regimental S2 after Clarence Hester had been promoted to major and appointed division G2. And the battalion S4, Lieutenant Alfred Winter ("No 's'," Winters always stressed) was a "goof off" who was still missing after he walked off the line at Noville.

The work was burdensome, but one job Winters gladly performed.

"You wanted to see me, sir?" Speirs said, standing before the table that served as Winters' desk.

"Yes," Winters said. "I put Carwood in for a battlefield commission. Colonel Sink approved it."

"And I would support the colonel's decision," Speirs said.

"Carwood will be officially notified shortly, but why don't you tell him?" Winters said.

*   *   *

Replacements arrived in Hagenau on February 15, including two new second lieutenants for 2nd Battalion: Hank Jones and another shavetail named Fitzpatrick. Both were West Point graduates, class of June 6, 1944: D-Day.

As a rule, Winters met and spoke with new men, especially officers, partly so they got to know each other, and partly to take their measure, but being short-staffed he postponed that meeting and assigned Jones to Easy Company and Fitzpatrick to Fox.

A patrol across the Moder was scheduled for that same night, and Winters handed the job to F Company. Unknown to him, Cox allowed Fitzpatrick, a young man far higher on eagerness than experience, to go along. In the darkness, Fitzpatrick stepped on a German schu mine and died from shock and loss of blood.

Winters was steamed at Cox. There was no way he would have permitted a green replacement officer to go on such a patrol. He also chastised himself for not having taken the time to meet Fitzpatrick, but rather assigning him to Fox sight unseen. It was the first and last time that would occur. Years later, thinking about the man he never knew, Winters lamented how fate was so cruel to the young replacement officer.

Still fuming over the needless loss of Fitzpatrick, Winters' mood was not enhanced next day when Nixon came to him with new orders.

"Colonel Sink wants you to send a patrol across the river for a prisoner snatch," Nixon said. "Division wants info on enemy troop strength, unit identification, deployment, whatever we can learn."

"My God, Nix," Winters moaned. "Doesn't anyone realize how tough a job it is to approach a man with a rifle or behind a machine gun, who is in a defensive position, and persuade him to come with you as your prisoner of war? And what's it going to accomplish? All we're going to find over there are enlisted men. And what can they tell us? Their guys are probably dumber than ours, and our fellas don't know what the hell's going on. And there's a real good chance of someone getting hurt and us having nothing to show for it. I don't like it."

Earlier in the war, Winters would never have griped about such an order because it was a tactically sound decision. One sent out contact patrols as a means of intelligence gathering. But at this stage of the war, men were no longer willing to take needless risks. Nor was he willing to risk men's lives on dangerous and pointless patrols. No one wanted to become what could be the last casualty. Winters was also keenly aware that the men were tired and manpower was thin. Instead of having two battalions on line and one in reserve, Sink reversed it, placing one on line and two in reserve. Since 2nd Battalion was now holding the line, this headache patrol fell in Winters' lap.

Winters knew that in complaining to Nixon, he was preaching to the choir. Besides, orders were orders. He sent for Lieutenant Speirs.

"Sir?" Speirs said when he arrived at Winters' HQ.

"Division wants a prisoner snatch," Winters said. "I need a patrol to cross the river and bring back some live Krauts. Pick your men carefully and make sure at least one speaks German; that'd be either Liebgott or Webster. Any idea who you want to lead it?"

"Ken Mercier," Speirs said without hesitation.

"That's who I had in mind," Winters said. "We've got some captured German rubber dinghies for the crossing, and we'll give the fellas some time to practice with them. I'm thinking we'll go on the eighteenth. Gather your men and I'll brief them on what I want."

As rumor of the patrol seeped through the ranks that day, Lieutenant Jones sought Winters out. Snapping to attention, he said, "Sir, I heard there's a patrol being sent across the river. I'd like to volunteer."

Winters looked at him with an appraising eye. "Cocky young man," Winters thought, but he admired the officer's eagerness.

"Request denied," Winters said. "You have no combat experience."

Dick at age eight, with his cousins Jane and Jack Gardner and an unidentified neighbor

Richard N. Winters, Dick's father, as a young man

Winters speaks with
Aunt Lottie and his
mother, Edith, on
Arch Street in
Ephrata, circa 1955.

The soldiers of the 506th regiment
head for a jump.

The wreckage of Captain Thomas
Meehan's plane, June 1944

Easy Company men head to Bastogne.

U.S. Army

E isenhower attaches a unit citation to the 101st Airborne flag.

U.S. Army

V ictims of the SS at Landsburg prison camp lie in rows.

American soldiers enjoy a relaxing moment on Hitler's mountain balcony. From left: Joe Zielinski, unknown, unknown, unknown, unknown, Steve Mihok, Lewis Nixon, Dick Winters, unknown, Lloyd Cox, and Harry Welsh.

Major Dick Winters, Lieutenant Thomas Peacock, and Lieutenant Jack Foley pose outside the Kaprun ski lodge.

M ajor Dick Winters in Holland, 1944

U.S. Army

Winters and Lewis Nixon

Intelligencer Journal, Lancaster, PA

Dick Winters sorts through his fan mail in his home office in 2002.

Courtesy of Susan Smith Finn

Winters and Frank Perconte at a
reception prior to the 2002 Emmy
Awards

Courtesy of Bob Hoffman

Grace Nixon, Dick Winters, Ethel
Winters, and Tom Hanks, with the
Emmy awarded to the HBO film
Band of Brothers, in September 2002

"Begging your pardon, sir, but I need to get that experience sometime."

"True, but not now. This will be dangerous enough for experienced fellas."

The patrol assembled in front of a house near the river, in plain view of the Germans. Winters, clutching a map, began outlining the plan, gesticulating as he spoke and causing some men to worry that a German artillery spotter would see him and direct a shell his way. None came. Evidently, no one was looking. Or no one cared.

Winters pointed to a large building across the river.

"That's your objective," he said. "We know the Krauts have an OP in there. Because of the current, the patrol will cross the river upstream on our right flank, by D Company's OP, and approach the objective. Once you reach the Kraut OP, Mercier, get your flankers out to provide security, then go in. Put a rifle grenade into the building, and close in fast. Get more grenades into the basement windows. That'll stun the Krauts inside. Get in, grab some POWs, and get out. But before you leave, I want a satchel charge on a delayed timer hidden in the building. With any luck, the Germans will reoccupy it before the charge goes off. Get back to the boats as fast as you can. Mercier has a whistle that he will blow when you're pulling back. That's the signal for the covering fire to open up. You'll have blanket support. We have a 57 mm anti-tank gun, a .50 caliber and several .30 caliber machine guns, as well as mortars covering your every move. They've zeroed in on every known or suspected enemy position, so woe be to any Kraut fool enough to lift his head."

Winters looked around at the grim-faced men. The plan was as perfect as he could make it.

"This patrol has two objectives," he said. "Division wants prisoners. So do I, but mostly I want you all back unharmed. Be careful."

As the gathering broke up, Jones again approached Winters.

"Sir," he said. "I'd like to go on this patrol. I feel I really need the experience."

Winters again stared at the young man, then nodded.

"Okay," he said, knowing Jones was correct. "You can go. As an observer. Mercier's in charge. You do what he says."

★   ★   ★

The patrol moved out on the night of February 18, stopping first at D Company's outpost to gobble down sandwiches and coffee before heading for the boats. The lead dinghy trailed a rope out behind it. Once across, the rope was tied to a pole. The next boatload of men used the rope to pull their way across but the third dinghy, carrying Melvin W. Winn, Roy Cobb and Thomas A.

McCreary, capsized, dumping the trio into the icy water. They emerged, drenched, cold and sputtering, righted the boat and tried again. Again the recalcitrant dinghy dumped them out and they gave up.

Winters stood apprehensively on the riverbank, staring across at the target building. He hated the waiting and the stupid, senseless mission, and he prayed the men would all come back safely. The time moved excruciatingly slowly. Then a dull boom rippled from the darkness beyond the Moder. Mercier's rifle grenade, Winters thought. More low booms rumbled. The patrol was charging the OP. Then silence. The patrol was inside, Winters knew. More waiting. The silence beyond the river became worse than the crack of the grenades. What the hell was happening?

The rattling of small arms fire erupted and tracers began knifing through the dark like fast-moving, deadly fireflies.

Come on, Winters thought. Blow the whistle. Blow the whistle.

The wait gnawed at Winters' gut. Then it came, the sharp bleating of Mercier's whistle. Instantly the covering fire came to life, led by David Webster's machine gun. German and American tracers crisscrossed each other in a lethal light show. In the dim glow of thin moonlight reflecting off snow, Winters now could see the patrol, a flock of shadowy figures racing pell-mell toward the black ribbon that was the river, some stopping to send a burst of fire back at their unseen pursuers. The patrol reached the river and there was a flurry of activity as men launched the dinghies and jumped inside. Soon they were recrossing the river as quickly as eager hands could tug their way along the rope.

Mercier was smiling from ear to ear when he reported to Winters a few minutes later. The patrol had come off textbook perfect. The GIs had grabbed three Germans, although one was so severely injured from the grenade blast that he had been abandoned on the far bank. The other two, a pair of somber-looking *Feldwebels*, were safe and sound. However, the patrol was not as "textbook perfect" as it had first appeared. Private Eugene Jackson had charged into the building before the last grenade, his own, had exploded. It practically detonated in his face, sending a fragment of steel burrowing into his brain. Do what he might, Doc Roe was unable to save the young man. In almost unendurable pain, Jackson died at the aid station.

Winters knew Jackson and hated the loss of a man who, he felt, was needlessly sacrificed. It was a poor exchange for the two captured sergeants who, as Winters had predicted, had no information to disclose. Jackson's death was also somewhat personal. He was from Winters' hometown of Lancaster, although Winters had not known him then.

Next morning, Winters again stood at the riverbank expectantly watching the house the patrol had hit. Seconds ticked by. Then the planted satchel charge blew, smoke pouring from every window in the structure. Winters never discovered if the outpost had been reoccupied or not before it blew, but he was satisfied. That satisfaction didn't last long. Later that morning Colonel Sink visited Winters at his HQ, accompanied by Colonel Joseph B. Harper, commander of the 327th Glider Regiment.

"That was a fine job your men did last night, Dick," Sink said. "Good work."

"We lost a man, sir," Winters said, wanting Sink to know the price paid for two prisoners who had little to offer in the way of vital intelligence. "Private Jackson."

"Regrettable," Sink replied. Then, "I'd like another patrol tonight. More prisoners."

Winters couldn't believe his ears. He reddened with anger, but simply uttered a "Yes, sir" and saluted.

"He's showing off for his drinking buddy, Harper," Winters complained to Nixon when the two were alone. "It seems we were the first regiment to send out a patrol that successfully brought back any POWs, and now he wants to brag and show everyone else how easy it is."

"He knows about Jackson?" Nixon asked.

"Yes, he knows. He called it 'regrettable.' Jesus, the Germans are going to be on the alert. The chances of losing the entire patrol are a heckuva lot higher than the chances we'll capture any Krauts."

"So what are you going to do?" Nixon asked.

Winters thought, then said, "Find Speirs. Have him assemble the same men in the same place in an hour. I'll brief them."

The glum faces of the men destined to make yet another patrol told Winters that they, too, were fully aware of their chances against an alerted enemy. Winters and Nixon joined the group.

"Men, I want you to know I'm proud of the job you did last night," he said. "You pulled it off perfectly. The loss of Private Jackson was an unfortunate tragedy. Colonel Sink's proud, too. So proud he wants another patrol tonight. So here's the plan. You'll cross just like you did last night, same place. With that Kraut OP knocked out, you'll have to move deeper into the town, look for another objective. When you grab the prisoners, pull back just like before and blow the signal whistle. The covering fire will make the Krauts keep their heads down again. Jump-off time will be an hour later than last night."

He paused and took a deep breath before he spoke again.

"Now relax; get a good night's sleep. Sergeant Mercier, when you report to me tomorrow morning, you'll tell me you entered the town as planned but could get no live prisoners." All faces turned toward him. "And if anyone asks any of you about the patrol, you'll tell them just what I told you. The patrol was unsuccessful. Understood?"

The men nodded, smiles of relief beginning to crease their faces.

Speirs grinned and saluted. "Yes, sir," he said.

Winters knew he'd just risked his entire military career, and a likely court-martial, by intentionally disobeying an order from his commanding officer. But he was damned if he'd risk any more lives on a foolhardy mission that had little chance of success and a very large chance of turning into a disaster. It was a risk he willingly took.

"I knew I was getting out as quick as possible after the war was over," Winters said years later. "I had no fantasies of making the army my life. If I had any idea of making the military a career and be a career soldier, would I have disobeyed an order and not sent those men? If someone is going to make it his career, he's not going to have it on his efficiency report 'refused an order.' What kind of officer is that?"

Lieutenant Ralph D. Richey Jr. of F Company, now attached to Winters as S2, said, "That was a classic, sir. You should write that one up for the future."

"No, Lieutenant," Winters said. "That's one report that will never be written."

Machine guns and mortars from 2nd Battalion opened fire late that night, sending a stream of tracers dancing through the darkness. Winters stood on the riverbank watching, but no American soldier crossed the Moder. The men the blazing weapons were supposed to be covering were asleep in their billet.

"Sink wasn't being mean when he ordered that second patrol," Winters said looking back fifty-eight years later. "He was proud of what we had done. But it was a dumb, dumb decision."

Winters filed no after-action report on the patrol that never was, nor did Sink ever request one. Perhaps he knew the second patrol never occurred, perhaps he didn't. Either way he said nothing.

★   ★   ★

The day after the phantom patrol, February 20, 3rd Battalion relieved Winters' men and they went into regimental reserve. As 2nd Battalion was loading onto trucks, Nixon delivered a package for Winters. He handed it to his friend. "This is from Colonel Sink," Nixon said. "Guess he forgot your birthday last month."

Winters opened the small box and found himself staring down at a pair of golden oak leaves.

Nixon saluted. "Major Winters," he said.

By February 23 the 101st was on another truck convoy, rolling for Saverne in France, having been relieved on the line by the 36th Infantry Division. At Saverne, the division boarded a train, the men climbing into straw-filled 40 & 8s for the eighteen-hour train ride back to Mourmelon. As the locomotive chugged away from the front, Winters began to realize this was the first time since December 18 that they were not in danger of being shot at. The 101st had endured seventy-two days of winter combat, served under two different army groups and four corps. They had fought 11 enemy divisions and covered 352 miles of mostly snowy, treacherous roads.

During the month of February, the 506th had suffered forty-four casualties, including three enlisted men and one officer—the unlucky Fitzpatrick—killed.

As the train jolted to a halt in Mourmelon the men were greeted by the 502nd Regiment's band blaring out its repertoire of martial music. One disappointment to the men was that this time they would not be billeted in barracks, but rather sleep on folding cots in twelve-man olive drab wall tents.

The troops were given light detail and kept in shape with calisthenics. Replacements arrived, duffel bags slung over their shoulders, and there were training classes and weapons demonstrations. On March 7 instructors were showing the use of a new baseball-style grenade that was armed not by the release of a lever, but by the wrist action of the thrower. During the session, a grenade exploded prematurely, wounding eleven men including the 101st Division's executive officer, Brigadier General Higgins, and Colonel Harry Kinnard, divisional G3.

The day after the accident, Sink issued a memo officially realigning his staff, and handing out promotions. With his regimental XO, Colonel Charles Chase, transferred to division to replace the wounded Kinnard, Sink moved 2nd Battalion's former commander, Lieutenant Colonel Strayer, into the XO slot. Captain Herbert Sobel was also officially named regimental S4, a post he had held unofficially for months.

Winters used this opportunity to bolster his staff. With Welsh still out, Winters tapped Lloyd Cox, now promoted to captain, as his XO. He had considered naming Joe McMillen of D Company. He liked McMillen, a very relaxed officer, quiet yet confident. "You know you're talking to a man when you talk to him," Winters later said. "He was a great leader and was there for the men the whole time." In the end he decided to leave that capable officer where he was. Appointing Cox, however, was somewhat uncomfortable for Winters. By right of the army's seniority system, Cox technically outranked Winters, yet it was Winters who now wore a major's oak leaves and commanded the battalion.

Bonning became Winters' S4 supply officer. Richey, one of Winters' favorite staff officers, would split his time between S1 and S2 duties until Welsh's return, and First Lieutenant Thomas A. Rhodes Jr. was placed in command of Headquarters Company.

For his S3, Winters soon reclaimed the man he wanted most. Ever since Lewis Nixon had been elevated to Sink's staff, the colonel had become increasingly frustrated with the man's drunkenness. In late March Sink had assigned Nixon to jump as an observer with the 17th Airborne Division during Operation Varsity, the assault on the Ruhr, the industrial center that still propelled Germany's sagging war machine. Nixon was jumpmaster and in the first seat by the door. On March 24, as the plane lumbered over the drop zone, it was hit by flak. Nixon and three others managed to launch themselves out the door before the plane exploded. A day later Nixon was back with the regiment, and while he was drowning the memory with Vat 69, Sink was visiting Winters' headquarters.

"I have a problem, Dick," he said. "It's Captain Nixon."

Winters knew what the complaint was, so it came as no surprise.

"Goddamit, the man's drunk all the time," Sink said. "I mean, I certainly tip a few myself at night and when off duty, but with him it's all the time. I can't get any damned work out of him. How did you find him to work with?"

"Captain Nixon and I get along very well, sir," Winters replied.

"That's what I had thought," Sink said. "Do you want him back? Can you use him?"

"Oh yes, I can use him," Winters said.

"You got him," Sink said. "Hell, every time I need him he's always here with you anyway. He may as well stay."

So Lewis Nixon, now the only man in the 101st to make three combat jumps, returned to 2nd Battalion.

Lipton's promotion to lieutenant also came through, and in a quiet ceremony, Winters happily handed him his discharge as an enlisted man, and pinned the gold bars on his friend's collar.

On March 15 Winters stood at attention on the parade ground at Mourmelon, watching General Dwight D. Eisenhower exchange salutes with General Taylor. Ike then bestowed a unit citation on the Screaming Eagles—the first ever given to an entire division—for their stand at Bastogne. It was a moment of intense pride for Winters and his comrades.

The stay at Mourmelon provided the battle-tested veterans with a chance to unwind and reflect. On March 12 Winters wrote DeEtta about his promotion to major. "You may wonder about this latest promotion. Well, I just got it last week. So it looks as if I can prove worthy of the job, if somebody of senior rank doesn't show up and take over and if my luck holds out, some day I may be a lieutenant colonel, say within the next six months.

"It sure was an honor to get the battalion for it means I've come straight up from junior second lieutenant to commanding officer in the same battalion in a period of 2½ years.

"As far as the promotion in rank goes, I don't give a damn. But I do like the job and the responsibilities that go with it."

One of Winters' favorite memories of Mourmelon during this time was watching German POWs marching back to the prisoner stockade after a day of working as orderlies in the nearby army hospital. The men walked with pride, in perfect step, often vigorously belting out some Teutonic marching tune. It was a beautiful sight, Winters recalled, and in admiration of their pride and discipline in the face of defeat, Winters specifically set aside time on most evenings just to watch and listen.

"I told myself that I always wanted to remember this beautiful moment," he would later say.

As March ended, so did the pleasant stay in Mourmelon. The men of the 101st climbed back onto the trucks, this time bound for the west bank of the Rhine, the last obstacle to the heartland of Germany.

CHAPTER 11

"Now I Know Why I'm Here."

April 2–May 8, 1945

Major William Leach was not a combat leader. His job was regimental intelligence officer, a position in which he excelled. But he had never led a patrol into action and his uniform sported no battle decorations. Perhaps that's why, on April 12, 1945, he decided to lead a four-man patrol across the Rhine.

Since it arrived at the Rhine on April 2, Winters' battalion had held a line between the towns of Worringen and Sturzelberg. Across Germany's fabled river were visible the spires of Dusseldorf and, beyond, the Ruhr pocket where hundreds of thousands of German troops still held the Americans at bay. Duties had been light. Winters sent out a few contact patrols and occasionally had artillery shells lobbed over the river, just to let the Germans know the GIs were still there.

Located within Winters' section was the town of Zons, which the young officer found especially appealing. Dating back to the 1400s, it was a medieval village in the true sense in that it included a castle, complete with a moat, and stone walls suitable for storming with catapults and battering rams. Winters wondered how many times hostile armies had attacked those walls in the town's 500-plus years of existence. Compared to the destruction he had seen in other German cities, some of which, he wrote, ceased to exist except for a few people wandering around amid mountains of rubble, Winters was glad the Air Corps had spared Zons.

As spring arrived, and the warming sun melted the snow and brought the first buds to the trees, Winters was more determined than ever to take no chances with the lives of his men. Yet he had to carry on the business of war. On April 8 Winters was ordered to send a patrol across the river. He selected the area directly across from Sturzelberg, opposite the battalion's left flank. Scanning the landscape 350 yards across the Rhine with his binoculars, he saw no signs of enemy activity, just farmland and an orchard.

Winters tapped Harry Welsh to lead the patrol. Welsh had resumed his job as battalion S2 upon his recent return following his wounding at Bastogne. However, at the briefing it was Winters, and not Welsh, who planned the patrol, lacing it heavily with safety guidelines. Winters told Welsh where the patrol would land and the route it would take along the opposite bank.

"Every step will be covered by artillery," Winters said.

Welsh was upset at the restraints being forced on him.

"Christ, Dick," he complained privately. "I'm leading this patrol. I've done this before. Give me some leeway here."

Winters refused to budge. He didn't want to send the patrol at all.

"What I've laid out here is the best way to insure that no one gets hurt," he said. "That's the key thing. I want no casualties. There's no room for discussion. You'll do it my way, Harry."

The patrol came back unscathed.

Another patrol four days later wasn't as fortunate. Led jointly by the newly promoted First Lieutenant Staplefeld and a Lieutenant Perdue, both of Fox Company, the patrol cautiously probed the lone German position on the western side of the river. Here the Rhine looped eastward between Zons and Sturzelberg, creating a concave salient or bulge. Moving forward in the dark, Perdue tripped a booby trap and was wounded. Alerted, heavy German small arms fire forced the patrol to withdraw.

That same day, April 12, Leach elected to lead his own foray. He decided to cross the Rhine on 2nd Battalion's left, and ordered Winters' friend, photographer Al Krochka, to take to the air in a Piper Cub to photograph the eastern shore. Of particular interest were any machine gun emplacements or other strongpoints. Krochka did as ordered and the low-flying, lumbering plane predictably drew ground fire. Krochka got the photos, but at the price of an arm wound that earned him a Purple Heart.

Winters was informed about the patrol.

"Damned fool," he muttered. He turned to Welsh. "This sounds like an ego trip, Harry. Alert Fox Company. Have them be on the lookout and not to get trigger happy."

"Yeah, right," Welsh said.

Then he forgot.

That night on the lonely, darkened Rhine River, Leach's patrol was spotted by alert American sentries. Machine gun fire from Fox Company's 2nd and 3rd Squads raked the water, sweeping the hapless soldiers, some with the words "don't shoot" screaming from their lips, from their bullet-riddled boats. Six days later the bodies of Leach and his four men were fished from the Rhine downstream, at Sturzelberg. In his heart, Winters held two people responsible for the senseless tragedy. Mainly he blamed Leach for taking out a patrol that was a high-risk venture for little or no purpose. He also found fault with Welsh who, as he had when Moose Heyliger was wounded six months earlier, failed to alert those most in need of alerting.

"He heard me," Winters later said of his friend. "But sometimes he didn't absorb what he was hearing."

The bad news of April 12 did not stop with the loss of Leach and his men. All along the battlefronts, both in Europe and Asia, GIs learned that President Franklin D. Roosevelt had died in Warm Springs, Georgia. This was disheartening news at a time when spirits over the war's inevitable outcome were beginning to soar. Many of the young soldiers could barely remember a time when Roosevelt was not their president.

"It left us with a great sadness," Winters wrote. "We have lost a good leader and a good man."

Occupation duty, for that's how Winters described the battalion's stay along the Rhine, was basically police work: keeping the local population in line, and making sure the enemy across the river stayed across. This lull in action allowed Winters to grant some men leave time in Nice, France. He also turned his attention to an important letter from DeEtta. Words like "love" and "marriage," evidently used in her note, forced Winters to face feelings the war had denied him the right to ponder.

"It's impossible for me to write my true feelings under present conditions," he wrote on April 10. "When you're fighting as a front line battalion, there is just no spare time. . . . Now you talk about meeting somebody like me and falling in love with him. Hell . . . I am just like a million other guys."

He told DeEtta his time was too preoccupied with weapons, targets, harassing fire, grazing fire, chow, transportation and base of fire to think about personal feelings. "All I know is that I am in no position to say I love anything or anybody. So there's but one thing to do. Wait till the war's over and then I'll start out on that subject. I hope to use my head, not the heart. Well, not too much."

In her letter, possibly in a pique of temper or frustration, she referred to him as a brass hat. He took offense.

"If I hurt your feelings, pardon me, I didn't mean to but I just didn't want anybody standing around waiting for me when I come home. Or have anybody with any ideas. Of those who have worked with me in the army there are only a few of them that really know and understand how I feel and think about life in general. Guess there's really only one, Lt. Welsh, a good little Irishman. At home there are my folks, and that's it."

Winters wrote home, describing the destruction of German cities, many of which, he recalled, had been leveled. But he felt little remorse for the devastation, and considered it just medicine after the misery German forces had visited on civilians and cities in other countries.

These feelings gave Winters little room for concern over German civilians when it came to selecting his CP. Finding what he considered the nicest house, he simply knocked on the door and told the people they had fifteen minutes to get out, but to leave the beds, silverware and cooking utensils.

"It's a very nice way to fight a war," he wrote. "Much better than Normandy, Holland or Bastogne."

One major thorn in Winters' side was the displaced person camps, where masses of people the war had jarred loose from their homes were being gathered by military authorities. The army had a nonfraternization rule, but army rules are made to be broken, especially by bored enlisted men, and officers found it hard to enforce. GIs were not above using food or other items to purchase a wide range of services from the DPs, including sexual favors.

The enemy, meanwhile, cared little that the war was winding down, and seemingly less about the DPs or, for that matter, German civilians in the combat zone. On the evening of April 15, two dozen 88 mm shells whistled in on Fox Company's position, killing a baby and a young boy and wounding six civilians and two soldiers. At 1 A.M. thirty indiscriminately fired rounds burst on the American side of the river, killing a girl. Another twenty-four-round barrage later in the morning injured no one. After each shelling, Winters ordered return fire.

Not all the heat was coming from the Germans. With the war visibly ending, DeEtta's letters continued to turn toward her future and, possibly, *their* future together. Winters resisted being pressed.

"You don't want to have any disagreement until after the war? Fine!" he wrote. "For I am not a fighting man and after this war's over all I want is a blissful state of tranquility and that's all. All I ask of the world is 'let me alone.'"

He added on April 20, "Tender thoughts are to me something I took off and left behind in the marshaling area prior to the start of this war. There's no time for them." This sentiment was not specifically aimed at DeEtta, but everyone in general, including his dead comrades.

"I think earnestly about the dead," he wrote. "But there's no time to mourn for them."

It was in this letter that he first mentioned the possibility of transferring to the Pacific Theater once the fighting in Europe ended.

"Looks like June should see the end of the war but when I am true to my-self, I realize that it'll be another two years at best before I get through with the CBI and home. Sure seems like a long time looking ahead, but if a fellow just takes it one day at a time it's not so bad."

The reason he allowed his thoughts to wander to the Pacific was because, two days earlier, on April 18, the Ruhr pocket fell and 325,000 German troops became prisoners of war. Enemy resistance was visibly collapsing and life was becoming ever more bearable for the GIs. The day after the Ruhr fell, supplies arrived. Each man got a pair of new socks, three bottles of Coca-Cola and, best of all for many, two bottles of beer.

On the afternoon of April 21 Winters was enjoying a bottle of the Coca-Cola when Sink arrived at his command post with news.

"Dick," he said. "Get Second Battalion packed up. We're heading for Bavaria. Eisenhower and the top brass think the Hostile Boys, at least the most die-hard of them, are flooding into that area to set up a redoubt, a strong-point, a last stand or whatever. We're to try to prevent that. We'll leave by truck tomorrow at eleven hundred, then transfer to trains. The trip will be nonstop and rapid, so each man is to be issued five K-rations."

★   ★   ★

The trip to Bavaria was roundabout. To get to Maastricht, Holland, where a train awaited them, the men were trucked through Luxembourg and Belgium, at times passing over the battlefields of the Bulge. Memories flooded back as the shattered countryside, still littered with dead vehicles, rolled by. Once on the trains, destroyed and damaged sections of track forced the engineers to take the long route through Holland and into France. April 23 and 24 found the men still on the train, whose wheels beat a monotonous clackity-clack through France and back into Germany. Men grew weary of the trip and the food, joking, "Damn the K Rations, full speed ahead."

On April 25 the division arrived back in Germany, this time in the town of Widden, where the rugged terrain prompted the password "Rough" with the countersign "Rider."

Loaded onto DUKWs, the part-land, part-amphibious vehicles that could roll along roads or ford rivers depending on the need, the convoy turned southeast toward Ludwigshafen, Mannheim, Heidelberg and Ulm. Halting in Buchloe at the foot of the Alps, the true cruelty of the war was about to hit Winters.

About three miles down the road sat the medieval town of Landsberg and Landsberg Prison, a stoutly built compound with towers adorned by onion-shaped roofs, whose claim to fame being that it had once housed the present German leader.

Following his blundering attempt to overthrow the Bavarian government during the Beer Hall Putsch of November 1923, Adolf Hitler spent thirteen months behind these walls. But it was an incarceration in name only. Catered to by prison officials, Hitler, who had garnered a considerable local following, had been granted unlimited visitations and his cell door was not only unlocked, but often stood open. In that cell, with the help of his secretary, Rudolf Hess, Hitler had dictated the text of his political testament, *Mein Kampf*, a hate-filled tome in which the former highly decorated Austrian corporal outlined in painstaking detail his future plans. Unfortunately for the Germans, and for the world, few paid attention, which was why Winters and his men were now bivouacked in nearby Buchloe.

At the prison, GIs discovered that Hitler's former cell had become a national shrine. A bronze plaque above the door proclaimed, "Here a dishonorable system imprisoned Germany's greatest son from November 11, 1923, to December 20, 1924." Perhaps, then, it was fitting that during the twelve years of the Third Reich, Hitler had erected a new style of prison here near Landsberg, far more sinister than the one the German dictator himself had been subjected to.

On April 27 elements of the U.S. 10th Armored Division had stumbled across the first of six concentration camps scattered around the Bavarian landscape, satellite camps for the main killing center at Dachau, near Munich, some forty miles to the east.

Two days later Winters and his men got their own firsthand look at this by-product of National Socialism. Dismounting from their vehicles, Winters gave orders to clear Buchloe of all weapons. He dispatched a platoon from Fox Company to patrol the woods south of town and pick up any German soldiers, particularly SS men, who might have taken refuge in the countryside. He sent other patrols out to secure his flanks by making contact with units to the left and right, especially those on his right since that was where the French were supposed to be. However, General LeClerc's men had a habit of disappearing.

"We imagined they were looting their way across Germany," Winters said later. "We figured they'd fill up their trucks, run them back to France to unload, then return for more."

The French also confounded Winters because the colonel acting as liaison between LeClerc and the 506th was always accompanied by a beautiful woman.

"And all I ever had was Nixon," Winters later remarked with a smile. "It wasn't the same."

Winters had just settled into his CP when his aide, Private Zieleski, told him a messenger had arrived from Fox Company. They had found something Winters should see. Going with the man, they entered a fine house. In the main hallway just inside the door, a man and woman dangled from a rafter. Winters looked at the two bodies, then to Staplefeld.

"We think it's the *Burgermeister* and his wife," Lieutenant Staplefeld told him.

Winters just nodded and said, "Cut them down."

The next find was far more hideous. Sergeant Percante came huffing and puffing back to town to report that his patrol had found something of horrific proportions.

"What, Frank?" Winters asked. "What is it?"

"I'm not sure what the hell it is, sir," he said. "Some kind of prison camp, but you gotta come."

Winters spotted his driver, Alton M. More.

"More! Get the jeep. Nix, come along."

Grabbing Nixon and a platoon of Easy, the little convoy roared out of town.

Winters found the patrol outside a large barbed wire compound. As his jeep halted the patrol's leader, Sergeant Randleman, approached. Lining the wire on the inside of the compound was a large clot of emaciated men, many wearing striped clothing, all looking more dead than alive. Winters did not know what to make of the pathetic spectacle that greeted his eyes.

"Bull?" he asked inquiringly.

Randleman just shook his head. As Winters approached the locked gates the men inside dropped their eyes and lowered their heads, much the way a whipped dog does when beaten. Winters ordered the gate opened. It was and the soldiers walked inside. The prisoners parted like the Red Sea before Moses.

The camp was large, with rows of primitive huts half dug into the ground. These huts were five feet high and twenty-four feet long, so a man could not walk around inside without hunching down. They reeked of filth and death. In fact, the entire area stank. Winters had noticed the stench as he approached the camp, recognizing it as the aroma of dead flesh, but he could not fathom the source. Until now.

Aside from the walking, louse-ridden skeletons milling around the camp, there were the innumerable dead. Hundreds were laid out in neat, straight rows, as if in some sort of macabre dress parade. Some wore the striped prison garb, others were semiclad or nude, with sunken cheeks and chests, gaping mouths and vacantly staring eyes telling a silent story of terror. Some of the dead lay in blood-splattered heaps and still others were sprawled individually where they had fallen. A few huts had been burned, and in the smoldering wreckage charred bodies told another grim tale.

"These men are starving," Winters told Lieutenant Richey. "In the cellar of my headquarters are large wheels of cheese. Get them out here, and bread too if you can find some. And send Liebgott to me."

Richey hurried off.

Winters got on his radio and made contact with Sink.

By the time Sink arrived Winters, thanks to the German-speaking Liebgott, knew most of the story; of how this was a slave labor camp that housed Jews, Gypsies, political prisoners and anyone else the Nazis considered to be *untermensch,* or something less than human. He heard how, as news of the American approach spread, the guards went on a killing rampage; locking some prisoners in their barracks, then setting them on fire, and shooting other prisoners until they ran out of ammunition. Then the guards fled, leaving their crimes behind.

"We've come across several of these camps in the vicinity," Sink told Winters as the two walked among the dead. "Bastards. I have some good news, though. General Taylor has declared the area under martial law. Starting tomorrow the good people living around this camp will be out here helping to bury the dead."

Winters nodded with satisfaction and said, "And I'll be here to watch."

The regimental physician, Major Louis Kent, had arrived with Sink and ordered a halt to Winters' food distribution. He told Winters that the weakened condition of the starving men dictated that their food intake be carefully prescribed. Otherwise, he cautioned, they would gorge themselves and many would die. The task of telling these starved men, who saw the Americans as saviors, that they had to go back inside the camp fell on Liebgott.

"I can't do that, sir," Liebgott pleaded.

"I know, Joe. But you have to. It's for their own good until our medical people can check them out."

Liebgott did as ordered, but it was "a very tough job," Winters acknowledged.

As medical teams moved into the camp Winters felt revulsion welling up inside him. He had never expected to see anything like what he was now witnessing. Even if he had been prepared and had heard the rumors that had been circulating after the first camps had been discovered, he later said, the reality would have been far worse than anything he could have anticipated. In his darkest dreams, Winters had never imagined that man could inflict such cruelty, punishment and torture on other humans. It was a sight that would be burned into his memory for the remainder of his life.

"Now I know why I'm here," Winters told himself.

★   ★   ★

The day after Winters encountered the nightmarish scenes near Landsberg, Adolf Hitler, the architect of so much misery, killed himself in his Berlin bunker even as, overhead, Russian troops prowled the once-regal hallways of the ruined Reichs Chancellory.

Winters received the news a day later, and while many GIs used their beer ration to toast the Führer's death, Winters, weary from so much killing, recorded it in his journal with just a single-line entry. "May 1, got the news that Hitler is dead."

May 3 found the 506th on its way to the German town of Thalham. Rolling through the countryside, largely untouched by war, the convoy was occasionally stopped by sporadic gunfire from token pockets of resistance. During most of the trip Winters sat back in his jeep, enjoying the ride as More whisked him along the famous Autobahn, the modern four-lane highway system that was one of Hitler's better ideas.

The scenes here along the Autobahn proved a stark comparison between victory and defeat. On the grassy median strip dividing the highway marched long lines of German soldiers, all weaponless and headed west. On both sides of this field gray column and stretching as far as the eye could see, American trucks, tanks, jeeps and other assorted vehicles barreled eastward. Sometimes the convoy passed a large gathering of prisoners sitting on the grassy shoulders lining the Autobahn, taking a break. But whether marching or resting, in almost all cases the German soldiers were guarded by just a handful of GIs.

Winters watched the prisoners trudging by with something bordering on awe. Though beaten militarily, they did not seem to be defeated in spirit. Units walked in step, heads held up proudly as if to say "You beat our army but you didn't beat me." The Germans, in turn, were equally awestruck as they watched the endless stream of American vehicles flowing by. The one expression shared by men on both sides was curiosity as they studied each other, one rolling east, the other tramping west.

"I wonder what they're thinking," Nixon said.

"Probably the same thing I am," Winters replied. "Just leave me alone. All I want to do is get this over with and go home."

"Speaking of home," Nixon said, "what are your plans when this is all over?"

"I haven't given that too much thought," Winters admitted. "Why?"

"Well, you know my dad owns Nixon Nitration Works and I thought maybe you'd want to . . ."

"You figure you've worked for me almost since we got into combat, and now you want me to come to New Jersey and work for you," Winters said.

"Unless you've got something better lined up," Nixon said.

"I don't," Winters said. "I'm not even sure how I'll fit back into civilian life after all this. I'll think about it, Nix."

In Thalham, Winters billeted his men in German homes, sending the occupants packing. The death and suffering of the concentration camp had hardened Winters, and the pleadings of the German civilians not to be forced from their homes fell on deaf ears. Nor did Winters any longer try to curb his men's excessive looting of German homes. He figured that, torn from their civilian lives and forced to endure the horrors and hardships of war, the troops had earned whatever they could cart away.

As he was settling into the house he had cleared for his CP, Winters was called to the radio. It was Colonel Sink.

"Dick, I want you to draw extra rations and ammo. We're pulling out first thing in the morning for Berchtesgaden," Sink said.

A thrill ran through Winters. Berchtesgaden! Few places outside of Berlin were more closely identified with the Nazi cause. Everyone knew about this mountaintop retreat Hitler had built for himself. While in college, Winters had seen photographs in the newspapers of Hitler entertaining Italian dictator Benito Mussolini, British prime minister Neville Chamberlain and French premier Edouard Daladier at his chateau, the Berghof, with its huge picture window giving a panoramic view of the Alps. Here the Führer conducted the shameful negotiations that led to the Allies meekly handing over Czechoslovakia and Hungary and thinking they'd walked away with an honorable peace when all they'd done was postpone war. Winters recalled photos published in *Life* of Hitler entertaining guests, usually high-ranking Nazi party officials, on the veranda of the Eagle's Nest, a stone guest house perched on the tip of a mountain ridge. The building had been a birthday present to Hitler from his cronies and was accessible by a gold-lined elevator shaft.

The idea of capturing Berchtesgaden excited Winters, but he knew the town would be a magnet for every other Allied unit in the area. He wanted to get there first.

Next day the 506th was back on the Autobahn, heading swiftly toward Salzburg. Fields, farms and villages sped by while prisoners continued to stream to the west. They'd gone about forty miles before leaving the Autobahn at Siegsdorf, turning right onto the road that would take them to Berchtesgaden.

Eight miles later the convoy ran into an enormous traffic jam. It was the French 2nd Armored Division.

"What the hell are they doing here?" Harry Welsh said as he and Winters climbed out of their jeep and studied the snarled mess. "They're supposed to be on our right flank."

"No wonder we haven't been able to find them," Winters said. "Looks like we'll be here a while. Have the men get out and stretch."

Winters had little respect for French soldiers. Still, he now allowed his men to mingle among them, fostering what Winters called some international good fellowship.

The French had been stopped by a blown bridge that had once spanned a ravine. Attempts to install a temporary bridge were met with plunging fire from German machine guns across the gorge.

Winters offered to solve the problem of the harassing fire. At Mourmelon he and his men had been briefed on two new weapons, the jeep-mounted 57 mm and 75 mm recoilless rifles. At Thalham, the battalion had been issued four of the new guns.

"This gives our men a good opportunity to learn how to use them," Winters told Welsh. "Get those guns up front."

The gun crews had learned their lessons well, and well-placed rounds from the recoilless rifles soon dissuaded the Germans from hindering the engineers' further work on the bridge. But the lengthy delay was making Winters bored and irritable. He walked along the line of stopped American vehicles until he found Sink.

"Colonel," Winters said. "This is not getting us anywhere. Let me send out a platoon and see if we can find a way around this position."

"No," Sink said. "I don't want anybody to get hurt. Not now. We're too close to the end."

Winters knew Sink was right, and there was irony in the fact that Winters, who usually preached caution, was now having it lectured to him by the same man who ordered two ill-advised prisoner snatches at Hagenau. Still, Winters was disappointed. That disappointment didn't last long. Within an hour Sink had rethought the idea and sought him out.

"Dick, God knows how long we're going to be stuck here; overnight for sure," he said. "Turn 2nd Battalion around and get back to the Autobahn. See if you can outflank this roadblock and get into Berchtesgaden ahead of these bastards. When you get there, find the hotel, the Berchtesgaden Hof, and put guards on it. General Taylor wants it for his CP."

"What about the Eagle's Nest and Berghof?" Winters asked.

"Major," Sink said with a wry smile. "You're an excellent tactician. You

take and hold whatever you feel is of strategic importance to secure your position."

Winters backtracked the battalion to the Autobahn, getting as far as Bad
Reichenhall, only to be stopped by another blown bridge. Army engineers
were already at work, so Winters' men bedded down for the night. The new
span was completed by early morning. Winters saddled up the battalion and
they raced on into the lofty Alps.

⋆   ⋆   ⋆

The convoy led by Winters' jeep entered Berchtesgaden at 12:30 on the afternoon of May 5. In this picture-postcard village, the elite of the Third Reich
had once gathered to relax, play and gloat over their many successes. Atop
the towering, snowcapped mountains high above the fairy-tale Alpine village,
Hitler could look out over his world, created by his own relentless determination and held by a steel fist.

Now Hitler was gone. His "thousand-year Reich" was in its final death
throes, and there was no mistaking the fact. On that sunny May day, Berchtesgaden lay as silent as the fallen Führer. White bedsheets proclaiming that
defeat fluttered from windows, but few people were to be seen, many having
either fled or gone into hiding.

Winters' first objective was the Berchtesgaden Hof, which he readily located. Ordering Lieutenant Richey to have Fox Company place double guards
around the building, Winters and Welsh entered the hotel. Service staff scurried away like cockroaches exposed to sudden light, cowed by the sight of the
conquerors in their combat fatigues. In the main dining room Winters saw a
waiter packing silverware into a four-foot-long, velvet-lined wooden chest.
The man looked up from his work as Winters entered the room, then fled out
a side door. Studying the silverware in the chest, Winters decided to engage in
a bit of souvenir hunting himself, but knew it was too much for him to handle.

"Harry, why don't we split this up?" he asked. "I'll take half with me, you
give the rest to Kitty for a wedding gift."

Welsh agreed, and the two friends split the set down the middle.

That was the extent of 2nd Battalion's looting of the hotel. The main task of
ransacking it would be left to regimental and divisional staff officers, who did
such a thorough job that Winters later mentally kicked himself for not giving
his own men dibs. He would not make that mistake again.

The hotel secured, Winters assigned 1st Platoon of F Company to guard
strategic positions around the town, and had other units seize all key houses.
This was done without resistance.

Winters saved the cream for Easy Company. He ordered Speirs to take his men up the mountain to Hitler's residential complex. This huge, sprawling area was, in fact, a military compound. Besides Hitler, Reichsmarshall Hermann Goering, Party Secretary Martin Bormann, and Minister of Defense Albert Speer all had homes here, surrounded by a private cadre of elite SS troops housed in several barracks buildings. Machine gun and antiaircraft positions bristled all around the mountain retreat, and most of the site was connected by underground tunnels and bunkers that ran as deep as a hundred feet beneath the earth. A subterranean radio room kept Hitler in touch with all points in his empire, and quaint guesthouses were available for his visitors.

While Easy was eagerly scurrying up the mountain, Winters arranged for the lodging of his men and his own accommodations. He put his company officers in three of the nicely built, elegantly furnished houses that had belonged to various Nazi party officials. These houses were scattered along a hillside, far enough apart to allow for privacy, yet close enough for convenience. Selecting the choicest of these for himself, Winters sent one of his staff officers, a new lieutenant named Robert H. Cowing, to secure it.

"Tell whoever is there they have fifteen minutes to get out," he told the young man.

Moments later Cowing was back, looking sheepish. "I'm sorry, sir," he said. "The people said no, they will not move out."

Cowing had not been hardened by war, nor by the sights of the camps not a hundred miles from where they now stood.

"Follow me, Lieutenant," Winters said. "I'll show you how it's done."

Approaching the door, Winters hammered on it loudly. A woman answered, a stern look on her face.

"We're moving in now," he told her in a harsh tone. "*Raus!*"

The couple did as ordered. Winters did not know where they went, nor did he care. People like them, he reasoned, were responsible for all the misery he'd seen in the concentration camps, and he had no sympathy for their problem, nor did he feel he owed them any explanations.

Winters gave the men free time in Berchtesgaden. The GIs relaxed and took time to go sightseeing, often in confiscated Nazi trucks or staff cars. For souvenir hunters, the town was a treasure trove. Yet not once did discipline become a problem. They were kids in a candy store, yet everyone behaved.

One souvenir hunter struck gold. As Winters was walking to his jeep that afternoon, he saw his driver looking through an oversized book.

"What do you have there, More?" he asked.

More's head jolted up. Startled, he closed the book. He looked at Winters, then cast furtive glances left and right.

"Promise you won't say anything, sir?" More asked. Winters crossed his heart with his right hand. More opened the book to reveal it was a photo album with neatly mounted pictures of Hitler, his mistress, Eva Braun, and other Nazi bigwigs enjoying themselves at the Führer's home. "I found it at the Eagle's Nest."

"Very nice, Alton," Winters said, flipping through the pages. "It'll be our secret."

"Thank you, sir," More said and returned to the book to a hiding place he'd fashioned under the driver's seat of the jeep.

The next day Winters went walking alone. He realized the foolishness of this, especially had there been any fanatical, die-hard Nazis left prowling the area undetected, yet he wanted to take advantage of this once-in-a-lifetime chance to explore Berchtesgaden. He next drove his jeep up to the Berghof. Hitler's grandiose mountain chateau had been thoroughly worked over by the Army Air Forces, leaving its roof holed and its walls pockmarked from bullets and shrapnel. The large picture window, which could be lowered to let in the alpine breezes, was gone, the frame gaping open to reveal a ruined interior.

A short distance to the east Winters discovered a large building that proved to be Luftwaffe chief Hermann Goering's officers' quarters and club. He entered cautiously, moving room to room. In one he found a man lying next to a bed, facedown in a pool of dried blood, a Luger next to him. The dead man was Luftwaffe General Gustav Kastner-Kirdorf who, two days earlier, had put the muzzle of the pistol into his right ear and pulled the trigger in defeat. Continuing on, Winters came to a cellar entrance. He flipped a wall switch; no electricity. Slipping his flashlight off his belt, he lit it, drew his automatic from his holster, and descended the stairs. Kicking open several doors, he soon came upon a wondrous sight. One doorway opened up to a room fifty feet in length, thirty feet wide and ten feet high, with each wall lined with floor-to-ceiling wine racks. Winters estimated he was looking at 10,000 bottles of wine, probably looted from every corner of Europe and stored here for the enjoyment of Goering and his officers.

Retreating from the house, Winters returned to his HQ and ordered Fox Company to place a double guard on the building, then went in search of Nixon. He found his friend, drunk as usual.

Leaning over him, Winters said, "Nix, once you sober up I'll show you something you have never seen before."

Worried that drunkenness could get out of hand once news of the wine cellar got out, Winters issued an antidrinking order, putting all of his men on the wagon for seven days. He knew it would not be obeyed totally, and later admitted it was one of his most foolish directives, but at the time he was looking to keep things under control.

"I didn't want a drunken brawl," he said years later.

Next morning a bleary-eyed but sober Nixon approached Winters and said, "What was it that you said you wanted to show me?"

"Follow me," Winters said.

The two jumped into Winters' jeep and sped off. Arriving at the officers' club, Winters took Nixon to the cellar. As Winters recalled, Nixon looked as if he had died and gone to heaven. This was especially true after what Winters said next.

"This is yours," Winters told his friend. "Take what you want, then have each company and battalion HQ bring around a deuce and a half and take a truckload. You're in charge."

An expert on booze, born of experience, as well as a wine connoisseur, Nixon selected the finest bottles in the stock. (In his book, *Parachute Infantry*, E Company Private David Kenyon Webster complained that Goering stocked only inferior grades of wine. The truth was, Webster got there after Nixon had chosen the cream of the crop.) The wine cellar was then opened up to the rest of 2nd Battalion. After the men had made their selections, Winters lifted the guards and the remainder of the bottles were left for later looters.

Pilfered wine wasn't the only thing discovered by the GIs in Berchtesgaden. During one excursion Winters and Nixon came across a rail siding where a group of decidedly unfriendly civilians hovered protectively around two boxcars. Winters stopped the jeep and studied the men.

"What do you think?" Nixon inquired.

"I think common sense tells us to leave them alone," he said, and they drove off. The incident was reported, however, and MPs from division moved in and the civilians were dispersed. Opening the cars, the MPs discovered stolen artwork.

The news every GI in Europe was hoping for arrived on May 7. Winters received a dispatch from Colonel Sink.

"Effective immediately. All troops will stand fast on present positions. German Army Group G in this sector has surrendered. No firing on Germans unless fired upon. Notify French units in vicinity. Full details to be broadcast, will be issued by SHAEF (Supreme Headquarters Allied Expeditionary Forces)."

Winters took the memo to the Eagle's Nest, where he read it to his officers, who had gathered there to enjoy the magnificent view from Hitler's patio. The men listened, then, after allowing a few moments for the news to truly sink in, broke out in grins and handshakes. They next cracked open some of Goering's wine, posed for Krochka's camera, and partied on the same spot where Hitler had entertained before them. The war was over. They had made it.

★   ★   ★

The war in Europe ended officially the next day, May 8. While the fighting had ended, there were still objectives to be taken. Even as German General Alfred Jodl and Field Marshal Wilhelm Keitel were scrawling their signatures on the surrender documents at Eisenhower's headquarters, Winters got orders to pack up 2nd Battalion; the division was moving into Austria. The order also stated that all captured German staff cars were to be left behind. Every man knew what that meant. Rear echelon staff officers were going to claim them as souvenirs. So Winters turned a blind eye as his men got careless. Cars were accidentally driven off cliffs or engines were allowed to run without oil. Sergeant Talbert heard that one car, supposedly used by Hitler himself, had bulletproof windows.

"They really are bulletproof, sir," Talbert told Winters. "Unless you use an armor piercing round," he added with a smile.

"Then they shatter?" Winters asked, shamming innocence.

"Oh, yes, sir," Talbert said.

"That's very interesting." Winters said, and let the matter drop.

The convoy that departed from Berchtesgaden bound for Zell am See, Austria, at ten P.M. that night was a mixed bag of U.S. Army and captured German trucks. Each company in 2nd Battalion had given special priority to its load of liberated booze, packing the bottles as carefully as if they were gold bars. This move into Austria was unlike any other in Winters' wartime experience. Headlights blazed on full beam from every vehicle. Inside the trucks the mood was high-spirited, a far cry from the usual somberness. It was party time, Winters recalled, a time for celebration. It was a night to remember.

Rolling south toward Austria, Winters and his battalion left Berchtesgaden behind, but sixty years after the war controversy still rages over who was first into that jewel of Nazism. In their history of the 101st Airborne, *Rendezvous with Destiny*, authors Leonard Rappaport and Arthur Norwood Jr. substantiate a claim by veterans of the 7th Regiment of the 3rd Division that they first had the honor of taking the town. Winters has always contested that view, drawing on his own memories, a journal kept without his knowledge by Lieutenant Staplefeld, and Krochka's photographs.

"If they were the first ones there, where'd they go?" Winters said during an interview with this author. "It was a small town and, aside from service personnel at the hotel and a few civilians, we didn't see anyone else."

If the old military adage is true that the British fight for King and Country, the Russians fight for Mother Russia, the Germans fight for the Fatherland and the Americans fight for souvenirs, then Winters' claim carries much validity. When they arrived, the posh Berchtesgaden Hof was unlooted, the German staff cars untouched and Goering's wine cellar was intact, a condition all but implausible had any American troops gotten there ahead of Winters and his men.

"As it stands in *Rendezvous with Destiny* we were latecomers," Winters said. "But I assure you, members of 2nd Battalion and the 506th have different memories and pictures to prove that we didn't do too badly in getting our share of the loot at Berchtesgaden during the last days of the war."

CHAPTER 12

"The Spoils of War."

May 9–November 4, 1945

The convoy carrying Major Richard D. Winters and the men of 2nd Battalion braked to a halt in the picture-postcard town of Zell am See just as the first rays from the morning sun had begun to paint the snowcapped peaks of the Alps.

En route they had barreled past thousands of former German soldiers, far more in number than the GIs guarding them, who gawked at the convoy in wonder.

"If I were a German officer I'd think it impossible that this army beat us," Winters thought. "We have no military demeanor. Our trucks are nondescript and beat-up, our tanks are nowhere near as formidable as their Tigers and King Tigers, our uniforms are faded and slovenly."

The trip had been rapid, so much so that at Saalfelden they had unknowingly roared straight past the headquarters of Field Marshal Albert Kesselring, the regional military commander. Second Battalion had been directed to proceed through the lush valley and occupy the villages of Kaprun and Bruck in the foothills of the Alps. It was these towering mountains that had finally halted the German retreat south. The few gaps through the lofty peaks leading to northern Italy, still under Nazi control, were blocked by snow. The German retreat had simply run out of room, and roadblocks now being set up by the 506th and other American units gave the enemy no place to go. So they came out by individuals, by squads, by companies, battalions and regiments, with their hands on their heads.

"The war ended about as gloriously as I'd ever hoped," Winters wrote home. "Berchtesgaden was really the heart of Germany, not Berlin, and it was quite an honor to be in it. Goering, Kesselring, generals by the dozens and

Krauts by the thousands. Never saw anything like it. They were backed right up to the mountains and no place to go. Then they threw in the towel and started coming out of the hills. Days before the final surrender we all knew it was over. There just wasn't any fighting, thank God."

Winters established his headquarters in the Hotel Kaprun in the center of the town. Companies were billeted in nearby houses and sentries were given the password "Twain—Mark." Shortly after he had set up his HQ, Winters sent a message to the local German military commander, a colonel, to report to his headquarters. The officer, a staff member in tow, dutifully showed up in full uniform, decorations on full display, pistol in a holster on his right hip.

"Major," the German said through his English-speaking staff officer. "I wish to surrender my command."

He laid his pistol, a thoroughly cleaned Luger, on the table Winters was using for a desk.

"Very well, Colonel," Winters said. "What I want you to do is spread the word through the valley that all weapons are to be turned in. You can deposit them at either the airport, the school or the church." He picked the Luger up from the table and handed it to the colonel. "Officers may keep their sidearms, and so may any military police."

Winters felt silly in his disheveled uniform giving orders to this fancily dressed, bemedalled officer twenty years his senior, but he continued.

"Tomorrow I will come out to inspect your camps, your kitchen and your men."

"It will be done," the colonel said. The two men exchanged salutes and the German left.

The colonel was better than his word. Next day when Winters and Nixon toured the areas where the weapons were to be collected, they found heaps of military rifles, pistols and knives. But also lying amid the piles were civilian hunting rifles, target rifles, pistols, hunting knives, and even antique firearms. Winters' order merely referred to military goods, but German efficiency took care of the rest. Winters just shook his head and laughed.

At the German camp, Winters found the soldiers lined up in formation for his review. They were neat, well dressed and fit. Winters felt a tinge of envy at the type of discipline that could make even a defeated army look so proud. The camp was orderly and the kitchen clean, with large pots of potatoes cooking over the fires.

Nixon asked Winters on the ride back to Kaprun why he had done the inspection. "You didn't have to, Dick. Remember, these guys are prisoners. They're not an army anymore."

"The fighting's over, Nix," Winters told him. "We now need to reopen the channels of communication between us and the Germans, and keep them open. To do that, we have to build some mutual respect. Humiliating them will do no good."

Next day the German colonel sent his English-speaking officer, also a colonel, to Winters to act as liaison between the two sides. The two men warmed to each other and were soon swapping war stories; Winters telling him about Bastogne, and the German recalling the bitter cold of Russia, where merely touching the freezing metal of a tank pulled the skin off one's hand.

"You know, Major," the German said. "Russia is the real enemy. Our two countries should never have fought each other. Our armies should join hands and wipe out the Russkies."

Winters shook his head. "No thanks," he said. "All I want to do is get out of the army and go home."

"Get out? But you are an officer," the German replied.

"Only through an act of war," Winters said.

In fact, Winters was not thinking of home, at least not yet. Even as he spoke, he wrote to DeEtta, saying, "Now that this war is over in Europe I've been thinking what's the use of sitting around over here for six months or so as occupation troops. So my friend Captain Nixon and I plan to take off for the CBI or at least tomorrow we're going to ask for a transfer to some parachute unit in the CBI, or any good infantry unit for it's going to be no good sitting around here. You gotta die sometime so why not?"

★   ★   ★

The fighting had ended, but peace carried its own set of burdens. Winters was now inundated by prisoners, both German and American, and innumerable DPs.

"What a hell of a mess this place is over here," he wrote on May 11. "You have thousands and thousands of Allied prisoners of war, millions of displaced persons who are really slaves, brought here to work from other countries, and now thousands of German soldiers. They all want something. They need help, food, medical care, everything."

Mostly, they wanted to go home to their families, but after the scenes at Buchloe, and reports of much larger killing centers captured by the Americans, British and Russians, Winters knew that, for many, there'd be no home or family to go back to.

Winters' six-hundred-man battalion now had in its possession twenty-five thousand German POWs and, since May 10, he had been shipping them by truck or train to stockades established around Nuremberg and Munich. One shipment consisted of a trainload of SS soldiers: men, women and even captured horses. Because they were the main tool used in the mass killings at the death camps, SS personnel were dispatched to Nuremberg, once the site of Hitler's massive Nazi Party rallies, and now the place where a war crimes commission was being established. Winters placed this train of prisoners under the watchful eye of Lieutenant Staplefeld. The young officer dropped off his cargo as ordered and hitched a ride back to battalion on May 12.

Still aware that there were likely to be German holdouts in the hills, traveling alone or in small groups, Winters sent out patrols each day to cruise the secondary roads or mountain trails in jeeps. Their mission was to locate these stragglers and direct them to a POW compound at the Kaprun airport. To Winters' great relief, the Americans suffered no casualties, even though riding in open jeeps made them, in Winters' favorite expression, "sitting ducks."

Perhaps more troublesome for Winters than the German POWs, who at least had a command structure to function under, were the DPs; thousands and thousands of them, mostly Poles, Hungarians, Czechs and even Germans. Feeding them was beyond Winters' capability, so he sorted them by nationality and managed to line up transportation that got them on their way home, or to what was left of it. Within two weeks, most had departed.

Upon his arrival in Kaprun, Winters had established curfew hours as between 6 P.M. and 6 A.M. Everyone in the village meekly complied, or almost everyone. At 6 P.M. exactly on the first day of the curfew, one aging, bald-headed Austrian man in lederhosen, the traditional alpine attire, strode out into the middle of the empty square, put his hands on his hips and struck a defiant stance. He glared at Winters and his staff, who stood in a clump on a hotel balcony, defying the major to place him under arrest.

After a few minutes of this silent standoff, Lieutenant Richey turned to his commander.

"Shall I have him arrested, sir?"

Winters shook his head. "No, Ralph," he said. "Let him alone. Let's just watch for a while."

Soldiers glanced at him curiously and the townspeople, off the streets but still gathered in their doorways, watched quietly. Five more minutes passed. Then ten, and soon people in the doorway started to giggle at the man. The laughter increased as the tension broke and before long, thoroughly embarrassed, the old man dropped his arrogant stance, lowered his eyes and headed for his home.

Winters smiled at Richey. "If we have no trouble with the people after a week," he said. "Lift the curfew."

*   *   *

In the days between the capture of Berchtesgaden and the occupation of Kaprun, a number of notable events occurred involving the 506th PIR. Members of the regiment had captured Field Marshal Kesselring, and Winters' own company, Easy, had accepted the surrender of General Theodor Tolsdorf, commander of LXXXII Corps. Shortly after that, men of the 506th captured Julius Streicher, the publisher of the hate-filled, anti-Semitic, and often pornographic newspaper *Der Sturmer*. A blustery, bullet-headed man, whose anger burned from his dark eyes, Streicher was one of Hitler's most trusted supporters and ranked high on the Allies' Most Wanted list. He was dispatched to Nuremberg, where he would eventually climb the thirteen steps to the gallows.

On May 18 a different sort of celebrity visited Kaprun: Colonel Charles A. Lindbergh, Lucky Lindy, who had made the first trans-Atlantic solo flight from America to France in 1927, visited the 506th. Lindy, an air enthusiast, was touring the area to inspect German rocket- and jet-propulsion technology.

At a dinner in Lindy's honor, hosted by Sink and attended by his top officers, the aviator asked why Sink had set up his HQ where he did rather than the more attractive opposite side of the picturesque lake.

"Why, goddamn it, the houses we were supposed to occupy are full of German wounded and evacuated children," Sink told Lindy. "We ought to kick them all out, but we won't do it."

Lindbergh liked that answer, later calling Sink "a real fighter" yet "a man who had not been warped by the hatreds of war. I wish to God we had more like him."

That evening the group went for a ride on the alpine lake aboard a "liberated" excursion boat. Winters recalled the sunset over the lake as it reflected the soft colors of the mountain peaks.

With the coming of darkness, Lindy was guest at a party which featured plenty of Goering's wine. No one, apparently not even Lindy, thought that this might be uncomfortable for Lindbergh, who had been wined and dined by the Reichsmarshall in 1938 and had become so convinced that the Germans could never be defeated in combat that he became one of the principal anti-war speakers for the American First Committee. Now he was gaily sipping the wine of his vanquished former host.

"You know we captured Fatso Goering not too far from here," Sink said, feeling the effects of the alcohol. "His Frau is still living down the road a piece. We have some German soldiers guarding her and some American soldiers guarding the Germans." Sink laughed and uncorked an excellent bottle of Rhine wine. "Goering's private train is down there, too. You ought to see the way it's fixed up. Why, the highest-ranking men in the German army are all around here." He waved his glass, wine sloshing over the rim. "More generals than you ever saw before in one place. And we have them all."

*   *   *

The night of May 16 found Nixon, Welsh and Winters—the Three Musketeers Winters had begun to call them—seated on the balcony of his battalion HQ, shooting the breeze. The drink that pleasant evening, from which Winters abstained, was a 1928 vintage champagne from Goering's stock. Topics ranged from asinine, flashy military parades to snafu officers they had known, such as Dike and Sobel.

This latter, in fact, had just sent out a memo as regimental S4, ordering that all nonessential military items no longer needed for combat be collected and returned. This included the silk maps of Normandy the men had been issued prior to D-Day. Failure to return these, Sobel warned, carried a $75 fine. Winters had sewn his map into the belt lining of his GI pants and there it had remained through four campaigns, so it held strong sentimental value. Taking his cue from McAuliffe, Winters said "Nuts." He neither returned the map nor paid the fine. It was this type of mentality that reinforced his decision not to make the army a career.

Now the three friends sat together, in the shadow of the Alps, sipping fine champagne. Winters played with a Luger he had just gotten, one of several handguns given him by surrendering officers, and squeezed off occasional, random rounds.

The topic of transferring to the Pacific came up again. Winters and Nixon were determined to move on, but Welsh, Winters knew, had a little Irish lass waiting for him in England.

"So, since love has all this power to make people go crazy, he's had it— poor boy," Winters joked.

Winters had a woman on his mind, too. That same day he had written DeEtta, "What say you come over for a little vacation. If you like the mountains, you'd love this. You could have any cottage, castle or home you'd want in this valley or the three others in my sector of fifty miles by thirty miles. If you'd want to take an airplane ride, boat ride, automobile, jeep, tank, go horseback riding, mountain climbing, all you'd have to do is say the word and your every wish would be my desire.

He promised DeEtta "any number of servants" she wanted and that she'd never have to "lift a finger." "That's the spoils of war, the price of defeat for the loser and payment for the victor."

After a few days of relaxing in Austria, Winters knew it was time to get the men back in shape for war. Word had come down that the 101st was slated to be deployed to the Pacific, so Winters reestablished a regimen of calisthenics and athletic programs. Rifle ranges were laid out for the men to sharpen their marksmanship skills, and close order drill and reviews were reinstated.

Men watched newsreels of the fighting on Okinawa, which had been invaded on April 1, and where the bitter fighting against a foe determined to die had cost thousands of American lives. If that was the cost of Okinawa, every man thought, what will be the price of landing on Japan itself?

By contrast, the end of the war in Europe had been easy on the 506th. Only twenty-five men had been hit in April, including five dead, and in May two men had been killed and one wounded, all from 3rd Battalion and all on the road to Berchtesgaden.

As much as he could amid the preparations to return to war, Winters gave his men R and R time by having tennis courts and baseball fields set up. He also utilized a ski lodge on a mountainside behind and above Kaprun. The ski lift itself was not working, and men would have to climb the snowy slope, but the exercise would do them good and many took advantage of the opportunity, so Winters set up a program that rotated platoons every seventy-two hours. Any man who preferred not to ski could hunt mountain goats or simply go into the mountains to pluck edelweiss to stick in his cap, the traditional German symbol of a true alpine climber.

As the men relaxed and played sports in the warm May sunshine, often stripped to the waist, Winters could not help but notice that nearly all carried scars. Some had as many as three or four. And these men, he knew full well, were just those who had received minor wounds. These scars became a badge, creating among the men a mutual, unspoken bond of respect and a fierce, loyal pride towards the unit. Just recently Private First Class Joe Hogan, whom Winters would forever recall as trying unsuccessfully to break the tension by singing on the flight to Normandy, only to be drowned out by the plane's engines, had gotten into a fierce argument with a GI from another outfit.

"My Company E will lick your company in fifteen minutes," he snapped at the man. "And if you wait until the guys who are AWOL come back, we'll do it in five minutes."

Meanwhile, the wait in getting the 101st transferred to the Pacific Theatre was working on Winters' nerves. If he was going to go, he wanted to go now, and not be forced to sit around in Austria until the army was good and ready to send him. To hurry the process along, Winters put in for a transfer to the newly formed 13th Airborne Division, which had arrived in France too late to see action. He assumed his experience would be a godsend to the rookie paratroopers. On May 26, Winters was called in for a personal interview with the 13th's commander, Major General Elbridge G. Chapman.

Looking over Winters' personnel file, Chapman assured the young major that he'd love to have a man with his skills and leadership capabilities had the 101st not been earmarked for the Pacific itself. But since that was in the cards, he told Winters, the men he now led deserved to have him at their head. The transfer was denied.

"Stuck, damn it!" Winters wrote that evening.

The cessation of hostilities, shell fire and aerial attacks had not eased up the problem of getting adequate supplies to the men up front, especially when it came to food. The difficulty was not that America was not sending enough. Rather, it was how many hands it passed through before it got to the men on the line. They were at the end of a long supply pipeline that stretched to the coast of France. From the time the food landed on the docks at Cherbourg or Le Havre, greedy clerks and selfish officers along the route began picking out the best items. Some ended up in their own bellies, the rest found their way to the black market or onto the pantry shelves of a mistress.

Winters and his men were left with an overabundance of dried potatoes and tomatoes—not the stuff to put meat on their bones—and they began losing weight. To supplement their menu, more and more men took to hunting. Some mountain goats were shot, as well as elk, and even a few cows, but the shortage continued. Winters complained to Sink, but the colonel never chose to visit the battalion's chow lines and nothing changed, perhaps because Sink himself was powerless.

Winters tried his own hand at hunting. Hiring a local guide, the pair climbed high into the Alps, well above the altitude where trees and grass ceased to grow; higher even than some of the ragged clouds. Their quarry was a herd of mountain goats that the guide spotted on a ledge below and to the right of where the two men now stood. Edging forward cautiously on the snow, Winters raised his rifle, sighted one in, and prepared to fire. Just before he squeezed the trigger, his weight shifted and he slipped, tumbling over the ledge. Landing on a steep slope, Winters began sliding downward on his back, fighting frantically for a grip on the snowy surface. He finally managed to jam his rifle butt into the snow and ice and bring himself to a stop.

Badly shaken, Winters rolled over onto his belly. He was bruised and sore. A trickle of blood flowed from his mouth where his binoculars had slammed into his face and broken off a tooth at the gum line. Even worse, the mountain goat he had been trying to shoot was still on the same ledge, only now it was above him, looking down as if gloating. Angered, as if the goat was to blame for nearly succeeding in doing what the Germans had failed to do in eleven months of combat, Winters opened the bolt of the rifle, blew the snow from the muzzle, then closed the bolt. Taking aim, he squeezed off a round. The goat dropped, sliding down the same slope until stopped by a snow bank several yards beyond Winters.

The guide worked his way down to Winters' side.

"Are you hurt, Herr Major?" he asked.

Winters sat up but did not try to stand. His knees were shaking and his legs were weak from shock.

"I'm okay," he told the guide. "Tell you what. If you want that goat, you can have it. All I want are the horns."

As the guide retrieved the goat, Winters made a promise to God that he'd never go mountain climbing again. He kept the horns, but not the promise.

Now Winters needed a dentist, but he'd be damned if he'd go to Shifty Feiler, the man who'd butchered his teeth just before D-Day. He found a civilian dentist in the village who did such a good job that Winters made a deal. First, he found other accommodations for the GIs who were billeted in the dentist's home. The doctor had complained to Winters that the men were disrespectful of him and his property. In addition, Winters knew other men had dental needs and that most feared Feiler as much as he did, so he arranged for the civilian dentist to see twelve Americans per day as patients. Even Colonel Strayer, the regimental XO, dropped by the man's office.

* * *

On May 29 Winters was awarded a Bronze Star to go with his DSC, Purple Heart and other decorations. The medal was courtesy of General Taylor, who ordered that every man who fought in Normandy, Holland and Bastogne, or who fought in two of them but missed the third while recovering from wounds, receive the medal. Winters proudly added it to the array of ribbons already on his chest, but what pleased him even more was a package he got from Al Krochka. A fellow Pennsylvanian, Krochka had spent the better part of two years photographing the men of the 101st. With the war now over, the fact that he shot more with a camera than with a gun seemed to haunt him.

"I went through the entire war and never got a chance to pick up much in the way of souvenirs," he told Winters. "If you happen to have a nice Luger to spare, Dick, I'll trade you it for an entire set of Easy Company pictures, from Toccoa to Berchtesgaden."

"You've got a deal," Winters said to his friend. He did not own a camera and badly wanted the photographs. The trade was made.

Winters later discovered that Krochka had produced sets of prints for every company in the regiment and made a similar deal with their commanders, his main goal being to gather enough war mementoes to sell in Paris and finance for himself a rousing good furlough. Winters chuckled when he heard the truth. It was okay. The two remained lifelong friends.

Life at Kaprun was relaxing, but monotonous. Winters' day began at 7 A.M. with breakfast, then paperwork. Next he inspected the guards, the quarters and the kitchen. From lunchtime on, his time was his own. He wrote, joined in games of baseball or volleyball, exercised or went for a run. Evenings, at least as far as Nixon and Winters were concerned, were often spent together ribbing Welsh, who was eagerly anticipating his marriage to Kitty Grogan, an Irish woman he met while in England. Welsh's two friends tried to convince him that well before their marriage four months hence, some 4-F would sweep her off her feet.

"If some draft dodger doesn't nab her and you do happen to get married," Nixon said, "Dick and I will steal her and hide her away for the duration of your leave. Unless you hire us to protect her."

"And what might that cost me?" Welsh said, playing along.

"One quart of scotch," Nixon said.

"And a quart of ice cream," Winters added.

Welsh did not hire them.

Nixon was having his own female problems. Several months earlier, his wife in the States wrote that she wanted a divorce. Winters knew her somewhat. She had taken a house near Camp Toccoa while the 506th was in training, and Nixon had often invited Winters to the house for meals or conversation. Now she was leaving and taking everything, including Nixon's dog, which possibly angered him more than her departure.

In May, Winters convinced Nixon to write to his wife for the first time since the previous November. Nixon protested at first, claiming he had nothing to say to her, only to his dog, but he relented. Possibly it was Winters talking him into it, or possibly it was the effect of the vodka, vermouth and rum he and Welsh were mixing.

As Nixon sat down to write, Winters jotted to DeEtta that Nixon was "quite a guy."

"I've known him for three years, and lived and slept beside him for two," he wrote. "This guy loves one thing at this stage of his life: a bottle of spirits or a fight. He's OK in a fight, but Jesus, outside of that he's absolutely the most undependable man you'd ever want to meet."

Winters noted that during their time overseas, Nixon had dated only one Englishwoman. She was "anything but beautiful" Winters said, but she was "a good listener and companion." He expected Nixon to remain in England after the war.

Sitting alone in his headquarters in Kaprun on the evening of June 5, the night before the anniversary of D-Day, Winters grew introspective.

"Feeling awfully restless and uneasy this evening as my thoughts go back to what I was doing exactly one year ago this minute," he wrote. "I was putting black, yellow, green and brown face paint on my face, ears, neck and hands, checking my equipment and answering a stream of questions. Oh, what a night."

His feelings were shared by many. Officers and men alike held parties that night, and liquor and memories flowed freely. Even Colonel Sink, a liberal imbiber of spirits himself, got into the festivities with a bash for his officers at his HQ, the Hotel Zell. Winters dropped by and was probably the only man to leave sober.

★   ★   ★

Winters had yet to tell his mother back in Lancaster that he planned to go to the Pacific, but she must've sensed his feeling. In mid-June she urged him not to go fight the Japanese. "You've done your part," she wrote. "Be smart and come home."

But Winters could not justify going back home while others were still fighting. On June 19 he wrote, "I feel that God has been good enough to let me get through this war. As a result I am combat wise and in a position to do some good to help a lot of men. I know I can do the job, better than or as well as any of the rest. How can I sit back and watch others take men out and get them killed because they don't know; they don't have *it?* Maybe I'll get hurt or killed for my trouble, but so what if I can make it possible for many others to go home. Their mothers want them too, the same as mine. So what else can I do and still hold my own self respect as an officer and a man?"

He next informed DeEtta that his immediate plans did not include marriage.

"This isn't what you want to hear or have me write. Actually, I should write all about love and how sweet you are and all that stuff. I could if I wanted to. I know all those words from the movies and magazines. But that wouldn't be right. I don't feel that way and I don't want you to think that way. What I want is for you to get married to some good guy who comes along. There are always a couple around. You need a husband and a family to be really happy.

"I like and enjoy seeing you write 'Love, De' and all that stuff, but I don't want you to actually feel that way because it's just going to end up with you getting hurt."

Winters wrote that, so long as he was in the army, he wanted no close ties.

"As a soldier, I don't want any more people than possible to even know me. It's no good. If a soldier lives, OK. He gets out of the army and forget it. If he doesn't live, OK. There are just that many fewer people who feel the toll of war."

In Germany, the toll of war continued to be felt even though bullets had ceased to fly. Losses in Winters' battalion included Easy Company's Sergeant Darrell "Shifty" Powers, a Toccoa man, who was severely injured when a truck he was riding in on the first leg of his trip home to the U.S. collided with another truck. One man was killed. Shortly after that Private John A. Janovec, another E Company man, was killed when he fell from a moving vehicle, fracturing his skull, and First Lieutenant Andrew E. Tuck III of Fox Company died in an accident on July 7, shortly after posing for a group photo with Winters and other battalion officers, including Strayer, who stepped into the picture.

The most senseless loss, though, occurred when Sergeant Charles E. Grant was shot by a drunken GI. Grant had been in a jeep with two privates, moving between roadblocks, when they stumbled across the man, waving a pistol. He had shot and killed two Germans. Two British soldiers, a major and a sergeant, had also been stopped by the gun-wielding man. In the melee that followed, both the British soldiers were killed and Grant had a bullet in his brain. The GI fled. An American doctor proclaimed Grant dead, but Captain Speirs, unwilling to quit, raced the injured man to another town and found a German surgeon, a specialist, who saved Grant's life.

Winters, who was writing to DeEtta on that night of June 28, was stunned by the news, although he made no mention of it to her. Grant was one of the company's most competent NCOs, not to mention a longtime friend and one of the sergeants involved in the Sobel Mutiny. Winters sent out orders to find the man who was responsible but Speirs had already done that. The man was apprehended and beaten bloody by Grant's buddies, several of whom threatened to kill him, before being turned over to the MPs. Oddly, Winters and the others heard nothing about the soldier's fate once handed over to military justice.

"I would assume he was court-martialed," Winters said later when asked about it. "But I wasn't told anything. That's the way the army is."

Which may be why so many men now wanted out. But getting out depended on the number of points one had earned, and the army was stingy with handing them out. Under the Advanced Service Rating Score established by the army, men received one point for each month of service between September 16, 1940 and May 12, 1945. They also got one point for each month spent overseas during the same time period. Five points were awarded for every decoration, including the Purple Heart, and five points were awarded for each small bronze campaign star a man could pin on his theater ribbon. Lastly, men were given twelve points for each child back home under the age of eighteen, with a limit of up to three children, or thirty-six points. A man needed a total of eighty-five points to qualify for a trip home.

Under those guidelines, however, a GI who had been in the service for three years and had spent two years overseas in combat would have only sixty points. If he had a Purple Heart, Silver Star or some other decoration and one child back home, his total would be seventy-seven points, eight short of what he needed.

Despite all the combat they had seen and the hardships they had suffered, very few men in the 101st had acquired enough points to qualify. And even if one did have the needed points, a boat ride home still wasn't guaranteed. By May 8, Winters had an even 100 points, more than any other officer in the regiment, but he remained in Germany and fully expected to be sent to fight in the Pacific.

But some men did get home. By late June two entire parachute divisions, the veteran 82nd and the 17th, had been dismantled as men were sent home or, in the case of the 17th Airborne, sent to replace men in other units who had been shipped home. One regiment of the 101st had also been dissolved. This put many ranking officers, mostly colonels and lieutenant colonels, out of jobs. Some of those officers were assigned to Sink who, on June 28, assigned a lieutenant colonel from the 502nd Regiment to command 2nd Battalion. This bumped Winters, with less seniority, back down to XO.

In a letter home Winters called the demotion "a good sock on the chin," but he knew about the other units being dismembered and added "it had to come."

Despite his promise to God following the mountain goat incident, Winters continued to visit the ski lodge, often skiing with lieutenants Peacock and Foley. He also wandered alone through the lush woods. The stunning beauty struck a religious chord in the young officer.

"While in the mountains I found a church of my own," he wrote. "The aisle is two mountain ranges down which you can see for 10 miles at least. At the end there's just a series of mountain peaks. A storm came up and the dark clouds covered everything but the far end, where the sun shone through on those many peaks. The color was all shades of rose, a light, soft rose, nothing hard or bright, but just rays of light coming through the clouds. They were the most beautiful stained glass windows I have ever seen or hope to see. What a wonderful place to pray. What a magnificent church."

By July Winters was becoming more and more aware that the end was coming for the 506th Regiment, and Easy Company in particular. Winters looked around at the familiar faces of the men. Many he had known for close to three years. He remembered their young, eager faces in that first parade formation back at Toccoa; their youth, their vitality and their optimism for the future. He recalled them loaded down with jump gear as they boarded the planes for Normandy, each man excited, yet lost in thought and determined not to let his buddies down. He recalled the mud and misery of Holland, and the snow and ice and lack of hot food in Bastogne, with tree bursts thrown in for good measure. He thought of men like Joe Toye, Bill Guarnere, Ed Tipper, Leo Boyle and the many others who had been severely wounded and were back home in the States or still recovering in military hospitals, bearing the scars of war. He thought of Buck Compton who, even though still in Germany, and who sometimes dropped in to visit his comrades, bore his own emotional scars. And Winters thought of men like Thomas Meehan, George Lavenson, Punchy Diel, Bill Dukeman, Skip Muck, Alex Penkala, Don Hoobler, Bob Van Klinken and the forty-four others of Easy Company, plus the thirty-seven men of Fox Company and the thirty-eight men in Dog, all of whom would never enjoy the peace they had fought for.

Some men remained, however. In early July Welsh, whose transfer out was already in the works, decided to stay on despite his eighty-five points.

Nixon was still there, too, and happier than he had been in a while. On July 2 Winters wrote that his friend had just returned from a furlough to England "looking better than I've seen him for 6 months at least."

"His eyes are all sparkle and he's not near as bitter," Winters wrote. "I think, in fact I know, he's going to ask or tell his wife to get a divorce and jump in a lake, and marry his ETO wife. For Nix and all concerned, it's the best. This skinny English girl seems to have what it takes to make him happy, namely honesty and sincere love for him. That's something his present wife never understood. She was just interested in the Nixon millions and Nix, as a result, lost all faith in women."

Winters' sister, Ann, was eagerly anticipating her brother's return and badgered him to take her to New York City. Winters had taken Ann, then twelve, to the city before he shipped overseas, treating her to Olsen and Johnson's show, *Sons of Fun.* He recalled that she had a great time, laughing until she cried. Next morning she wanted to do more and Winters, trying to grab a few extra minutes of sleep, slipped her $5 and told her to go have breakfast in the hotel dining room.

"It was a pretty big thrill for a twelve-year-old pig-tailed kid," he recalled.

*   *   *

Even though Winters had already told DeEtta that marriage was not in his immediate future, the two continued to discuss the topic frequently. In a long letter on July 9, Winters asked her what love was.

"Everybody talks about it, like you would a beautiful church or a sunset or a painting" he wrote. "It seems to be something holy. In fact, when somebody asks me 'haven't you *ever* been in love?' and I answer 'I don't think so,' I feel just like you do when these hard working Christians stop you on the street and want to know if you're 'saved' or 'ready to meet your maker.'

"Hell, I don't know! I go to church. I read the Bible, pray and do what I think is right, but I've never had any assurance that I was going to Heaven and I am not at all sure if I am saved. It's the same with love. I don't know. Do you feel different, act different? What is it?"

Back home in Lancaster, meanwhile, Winters' parents fretted over their son going off to the Pacific. The elder Winters wrote that it appeared as if he and the family would have to "continue to sit tight and wait under the same old tension" and do their best to be "parentroopers to a paratrooper."

Richard Winters had expected that his son would be promoted to lieutenant colonel within ten days of his elevation to major and being made battalion commander back in March, and voiced disappointment that it never occurred. He also predicted his son would be gone another six months at least, and that he would likely "make a career of soldiering."

*   *   *

If Winters had been contemplating the military as a career, the army's next move would have gone a long way toward dissuading him.

On July 30 the 506th, duffel bags packed, left Germany aboard a convoy of trucks. This trip, their last as a regiment, ended at Joigny, an ancient French village with narrow, cobblestoned streets located eighty miles southeast of Paris. Camp conditions were deplorable to the point that Winters considered it little better than one of the concentration camps he had helped liberate three months earlier. It was crowded, dirty and its previous occupants, the 13th Airborne, had built makeshift latrines by the simple method of digging slit trenches. By the time Winters' men arrived, space for new latrines was nonexistent, so he ordered that lumber be acquired, by theft if necessary, to be used to construct honey-bucket latrines, where refuse goes into drums that are emptied regularly by whatever poor souls drew honey-bucket detail that day.

Bathing was relegated to two faucets located one hundred yards from the men's quarters.

"Hell," Winters complained to Nixon. "The men live like pigs. And nobody seems to give a damn."

Winters ordered the construction of washstands with hot water, where the men could shave and bathe under a roof and out of the weather. He wondered how the 13th Airborne had withstood it for seven months.

Winters had managed to scrounge up an acceptable billet for himself, clean and modern with, amazingly, a private bath.

During his stay in Joigny, Winters seldom visited the town, preferring to spend his time running and playing football or baseball.

The news that the Japanese had surrendered reached the GIs on August 15 and was greeted with a collective sigh of relief by the men of the 101st. Parties that night were even more enthusiastic than on VE-Day because now the troopers knew they were heading for home, and not the hostile shores of Japan.

News of the end of the war left Winters far less excited than the men around him. He had seen it coming, he said, and now just wanted to get the hell out of the army.

"I can see in the wind just how this army's going to be, or at least close enough so that I can appreciate the fact that I don't wish to be associated with it in any way," he wrote. Officers, he said, were allowing their men to grow lazy, mentally and physically.

With the war now definitely over, Nixon reiterated his job offer.

"You'd be personnel manager," Nixon told him. "We don't have anyone doing that job. It'd be a new position you'd be creating. And you'll make the same salary you're making now, so there'd be no pay cut."

Winters again agreed to think about it, although he didn't put much stock in the offer, keenly aware by experience of Nixon's personal unreliability.

In keeping with the gaiety of VJ-Day, Winters managed a seven-day furlough, which he finagled into fourteen days, for both himself and Nixon, and they traveled to England. While Nixon went off to visit the woman who would soon become his second wife, Winters headed for Aldbourne. The village seemed at peace again. The tanks, trucks, jeeps and soldiers were gone, allowing the town to resume its pastoral tranquility. But to Winters, who had not known it before it had become a military base, it seemed desolate.

As he walked along the familiar streets he was recognized. Townspeople shook his hand, patted his back and welcomed him. Reaching the Barnes' door, he stopped, recalling the last time he had passed through it on his way to Holland. He entered. Mrs. Barnes greeted him.

"Richard," she said, and embraced him. She was pleased beyond words to have him back. As he stood there with her, he realized how empty the house was. Francis Barnes was dead and Elaine Stevens had returned to her family in London. As he had predicted, Mrs. Barnes kept his old room ready for his return, and he eagerly took up residence. The next day he and Mother Barnes carried fresh flowers to the cemetery, one bouquet for Mr. Barnes and one for the son the war had taken.

Sunday at the Barnes' church was Children's Sunday, a ceremony he had missed a year earlier, but wanted to attend since many of his young friends would be taking part in the program.

Winters spent ten of his fourteen days in Aldbourne, catching up on his reading and his sleeping, and going for long walks and runs, not unlike two years earlier. Taking some of his accumulated pay, Winters bought some new gardening implements. He weeded and hoed Mother Barnes' backyard garden.

On the eleventh day of the furlough, he departed for London, leaving behind Aldbourne and his English mom. It would be the last time the two would meet, although he remained in contact with her until her death in the 1970s.

Arriving in a London where buzz bombs were no longer singing overhead, Winters saw several shows, viewing them with a critical eye. He took in productions of *Happy and Glorious* and *The Lady From Edinburgh*, both of which he deemed "damn good." He also saw *Sweeter and Lower* ("fair"), *Johnny Frenchman* ("fair") and *A Bell for Adano* ("poor, damned poor"). The young officer stopped by a club and caught a musical act featuring entertainer Eddie Bracken ("poor plus").

Winters had picked up one British affectation while on leave. He had taken to carrying a swagger stick. He admitted some might call him prissy, but if they did, he said he'd readily knock their blocks off.

Back in camp after his leave, Winters was strolling down a deserted company street one afternoon when a solitary figure approached from the other direction. Winters instantly recognized the familiar shape of Captain Herbert Sobel. The former commander of Easy Company and his former XO had not had any direct contact since shortly after the court-martial incident seventeen months earlier. Now they were alone, about to confront each other on an empty company street.

Sobel pretended he hadn't seen Winters, or at least did not recognize him, both of which were impossible. He brushed past. Winters stopped and turned.

"Captain Sobel," he snapped.

Sobel stopped and turned to face Winters.

"We recognize and honor the rank," Winters said.

Sobel came to attention. "Yes, sir," he said, and saluted.

Winters returned a crisp salute. Sobel dropped his hand, spun on his heel and tromped off. Winters watched him go with an air of satisfaction. Any debt that man had owed him for the hard times of the past was now repaid in full.

* * *

The end of the war brought rapid changes to the 506th. On August 11 Colonel Sink was promoted to brigadier general and made assistant division commander. The regiment was handed over to Sink's wartime XO, Lieutenant Colonel Charles Chase.

Eleven days later General Taylor left the 101st for good, becoming the superintendent of West Point Military Academy. Sink would soon follow him there.

Meanwhile Winters was still stuck in France, and for him things were getting worse rather than better. In early September Nixon was rotated home, which Winters wrote was "just dandy." It left him, he said, about as lonesome as a lovesick swab who married a Wave on an eight-hour pass.

Even worse than Nixon's shipping out was the fact that Chase had declared Winters as essential, all but guaranteeing he'd be in Europe until the 101st was phased out. For Winters, who now had in excess of a hundred points, the decision was infuriating.

"Do you smell something burning?" he wrote DeEtta. "Don't worry. It's just me."

His anger did not prevent him from making one last parachute jump on September 20, a demonstration jump and his first since Holland, a year plus three days earlier. It was strictly voluntary and earned each man a cash bonus of $100.

A day before the jump, Winters heard that a boatload of high-point men from the 82nd and 101st Airborne divisions, including himself, would set sail for the States on December 2, just over two months in the future.

He wrote DeEtta, "Now that I've got the news I can hardly believe it, that I've been lucky enough to live through this whole damn mess and get a round trip ticket home. Home! My gosh, will my folks even know me? Will I know them? My sister? Chow? Water, hot water? Milk? I really haven't had any in over two years, not real milk with calcium in it."

Impatient to get home, a week later Winters heard even more exciting news. All eighty-five-point men, and a certain number of high-point officers, would be leaving for the States in October. He stormed into Colonel Chase's office to plead his case.

"I've watched you grow and develop ever since Toccoa, Dick," Colonel Chase said after Winters' fifteen-minute diatribe. "You've been a fine officer and an excellent leader. And I know I speak for Colonel Sink, there, too. You've done your service to the regiment, and I'll do good by you."

Orders were cut. Winters, now with 108 points, would soon leave the 101st forever and be transferred to the 75th Infantry Division, which was being used to funnel high-point men home. Winters was more than ready. With the exception of Captain Speirs, who planned to make the army a career, and Harry Welsh, almost all his friends had departed. Easy Company was all but gone; everything was coming to an end. Saturday night, Winters' last week-end with the 506th, he attended two farewell parties, one of which included a clambake.

Chase did Winters another favor. Throughout the last months of the war, Winters had been promoted to battalion XO, battalion commander and major, all of which circumvented the army's seniority policy. With an eye to possible future controversy or questions regarding Winters' service, Chase spelled it all out in writing.

"This will certify that Major Richard D. Winters served during combat as a battalion executive officer with the 506th Parachute Infantry from 10 October 1944 until 20 February 1945 while holding the rank of captain. Throughout this time there were captains assigned to the regiment who were senior in rank to Major Winters.

"This will further certify that Major Richard D. Winters served during combat as a battalion commander with the 506th Parachute Infantry from 10 March 1945 to 9 May 1945 while holding the rank of major. During part of this period from 16 April to 9 May 1945 there was a major assigned to this regiment who was senior to Major Winters."

With home staring him in the face, Winters gave more thought to Nixon's job offer. His father opposed the idea. The family had been without him for al-most three years, and once he was home, they wanted him to stay there and find work in Lancaster. Winters knew he'd be comfortable living at home, but worried it might tie him down. He refused to be a single man stuck in one place "like a married man with six kids and an $18 a week job."

October 7 still found Winters in France. The date of the boat's sailing had been pushed back to October 11, and Winters said if another week still found him in Joigny, he'd scream. Not only was he upset about the delay, but he was becoming increasingly irritated with the new officers and soldiers arriving to take up occupation duty. Winters considered them to be poor examples of soldiers in both training and discipline, and he thanked God the fighting was over and he would not have to lead them into combat.

Lieutenant Richey, one of Winters' favorite aides, brought some nurses to camp from Paris and introduced them to Winters. Out of practice in dealing with young American women, even ones like these whom he considered unattractive, Winters recalled that he stammered like a "big, overgrown kid of twelve." Still, he had an enjoyable evening.

A day or two later Winters and Welsh boarded a train bound for Camp Pittsburgh in southern France, last stop before the boat home. Winters called the ride a three-ringed circus. Military officials had their hands full keeping "1,150 GI monkeys" from riding on top of the cars where trees and low bridges were a threat, hopping off while the train slowly passed through towns to either kiss women or to relieve themselves, and then run after it again to be pulled into another car by their buddies.

Arriving at Camp Pittsburgh, the homeward-bound men sat for another two weeks, during which time Winters was so eager to leave he felt like tearing the camp apart. With 108 points, he told DeEtta, he felt as rare as a man in a Wave's barracks.

Winters was made XO of the 2nd Battalion, 290th Infantry Regiment of the 75th Division, noting that it was almost the exact same job he had a year ago with the 101st. Camp Pittsburgh was boring and the army began issuing three-day passes. This pissed Winters off.

"I came here to go home, not to go on a three-day pass," he complained to Welsh.

One night Welsh, getting drunk to forget how bored he was, nearly got into a scrap with another GI. Winters prevented any injury by getting between the two men, and smoothing things over by telling the GI that Welsh was "a bit off" thanks to too many mortar and artillery shells.

The end soon came. On November 1, Winters led the 2nd Battalion aboard the Liberty ship *Wooster Victory* in the harbor at Marseilles. Winters had commanded the battalion for about a week after its CO was transferred out because he lacked enough points to make the trip home. On the early morning of November 4, the ship weighed anchor and slipped out of the harbor. Rounding the coast of Spain, it cleared the Straits of Gibraltar and headed out into the Atlantic Ocean.

Major Richard D. Winters, late of the 101st Airborne, was heading home.

CHAPTER 13

"I'll Bet You Thought I Was Gonna Shoot You."

November 25, 1945–December 31, 1951

The train carrying Major Richard D. Winters home from the war arrived at Fort Indiantown Gap on the evening of November 25, 1945, just five days before the 101st Airborne Division was declared inactive. The sprawling training center for the "Bloody Buckets" of the 28th Division, so nicknamed because of the red keystone emblem on their sleeves, was alive with activity. While some men packed their duffels to ship overseas for occupation duty, others like Winters were unpacking theirs in preparation to resume their civilian lives. There were even a few German POWs left in camp, holdovers from the days in the not-too-recent past when Indiantown Gap included a prison camp for captured enemy soldiers. Some of the former POWs pleaded to stay in America after the war, knowing their future in the U.S. would be brighter than in the shattered remains of the Fatherland, but the appeals were denied. Now they awaited transportation back home to whatever might await them there. Some would eventually find their way back.

Separation papers in hand, Winters called his home. His mother answered.

"It's me," he said.

"Son," Edith Winters said. "Thank God. Where are you?"

"Indiantown Gap," he told her. "I'll be home as soon as I can get a ride to Lancaster."

"Your father and I will leave now," she said.

While he waited for his parents to make the drive from Lancaster, less than thirty miles to the south, their home-from-the-war son spent his time sprucing up for them. He vigorously polished his brass and donned his crispest Class A uniform, resplendent with his array of ribbons above his left breast pocket and the gleaming golden oak leaves of a major on his lapels.

"How far I've come in three years," he thought as he primped himself in the mirror.

The trip that brought Winters home had been a far cry from the voyage to England aboard the S.S. *Samaria* twenty-six months earlier. On that trip, he and his comrades were sailing off to adventures and perils as yet unknown. As they glided by the Statue of Liberty and watched it recede in the ship's wake, each man stood in silent reflection, eager for the future, yet fearful. During the cruise, the men tried to keep fit as best they could in the cramped conditions of the ship, and while they gambled for relaxation, military discipline was maintained.

That was not the case aboard the *Wooster Victory*. Winters, as the ranking officer on the ship, was in command, but he was not in command of an army. Instead he was trying to control a boatload of men to whom the regimen of military life became less and less important with each mile the ship covered across the broad expanse of ocean. They gambled, of course, but there was fighting, drunkenness, thievery and other breakdowns in discipline as the soon-to-be civilians took on a "fuck you" attitude toward anything military.

"They were all getting out of the army, getting ready to be discharged," he later remembered. "That made it very difficult to keep any kind of discipline and to keep those men under control."

Winters was never so glad to see the Statue of Liberty as he was on November 20, 1945, the day the *Wooster Victory* slipped past her into New York harbor. He stood and watched Lady Liberty pass the port side of the ship and heaved a sigh. Damn, but he loved the sight of that woman, all 450,000 pounds of her.

★   ★   ★

His mother was as good as her word and, within the hour, Winters saw the family Oldsmobile arrive at the Lebanon County military base. It was the first time Winters had seen his parents in almost two years, and he was first struck by how gray his mother's once-lush, brown hair had grown during his absence.

"Mother," he said. "You're completely gray. Are you all right?"

She melted into his arms and cried as he hugged her. He had tears as well. His father, on the other hand, showed no outward emotion, but stood quietly by.

One of his first orders of business was to write to DeEtta, trying to arrange a time and place "and atmosphere so that I can introduce this stranger, Mr. Winters."

"Arrived home Saturday night as Mr. R.D.W.," he wrote on November 26.

"Never had a chance to read your letters dated from 4 Oct. to 17 Oct. waiting for me, with neighbors and relatives keeping me occupied all day."

He mused on the idea of hoping to see her in person while still in her Wave uniform, and said a photo she had sent him in her uniform was "pin-up grade triple A."

With civilian fashions just starting to become more readily available, Winters continued to live in his military uniform, even donning his full dress regalia, complete with ribbons, for a final formal color portrait at the photo studio inside the ornate Watt & Shand department store in downtown Lancaster.

"Things seem to be very nice back here," he wrote. "So clean. Lots of food, heat. Now that's something, heat. Everyplace you go, it's warm. All homes and rooms are heated. I'd almost forgotten how nice it is to be warm and comfortable in the wintertime." He also made a vow to buy up all "the darn chocolate I can eat for a couple of weeks. This diet of milk, ice cream and eggs is just wonderful."

But not everything was as wonderful as he painted it. As the days dragged on, Winters found it harder and harder to blend back into a way of life that did not carry with it the possibility of violent death.

One morning while hiking through the Woodland Hills section of Lancaster, which Winters referred to as the "well-to-do part of town," a young boy walking passed him dragged a stick across a picket fence. The resulting *Brraaaappp* sent Winters diving for the ground.

"I picked myself up out of the gutter," he later recalled. "There was no thought, it was all reaction. You are tight. You're still fighting the goddamn war, and that was a machine gun."

Winters also found himself withdrawing from men his age who had stayed home while he and his comrades were fighting in the mud and snow of Europe.

"I was bitter," he said. "I'd lost my respect for the men who did not go into the service. I didn't really want them as a friend."

He missed the day-to-day contact with the friends he had made in the army, the people he cared most about right now, and found he had considerably more trouble sleeping at home in his own bed than he ever did in the army.

"I was exhausted mentally," he said years later. "Absolutely exhausted."

In the waning weeks of 1945, Winters had no job and no direction for his life. His family understood this, and gave him space to adjust, never pushing their son in any direction, but letting time take its course. One of the hardest adjustments for the twenty-seven-year-old veteran was that of no longer being in charge, of no longer being a person who commanded obedience and who was burdened with responsibility.

"You expected attention and you expected respect, and now of course, you're not going to get it," he recalled. "You're a civilian."

Though he sorely missed that environment, Winters gave no thought to staying in the army past January 22, the date his discharge would officially take effect.

"I just wanted out," he said.

Home from the war, Winters was in no hurry to get a job. He had saved $10,000 during his time in the army, much of which he had sent home. Of his savings, about $7,000 was used to pay off the family home on West End Avenue. The remaining $3,000 was his to live on while he tried to readjust.

One attempt to help the young man reaccustom himself to life was an invitation from a family friend to go deer hunting, a time-honored Pennsylvania tradition. He agreed, though not without prodding from his father, who thought it might be a good first step back to normalcy for his son. On November 30 the hunting party set off for the mountains of northern Pennsylvania.

"I didn't want to go deer hunting but thought, 'You gotta get with it, it's tradition in Pennsylvania,'" Winters said, recalling the incident years later.

He had never hunted during civilian life, having neither the interest nor the time, since he went straight from high school into college and then into the army. And, aside from the mountain goat incident at Kaprun, and its painful consequence, he had not hunted while in the army. It gave him no pleasure. He hoped this hunting trip might prove fun. It didn't. While the men with him enjoyed themselves, Winters was unhappy the entire week. It proved especially difficult when he was actually confronted with several white-tailed deer while out in the woods.

"The fellow who was in charge of planning the hunt posted me along a narrow trail," Winters recalled. "I waited and suddenly about four deer came bounding down the mountainside and stopped barely twenty feet from me. But I couldn't shoot. I couldn't even think about lifting that rifle. I was done. I did not want any more killing."

Dick Winters the civilian was evolving from Major Dick Winters the soldier, who had evolved from Dick Winters the college graduate. The student had been a boy, with a boy's eagerness for life and dreams of the future. The soldier was a decisive, confident leader who had taken men into battle under almost unendurable hardships, seen his friends killed and maimed, and who had killed at least seven of the enemy. The civilian was now trying to reclaim a life he no longer recognized. War had changed him, and the sensitive, friendly boy who had marched off to Camp Croft had returned an embittered man who began divorcing himself from his past. This included his best friend for the past three years.

In a December 15 Christmas card to DeEtta, who by now knew she and Winters would never be anything more than friends, the ex-soldier wrote that he felt like "a heel, a dishrag."

"Thanks and good-byes and all the other chit chat is just so much extra wasted time and effort when you know the party of the second part is in harmony with you on all feelings, be what they may.

"Dad has this record of 'People Will Say We're In Love.' Reminds me of a couple I once knew, so there's that tricky smile on my lips and a wee bit of a twinkle in my eye as I listen."

Winters and DeEtta allowed themselves one more chance to relive their wartime friendship. As DeEtta was being discharged from the Navy, Winters borrowed the family Oldsmobile and drove to Washington, D.C. There Winters escorted DeEtta and a girlfriend around the city, seeing all the sights of the capital. At night, DeEtta and her friend returned to their room at the YWCA and Winters retired to the YMCA. After three days, it was time to leave. There would be no more contact between them until an unexpected phone call fifty years later.

"She was going back to Asheville, and I was looking for a job, and that's about the way it ended," Winters said of DeEtta in 2003. "Her friendship meant so much to me. I can't help at times but wonder, maybe I should've married her because she was a good, close friend. But I had no job. I didn't know what I was going to do, or what I wanted to do. It was a difficult time. If I'd had a job and was making a living on my own, established, it could very well have been a whole lot different. At night when I say my prayers, she's one of the people I remember."

★   ★   ★

Winters was not only separating from DeEtta, but people in general. When friends came to visit, he refused to see them. This included the wife of fellow F&M graduate Rick Burgess, the army friend Winters loaned $125 while at Camp Croft so he could get married. The new Mrs. Burgess stopped at the house to welcome him home, but he would not go downstairs to greet her.

"Naturally I hurt her feelings, but I didn't want to see her," he said. "I didn't want to see anybody."

He took in some movies and did what he pleased. His family did not push him, giving him space to reaccustom himself to postwar life. Winters had also done no active job hunting, but offers came to him. At the hunting camp, one of the deer hunters asked if he had found a job yet. Winters told him he hadn't. A few days later the man knocked on Winters' door and offered him a job as a truck driver. He turned it down.

Days later the owner of New Holland Supply Company, a Mennonite man who knew Winters' grandfather Serenus, called on the house. The company manufactured hay balers for area farmers. Winters was offered a job as assistant personnel manager, although he would first have to put in time on the factory floor so he could learn about the various jobs. Winters said he'd think about it.

But the offer from Nixon was still in Winters' mind. At about the same time the man from New Holland Supply made his offer, Nixon again called his army buddy.

"Job's still open, Dick," he said. "Let's get together and talk about it."

Winters liked the idea of seeing Nixon again, and agreed.

"I'm in New York right now," he told Winters. "My mother's here."

"I thought she lived in San Francisco," Winters said. He knew Nixon's parents were divorced and that the elder Nixon, Stanhope, was married to a woman whom everyone simply called "the blonde."

"She does," Nixon said. "But she's in the hospital here. I'm staying at the Yale Club. Grab a train and I'll meet you at Pennsylvania Station."

Winters agreed. For the young man, going on his first real job interview was a big deal. Still having no civilian clothes suitable for the occasion, Winters got out his dress uniform and had it pressed. He polished the brass buttons and shined his jump boots.

Nixon met Winters at the station. The first thing he noticed was that his friend was in full uniform. "Thought you were eager to be a civilian?" he asked.

"I'm working on it," Winters replied. "Just give me time."

Nixon flagged a cab that took them to the posh, twenty-story Yale Club at Vanderbilt Avenue and Forty-Fourth Street, and began showing his former commander off to his alumni friends. The next stop was the hospital where Nixon's mother was a patient.

"She was very, very nice and pleasant," he recalled. "I can remember her very definitely trying to say nice things, the right things, like 'I've heard a lot of good stories about you' and so forth."

When the sun went down the two wartime comrades went out on the town, or rather, Nixon took Winters out on the town. Not surprisingly, Nixon dragged his friend to nightclubs and bars, where the young man from Lancaster would sit, fidgeting in his chair, while Nixon downed drink after drink.

"I was not used to that kind of thing at all, it was all new to me and I was very uncomfortable," Winters recalled. "But there I sat all prim and proper."

Ironically, although it was Nixon who was getting drunk, it was Winters who nearly got into a barroom brawl. While the two were sitting at a table at one of Nixon's nightspots, a man who had had almost as much to drink as Nixon staggered up to the pair. He spotted Winters' uniform, the brass buttons and golden oak leaves gleaming in the light.

"Well, well," he said in an alcohol-laced voice. "Lookee here. We got a soldier. And an officer to boot. What are you doin' here, General?"

Winters ignored him.

"Hey, General, are you deaf?" he prodded.

"Blow," Nixon told the man.

"I ain't talking to you, fella, I'm talkin' to this nice, neat-looking soldier boy."

Winters saw anger flash in Nixon's eyes, and his own slow fuse was starting to burn.

"Look at that fruit salad," the man said, noting Winters' array of ribbons. "You must be a hero, General. Are you a hero?" Winters did not respond. "Are you too good to talk to me? You're not a hero. You're a sucker."

Winters had just about enough of this drunken fool when a waiter, knowing trouble when he saw it, hustled over and snatched the man by his upper arm.

"Why don't you find a nice corner somewhere else to drink?" he said and shouldered the man to another part of the room.

"I could barely hold myself in," Winters said later. "I was getting ready to kill that son of a bitch."

A cab delivered the pair back to the Yale Club. Nixon handed the man a fifty dollar bill to pay the fare and asked for change. The hack driver took a look at Ulysses Grant's picture, then at his drunken passenger, and hit the accelerator.

"Hey!" Winters yelled as the cab disappeared into traffic. "He just . . ."

Nixon waved him off. "What the hell, don't worry about it," he said.

The next day Winters met Nixon's father, Stanhope. One look at the two and Winters realized that the acorn did not fall far from the tree. Stanhope Nixon was a hard drinking womanizer who did not hesitate to speak his mind. He was also a stern businessman and he laid the job offer on the table for Winters' consideration. Winters still had the New Holland job pending and had to decide. The main drawback to that job, though, was the fact that he would have to start work at 6:30 or 7 A.M. and work until late into the evening. And while he did not mind getting up early, the prospect of being cooped up in a factory was hard to accept for a man who had spent the last three years living in nature.

"My God, I'll never see the sun," he thought.

He accepted Nixon's offer.

In January 1946, against his parents' wishes, Winters left the family home in Lancaster and moved to an apartment in New Brunswick, New Jersey.

★   ★   ★

Nixon, New Jersey, does not appear on any maps. A small postal district, it is located along, and south of, Woodbridge Avenue between Bonhamtown and Piscatawaytown in what was called Raritan Township until 1954, when voters—given a choice between Nixon and Edison—narrowly selected the latter in honor of the region's most famous inventor. The post office occupying the corner of Plainfield and Woodbridge avenues is still known as the Nixon Post Office.

The Nixon family, for whom Winters was now going to work, had been prominent in local industry since 1913, when Lewis Nixon, grandfather and namesake of Winters' friend, founded the Nixon Nitration Works. Earlier, Nixon had owned and operated the Crescent Shipyard at nearby Elizabeth, New Jersey. There, on May 17, 1897, his company had developed and launched the United States Navy's first submarine. Named the *Holland VI* after its inventor, John P. Holland, the fifty-three-foot-long, seventy-five-ton sub was powered on the surface by a gasoline engine and underwater by a series of batteries and electric motors. It held a crew of six. The Navy, which paid $160,000 for the sub, commissioned the boat in April 1900, after having ordered six more. It was sold for scrap to the Brooklyn Navy Yard in 1930.

By the time Winters arrived in New Jersey, however, the shipyard had been phased out. But the family still had a booming business in the Nixon Nitration Works, which was a manufacturer of cellulose nitrate, a plastic using a nitrate base, making the material flexible but also flammable. The company's product was then sold to various other firms to be molded into whatever product the company produced.

Although owned by the Nixon family, the company's day-to-day operation was run by its president, Charlie Shuster. When Winters arrived for his first day of work, he found the company could not provide him with an office, so he was shoehorned into Shuster's already cramped quarters. Taking up his duties, Winters discovered that, initially, he had none other than being Shuster's errand boy. Despite that, and the fact that he found Shuster to be loud, outspoken and domineering, he grew to like the man and the two developed an excellent working relationship.

Winters' favorite employee at Nixon Nitration was Blanche Blaine, the middle-aged, former live-in lover of Stanhope Nixon who was offered the job of being his personal secretary after he dropped her to marry the blonde. Now married herself, Blanche and Winters developed a close friendship. Many times she invited the young man to her home for dinner.

"I'm trying to figure you out," she told him one day. "You're funny as hell. You don't run around with women and you don't drink. You just don't fit in with the Nixon crowd."

"Is that bad?" he asked.

"No," she said. "It's refreshing."

When he wasn't at Blanche's having dinner, he was at Lewis Nixon's home in Princeton, where Nix and his wife, Irene, the British woman from Swindon he had brought to the States and married shortly after his discharge, would wine and dine him. Sometimes these little get-togethers involved just the three of them and other times Nixon invited other friends as well. Either way, it always ended up the same, with everyone except Winters sitting around drinking.

"Nixon and I always remained good friends," Winters reflected years later. "But our relationship after the war was tough. The thing that kept us together was the bonding that we had from the war, because to visit with Nixon was to sit there and watch him get drunk. That's no fun when you're sober. So I'd sit there until I got tired, then I'd get up and go to bed. It was the only thing I could do."

Winters also began taking night classes at Rutgers University, majoring in business courses and personnel management. On weekends he often hopped a train for Lancaster, where his father would pick him up at the station.

Although he worked for the Nixon company, Winters soon discovered that he seldom saw any of the Nixon family; at least, not at the plant. Stanhope had a home near New Brunswick that he called Farenton Lake, but much preferred to spend his winters in Florida. En route, he took in the Kentucky Derby and other races, laying down liberal bets. As spring arrived, the elder Nixon traveled back to New Jersey, where he spent the next month to six weeks looking over operations and giving instructions, before heading for his summer home in New England.

The younger Nixon would come to the plant from his home in Princeton once or twice a week to get his mail and pick up his paycheck. This attitude troubled Winters, who understood that his friend did not have to work, but felt Nixon needed to take on some type of responsibility. One day at lunch he was no longer able to contain himself.

"Nix, why in the hell don't you take a job around here?" Winters asked.

"There's a lot to do. They can use you. Someone from the family should be here."

The warmest, most pleasant smile Winters had ever seen creased Nixon's face. "Dick, I can't take a job," he said, as if the answer were obvious. "If I take a job, I'm taking work from somebody else and that would bother my conscience."

"That's the way he was," Winters said fifty-five years later. "He was the same way in the army. His drinking interfered with the mundane details of administration, but he was a good communicator. He had the ability to talk and explain tactics and background to the men, and give them insight on the job they were supposed to be doing. He just was not a good administrator as far as going over details. He delegated that to underlings."

*   *   *

Seven months after taking the job in New Jersey, Winters was suddenly called home. His father, Richard Nagle Winters, had long suffered from bleeding ulcers, a condition he treated with a bland diet and lots of milk. But his illness worsened and on July 30, 1946, five weeks short of his fifty-fifth birthday, he died.

Standing by the graveside at the Ephrata area cemetery where generations of the Winters family lay, Dick Winters recalled his father's sense of humor and the love of music that often led him to break out in song with friends and family. With a smile he also recalled his father's quirks. Often he took his children to a movie and, invariably, soon after they were seated, he'd relocate them elsewhere, utterly annoyed by someone sitting close by.

An antiunion Republican, the elder Winters voted against Franklin D. Roosevelt in four straight presidential elections and it was not without humor that Dick Winters recalled the heated debates between his father and his Aunt Lottie, a Democrat, as brother and sister bickered over the president's policies.

For his mother, the loss of her husband proved a difficult time, so Winters stayed at home for a few days until he was satisfied that she and his sister Ann, now fifteen, were fine. He then headed back for New Jersey.

*   *   *

The next eighteen months proved uneventful as Winters worked to establish himself within the company and to define the job of personnel manager. His life was now into a routine, but in early 1948 that routine would undergo a drastic change.

By now Winters had given up the apartment in New Brunswick for a house in Metuchen, commuting to work by train. His daily ritual included a morning stop for breakfast at a Greek-owned restaurant near the rail station. Of late, Winters began to notice a slender, attractive young woman who came into the restaurant, bought a newspaper, and then headed for the station.

Her name was Ethel Estoppey. A graduate of Rutgers, where she had majored in psychology, she now worked for the college in the placement office, where her job was to assess the qualifications of veterans graduating from the school and work to help them find jobs. Winters, of course, did not know any of this. All he knew was that something about her struck a chord deep inside, and on this day he decided to act.

Following her to the rail station, he stopped beside her on the platform where they awaited their train. After a few moments of silence, he introduced himself and engaged her in some small talk. Finally working up the courage, he asked, "I, ah, was wondering if you would be interested in having dinner with me maybe Saturday night."

She turned and cast an appraising eye on the tall, young blond-haired man.

"Well, who do you know here in town that I might know?" she asked.

Taken aback at being asked for references, he said, "No one, I guess. I'm new in town. I really don't know anyone. I'm the personnel manager for Nixon Nitration Works in Nixon."

She pondered that while her train arrived. As the doors slid open and she prepared to board, she said, "I'll think about it."

Later that day the phone rang in the office at Nixon Nitration. It was answered by the receptionist. The caller was a woman who asked if someone named Dick Winters worked there.

"Yes, he's our personnel director," the receptionist replied. "Shall I connect you?"

"No, I was just checking," the caller said and hung up.

The next day Ethel accepted Winters' dinner date.

Winters was so obviously pleased that Blanche asked him what was up.

"I've got a date," he told her. Blanche broke out laughing. Winters got defensive. "What's the matter? Don't you think I can get a date?"

"It's just so out of character," she replied. She then asked who the lucky lady was. Dick told her. "So where are you two going?"

"I don't know yet," he replied. "Any suggestions?"

"Try the Princeton Inn," she said. "You can even use my car."

Dick and Ethel had a pleasant evening and she immediately accepted his offer for a second. Then a third. The two got caught up in a whirlwind romance and on May 16, 1948, just a few months after they met, they were married in New Brunswick. Unfortunately Blanche could not make the wedding, but she sent the couple a blanket that Winters cherished the rest of his life.

★   ★   ★

By 1951, Edith Winters was living alone. Her son, a married man and now a father after the recent birth of his son, Tim, was a busy executive in New Jersey. Ann, her daughter, had graduated from Lancaster General Hospital's school of nursing and was also now out on her own. Quite simply, the family home at 418 South West End Avenue was now too big for her, so it was sold and Winters packed his mother up and moved her back to Ephrata to be near her sister-in-law, Lottie. At first he found her a small second-floor apartment above a garage at 10 East Fulton Street. The garage was owned by a family friend, John Garman, who owned the Ephrata Sports Center in partnership with Alex Kilkuskie, the husband of Lottie's daughter, Jane Gardner.

"The Garmans were nice people. We'd known them for years," Winters recalled.

Winters was glad to have his mother back in Ephrata, just a short walk from her sister-in-law and the house across the street where she and her young family had lived in the 1920s with her late mother-in-law. The neighborhood was warm and familiar. Shortly afterward, Edith moved a few doors to the east, to 56 East Fulton Street, the small house where Lettie Hull once lived and behind which a young Dick Winters had fished in Gross Run.

Changes were also happening at Nixon Nitration Works. The plastics industry was evolving from the use of cellulose nitrate to acetate, and the company was not successfully making the transition. Possibly because of that, around 1950 Stanhope Nixon decided it was time to clean house and Winters, as personnel manager, was ordered to start firing people. It was a hard duty, despite the six months' severance pay each person received, and the whole thing left a bitter taste in Winters' mouth. Everyone, he later said, got "very, very nervous when they saw me coming."

"They were good men, but it was my job and I had to do it," he remembered.

Eventually the ax even fell on Shuster himself. But the ax was double-bladed; it struck down Shuster and elevated Winters to plant manager. This was a change that was not welcome. Winters had a few old hands left, but overall he now had several newer, younger workers not as familiar with the job as the men he had let go, and he did not have Shuster's years of experience to guide him.

Pressure mounted on Winters, who was constantly getting orders, either in writing or by phone, from Stanhope Nixon, telling him how he wanted things done.

"He'd write a letter, tell me what to do, tell me what he wanted, and that's the way I did it," Winters recalled.

Another problem Winters had to contend with was the elder Nixon's drinking, which was worsening. Unhappy with the blonde, he had taken to having an affair with his Japanese housekeeper, a woman named Lillian. Her husband also worked at Farenton Lake as groundskeeper, a job the elder Nixon so appreciated that each year he built the couple an additional new greenhouse all their own as part of their inheritance.

Sitting in his office one afternoon, Winters got a phone call from Lillian. "I must see you," she said, her voice heavy with urgency. "Can you come here?"

"I really can't, Lillian," he said. "What's up?"

"I must see you," she replied. "It's most important. I can't control him."

Winters had a bad feeling about the situation. "Look, why don't you call Sam Hoffman?" he said, naming the Nixons' attorney.

"No. It must be you. Please," she pleaded. "He respects you. No one else will be able to help."

Winters relented. "All right," he sighed. "I'll drop out later and say I'm bringing the mail."

When Winters arrived at Farenton Lake he found the front door ajar. He tapped lightly. No answer. He knocked louder. Still no response. Pushing the door open, Winters stepped into the house.

"Anyone home?" he called.

Stanhope Nixon appeared from an adjacent hallway, partially dressed and very drunk. In his right hand he held a pistol, its barrel leveled at Winters' chest.

"Oh, it's you," he slurred. "What do you want?"

After a glance at the gun, Winters locked his eyes on Nixon and slowly began to walk forward.

"You haven't been in the plant for a few days," he said. "I thought I'd bring the mail out here in case there was anything in it you needed to see."

Eyes locked on his boss, Winters continued walking the whole time he talked. As he got to Nixon, he reached out and gently pushed the gun aside. He then removed it from the man's hand. Opening the revolver, he found all six chambers had been discharged. Across the living room, Winters saw the screened-in back porch and six holes where Nixon had fired the gun through the screen door at some ducks on his pond.

Nixon chuckled. "I'll bet you thought I was gonna shoot you," he said.

Winters wasn't too damned sure what Nixon's intentions were. He laid the mail on a hall table, along with the gun, and left.

"This is it," he told himself. "I'm leaving. I need a job, but I don't need this."

Winters had now resolved to quit Nixon Nitration Works, although with a wife and a one-year-old son, not before first finding another job. What his next job would be, Winters had no idea. In December 1951, the army supplied the answer.

★   ★   ★

The Korean War had erupted with sudden violence on June 25, 1950, when Soviet-backed North Korean troops poured cross the thirty-eighth parallel. The United States and United Nations reacted swiftly, and troops were committed. However, they were too few to stop the well-armed hordes from the north and the U.N. forces were driven back, setting up a defensive area around the port of Pusan called the Pusan Perimeter.

On September 15, General Douglas MacArthur performed a brilliant end run, landing U.S. Marines at Inchon, well behind the front. Suddenly in danger of being cut off and destroyed, the North Korean tide receded as Communist forces were beaten back behind the thirty-eighth parallel. U.N. forces followed and, by the end of the year, had taken the North Korean capital of Pyongyang and, ignoring Chinese warnings, were nearing the Manchurian border. The Chinese reacted by secreting eighteen divisions, two hundred thousand troops, across the border and hiding them from Allied aircraft amid North Korea's tangled, mountainous landscape.

On November 25 this army was unleashed, creating what MacArthur called, "an entirely new war," and coming dangerously close to encircling and annihilating the U.N. forces. The war then bogged down into a bloody, grinding stalemate.

Winters was keenly aware of events in Korea and of the military's calling back of men who had served in the Second World War. Still, like many, he was hoping to stay out of the conflict. The army, however, was not of a like mind and his notice of callback arrived in the mail.

In a way, the callback gave him a natural out at Nixon Nitration Works, but his idea of leaving that job for another had not included getting shot at in Korea. Resolved to stay out of the war, Winters hopped into his car, a company car he had been given for his personal use, and drove to Washington, D.C. Crossing the Potomac into Virginia, he pulled into the parking lot of the Pentagon.

Winters had never been to the Pentagon before, nor has he been back since, but that day he was a man with a mission. Consulting a map of the building, he groped his way through the myriad of corridors to the office of the army's G1 in charge of personnel, Major General Anthony C. McAuliffe.

Winters entered the office and approached the desk of McAuliffe's secretary.

"Yes, sir?" she said. "May I help you?"

"Yes," he replied. "I'm Major Richard D. Winters. I served in the 101st Airborne under General McAuliffe at Bastogne. I'd like to see him for a few minutes if that's possible."

She looked at the young man in civilian clothes, then said, "Just a minute, please."

She rose and disappeared into the adjoining office. Moments later she emerged. "You may go in," she said.

For the rest of his life, Winters would be amazed by this gesture. He had no appointment nor had he notified anyone he was coming, yet McAuliffe was bidding him to enter.

"Major Winters," McAuliffe said, rising. "Good to see you."

He stuck out a hand and the two men shook. McAuliffe invited Winters to sit.

"I'm sure you don't remember me," Winters said, sitting. "I served under you at Bastogne."

"Oh, yes," McAuliffe said. "I remember you."

Winters felt McAuliffe was just being polite; that to the general he had been little more than a name on a roster. But he was not about to argue.

"What brings you to my office?" the general asked.

"Sir, the reason I'm here is that I received notice that I'm being recalled into the service," Winters said. "The first time, I volunteered for everything. I volunteered for the service in 1941. I volunteered for OCS. I volunteered for the paratroopers. I saw action with the division from Normandy to Austria, and I was proud to do it. But now things are different. I'm different. This time I'm married, we have a child and I have a job, which I think is important. I'd like to skip this one."

McAuliffe pondered this. Then, folding his hands on the desk, he said, "You know, Major, every year we graduate men from West Point."

"Yes, sir."

"And they're good men."

"Yes, sir. I agree. They're very good men."

"But they have no combat experience, Major. Can I make battalion commanders out of them?"

"No, sir," Winters conceded. "You can't."

"That's your answer, Major," McAuliffe said. "Men like you are too valuable. We need your knowledge and experience. I'm sorry."

Winters didn't like the answer, and felt McAuliffe used that same argument "ten times a day" on other officers who sought him out for excused duty. Yet it was the answer he had expected, and he felt McAuliffe's way of handling it was fair.

Like it or not, Major Richard D. Winters was back in the army.

CHAPTER 14

"I'll See You After I Make the Final Jump."

January 3, 1952–Fall 1988

Dick Winters, general manager of Nixon Nitration Works, officially became Major Richard D. Winters, United States Army Reserve, on January 3, 1952. Contrary to General McAuliffe's allusion to Winters resuming his role as battalion commander, the ex-paratrooper found himself stationed at Fort Dix, New Jersey, near enough to home that he was able to spend weekends with his family in Plainfield.

Winters had been originally assigned to Fort Campbell, where he was to rejoin the airborne, but the number of "superior" comments on his fitness reports struck a favorable chord with the brass at Dix, and Winters was retained and assigned to oversee basic infantry training.

It took less than twenty-four hours on the job for Winters to realize the enormity of his task. On his first full day of duty, Winters was ordered to chaperone a visiting general from the Pentagon as the senior officer observed a mock infantry attack. As the assault unfolded, Winters was appalled by what he watched. Men bunched up, officers failed to make good use of terrain or to advance their men under a hail of covering fire. Halfway through the exercise, the general turned to Winters. His eyes glanced down at the ribbons on Winters' chest, then back into his eyes.

"Major," he said. "How many of those men do you think are going to live through this attack?"

"Sir, they're all dead already," Winters replied. Then he added, "Sir, this is my first day back on active duty. I just took over this job."

"I'm sure you'll change this," the general said.

"Yes, sir, I'll change it," Winters answered.

Despite those assurances, it wasn't long before Winters realized he could not make the adjustments in the program that he felt were needed. What he could and did do was intensify the training, and refocus a few drills and maneuvers, but he could not change the overall regimen. The training program was set by the top brass, and they seemed unable or unwilling to make any substantial alterations. Winters was expected to work within their framework. He was, in his description, just another "cog in the wheel," and he grew to hate it.

Years later, he remembered, "It bothered me every day I was there, and it still bothers me, that these boys were being sent over there who weren't ready to go into combat."

By spring Winters was thoroughly fed up. Feeling, he said, like he was "working with the dregs," or with officers who just didn't give a damn, he longed to be back in a unit similar to the one he had served with ten years earlier, a group of men with pride and spirit and an urge to be the best. So, at age thirty-five, Winters put in for a transfer to U.S. Army Ranger school.

The transfer was granted and Winters found himself in familiar surroundings: Fort Benning. He enjoyed the training and the challenge of the Rangers because they shared his philosophy of doing one's best. Still, it didn't take him long to get off on the wrong foot with some of the ranking officers. A few weeks after his arrival Winters was assigned to a bevy of field-grade officers, mostly majors and lieutenant colonels, to observe the Rangers as they undertook a three-day field problem that included a mock night attack. At first Winters was excited. He longed to get back out into the wilds and live in the field. So he was horrified when he discovered that the officers would simply observe the Rangers as they left for the training session, and be there when they got back. Winters sought out the colonel in command.

"Colonel, I'd like to go along on the exercise," he said.

The colonel looked startled.

"No, no. That's out," he said. "That's not the way we do it, Major. This is an extremely arduous exercise, and it's hard enough on these younger men. This is a tough assignment."

"Respectfully, sir, I understand that. But I'd like to go along," he insisted. "I can't see the point in observing them if I can't see them in action."

The colonel again tried to dissuade Winters, but failed to budge the insistent major. Obviously displeased, the colonel finally relented.

Back in combat gear and helmet, fully loaded backpack and clutching a rifle, Winters trudged into the North Carolina wilderness for three days of hard living, surrounded by men, most of whom were fifteen years his junior. The three-day training exercise gave Winters the exhilarating opportunity not only to observe, but to participate in everything from lengthy hikes to cliff scaling.

"I did the whole damned thing," he later said.

In the wilds, men lived on field rations except for one day when providence provided unexpected, and far tastier, fare. Bivouacked by a roadside, Winters was beginning to shave, a holdover from the days when Colonel Sink ordered all officers to shave every morning, when a civilian truck carrying a load of chickens roared past. An improperly closed cage swung open and several chickens escaped, making themselves fair game for men living on K Rations. Winters caught one of the escapees, which was now destined to become his lunch. He restrained the flapping bird by tying it to his leg with a shoestring and returned to his shave. Winters lathered up his face, then scraped away the minuscule growth of whiskers with his razor. As he shaved, a movement on the ground caught his eye. Not far away, a copperhead snake was also anticipating a chicken dinner. Winters froze as the snake slithered quietly closer. Winters slowly reached down to his field pack, and withdrew his machete. With one quick, sure motion he killed the snake, giving the chicken a temporary reprieve. He resumed his shave.

With the coming of darkness, men donned combat gear and blackened their faces. Their assignment during the night attack maneuver was to seize an enemy command post. Winters accompanied the Rangers as they moved silently along a wooded trail. As the command center loomed ahead, Winters and the others spread out, dropped to the ground and began to creep forward.

Winters spotted one soldier at the command post, possibly a sentry, standing alone. Slinking through the underbrush as carefully, and as lethally, as the snake he had killed earlier, Winters stalked the man. He worked his way unseen behind the sentry, then leaped up. He wrapped an arm around the soldier's neck, closing a hand over his mouth to stifle any sound, and drew his other hand to the man's throat.

"You're dead," he whispered.

Winters was ecstatic. It was a sure kill. His training from ten years earlier had stayed with him. The sentry had never heard him approach. For Dick Winters, it was the high point of his entire military experience since his recall.

After the three-day exercise, the Rangers hiked back into civilization, and the thirty-five-year-old Winters marched right along. The younger men appreciated Winters' abilities and endurance, and poured respect on him. He returned their respect. However, the glowering looks on the faces of the observing officers plainly showed their dissatisfaction.

"They didn't appreciate me going out one damned bit," he recalled years later. "Basically, I was showing them up."

Winters quite likely would have been happy remaining with the Rangers for the duration, but the army had different plans. In September, new orders arrived. He was being sent to Seattle, Washington, to await a ship that would transport him to Korea. With a heavy heart and a sense of foreboding, he bade his wife and young son good-bye. Dick Winters was heading for his second war in eight years.

★ ★ ★

Or so it appeared.

Fort Lawton, Washington, was a bustling camp, with men waiting to ship out for the war-torn peninsula half a world away. On September 22, Winters sat in a room with a bunch of other officers, all of whom were bitching first, about being recalled, and second, about being shipped overseas. In the midst of this piss-and-moan session, a staff officer walked in and called the room to attention.

"There's been a new order," the man said. "Any officer who has been recalled involuntarily does not have to continue. He may resign and not have to go on to Korea. If there are any officers in this room who wish to take advantage of this order, please step forward."

Winters couldn't believe his ears and was on his feet before he even realized it. Looking around, he was amazed that in this room full of whining men, only one other officer, a captain, had risen.

"The only thing I can figure is they didn't want to go home and go back to work," Winters later said.

"Follow me, gentlemen," the staff officer said, and led Winters and the captain away.

Ushered into another office, a lieutenant colonel tried to convince Winters to stay in the service. Winters was just as determined to leave.

"Well, Major," the colonel said. "You're being very foolish. You should stay in. With your service record, you'd have a wonderful career in the army."

"I sure as hell don't understand this, sir," Winters replied. "If you keep sending me out where people are shooting at me, I'm not going to have much of a career in anything, and I'm surely not going to enjoy my retirement."

Before the day was out, Winters' separation papers were signed (his honorable discharge from the U.S. Army would follow on April 1, 1953). Now ex-major Winters was granted $263 in separation pay and $183.80 for a travel allotment, and he headed back for New Jersey. But not, as it developed, back to Nixon Nitration Works.

★ ★ ★

"I'm sorry, Dick," Lew Nixon told his friend when he reported back to work. "We didn't know how long you'd be gone, so Dad filled the position. You'll get six months' pay, though, and the company car is yours. I'll sign it over to you."

Winters took the news well, and certainly held no animosity against his army friend. But for now, he was a family man out of work.

At Rutgers, Winters had befriended the personnel director for the Johnson & Johnson plant in New Brunswick, and within weeks of leaving Nixon, Winters was back at work. His job was superintendent in the plant's roll room, where adhesive was added to cloth and then cut to make Band-Aids. At first Winters enjoyed this new career path. As was his leadership style in the army, he moved around the plant, talking to the workers, getting to know them and letting them get to know him.

But it didn't take Winters long to suspect that he had been hired less for his knowledge of adhesives, which was nil, than for his people skills. Labor problems were looming at Johnson & Johnson and a strike was in the offing that had it occurred, Winters later discovered, could have shut down the entire plant. The dispute centered around one man in Winters' department, a longtime maintenance employee whose primary job was to keep the machinery oiled.

Workers felt the general manager of the plant, a cost-cutting bureaucrat, was singling out the old oiler. As a result, labor and management were drawing lines in the sand and a walkout seemed imminent. Winters made it a point to get to know the oiler and found he liked the man, an emotion the oiler reciprocated. Winters intervened between the employee and management. The man kept his job and the walkout was averted. But it left a bitter taste in Winters' mouth that grew more sour with time. Within two years Winters had grown to loathe Johnson & Johnson, which he began to view as little more than a sweatshop.

"I asked myself, 'Who ever retired from this place? Nobody. They died of a heart attack or they had ulcers and had to quit,'" Winters told author Stephen E. Ambrose in 1990.

Winters didn't have ulcers, but in 1955 he did quit. He also quit New Jersey. Packing up his small family, which now included a daughter, Jill, born a year earlier, he returned to Pennsylvania. At first he didn't know what his next job would be. His mother suggested working at one of Lancaster County's many shoe factories, but Winters rejected the idea. He soon landed a job with Whitmore Laboratories in Lebanon, Pennsylvania, after the sales manager, a man Winters called Dutch Gardner, took a liking to him.

"He said I was tough and he could make something out of me," Winters recalled.

Whitmore Labs specialized in animal nutrition and health products, another totally alien field to the former airborne commander. Winters was hired as a salesman, calling on feed mills, hatcheries and farms in a sales territory that covered Pennsylvania counties west of the Susquehanna River, including York and Adams.

Winters worked hard studying and learning all he could in the field of animal nutrition. During this reeducation period, Winters recalled that Gardner was "very supportive," and helped him master the job.

"Like anything else, if you put your mind to it, you can learn it and make a go of it," Winters remembered.

Taking the job at Whitmore came at a cost. Winters was making only half of what he had earned at Johnson & Johnson, and he felt he had sacrificed the prestige he once had as a corporate manager.

"This is coming down the line about as far as you can go, prestige-wise," he told Ambrose. "You're a salesman, you know, a salesman or a farmer. Prestige is zilch. But I was keeping that promise to myself about the peace and quiet I wanted."

So, happier but poorer, the family struggled on.

Still saddled with the house in Plainfield, New Jersey, Winters moved his family into a small apartment in the historic town of Gettysburg, whose name in history had been etched in blood 92 years earlier. After the Plainfield house sold, Winters bought a home in the quaint Adams County town of New Oxford, whose centerpiece is a picturesque village green.

By 1957 Gardner had added Lancaster County to Winters' territory. The former paratrooper used the opportunity to fulfill a promise, the one he had made to himself in a dark Norman hedgerow on the night of June 6, 1944, about settling down on a quiet piece of land. Shortly after the Korean War, Winters had purchased a three-hundred-acre farm in Lebanon County. Unable to devote full time to the land as yet, another family lived in the small farmhouse and worked the land except for weekends. That was when Winters and his family came by. By 1955 he had begun construction of a larger house, working on it as time and money allowed. The house was finished by 1960 and Winters moved his family to the farm for good, working the soil in the moments he wasn't on the road for Whitmore.

Winters was content to work for Whitmore but in 1965 the company was purchased by Rome and Hawes, and, he recalled, "things changed dramatically." So Winters moved on, taking a job with Poorbaugh Grain Inc., where he found himself working in Lancaster on the seventh floor of the Greist Building, just a few floors above the office his father had worked in as a foreman for PP&L.

Poorbaugh had been strictly a grain operation until Winters brought along his knowledge of animal nutrition. So popular was Winters with his Whitmore clientele that many of them followed him, becoming customers of his new employer. To help entice them, Winters arranged to buy nutritional products from Rome and Hawes' competitors, who in turn gave him a price break. This allowed him to resell it to his customers, undercutting Rome & Hawes, and still make a modest profit. Winters was clearly putting his business education to work.

In 1968 Winters got a call from Glenn Trout, a plant manager at Hershey Foods. The two men had worked together at Whitmore Laboratories, and now Trout had an offer. He explained how Hershey, during the processing of its many chocolate items, is left with tons of by-products that cannot be used and are ultimately packed off to landfills—things like cocoa bean shells, opened bags of chocolate, peanuts, nuts, sugar and cocoa butter. For Hershey Foods, it was an ecological nightmare. For Winters, Trout felt, it was an opportunity.

"This material has high nutritional value, but we can't use it for anything," Trout said. "It could easily be converted for farm use. You're the guy to do it, Dick. You know every feed mill operator in the area."

"In essence, I became Hershey Foods' garbage man," he recalled, laughing.

At first this new endeavor was merely a sideline, as he tried to convince the owners of Poorbaugh that this was a viable source of animal nutrients. However, the company wasn't interested, so Winters quit and went into business for himself as the owner of R.D. Winters Inc.

Winters made arrangements to have the materials picked up at Hershey, which was then taken to feed mills to be ground up and blended into cattle food. Feed mills rejected some, saying it was too gooey for them to deal with, so he sold this directly to Lancaster County farmers.

"I don't think there's an Amish or Mennonite farmer there that I didn't deal with," he said.

The business venture proved successful and, a few years later, Winters purchased a home in Hershey, now dividing his time between it and his Lebanon County farm.

Dick Winters' life had now become the American dream of a home, a wife and two kids. While family members lovingly recall that Winters was not exactly blessed with a green thumb, he was a tireless worker who made both his farm and his animal nutrition business a success.

*　　*　　*

By 1970 Edith Winters, her frail body wracked by pancreatic cancer, was no longer able to live on her own, so her son moved her from her Ephrata home to his farm. In early February her health took an even more serious downward turn, and she needed hospitalization. However, a ferocious snowstorm had drifted over the long lane leading from the farmhouse to the road. Winters climbed aboard his farm tractor, which had a snowplow attachment, and tried to open a path for his car, but the stubborn snow was too much for the tractor. Winters hurriedly phoned the township office and spoke with the township manager, who obliged him by dispatching a snowplow. Between Winters' tractor and the township truck, the lane was opened and Winters bundled his mother into the car.

His destination was Ephrata Community Hospital, some twenty-five miles away, but snow blocked the roads and forced roundabout detours, making the trip even longer. Edith Winters was admitted to the hospital, but it was obvious to all that Dick Winters' gentle, loving mother was beyond recovery. Dick and Ethel set up a death vigil, with Dick taking the night watch, and Ethel spelling him in the morning.

On the morning of February 7, 1970, Winters had finished his stay and had to leave. It had been a quiet, yet eventful night. Around 4:30 A.M., as Edith lay near death, a man came into the room, a Bible in his hand. The man barely glanced at Winters, but with his eyes focused on Edith he leaned down to the dying woman and said to her, "Are you ready to meet the Lord?"

Anger flashed through Winters. His eyes burning, he rose to his feet, pushing his chair back with his legs. He began rounding the bed. The man looked startled and, accurately reading the look in Winters' eyes, quickly fled the room.

"I'd have killed that holier-than-thou son of a bitch," Winters recalled thirty-four years later.

Winters was now on the still-snowy roads, heading home; his job at Poorbaugh beckoned. Somewhere between the hospital and the farm he passed Ethel on her way to sit by Edith's bedside. She didn't get there in time. Edith Winters died shortly after her son said good-bye.

But the day had a double whammy in store for the Winters. Back at the farm, unaware that his mother was dead, Winters shaved, showered and dressed for work. Before he could leave, however, the phone rang. It was one of Ethel's relatives in New Jersey, bearing the news that Ethel's mother, Lilian Estoppey, had died that night.

"We ended up telling each other that our mothers had both passed away," Winters said years later. "What a night."

A few days later Winters, Ethel, their two now nearly grown children, and Dick's eighty-six-year-old Aunt Lottie stood shivering at the snow-swept Ephrata Township cemetery as Edith was laid to rest between her husband and her stillborn child, Beatrice. Before leaving, Lottie cast a glance to the Gardner plot some forty feet to the east, and thought about her own husband lying there. Eight years later, on July 2, 1978, she slipped quietly away and rejoined him. She had turned ninety-four just six weeks earlier.

★   ★   ★

Though the gap between 1945 and the present grew ever wider, Winters never forgot the war and the people who had played so important a role in his life. For more than two decades after he had returned home, Winters kept up a correspondence with Louie May Barnes, exchanging gifts and updating each other on news. Among the cherished gifts Mother Barnes sent her only sur- viving "son" was a small wooden tray with hand-carved wooden eggcups. The wood came from an old church and dated back four hundred years. Then, one day, the letters stopped. Francis and Louie May Barnes were reunited.

In 1965 Winters learned that death had also claimed his former com- mander. General Robert F. Sink, an early and enthusiastic proponent of air- borne operations, had made the last jump.

"He was a leader," Winters recalled, admiration in his voice.

A few others were gone, too. Among them, Marshall Clayton Oliver had died in 1956. Winters' jeep driver, Alton More, who had "liberated" Hitler's personal photo album at the Berghof in 1945, was killed in a car accident in 1958. David Kenyon Webster was lost at sea in 1961 and Albert Blithe, who had made the army a career despite his hysterical blindness episode at Carentan, had died in 1967. Among Winters' former staffers, the ever-faithful Ralph Richey died in 1970.

However, many of Winters' other former comrades were alive and healthy, even if time was turning their once-lean bodies to paunch and streaking their hair with flecks of gray. The men kept up with each other's lives through re- unions, where they fondly remembered the past, and though these were happy, social events, and the men were now all wearing civilian clothes, time and circumstance did not diminish the fact that Winters was still the CO, and the barriers between officers and enlisted men, though not nearly as pro- nounced, still existed and would continue to exist.

It was a job Winters willingly accepted. He never forgot these men. After the war he had packed up all of his company and battalion records and shipped them home, where his mother, thankfully, had saved them rather than discarding the boxes.

Winters had established an office in his home that was essentially an HQ, where he set up a file on each man. Into this file he placed not only their mil- itary records, but any correspondence he received from them, whether it was from a hospital after they had been hit, or letters he received after the war. In short, he kept everything that had anything to do with Easy Company and 2nd Battalion.

Other correspondences also found their way into Winters' rapidly expanding files. In early 1984 Winters received a letter from Louis de Vallavieille who, as a nineteen-year-old boy, had hidden inside his family home at Brecourt Manor while Winters and his men fought in the fields outside. De Vallavieille only knew Winters from what he had read in a book by ex-paratrooper George Koskimaki titled *D-Day with the Screaming Eagles*. The letter, in fact, written in French with an English translation, was addressed to "Lieutenant Charles Winters" and sent in care of the 101st Airborne Division Association. It eventually found its way to Hershey. The letter asked Winters several questions concerning the Brecourt fight, such as: did he recall talking to any civilians at the manor, particularly a man with "white hair and a moustache about 69 years old"; how many Germans did he find; what were the losses on each side; and any details of his brother Michel's wounding at the hands of a paratrooper. He hoped Winters would come to Normandy for the fortieth anniversary of the D-Day landings and that the two men could meet.

Winters did not get to France that year, but did revisit the field in 1985, along with Don Malarkey. The veterans, their hair now graying, once again walked the fields and hedgerows of Brecourt, along with de Vallavieille. It was eerily quiet. Bees now droned lazily where bullets once buzzed. Much of the tree line that once hid the four German guns was now overgrown by a tangle of vines, but the earth still bore the scar of the trench. As the landowner listened, Winters pointed out the progression of the battle; the tree Carwood Lipton climbed, fragile then but now grown to maturity; the place where John Hall died and the location of the German headquarters where he had found the maps. Malarkey recalled his mortar barrage of the house, unaware that the family was hiding inside.

The guns themselves, the object of the fight, were long gone, claimed by some postwar scrap metal dealer.

Winters had by now become good friends with the de Vallavieille family. He had stayed both at the manor house and at Louis de Vallavieille's lavish apartment complex in Paris, where he was impressed by the huge iron gate that ushered one into a courtyard surrounded by a stone wall. Inside Winters recalled the wide, circular stone staircase that wound upward "like something out of an old movie." The grounds included a stable and servants' quarters.

Two years later Winters returned, this time accompanied by Walter Gordon, who had recovered from the Christmas Eve wound at Bastogne that had left him paralyzed.

After once again walking the Brecourt battlefield, the men accompanied de Vallavieille to St. Marie-du-Mont, where his brother Michel, twenty-four at the time he was shot by an angry GI, was now mayor. Michel held no animosity for the shooting, and in fact had helped establish a Utah Beach museum nearby, and the arrival of the two veterans was a time of celebration in the town.

"I'm considered a member of the family," Winters recalled years later. "I certainly honor that."

In 2004 Louis invited him back for the sixtieth anniversary of D-Day, but Winters remembered, "I thanked them very much for the invitation, but I'm not going back."

On one trip he revisited Aldbourne, staring pensively at the cottage that was once his home. Then, taking flowers, he walked into the cemetery where the Barnes family lay. Stooping down over the graves, he laid the flowers by the headstone and muttered, "I'll see you later, after I make the final jump."

*   *   *

Looking back over the years at what he and his comrades had done, and the experiences they had shared, Winters grew more and more convinced that he wanted the company's exploits turned into a book. "It had been in my head for a long time that Easy Company has a story to tell," Winters said. "D-Day, Holland, the Bulge, Berchtesgaden. We'd been through it all from start to finish."

Winters shared his feelings with Carwood Lipton, Walter Gordon, Forrest Guth, Bill Guarnere and the rest, and he said nearly all "had the same feeling." The men of Easy discussed the possibility over and over, Winters recalled, so he began looking for a writer to take on the project. He found writers, but none shared his enthusiasm. One would have written the book provided he had sufficient incentive.

"How much money do you have?" he asked Winters.

"Hell, I don't have any money," Winters said disgustedly. "I'm working for a living."

So it went until 1988, when another writer unexpectedly entered the picture and forever changed the lives of Dick Winters and the men of Easy Company.

They were about to meet historian Stephen E. Ambrose.

CHAPTER 15

"I Think E Company Has a Story to Tell."

Fall 1988–Summer 1998

In the autumn of 1988 Stephen E. Ambrose, head of the history department of the University of New Orleans, was busily finishing up the third book of his three-volume biography of Richard M. Nixon, entitled *Nixon: Ruin and Recovery 1973–1990*. However, always looking ahead to his next project, the author was planning a book on D-Day, which he felt was the definitive battle of the war in Europe. With that in mind, and on the lookout for veterans to interview, he noticed that a group of World War II vets from the 101st Airborne was planning a reunion in New Orleans, not far from his home in Gulfport, Mississippi.

It was here that the men of Easy Company and Ambrose first met. The author sat down with the men and, after explaining his purpose, began the interviews. Winters saw this as an opportunity to get a bona fide author interested in telling the story he felt the company had to tell. Envisioning it as the men's story, Winters stepped back to allow the others to relate their experiences. However, as he listened he felt "some of the stories were pretty wild," especially when Lieutenant Brewer recounted his role in taking the guns at Brecourt.

"This is terrible," Winters thought. "Something has to be done about this."

Arriving home after the reunion, Winters sat down and, with the aid of his notes and diary, began poring over his memories. He next called Gordon, who lived a few miles from Ambrose in Pass Christian, Louisiana. He wanted to come to Louisiana and contact Ambrose.

"Gordon, what are we going to do when we get down there?" Winters asked. "I'd like to meet this guy, Ambrose. Can we look up the University of New Orleans and go visit him?"

"Sure," Gordon said. "I'll contact him and arrange it."

He did, and when Gordon told Ambrose the two were practically neighbors, Ambrose invited them to his home. On February 26, 1990, Winters and Gordon, along with Lipton and Guth, were ushered into the author's home.

"You do the talking when we get in there," Lipton said to Winters.

That suited him fine. He had cloistered himself away from the others the night before to reread his notes in order to "get primed up for this thing."

Winters recalled that Ambrose's home was "nice, but modest." The author escorted the veterans to his work area, a loft above his garage.

"Come on up," Ambrose invited, and the men climbed a stairway to Ambrose's "very humble" office.

Books were everywhere, Winters recalled. This was the author's library, with makeshift bookshelves made from plywood boards laid across cement blocks. When he needed additional shelves, he simply added blocks and another board. Even Ambrose's desk was a large sheet of plywood sitting atop concrete blocks, and his chair was a Western-style saddle mounted on a wheeled, swivel base.

Once everyone was settled into chairs and Ambrose was on his saddle he said, "Okay, tell me your stories."

"We're here basically to see how we can contribute to you and your project," Winters began. "And the big thing in our contribution that I think we can make is the job that we did, that is Easy Company, on D-Day."

"That's what I want to hear," Ambrose said. "That's exactly it."

Winters began to relate the Brecourt fight, telling Ambrose that past accounts of the action around Causeway 2, especially those done by historian S. L. A. Marshall, had been "very, very vague" and often "have not been accurate." Ambrose offered to pull out a map as they traced the action, but Winters had his own map.

One matter Winters wanted to clear up was Brewer's account of the assault at Brecourt Manor.

"Bob Brewer wasn't there," Winters said. "He's a good man and I don't understand what happened there, but he made a comment that he took it and that Lieutenant Compton was with him. That is not true. Lieutenant Compton was with us. He played a major part in taking the battery."

The interview went on for several hours, interrupted only when Ambrose's wife, Moira, announced that dinner was ready. The veterans joined the Ambroses in a meal centered around roast beef, and shared a few drinks. The alcohol loosened Ambrose's tongue and at one point in the talks, drink in hand, he reared back in his chair and said, "You know what? I think I am the best military historian in the business today."

This statement shocked Winters, who had never heard of Ambrose before New Orleans, although before this meeting he and the others had all read Ambrose's book *Pegasus Bridge*, about the seizing of the Orne River bridge by British glider troops under Major John Howard early on D-Day morning.

"That takes a helluva lot of ego," Winters recalled later. "He might be well-known, but I didn't know him."

Ambrose later proved it was true, at least to Winters' satisfaction, and the two would prove to be an ideal team, also developing a personal friendship.

"He treated me wonderfully," Winters later reflected.

At the conclusion of the interview, Ambrose told the Easy veterans, "I think E Company has a story to tell. You've been to D-Day, Holland, Bastogne, Germany, the Holocaust, VE-Day at Berchtesgaden. It pulls the entire war in Europe together. Let me think about this fellows; I'll let you know."

The four men returned to Gordon's home with mixed feelings. Winters, Guth and Gordon thought they had been blown off by the author. They felt Ambrose would not be in any further contact. Only Lipton remained optimistic.

"I think he'll call," Lipton said. "I think he'll get in touch with us."

He was right. Within weeks Winters got a note from Ambrose telling him to get the men's stories together. "Let's try it," Ambrose told him.

Ambrose envisioned a book about their exploits as a filler, Winters later recalled, something to write and get out on the market while he worked on his lengthier D-Day project.

Winters, Gordon, Guth and Lipton split the company roster into equal portions and began contacting their comrades, asking for their memories.

Almost all seemed to be enthused, although some needed prodding.

"Malarkey would write and come in with good stuff, but he was always a step late," Winters remembered. "Like, we were on Holland, and he'd come in with Normandy. I'd say, 'Shit, Don, get on the ball and get me Holland. We're gonna hit Bastogne next.'"

When Winters had all of the notes from the men, he and Gordon returned to Ambrose's home and laid them before the author. Ambrose flipped through them, read passages here and there, and smiled.

What had sparked Ambrose's interest, he said in a handwritten introduction for *Band of Brothers*, a copy of which he forwarded to Winters, was not just the veterans' stories, but the "remarkable closeness" they seemed to share fifty years later.

"It is something that all armies everywhere throughout history try to create but seldom do," he wrote. That elusive, rarely achieved bond was "never better" illustrated than with the men of Easy. "The only way to satisfy my curiosity was to research and write a company history," Ambrose added.

Ambrose and Winters now were in frequent contact as work on the book began in earnest. The author visited Winters at both his home in Hershey and at his farm. In August 1990, Ambrose sat down at the farm with Winters, Guth, Harry Welsh, Joe Toye and Rod Strohl for a lengthy interview. This session covered the war years and was punctuated by numerous personal stories, including the theft of personal items from storage while the men were overseas, and from men who had been wounded.

Strohl recalled being hit at Carentan. He was sent back to Utah Beach for evacuation. "I was hit in the feet so they took my boots off and tied them to my stretcher," he told Ambrose. "I had a .45 and pair of boots when I went to sleep on the beach that night. The next morning when I got up I didn't have the .45 and I didn't have the boots, and I thought to myself that was pretty chickenshit of the guys who were there to steal the boots off a wounded soldier."

Toye told Ambrose that wounded paratroopers had an advantage over regular infantrymen after they had recovered and were ready to go back on the line.

"We were specialized troops," he said. "They sent us right back to our outfit. Those other poor infantrymen, they kept them there and sent them to a place called Fiji Farms and they just pushed them in any infantry outfit that . . ."

"Needed men," Winters finished.

"There was a tremendous amount of complaining about that, and it was a terrible mistake," Ambrose admitted. "That's one place where the Germans had it way over the American army. They always kept their units together as units."

During the interviews about Bastogne, Winters commented that he hoped the U.S. never fights the Germans again. "They are tough," he said. "You get to Berchtesgaden, you get to Austria, and you're eyeball to eyeball with them, you know. They have my respect. They were good soldiers."

Ambrose questioned Winters about his style of leadership, impressed by Winters' rapid climb from private to lieutenant to company commander to major and battalion commander. He asked if Winters was given good junior officers to serve under him.

"We had weak lieutenants and we had some good ones, but they were few and far between," he said. "What you do in a pinch is talk to the sergeants. The lieutenant might be there, but I'm talking to the sergeant. And I get the job done."

Over forty years after the fact, Winters' bitterness toward General Taylor for not being with his men when the Bulge erupted still showed. He talked about the hardships the men endured while "Taylor was coming back from Christmas in Washington."

"That's not quite fair," Ambrose interrupted.

"Isn't it?" Winters replied.

"He was called back to testify . . ." Ambrose began.

"I don't want to be fair," Winters stated.

"Okay," Ambrose said. "All right. All right."

Winters appreciated the job McAuliffe did but said Taylor "tells you what you do here and tells you what you do there. He has to run everything."

Winters spoke about the strain of combat. He said that by Bastogne many, himself included, had "reached the third stage."

"Sooner or later I'm going to get it," he said. "I just hope it isn't too bad. But there was never a fear in me that I was going to break. I just felt I was going to get hit sooner or later."

After these interviews, Ambrose began visiting other Easy Company men at their homes, stopping in West Virginia with Lipton and Philadelphia with Guarnere. He then flew to the West Coast to visit with Malarkey and the men there. Other interviews, like one with Shifty Powers, were done by telephone. Overall the men were cooperative and enthusiastic, with one notable exception. Lewis Nixon took no part in the book.

"He did not want to talk about it," Winters later said of his friend. "He did not outwardly object, but he had a habit of pooh-poohing every idea that came down the road."

Another who took no part in the book was Easy's former commander, Captain Herbert Sobel. After leaving the army he had returned to Chicago an embittered man. Over the course of the next several years he married, took a job as an accountant, divorced, and grew apart from his children. Sobel blamed the men of Easy Company for much of his trouble and refused to reconcile his differences with them, even after Bill Guarnere paid his former commander's dues to the 101st Division Association in hopes of getting Sobel to a reunion.

In 1971 a distraught Sobel shot himself.

"Wouldn't you know the poor guy botched it?" Winters said.

While the attempt did not end his life, it added immeasurably to his misery. Severely injured, Sobel lingered for seventeen years in an army hospital before finally succumbing in 1988, just as the book was getting underway. In the years since, many of the surviving members of Easy credit Sobel and his harsh policies with helping to forge them into a first-rate fighting unit. Winters never bought into that belief.

"He didn't make us a better outfit," he said in 2002. "He just made things worse than they had to be."

In order to do on-site research, Ambrose and Winters traveled to Europe in 1989 and walked the old battlefields. The trip was made aboard a tour bus and included a number of veterans and invited guests. After a stop in Holland, where Winters posed outside the former 2nd Battalion HQ by the distinctive Schoonderlogt arch, duplicating a photo taken of him in full combat gear in October 1944, the tour continued into Belgium. In the Bois Jacques outside Foy, on a day when the warm, summer weather was considerably more agreeable than it had been forty-four years earlier, Ambrose began talking about Easy's deployment for the attack on Foy.

"You take it from here, Dick," Ambrose said.

He did. Although the tree line was now further from the town than it had been in 1945, Winters accurately pointed out his defensive positions.

"I had machine guns set up to provide suppressing fire there and there," he said, pointing, "and there where Moira is standing."

As if it had been staged, at the mention of her name, Ambrose's wife began pawing at the cultivated field with her shoe. After a bit she stooped to pick up several objects. They were .30 caliber shell casings. Ambrose gaped in disbelief.

The tour ended in Salzburg, Austria, where Ambrose and Winters bade good-bye to the group. Then, renting a car, Ambrose, Winters and Moira headed toward Munich the next morning because the author had arranged for Winters to sit down with his old nemesis, retired Colonel Frederick von der Heydte, the man who once led the 6th Fallschirmjager Regiment that went nose to nose against the 101st on D-Day, at Carentan, and in Holland and Belgium.

"I'm letting you do the talking," Ambrose told him.

Von der Heydte's estate was in a small village and was surrounded by a tall, brick wall designed specifically to keep out the public. Passing through an iron gate around nine, Ambrose parked the car in the courtyard and the trio knocked on a heavy door. They were greeted by a young woman, the former paratroop commander's daughter, who escorted them inside.

"He's been very nervous knowing that you were coming today," the woman said, leaning over Winters' chair.

"I'm more than a little nervous myself," Winters replied.

She then left them to cool their heels until the man made his entrance.

Winters had prepared for this meeting by jotting down notes and bringing along maps. He mostly hoped to compare memories from D-Day through the fight outside Carentan, and the battles in Holland around Vechel and Uden.

Winters found von der Heydte, after the latter made his entrance, to be "the perfect gentleman." After their initial greeting, translated by the colonel's daughter, whose English was adequate but hardly fluent, Winters laid out a map on the coffee table. Von der Heydte recognized it immediately.

"*Ja*, Brecourt," he said. "Ste. Marie-du-Mont."

Von der Heydte was fully aware of the fall of the four guns at Brecourt, he told Winters. Though the artillery unit was not part of his regiment, they were in his defensive area. He recalled to Winters that he had climbed into the bell tower in Ste. Marie-du-Mont early on the morning of June 6 and had seen the ships off shore.

"I knew immediately this was the invasion and not a diversion," he said.

Moving on to Carentan, von der Heydte told Winters about his plight, of being cut off from communication with his superiors, of being unable to be re-supplied with food and ammunition because of Allied air superiority, and of the immense pressure the U.S. forces were putting on his meager defenses. He recalled Colonel Cole's attack on the town that led to Cole getting the Medal of Honor.

"I was low on ammunition," he said. "I considered withdrawing even though we had the Americans pinned down. I was unable to get any artillery support. I had just started to order the men out when the Americans attacked."

After lunch, served by von der Heydte's daughter, the discussions continued. At one point, a curious Ambrose, possibly feeling the two veterans were keeping him out of the loop, rose and walked around the table behind von der Heydte for a better look at the map the two men were poring over. Throughout the meeting, a German shepherd had been lying passively by the old colonel's feet. As soon as Ambrose moved behind its owner, though, the dog growled.

Von der Heydte barked an order and the dog stopped. The colonel apologized and said the dog didn't allow strangers to get behind him.

"Oh, I'm sorry," Ambrose said; then, returning to his chair, muttered, "Goddamn that dog."

The interview ended late that afternoon and the small group returned to its hotel in Munich. Winters felt very good about the day, knowing that the meeting had given each man a great deal of insight into understanding the mind and tactics of the officer he opposed.

"I told him how many men I had the first day and how our numbers grew daily," Winters recalled. "It came as a revelation to von der Heydte. He told me, 'I had no idea we were outnumbered that badly.'"

* * *

As the book began to take shape, Ambrose mailed chapters to Winters for his approval. Winters scanned the typewritten sheets, many with Ambrose's handwritten notes crammed into margins or between the double-spaced lines.

"The first chapter started off, it was terrible," Winters recalled. "We redid that one about three times, then we were off and running after that. But it was tough getting that first one under control."

Winters jotted notes, critiques and comments on the pages. "He took a few of my comments," Winters said of Ambrose. "The rest he just ignored."

Winters worked closely with both Ambrose and his editor, Alice Mayhew, at Simon & Schuster. Winters was kept informed of each step the book went through from initial editing to final print. He recalled that Ambrose was easy to work with despite a dominating personality that let everyone know who was in charge.

"When you talked to him, you might make some comments and you might think he never heard you, but he did," Winters remembered. "He heard you."

During these final phases, Winters was given an inkling of the possible success of the book.

"Alice has read the book," Ambrose told Winters over the phone one day. "And she said that with my biography of Eisenhower, I did okay. With Nixon I did good. But *Band of Brothers* is the best book I've written to date."

The book came out in 1992 and Winters agreed, saying it was all he had hoped it would be. But not everybody was happy with the final product. Shortly after the book's release, Ambrose received a phone call from a woman identifying herself as the sister of Captain Sobel. She took offense with the way the book depicted her brother, claiming it was not the way she remembered him. Ambrose neatly dodged the issue.

"I'll give you Dick Winters' phone number," he said. And did, although he quickly called Winters to forewarn him.

"That was nice of you," Winters replied with a hint of sarcasm.

When Sobel's sister called, Winters listened with a sympathetic ear. She told him of a "nice guy with a good sense of humor and a good brother." They talked at length and he invited her to the next reunion, which would be held in Philadelphia. She agreed to attend. She also sent Winters copies of letters by friends of Sobel's who served under him while he was at Culver Military School. They recalled more delightful moments, although there were complaints about Sobel's nitpicking. In the end, she half convinced Winters that Sobel wasn't as bad as he seemed to appear.

"We had not known Herbert as well as we could have," Winters conceded during an interview with the author. But that still did not excuse his behavior or his tactical deficiencies. A military academy is one thing, the army is another. "For us it was the real army, and it's life and death and you're going to go into combat with this man, not just school, so you take it a little different."

The success of the book amazed both Winters and Ambrose, and helped forge a lifelong bond between the two men. While still not the focus of world-wide attention he would become seven years in the future, Winters now began to get speaking engagements and a modicum of fame. A few fan letters began to come in, as well as requests for autographs, but nothing surpassed the phone call that came to his home one night a year or two after the book appeared.

"Are you Major Winters of the 101st Airborne?" a woman's voice inquired when Winters answered the ring.

"Yes I am," he replied.

"Do you remember a DeEtta Almon from Asheville, North Carolina?" the woman continued.

"Yes," he said. "Definitely. I have very good memories of DeEtta."

"Well, I'm her daughter," the woman said.

Winters was struck speechless. Then another woman's voice, this one much older, came through the phone's receiver.

"Hello, Dick?" DeEtta said.

Years melted away as he heard a voice he had not heard in almost half a century.

"My God," he said, and the two chatted away.

DeEtta Almon, now DeEtta Robbins, had found the love Dick had told her was waiting for her in one of his last letters. She had married Johnnie Spurgeon Robbins and was the mother of two daughters. Living in Wilmington, North Carolina, she had heard about the book and knew that the man featured most prominently in it was her long-lost, but never forgotten, friend.

Near the end of the conversation DeEtta said, "Dick, I saved all the letters you sent me. I have them here. Would you like them back?"

Realizing the treasure trove of long-forgotten feelings he had written in them, both about her and his life in general throughout the war years, Winters replied, "My God, yes. I'd like that."

Soon afterward two packages arrived containing 117 letters, many in their original envelopes. They sat in his office for several days, Winters not having the nerve to open them.

Eventually he did and, with Ethel's help, retyped all the letters (with Ethel correcting his poor punctuation), made copies, and bound them in book form.

"I knew there was nothing improper in them," he recalled about sharing them with Ethel. "Our friendship was strictly platonic, so there was nothing I had to hide from my wife."

In May 1996 Winters and his wife made a trip to North Carolina, where he presented two copies of his "Letters to DeEtta" booklet personally to DeEtta for her birthday. Now wrinkled with age, but her hair still bright red and her eyes still aglow, DeEtta posed with Winters for photographs, the two all smiles, arm in arm, making one wonder about what might have happened had the fates been different.

It was a very emotional visit for Winters as the two caught up on each other's lives and shared memories. The Winters stayed in North Carolina for several days, then left. The two former pen pals remained in contact until DeEtta's death in February 2001 at age eighty-eight.

* * *

As the fiftieth anniversary of D-Day approached in 1994, Ambrose made plans to lead a group of invited guests to the ceremonies in Normandy, with stops at Ste. Mere-Eglise and Carentan, and one of the first people he contacted was Winters. The seventy-six-year-old veteran agreed immediately and wrote out a check for $10,000 to cover the trip for himself and his wife.

The group, which included many veterans but only one other Easy Company man, Ed Tipper and his daughter, arrived in England and boarded the *Black Prince*, a cruise ship Ambrose had chartered for the trip. On board, Winters discovered Ambrose had given him Stateroom 1.

"Ambrose and the elite were one deck above us," Winters recalled. "But at least down where the common people were, we had stateroom number one."

The cruise was arranged so that at dawn on June 6, the hour the preinvasion barrage began, the *Black Prince* was cruising just off the Normandy coast. Almost all the veterans were on deck, looking shoreward, lost in their memories of smoke and flame fifty years earlier. Winters, however, had already been ashore for more than four hours and was not impressed with the predawn beaches, so he did not go on deck.

"Aw, hell," he told Ethel. "Let 'em go. Let the rest of them talk."

He had decided to lounge in his stateroom and was shaving when the voice of Ambrose, who wanted all veterans topside, boomed over the public address system. "Dick Winters, you're wanted on deck."

"Oh my God," Winters said, then dressed hurriedly and went up.

Leaving Normandy behind, the *Black Prince* sailed into the Caen Canal and docked at Caen. Two other ships were already tied to the wharf, one chartered by newsman Walter Cronkite and the other the royal yacht of Queen Elizabeth. Anchored beside the yacht was a British submarine whose crew closely guarded Her Majesty's ship.

"We were in pretty good company," Winters remembered.

After traveling 6,000 miles to be at Normandy on D-Day, Winters did not get to the ceremony overlooking Omaha Beach. Just prior to boarding one of the chartered buses transporting guests to the ceremony, Ethel became ill, and Winters dutifully stayed behind and watched it on TV. After the ceremonies, though, he did catch up to the group for the trip to Ste. Mere-Eglise and Carentan. In that town where they had fought so hard fifty years earlier, much had changed. The building where Doc Neavles had set up his aid station was gone, but Ed Tipper was able to locate the place he had been so severely wounded. Winters pointed out the intersection where he had been struck by the ricocheting bullet, and recalled an argument he had had with Lipton a few years earlier when they revisited the town.

"I showed Lipton where he had been when he was hit by mortar fire and where I was when I got hit, but he insisted 'No, this isn't the road,'" Winters said in 2003. "Well, it was the road. I can recall exactly where I was hit. I remember it. He and I nearly killed each other over that."

After Carentan the bus began its return trip to Caen. Passing Ste. Mere-Eglise, Winters spotted several German buses parked by a German military cemetery. On the buses a sign read 6TH FALLSCHIRMJAGER. These aging veterans prowling through the cemetery, recalling fallen *kamaraden*, were the same men Winters and his soldiers had fought against over this very ground. Winters yearned to get off and talk with them, but the bus had a schedule and the opportunity passed.

"They were going through the German cemetery," Winters said. "I would have given anything to be able to have gotten off that bus to go see if I could find some guys I could talk to, who would remember D-Day night, Carentan, and so forth. But there they were and we were going by on that damned bus and I had no way to get off."

Stopping at the American cemetery overlooking Omaha Beach, Winters walked among the neatly lined rows of crosses and Stars of David, finding a few familiar names. Then it was back to Caen and the *Black Prince*.

Getting to Caen was no easy feat. The narrow Norman roads were no match for the number of vehicles moving along them between the beaches and the inland battlefields; many of them, Winters recalled, period jeeps and trucks owned by the hundreds of World War II reenactors who had flocked to Normandy.

The bus was hopelessly delayed and by the time it reached Caen, the *Black Prince*, with a schedule to keep, was steaming down the canal. The group's escort, however, waited, and told the driver there was a chance to catch the ship as it passed through the locks and into the English Channel. The bus hurried ahead, arriving just as the ship was entering the locks. The stranded group met it at the last set of locks. The sides of the ship were close to the edge of the canal but not so close that Winters, Ethel and the rest of the guests could board without having to practically leap onto the deck.

"That's how we got back on the ship," Winters said with a chuckle.

This trip, like the others Winters had taken back to revisit the scenes of so much danger and death, left him exhausted. Returning to those fields, he said, "wipes me out." "Especially England and D-Day," he added. "Once I get finished with England and D-Day, I calm right down. I can go through Holland, Bastogne and so forth, and look at it like a normal man. But it's very, very emotional to go to England and to France."

*   *   *

In 1995 Winters was stunned by the news of the death of his best wartime friend, Lewis Nixon. Pondering his friend, Winters found solace that, with the help of his third and last wife, Grace, whom he married in 1956, Nixon had managed to pull his tumultuous life together and the couple spent much time traveling.

That same year death claimed another man Winters felt close to. Joe Toye died in his hometown of Reading, Pennsylvania, and Winters was asked to give the eulogy. Addressing the crowd, which counted many Easy Company men among its number, including Bill Guarnere, who had lost his leg trying to pull a severely wounded Toye to safety in the snowy Bois Jacques, Winters recalled events from the past.

"On January 1, 1945, the German Air Corps made their last big bombing raid of the war," Winters said. "They smashed Bastogne, they bombed our front lines. Joe caught a piece of shrapnel in his right arm. This was his third Purple Heart. He was evacuated to Bastogne for first aid treatment. The 101st was no longer surrounded at Bastogne. Joe could have been evacuated to a rear echelon hospital. Instead, Joe preferred to return to Company E. As he was walking across a snow-covered field to the left of the battalion CP, I saw him with his right arm in a sling going back to the front line. I cut across the field to stop him. I said, 'Joe, you don't have to go back on the line with one arm. Why don't you take it easy for a couple of days?' I'll never forget his answer: 'I want to be with my buddies.'

"Two days later he was caught in a heavy artillery barrage and he lost his leg. That kept him from joining his buddies on the front line then, but that did not stop him in the next fifty years from joining his friends at their annual reunion.

"Today, I know Joe has joined his assistant squad leader, Corporal Jim Campbell, who he lost in Holland, and all the rest of his buddies who have preceded him—in Heaven."

Two years later, on April 19, 1997, death overtook Walter S. "Smoky" Gordon, and a year later the little Irishman from Pennsylvania, Harry Welsh, made the final jump as time continued to take a toll of Easy Company's roster.

* * *

In Hershey, during these years, Winters had by now retired from his animal feed business, devoting full time to documenting the lives of the men of Easy Company and keeping their story alive as invitations started rolling in for public appearances. The number of requests was not overbearing, but steady to the point where it kept him as busy as he was while working at his job.

"I tell people I didn't retire," Winters told this author with a smile. "I just changed careers."

But life was about to get a lot busier for the aging veteran. Arriving home one evening in 1998, Ethel checked the telephone answering machine. There was one message. It was from Ambrose.

"Hi, this is Steve," the gravelly voice on the tape said. "This is not going to be a short message. I have a letter from Tom Hanks and he wants to buy the *Band of Brothers* and he has sent me the HBO show he did called *From the Earth to the Moon*, twelve parts. He said he wants to do the same with *Band of Brothers*. He wants to do twelve parts following the 101st Airborne from training to postwar Germany. It would make a magnificently textured story, which needs hours and hours to tell, and he wants to do it. I presume he'll want to play Dick Winters. Although I'm going to try to tell him Herb Sobel's the role for him. Anyway, I just wanted to share that good news with you. Bye."

That call would change Winters' life in unforeseeable ways, and threatened to end any dream that his final years might reflect the peaceful and quiet life that he had promised himself on June 6, 1944.

CHAPTER 16

"This Is Our Last Hurrah."

Summer 1998–September 2003

Primary filming of the miniseries that would tell the story of the *Band of Brothers* would take place on an eleven-hundred-acre lot at the Hatfield Aerodrome in Hertfordshire, England, a former World War II Royal Air Force base northeast of London. Here director Steven Spielberg had filmed his gritty 1998 combat classic, *Saving Private Ryan*. The lot would feature a twelve-acre village that was built in such a way that it represented eleven different European villages.

But before any actors were cast, before any storyboards could be drawn, and long before a single frame of film could be exposed, a script was needed. Here Hanks turned to the men of Easy Company and Dick Winters.

Winters had already met Hanks. Ambrose, who served as one of *Saving Private Ryan*'s historical advisors, was invited to that film's Hollywood premiere and he took along Dick Winters. The day before the actual premiere a small group of invited guests, including members of the Niland family, were given a tour of the Dreamworks studios. It had been the experience of Sergeant Frederick "Fritz" Niland that served as the springboard for Spielberg's tale. Niland, who served in the 101st Airborne, 501st PIR, lost two brothers killed in Normandy and a third was reported missing in Burma, although he later turned up alive.

Spotting Hanks at the premiere, Ambrose dragged Winters up to the actor. "Tom, I'd like you to meet Dick Winters," Ambrose said.

Evidently Ambrose had already regaled Hanks on Winters' remarkable display of memory during the trip back to Foy a few years earlier, because Hanks stuck out his hand and said, "Oh, yeah, I remember you. You're the guy who knew right where the machine gun was set up."

Later that evening, at a special showing of *Saving Private Ryan*, Spielberg rose to make some prefilm remarks. He then began to recognize guests, starting with Winters.

"This guy isn't too goddamn smart," Winters thought to himself. "Winters is at the end of the alphabet, not the beginning."

He listened as Spielberg also began to recount the Foy story, which had become one of Ambrose's favorite tales.

After the premiere, work began in earnest on *Band of Brothers*. Winters supplied Hanks with a four-volume set of his notes, the same material he provided Ambrose and, in 2003, this author. These looseleaf books contained personal memories, photographs, maps, letters from other Easy Company men, and company, battalion and regimental memos and reports. When he received them, Hanks wrote back, "You have sent me golden nuggets."

Hanks next dispatched head writer Erik Jendresen to go to Hershey and sit down with Winters to pull together the 250-page bible, or framework upon which the scripts would be based. Jendresen sifted through Winters' files and the two held several lengthy interviews in the second-floor office of Winters' Hershey home. For the next three and a half months they would be in contact "night and day," Winters recalled, both by phone and in person. Jendresen also spoke with other surviving members of the company, to get a well-rounded look at the action from their viewpoints as well. Once completed, sections of the bible were assigned to six other writers to spin into episodes of the planned series. Jendresen maintained contact with Winters once the film went into actual production, clarifying points and getting answers to questions that arose.

★   ★   ★

Principal filming for the miniseries, now scaled back to ten parts from twelve, began in April 2000 and lasted until December. Period vehicles and weapons were obtained, sets were built and, in many cases, later blown up, and uniforms made for the five-hundred speaking roles and ten thousand extras. Filming would take eight months and, before it was over, Home Box Office, which was footing the bills, would spend $125 million or $12 million per episode. (A "normal" TV episode costs between one and two million dollars per hour to produce.) This phenomenal amount was $60 million more than it had spent on Hanks' twelve-part *From the Earth to the Moon* and $70 million more than Dreamworks spent on *Saving Private Ryan*.

About six weeks into the filming, Winters and other Easy Company veterans were flown first class to England by HBO and given a chance to walk the set. Picking his way along the rubble-strewn streets of the mock village and seeing his friends, many of them now dead but brought back to life through the cast of young actors, tore at Winters' heartstrings.

"That was probably as emotional a time in my life as I can remember," he later noted. "I didn't handle it very well. That was the first time my emotions got to me. I froze up. I'd always been able to handle these things before. But my nerves got to me."

During the tour Winters was shown the extensive wardrobe section, with racks and racks of German, British and American military garb and civilian clothes.

"It was huge and very impressive," he said. "The producers demanded that it all be correct. They even had the same company who made our jump boots during the war make the boots for the film."

Winters and the other veterans were asked their advice on some matters, but in essence they soon realized they were there primarily to be observed.

"I wasn't sure myself why I was there at the time," he recalled. "But as I look back on it, what they were really doing was studying me. They were watching my mannerisms, my speech, my expressions, my tone of voice. They studied all of us very carefully, and it shows up when they made the film."

He also got his first chance to meet the young actor who would be playing Dick Winters, Damian Lewis. Winters recalled how Ambrose's editor at Simon & Schuster, Alice Mayhew, had told him if *Band of Brothers* had been made into a film years earlier, his role would have probably been played by John Wayne. Lewis was no John Wayne. Somewhat taken aback that he, a formerly blond-haired American, was being played by a redheaded Englishman, he soon got over the shock and found Lewis to be "a good guy" who studied him while they were together.

"We spent a lot of time talking," Winters said. "And he sat right beside me. This guy had been studying me very intently."

Indeed he was. The two men spoke several times during the ten days Winters was in England. Lewis would ask him both technical and trivial questions, down to how he wore his knife. Winters also corrected him on some things. In episode two, entitled "Day of Days," an utterly fatigued Winters plopped down to rest on a log. Winters informed Lewis and the writers that under no circumstance would he allow himself to take such a break, even for a few seconds. The scene was deleted.

Lewis found that Winters dealt with his experiences by militarizing his memories, replacing fear and emotion with the cold, hard fact of just getting the job done. Winters helped Lewis with his questions and concerns, but the actor's chief complaint was that the man he was portraying refused to discuss in intimate detail his wartime experiences. He also discovered that Winters commanded much respect and that he, in turn, would have to earn respect from Winters.

He did.

"Damian had no military experience going into this thing, but hell, I didn't have any either when I started," Winters told this author. "But he matures as he goes along and he becomes better and better as the thing progresses. By the end, he's doing a good job."

Ten days after arriving in England, Winters headed for home.

"I should have stayed longer, but it was very, very hard emotionally," he recalled. "I had to come home. The memories it brought back and the realization of what we were doing here, of re-creating all of this, was very, very emotional. And it got me down."

Winters never returned to the set.

Over the next half year, as filming progressed, Hanks sent Winters finished installments on tape for his critique. Winters would watch each episode, make his comments, then lock the tape away in a bank safe deposit box to insure that no one else saw it before the series was aired. Overall, Winters was pleased with the results. He felt the actors did an excellent job in their portrayals of the men of Easy and was impressed with the level of detail the production staff went to in order to capture the feel of the times. He was especially thrilled with the winter scenes around Bastogne, calling them "terrific" and "very realistic" although, he said, the snow was at times almost hip deep. Most impressive of all were the tree bursts depicted in the film, which gave Winters shudders of realism as the memory of exploding trees raining down jagged missiles of wood flashed through his mind.

The hardest part of watching the film was seeing everything happening again, and especially watching his friends get killed or wounded.

"Before the guy's wounded, I knew where he was going to be wounded," he said. "I knew when each man was going to get hit."

Of course, Winters didn't like everything. In episode seven, leading up to the attack on Foy, the film depicts the battalion CP as being under a canvas tarp. In reality, both Winters and Strayer, who was still CO at the time, shivered in frozen foxholes like the rest of the men.

"Who in the hell was the advisor on this episode?" Winters wondered. "The guy must've been English. He thinks like an Englishman. That looks like something you'd put up in the tropics. It's so dumb. He creates an atmosphere that you're in the tropics when you're caught in a snowstorm."

Winters also questioned what looked like sandbags helping to shelter the CP.

"We never had sandbags," he said. "Where the hell are you going to get sandbags?"

Winters also objected to episode five where, on his big night in Paris before being trucked to Bastogne, he rides the Metro and sees flashbacks of the German he shot at the crossroads. That, he said, never happened. "You always have flashbacks," he said. "But that was somebody's imagination."

He roundly hates the scene in the same episode where Damian Lewis keeps glancing at the French youth who, in the film, reminds him of the dead German sentry.

"It looked like I was trying to pick him up," Winters said. "I don't know where in the hell Jendresen's brain was when he came up with that. That was one of his worst ideas."

But if Winters didn't like some parts of the film, there were others he detested. One was the liberal use of the word "fuck." Winters acknowledged that the men were quite familiar with the word and used it, though their usage was far more limited than the film depicted, where, he said, the actors seemed to use it "six or seven times in a paragraph."

"The producers, writers, directors and the actors were all contributing their little part," Winters said in a 2003 interview. "And as far as I could see, the only part they were contributing was the word 'fuck.' And they kept using it more and more and more, and it was unforgivable."

One scene, later changed, that he totally objected to occurred in episode two after Damian Lewis reprimands Bill Guarnere, played by Frank John Hughes, after Guarnere opens fire on a German supply train before the order to fire is given. As Lewis walks away, Hughes muttered, "Dumb fucking Mennonite."

That and other usage upset him so much he wrote a stern letter to Hanks.

"I don't mind being called dumb behind my back, but not fucking Mennonite," he said. "It's not hurting just me, but a lot of other people. This was unthinkable."

The letter caught Hanks' attention and he phoned Winters. "Dick? This is Tom Hanks. How are you?" the actor said.

"Tom Hanks?" Winters replied. "You don't sound like Tom Hanks."

"Well, I'm in Chicago," Hanks answered.

"What other excuse do you have?" Winters snapped, feeling grouchy.

"I'm calling about your letter," Hanks said.

The two discussed the topic of foul language for nearly thirty minutes, during which Hanks basically told Winters that he and the directors didn't see it his way.

"Well, there's nothing I can do about that," Winters said. "But I can let you know how I feel. So there's only one way I can handle it. I can shun you."

"What?" Hanks said, taken aback.

"I can shun you," Winters said again. "Here in Mennonite country, we don't get mad. We don't sue each other every time something happens that we don't like. We don't throw a tantrum. We just shun you. We don't talk to you. We stop having anything to do with you."

The conversation was over but Winters followed it up with a second, more strongly worded letter, outlining his position. His goal was to get the story and the message of Easy Company out, and not cloud it over with harsh language.

A week later Hanks called Winters again.

"We're going to make the changes you asked for," Hanks said.

Changes were made, and usage of "fuck" was scaled back, but for Winters it was still used too much; a point he also raised with head writer Jendresen.

"This will be going into the homes," he said. "You're going to want to show it to schoolchildren. You don't have to see how tough you are."

But while Winters won the battle, at least in part, over the use of the word "fuck," he lost the one over the actual sex act itself. Winters issued a strong objection to the nude scene in episode nine where Tom Hardy, playing Private John A. Janovec, was in bed with a German girl, played by Isabella Seibert.

"You have a wonderful episode here," he told Hanks. "But why for the sake of ten or fifteen seconds did you run that sex scene? It was out of place completely."

"Dick," Hanks reasoned. "You have to remember it was a true story."

"No matter," Winters replied. "It was an episode that could be shown in any school, any place, any time, or any living room while your children are watching. Then you see that and bam, for any normal person, you've just ruined it."

Winters also pressed the issue with Jendresen.

"You're just not seeing it our way," Jendresen told him.

"Erik, how old is your daughter?" Winters asked. "Eight years old? Would you like your daughter to sit down in front of the TV and watch a scene like that?"

Jendresen was silent.

"That's my point," Winters said. "You can't show that in a school."

The scene survived the final cut.

Despite his objections, Winters, who had been nervous throughout the filming in hopes that Hanks and Spielberg "get it right," was more than pleased with the final result.

"I think they did an excellent job," he said. "You cannot re-create it the way your memory tells you it happened. That's impossible. But they did their best."

Concurrent with the filming of the miniseries was the accompanying documentary, *We Stand Alone*. For this, filmmaker Mark Cowen interviewed the veterans on their memories.

"The guys are all old, and ugly, and there's nobody exactly too smart these days," Winters joked about himself and his comrades. "But when they talk to you, it comes across very, very good."

Winters recalled that he spent many hours interviewing with Cowen, "and he used two or three minutes of that."

*   *   *

As the September airing date loomed, HBO began promoting the film through a series of premieres. Surrounded by a great deal of hype, the veterans and, at times, cast members, gathered to watch as segments of the film, as well as *We Stand Alone*, were shown.

One premiere was held in France that June. Winters didn't want to attend but felt obligated. HBO spared no expense to make his eight-day stay enjoyable, throwing a lavish welcoming party the first night for the men in Paris.

HBO made a limousine and driver available to Winters, day and night. Arriving in advance of the rest of the men, he had the driver take him to Brecourt Manor, where he visited the de Vallavieille family. On June 6, the anniversary of D-Day, he went with Louis de Vallavieille to lay flowers on his father's grave. He also walked the Brecourt field one more time, and visited Lipton's tree, now a far cry from the meager protection it had given the rookie sergeant fifty-seven years earlier.

"He was a target up there," Winters reflected.

In Normandy, Winters was housed in a chateau just behind Utah Beach, near where the premiere was to be held. Still awaiting the arrival of his comrades, he took the opportunity to watch the preparations for the premiere, and he got a lot of attention from the crew setting everything up.

The rest of Easy arrived by train the next day, followed by a mob of well-wishers and media, snapping photos and conducting impromptu interviews. One highlight was meeting Ronald Speirs for the first time since the end of the war. Standing in yellow rain slickers on the Normandy coast, the two veterans, all smiles, embraced for photographs. Privately, Winters frowned on Speirs' shooting of six German prisoners on D-Day, and felt his leadership style was based in part on the men's fear of him. Yet Speirs, Winters felt, was a top-notch combat soldier and a fine officer, who led his men competently and always did what was asked of him, giving "110 percent to the company."

The premiere ended back in Paris for a farewell dinner.

Another premiere, this one on July 22, took place where it all began, Camp Toccoa. Eighteen of Easy Company's surviving veterans attended, along with some of the actors. Episode two, "Day of Days," depicting the D-Day invasion, was shown in its entirety, along with teasers of the other nine installments, and the whole memory-filled event left lasting smiles on many faces.

"It was one of the greatest times in my life," recalled Bucky Simmons, vice president of the Toccoa/Stephens County Historical Society. "I sat in the same section as the vets and the actors during the viewing of 'Day of Days.' To sit there with the men on the screen and the men that the movie was based on was mind-blowing."

HBO shelled out more than $150,000 for the weekend premiere and reunion, booking an entire hotel, the Country Hearth Inn, for the 1,500 expected guests as well as reserving a restaurant to feed them. The entire town of Toccoa eagerly awaited the arrival of the former paratroopers turned media stars. Every store window in town sported signs reading "Welcome Easy Company."

Buses began rolling in that Friday. Along with cast and veterans were a number of invited guests including representatives of the French government. Veterans and actors alike spent time walking the old army base. For the vets, it was an emotion-charged time. While only one building remains standing—historians think it was either the PX or a storage facility although Bill Guarnere insists it was the old mess hall—Currahee still looms over the place, immobile, eternal.

Throughout the event, the actors stayed close by the men they portrayed. Hughes spent a great deal of time with Guarnere, Donnie Wahlberg and his bodyguard (a throwback to his rock 'n' roll days with New Kids on the Block) stayed near Carwood Lipton and Michael Cudlitz with Bull Randleman. Damian Lewis was not able to attend with Winters. It was an emotional day for both the cast members and their veteran counterparts, especially the latter. Following the screening in the auditorium of the Georgia Baptist Conference Center, Don Malarkey went off by himself, tears flowing from his eyes. A woman with actor Scott Grimes, who portrayed the Oregon-born veteran, turned to him and said, "Scott, Malarkey needs you. Go to him." The young actor raced over to the veteran's side and the two spoke softly. As Bull Randleman, with the aid of a walker, and his wife boarded the bus following the reception, Cudlitz hovered behind them, arms outstretched in case either stumbled. From Cudlitz's arm dangled Mrs. Randleman's pocketbook.

On Saturday morning, before the screening, the actors, feeling spry, decided to run up Currahee. With the veterans riding in vans to the rear, the actors set off in high spirits, but the mountain soon got the best of them. Hughes made it the furthest, but none made it to the top to touch the marker placed there some years after the war to commemorate the paratroopers' ordeal. Everyone continued on to the top in the vans, where Winters snatched a rock up off the ground and approached a still-puffing Hughes.

"You were my bet all along," he said and handed the young man the rock as a trophy.

That evening "Day of Days" was shown in surround sound, which added dramatically to the realism. Bucky Simmons, who was seated near the front, recalled looking back at the veterans as the C-47s on the screen came under intense antiaircraft fire and Meehan's plane was hit and went down in a ball of flame.

"Some of the men had tears in their eyes, the rest were ducking like the bullets were really flying past," he said. "Winters was just sitting there in deep thought."

During the fight in the trench at Brecourt Manor, when Hall was killed, Winters sat with his hands held up to his face, his fingers to his lips and his head tilted down.

"You could tell he was back in Normandy," Simmons recalled.

During the reception that followed, men mingled and talked about the film while three women dressed as the Andrews Sisters sang songs from the war years. Winters, emotionally and physically drained from the activities and the movie, stood off in a corner, just watching the festivities. Simmons approached Winters and spoke to him, sensing the fatigue in the veteran's voice.

"No one was paying Winters any attention," he recalled. "You would have never guessed that he was the star of the movie that had just been shown. He was like a regular grandfather. He talked about the town now and about other things."

As the September airdate for the miniseries approached, Damian Lewis arrived in America to reunite with Winters. The two posed for photographs for *People* magazine, both at the veteran's Hershey home and at the farm, which Lewis called "a charming little place."

*   *   *

Episode one of the ten-part series, "Currahee," aired on September 9, 2001, and was watched by ten million viewers. The afternoon before, Hanks phoned Winters to wish him well as the big moment approached.

"Hello, Ethel and Dick, this is Tom Hanks calling from Los Angeles,"

Hanks said in a taped message Winters has preserved. "It's about quarter after four your time. Sunday is the big premiere and I'm sure your phone has been ringing right off the hook."

He said he had called to wish them both a "peaceful and relaxing weekend" and that he, too, was looking forward to the premiere.

"It's exciting all the way around," he told them.

Hanks went on to say he hoped the couple would not "be bothered by too big a steady stream of calls and well-wishers.

"But here I've added one more," he said. "So I don't want to go on too much longer." Hanks said he would check in with the Winters later in the week to see how they fared. "Take care and God bless you," he ended. "Bye bye."

Two days after the premier, on September 11, 2001, terrorists crashed two jetliners into the World Trade Center in New York, a third into the Pentagon in Washington, D.C., while a fourth nosed into a field in rural western Pennsylvania. The unfolding tragedy took some of the wind out of the miniseries' success and viewership dropped to between six and seven million per episode. Those numbers made *Band of Brothers* the second most watched HBO series behind *The Sopranos*.

The series was universally acclaimed for its no-holds-barred accuracy in depicting the hardships and sheer terror endured by the World War II combat infantryman. But more importantly, from the viewpoint of Winters and his men, it transformed them from retired veterans living out their last years in tranquility into celebrities. Before the ten parts had all aired, the men of Easy Company were being sought out for public appearances and speaking engagements. Autograph seekers seemed to be everywhere.

Fan mail began slowly at first, since HBO didn't immediately release *Band of Brothers* worldwide, but staggered the series, starting in the United States, then moving on to England and Europe. As a result, the letters started to trickle in slowly but became a steady flow as the series debuted in country after country.

"I realized with Home Box Office that this would be released over the entire world," Winters said. "But I assumed it would all be released at once, but it wasn't. It was released in the United States first. And after it had its impact here, then it was released overseas in various countries around the world over a period of months. You could trace its movements by where the letters were coming from. So that, as a result, today you have the thing translated in Japanese, and now into Chinese. Can you imagine that?"

Winters always had anticipated a heavy response from American viewers, but never anticipated the way the exploits of him and his men would be received overseas, even from former enemies.

"I got a beautiful letter from a German living in Brazil," Winters recalled. "The fellow's uncle was in the German army during the war and was wounded at Bastogne. He slipped out of the hospital and got aboard a freighter for Brazil. He's now a deserter. He cannot return to Germany or he'll be punished. His nephew got the book and read it to him, and it brought back his memories. He thought it was wonderful. He was overcome with the book. Here is a German that I was fighting, going through all of this in Brazil all these years. He has a chance to have his nephew read him the book and it brings back his memories. It's overpowering."

Too overpowering, in fact. It didn't take long for Winters to change his phone number to an unlisted one and adopt a post office box instead of a street address. Still the mail and offers streamed in, including one from West Point Military Academy, where Winters, who never attended the school, was made an honorary member of the class of 1957, the same class as General Norman Schwarzkopf of Operation Desert Storm fame. Eventually, Winters spoke at West Point on "six or seven" occasions on the topic he knew best—leadership.

During one of those times a cadet asked, "What was your toughest challenge as a commander?"

Winters instantly replied, "To be able to think under fire. In peace the toughest challenge is to be fair."

From this speaking engagement in 2000, Winters was given one of the Four Freedoms Awards, Freedom from Fear, from the Franklin and Eleanor Roosevelt Foundation in a special ceremony at Hyde Park, New York.

Winters also has an open invitation to speak at Quantico "as many goddamn times as I want to."

"It's all a result of the book," Winters said of these opportunities.

Winters' theme, wherever he speaks, is leadership. "Ambrose once told me that if I ever go on the speaking circuit, I should talk about leadership," Winters recalled.

Ambrose reinforced that statement. In a letter to Winters in December 1995, Ambrose thanked the former soldier for "teaching me the duties and responsibilities of a good company commander." In the acknowledgment of his book *Undaunted Courage*, he repeats the message, crediting Winters for giving him insight into leadership.

On August 19, 2001, TV personality Charlie Rose interviewed Ambrose, whom he called the "preeminent World War II historian."

"If you had to serve in World War II, where would you have wanted to be?" Rose asked.

"Easy Company of the 506th Parachute Infantry Regiment of the 101st Airborne Division," Ambrose replied without a moment's hesitation. "Because the company commander, Dick Winters, was almost a Meriwether Lewis, he was that good. And if Dick told me then—or if he tells me now—to do something, I won't say, 'Don't you think . . . ?' I just do it."

Rose asked what made Winters so special. Ambrose replied it was "character, honesty, a firmness of purpose." He said, "Winters knows so much about the weapons, about the men and what they can do and how to lead an attack.

"He knows what a good company commander needs to know," Ambrose said.

*　　*　　*

The demands of stardom took a heavy price on some of the aging men of Easy Company. Many times Winters drove himself to the point of outright fatigue trying to keep up with his mail and an increasingly hectic public appearance schedule. Carwood Lipton, too, paid a price.

Lipton, plagued by emphysema and increasingly dependent on oxygen, spoke with Winters in late 2001. "You know, Dick, with all these offers I get from all over to talk and travel here and there, I'm going to keep going as hard as I can go," he told Winters.

"Not me," Winters replied. "I'm going to go as hard as my limitations will take me."

That December, while boarding a plane, Lipton's oxygen was temporarily removed from him. It took longer than expected to return it to the aging veteran, which seemed to have a disastrous effect. On December 16, two days shy of fifty-seven years from when he and his comrades were trucked into Bastogne, Clifford Carwood Lipton died.

"Removing his oxygen like that seemed to be the straw that broke the camel's back," Winters reflected. "After that, he went very quickly."

As acclaim continued for the *Band of Brothers* miniseries, it became more and more evident that the series was destined for awards. Shortly after Lipton's death, Winters was talking with Ambrose and brought up the subject of the Golden Globe awards.

"Steve, how are we going to make out in the Golden Globes?" Winters asked.

Ambrose quit talking and remained silent.

Winters thought, "Oh my God, I got him."

"You seldom get one step ahead of Ambrose," Winters said in 2003. "And if you did, you knew because he'd quit talking."

Ambrose quickly changed the subject.

"You know, I was talking to Alice Mayhew the other day and she told me since this hardcover copy of *Band of Brothers* came out in June, we sold well over a million and a half copies. That's all a spin-off from the movie."

In fact, *Band of Brothers* did well at the Golden Globes. Damian Lewis was nominated for Best Actor in a TV special or miniseries (he lost to James Franco, who starred as the troubled actor in *James Dean*). When he heard the news, Winters contemplated calling Lewis and volunteering to stand in for him in case the redheaded British actor couldn't make it to the ceremonies. "I was going to tell him that winning was a long shot, a very long shot, and to come all the way over here from England and lose might be embarrassing," Winters later said. "So I'll stand in for you, and if you win I'll say 'It's a true story and here's the real thing.'"

Winters never made the offer.

On April 8, 2002, no doubt spurred by renewed patriotism due to the war on terrorism following the 9/11 attacks, the miniseries was reshown by HBO, simultaneously touching off a new round of fan mail and demands on the veterans' time. The reception of this second airing, plus anticipation of the release of the video and DVD sets, slated for November, just in time for Christmas shopping, bore witness to the fact that *Band of Brothers* would be a heavy favorite at the upcoming 2002 Emmy Award ceremonies.

Accordingly, HBO began preparations for a big, Hollywood-style splash. All the surviving men of Easy Company plus one guest per veteran were invited, all reasonable expenses paid. Children of deceased veterans could also attend at their own expense, but with a reduced hotel rate. All the vets able to attend jumped at the chance with two exceptions: Speirs, who had called Winters from his home in Arizona and said he would not be present, and Winters himself.

Winters hadn't given the Emmys "a whole lot of thought," and when HBO sent his invitation, he did not respond. "It didn't make any difference to me," he recalled. "So I didn't say a word, yes or no. Nothing."

A few weeks dragged by. Then Winters got a phone call from Playtone, Tom Hanks' production company. A voice asked if he had returned his invitation. Winters said he hadn't and that he was undecided if he wanted to go or not.

"Tom definitely wants you there if you can make it," the man said.

Winters said he would think about it. This was followed by a call directly from HBO, which also wanted Winters to attend. Winters explained that he had health problems that included a weak heart and an ongoing struggle with Parkinson's disease, and was "not in the best of shape."

"We'll take care of you," he was told. HBO agreed to have a stretch limousine pick him and Ethel up at their door in Hershey. A wheelchair would await him at Philadelphia International Airport to take him directly to the plane. Another wheelchair and limousine would be waiting in Los Angeles and would be "at my beck and call" for the next five days.

"It was almost embarrassing," Winters told this author the day before he departed.

Nerves and anxiety caused Ethel to have trouble sleeping for several days prior to their departure, but her husband did not share the problem, recalling that he had slept "better than I have in a long time."

"I figured, why get excited," he said. "If I lived through the war, this is absolutely nothing."

As promised, the limousine stopped in front of Winters' door at nine on September 20. The Winters, along with his guests, Robert Hoffman and Michelle Kopecky from Lebanon, climbed in. Hoffman, an architect and longtime friend of the family, would assist Winters while on the trip.

Arriving in Philadelphia, the party boarded the plane to find that HBO had booked them in the first-class section, seats 1A through 1D.

"You can't do any better than that," Winters said. "Next you're up with the pilot."

In Los Angeles, Winters was met by Kirk Saduski of Tom Hanks' office. A limo whisked Winters and his party to the lavish Peninsula Hotel in Beverly Hills which Winters remembered as the most luxurious he had ever stayed in. Winters, his wife and friends, it turned out, would be alone at the Peninsula. The other eighteen veterans and their wives, slated to arrive next day, would be lodged at the St. Regis Hotel, where the ballroom was already being wired for a live feed from the Shrine Auditorium, site of the fifty-fourth annual award ceremony.

On Saturday morning, Saduski brought Grace Nixon to the Peninsula Hotel from her home in Sherman Oaks for breakfast with the Winters. The three enjoyed a pleasant visit before the day began. One stop on the agenda was to pick up Winters' tuxedo. He had sent his measurements to HBO, "right down to my shoe size," he recalled, which arranged for him to be outfitted in a fine black tux. Ethel had to purchase her own gown for the ceremony.

At seven on Saturday night, HBO hosted an Easy Company buffet for all of the guests. It was a grand affair, with the men reliving old times and marveling at the circumstance they now found themselves in. Other guests mingled too, snapping photos and getting autographs from the vets, as well as from cast members and writers who were present. Some of the children of members who had died asked the veterans about stories that might involve their fathers, hoping to complete a mental picture of their parent in his younger days.

Missing from the crowd was the man who started it all when he wrote the book. Stephen Ambrose was suffering from the lung cancer that would claim his life three weeks later. His son, Hugh Ambrose, stood in for his father.

"Dad wishes he could be here," Ambrose told Winters as the two shook hands. "He really wanted to see you and the other men again."

"You tell him we miss him," Winters sincerely replied.

Sunday morning, the day of the Emmy ceremonies, began with breakfast at the Peninsula. Joining Winters was head writer Jendresen, along with writers Max Frye, Bruce McKenna, Graham Yost and John Orloff. Winters had grown quite fond of these men and spent an enjoyable time chatting with them. As breakfast concluded, Jendresen's wife, Venus, recommended Winters have a massage before the evening's ordeal, and before long a masseuse arrived at the veteran's room, armed with a folding table and various oils. The massage so relaxed him that Winters nodded off and slept for several hours, putting him in "wonderful condition" for the night's exertions.

The miniseries, including the accompanying documentary, had been nominated for a total of nineteen Emmys, and as the time drew near to go to the Shrine Auditorium, one fear nagged Winters. He had been told by Hanks that if *Band of Brothers* won for Best Miniseries, he and Spielberg wanted Winters to go on stage with them for the presentation. However, the legs that once propelled him from airplanes were no longer strong or dependable, and he dreaded the few steps leading up onto the stage. He had hoped to enter from the wings instead.

"I don't want to embarrass myself or anyone else by going up those steps and not having my balance," he told this author in a preaward interview on September 19.

Emmy recipients had sixty seconds to speak. It was planned that Hanks would receive the award, say a few words, then turn the microphone over to Winters.

"Everybody's writing me on what to say," Winters said. "One of the writers said he'll help me, but I think I know what I want to say. The big thing is to thank them all for putting the film together, but I also want to make sure that I remember the men that we lost along the way, and the men that are there, so everybody is recognized. If I do that, I've done my job."

The limo picked Winters and his party up at the Peninsula Hotel at 5:15 that Sunday afternoon and took them to the star-packed Shrine Auditorium. Since the ceremony had begun hours earlier, all was quiet outside—the limos having already deposited their celebrity passengers—so Winters and his party were taken to a comfortable waiting area until it was time for them to be taken into the auditorium. As the moment for the announcement of the winner for Best Miniseries drew near, Winters was whisked into the auditorium in his wheelchair during a commercial break in the program. He took his seat in the third row, next to Hanks, and the wheelchair was quickly rolled away, to be taken backstage to greet him after the presentation.

When the announcement came that *Band of Brothers* had won the award, it put renewed energy into Winters. He rose and, using his cane and a little help from Hanks, negotiated the much-dreaded steps with ease. He felt no fear or nervousness as he was introduced by Spielberg, who stepped in for a far more nervous Hanks, although he did struggle to maintain his composure as his emotions swept over him. Then, as the nation watched, Dick Winters thanked Ambrose, Hanks and Spielberg, as well as the directors and writers for telling the story of the men of Easy Company. He then addressed the veterans themselves, all of whom were watching on TVs from the St. Regis ballroom. With a final thank you and salute to the audience, Winters left the stage to a standing ovation.

In the wings he was reunited with his wife and friends, who had been spirited out of their seats while all cameras were focused on the stage. Slipping out a back door and into the limo, they headed for a postaward party at the posh Spago Restaurant, skipping an invitation to the Governor's Ball. Missing the ball did not bother Winters. "They say everybody's anxious to get out of there," he said.

Cast, crew, veterans and family all converged on Spago. Grace Nixon was awaiting the Winters, and joined them and Hanks at a table. At Spago, a party fever raged. Men slapped each other on the back and shook hands in congratulations. Spielberg stopped by the table. The son of a World War II veteran, the director was thrilled by the standing ovations the men of Easy Company had received.

Monday was a calmer day, with Winters again getting together with Grace Nixon, this time for an interview about her husband with a writer from *World War II* magazine. The next day, their last in California, Winters and his party were again met by Saduski, who escorted them to Chavez Ravine where they, along with the documentary filmmaker Mark Cowan and actors Frank John Hughes and Ron Livingston, who played, respectively, Bill Guarnere and Lewis Nixon, watched the Los Angeles Dodgers lose a baseball game to the Colorado Rockies from the comfort of Playtone's plush executive skybox.

Winters, Ethel and their friends were up at dawn Wednesday for a 7:20 A.M. flight back to Philadelphia.

"We were tired but happy that we had a wonderful experience full of unforgettable memories," Ethel wrote. "A fitting climax to the *Band of Brothers* story."

Winters, while grateful and thrilled with the reception he and his men had gotten, took a different spin on the events of the past several days. "I feel this is our last hurrah," he told this author.

Winters has never been able to get over how Easy's story snowballed from a collection of memories to a book to an award-winning miniseries.

"I remember when I went to Ambrose and I said 'Would you tell our story?'" he said. "That's all I asked for, tell our story. He did, so he did his part and did a heck of a job and it's exceeded anybody's expectations."

"Everybody Wants a Piece of You."

The present

Within days of the airing of the first episode of *Band of Brothers*, Dick Winters, then eighty-three, found himself in the public spotlight. The miniseries kicked off a landslide of fan mail and adulation worldwide. From shortly after the series debuted up until the present, not a day goes by when stacks of letter mail and books for signing don't arrive at his Hershey home. By March 2002, the number of letters reached eight hundred. Incessant phone calls caused him to change his number several times, yet some determined fans manage to track down his address and show up at his door.

One of those was a teenager enrolled in a junior ROTC program at Odessa High School in Odessa, Texas. The young man wrote that Winters' character "mirrors a portrait of good moral qualities and a positive role model."

"In the series I saw my profession in a real perspective," he wrote. "I also saw depicted in your character optimism and courage. I believe you are a good man with outstanding qualities and one of the best infantry officers that I have ever heard of."

In February 2002, just four months before his graduation from high school, the young man's parents offered him the gift of a trip to Ireland. Instead, the boy opted for a visit to Hershey on the chance he might locate and meet Dick Winters.

"Would you be interested or available to visit with me at the end of May?" he wrote. "If so, that would certainly be a dream come true."

In May he showed up at Winters' door for a visit with the man he admired.

Ethel is in charge of her husband's mail. She also fields phone calls, although, Winters joked, she is "a little too tough.

"It's damned hard for somebody to get through to me on the telephone," he said.

For the most part Winters did not mind the interruptions too much, except at mealtime.

"'That's enough,' I'd think," he said. "'Now knock it off. Let me have dinner.'"

Ethel took on the job of arranging her husband's increasingly busy schedule of requests for public appearances and interviews from newspapers, magazines, TV and radio, although with interviews Winters has one hard-and-fast rule: the interviewer has to have read Ambrose's book.

"So many times people want to have an interview, which is nice, but they haven't read the book," Winters noted. "And that makes it tough."

Sometimes interviewers simply show up without calling ahead. Winters said a knock will come to the door and, upon opening it, Ethel is confronted with a TV news crew with cameras and lights.

"'This guy wants to interview you,' she'll tell me," he said. "And I'll think, 'Oh my God.'"

By 2003, the demand for Winters at public appearances had swelled beyond the capabilities of an eighty-five-year-old man. That January he was hosted at a special birthday party at the Hershey Veterans of Foreign Wars club, where he was accompanied by Forrest Guth and Clancy Lyall, an Easy Company replacement. Winters was presented with a replica of the 506th's flag.

In the months that followed he was interviewed by several newspapers, the invited guest at a dinner attended by Bastogne veterans and World War II reenactors, and featured in a special edition of the alumni magazine for F&M College. He was the grand marshal in several parades honoring veterans as well as the Hershey Centennial parade that September.

He was invited to luncheons with both his state and federal legislators in Harrisburg and Washington, D.C., and in April was invited to speak before a gathering of FBI agents and officials at the bureau's headquarters, where he received a standing ovation. That trip was also to include a tour of the White House by the Secret Service, but the tour, and a subsequent meeting with President George W. Bush, were postponed because of the president's schedule.

One honor Winters received that October was the Distinguished Alumni citation from F&M College. Prior to this, Winters had not been back to his alma mater since 1941. A few weeks before the event, he and Ethel, chauffered by this author, who served as his assistant, were briefed on what would happen that weekend. He also got his first tour of the campus in sixty-two years. Now unable to walk long distances, Winters paraded across the campus in a wheelchair pushed by this author. Moving in and out of buildings, some of which held memories for the former student, but most of which were new, Winters marveled at the school's growth.

The award ceremony was held October 24, during alumni weekend. The next day Winters was back again, this time as a featured speaker. This gave Winters the chance to publicly debut a new speaking tool aimed to ease the burden of his hectic schedule. With the help of a local filmmaker, Brian Kreider, Winters had put together a video tape entitled *Major Richard Winters . . . In His Own Words*. The presentation uses film clips from the miniseries overdubbed with Winters' own memories. The lesson, as always, was leadership, and the video was divided into segments. In each Winters discusses the leadership styles of men like Sobel, Speirs, Strayer, Sink and Lipton, as well as his own philosophies. It also covers action scenes and incidents, during which Winters tells why he made some of the decisions he did.

The film looks at the NCO mutiny in England, as well as Brecourt Manor, Carentan, the Island and Bastogne. The video gave Winters a much-needed break from public appearances. Organizations that wanted him to speak could, instead, now use the video, showing the entire two-plus hours or just the segments they wanted. A number did this, usually focusing on Bastogne and Brecourt. To Winters' dismay, few showed the Holocaust, which he considers one of the most important lessons the tape has to teach.

A month earlier, Winters had debuted this project at a private, invitation-only screening at the Hershey Cocoaplex theater near his home. Nearly a hundred friends and supporters attended. Between segments, Winters, seated in a high-backed chair, had Kreider stop the film. Then he flicked on a lamp on a small end table and added more memories to those being shown on the big screen. At the end, Winters' audience gave him a warm, standing ovation, shaking hands and congratulating him as they filed out.

Winters was ready to take his show on the road.

★   ★   ★

In late 2001 several of Winters' friends and supporters began a drive to correct what they viewed as an error made fifty-seven years earlier, the downgrading of his Congressional Medal of Honor nomination to the Distinguished Service Cross. A recommendation for the Medal of Honor was filed by retired Sergeant Major Herman W. Clemens and endorsed by retired Colonel Cole C. Kingseed and Stephen E. Ambrose. The three sent letters to U.S. Senator

Rick Santorum, outlining Winters' actions at Brecourt, and also touting his record as a commander.

Kingseed asked Santorum to support the request "while Dick is still with us." He continued, "Now is the time to honor this gallant officer, whose self-less service to the United States and the men of Easy Company, 506th PIR, inspire us all." He concluded, "I firmly believe that his intrepid leadership under fire merits the thanks of a grateful nation."

Clemens' letter told the Pennsylvania senator that Winters' actions at Brecourt "saved untold lives" and "positively affected the success of the invasion force landings beyond our ability to calculate."

Ambrose added his comments on February 6, 2002, telling Santorum, "Of all the leaders and heroes I have studied and interviewed—including some two dozen MOH recipients—none can surpass Dick Winters for courage, re-solve, wisdom, concern for his men, determination to get the job done, the havoc he wrought on the German companies and battalions, risk-taking and accomplishments."

In April 2002 Clemens submitted a recommendation form to the com-mander of army personnel requesting Winters be given the Medal of Honor for "conspicuous gallantry and intrepidity in action at the risk of his life above and beyond the call of duty." The recommendation included the three letters to Santorum, a copy of the official after-action report dated June 9, 1944, and affidavits from Don Malarkey and Carwood Lipton.

The recommendation moved quickly. It was approved by both houses of Congress and passed successfully through several civilian and military re-view boards, arriving on the desk of Acting Secretary of the Army Les Brown-lee in early 2003. There it stalled. That July, a number of Winters' former comrades took it on themselves to pay a personal visit to Brownlee. The "Band of Brothers" trooping into Brownlee's office included Earl McClung, Jack Foley, Ed Joint, Don Malarkey, Forrest Guth, Ed Shames, Darrell "Shifty" Powers and Joe Lesniewski. They were joined by former Pennsylva-nia governor and then Homeland Defense Secretary Tom Ridge. They urged Brownlee to act on the recommendation by signing it and sending it on to Sec-retary of Defense Donald Rumsfeld, the last stop before it reaches the desk of the president.

"It took a lot of guts and a lot of know-how to do that, and Winters was in charge," Guarnere told the Associated Press about the attack at Brecourt. "You don't realize what you're doing when you're doing it, because you'd say to yourself, 'You got to be nuts to do this.' I hope he gets the medal. He de-serves it."

In Decembeer 2004, outgoing Secretary Brownlee rejected the request, although supporters continue to push the effort.

But Winters doesn't fret over the Medal of Honor, nor does he talk about it, and he chooses to stay out of the proceedings completely.

"If I get it, that's wonderful," he told this author. "And if I don't, then I'm not getting all excited for nothing."

He prefers to focus on his fan mail, which, three years after the first airing of the miniseries, continues to flow into his Hershey home daily. Since Winters has an unlisted phone number and his address is a closely guarded secret, the envelopes containing the letters are a constant source of amusement to the veteran. Some letter writers use the description Ambrose gave in his book, sending their fan mail to Winters at "A Farm Somewhere in Hershey." Others send theirs to "Major Richard Winters, Easy Company, 101st Airborne Division, Band of Brothers, Hershey, Pennsylvania." A letter from Romania was addressed to the "Mayor of the city of Hershey." Hershey doesn't have a mayor, so a town supervisor took the letter to the public library, where he knew Ethel Winters volunteered, and gave it to her to deliver.

One very wordy fan sent his letter to "Mr. Richard (Dick) Winters, World War II hero and subject of the HBO Band of Brothers Series, Hershey, Pa. 17033," while a polite British writer addressed his envelope to Winters at "an address in or near Hershey." On the front of the envelope, he also wrote an apology to the post office "for not having the full address" and adding, "Would you please deliver? Thanks."

"You never know what to expect," Winters said with a smile. "If they have no address, they use their imaginations."

However they are addressed, though, Winters gets them. "The post office has been very kind to us," he told this author. "Every once in a while I go to the post office personally and thank them."

Winters enjoys his mail immensely and appreciates people's sentiments as well as their concern for him.

"They often apologize for disturbing my privacy, but they just want to say, 'Thanks,'" he said to this author in 2002. "They're very touching. I can only read so many, then I have to stop. It's very emotional."

Sometimes the writer shares a memory. One man living in Winters' hometown of Lancaster wrote that had lived in Holland as a child during the German occupation. He recalled being a witness to Operation Market Garden, the Allied invasion of Holland.

"On September 17, 1944," his letter reads, "I saw planes with gliders flying overhead for the air drop on Arnhem."

Some letter writers share memories and regrets at not having talked to their own uncles, fathers and grandfathers about their wartime memories, allowing them to pass on without leaving their stories behind. Almost all ask Winters to pass along their thanks to the rest of Easy Company.

"You can just read so many, then you can't take any more," he reflected.

Some of the writers tell him they do not know how they would have done had they been placed in the same circumstances as Winters. "It's natural," Winters noted. "I often wonder how I did it."

Winters' favorite letters come from overseas, especially Europe and England. He says these are "beautifully written and sincere," with sentiment borne of experiences American writers can't share.

"They or their grandparents lived through the war, so you have a spin-off from having lived through the war and the bombings," Winters said. "These letters are more meaningful. Over here, people talk about the war. Over there, they've lived it."

Letters from Dutch fans stand out, Winters noted. They are sincere, grateful and filled with emotion.

"Anytime you get a letter from Holland, you know it's going to be very, very good," Winters said.

As much as time and his health allow, Winters replies to each letter, sending the writer a personalized response and an autographed picture urging them to "Hang tough." He also signs *Band of Brothers* books, provided the sender has enclosed return postage.

Winters is flattered by the attention, and more than a little astounded at the adulation being focused on him and his men, although he feels it should be spread around equally to all World War II veterans.

"As I look at it today and as I see the response of people from all over the world, and it just keeps pouring in, I know this film has made a huge impact," he said.

But time continues to take a toll on Easy Company. With the death of Lipton in December 2001, about twenty-one of the men were still living. Since then, more have made that last jump. Strayer survived Lipton by almost exactly one year, dying December 18, 2002, just one week after Lester Hashey. (December is a rough month on Easy veterans. Winters' friend Burt Christenson died December 15, 1999.) John R. Korb died November 5, 2002; Patrick O'Keefe died February 8, 2003; and Donald King passed away on August 11, 2003. Bull Randleman, one of Winters' most dependable soldiers, died June 26, 2003.

These men rejoined their comrades who had gone on before, men like Popeye

Wynn, who died in 2000, Floyd Talbert (1982), Charles E. Grant, who survived his head wound from a drunken GI in 1945 (1984), Warren Rousch (1999), George Luz and medic Eugene Roe (1998).

Other friends of Winters were also gone by now, men like Moose Heyliger (November 3, 2001) and Clarence Hester (December 2000).

In early 2002, Winters learned of another death of someone near and dear to him. That January, a man named Keith Sowerby knocked on Winters' door in Hershey. Sowerby was from Aldbourne, and brought his children along to meet the man who helped make their hometown famous. It was a pleasant surprise for Winters, and during the conversation he told Sowerby about his memories of the Barnes family, of their first meeting on the benches behind St. Michael's, and of his going to live with the family and what it meant to him. He also brought up the name of his "kid sister," Elaine Stevens. Ann had kept contact with her after the war, but Elaine's letters stopped around 1950.

Sowerby told Winters about a BBC program entitled *Until We Meet Again*, which was aired weekly and which tried to reunite people who had lost contact with each other over the years. Winters hoped to find Elaine, and decided to give the BBC a try. He contacted the program and convinced them to help him locate her. In March, Winters was interviewed over the phone for *Until We Meet Again* by radio hostess Angela Lodge, and he told her about his desire to find Elaine Stevens. It worked, although not to the extent Winters would have liked. Shortly after the interview aired, Winters was contacted by a woman named June, who said she was Elaine's sister. June told him Elaine had moved to Australia when she reached the age of twenty, about the same time he had last heard from her. There she married and eventually had four children. But Elaine had died a few years before Winters' broadcast. Sadly, Winters thanked June, sent her a signed copy of *Band of Brothers*, and promised to keep in touch.

Time was also catching up to Dick Winters. By mid-2003 his Parkinson's disease was starting to slow him down. He agreed to speak at the Pennsylvania State Police Academy in Hershey. He also still visited historical societies and schools, as well as activities at Fort Indiantown Gap, where he had mustered out of the army in 1945.

However, distant events that required extensive travel, like an invitation to receive an honorary degree from the University of New Hampshire and a presentation of a medal of honor from the Daughters of the American Revolution in 2004, were more and more being rejected by Ethel, whose concern for her husband's health led her to begin reining in his social calendar.

"There's a time I could have made all these things, but Ethel's right," he told this author. "Where does it all end?"

In April 2004, *Band of Brothers* was aired by the History Channel. To accompany it, Winters taped an interview with the History Channel as well as the Pennsylvania Cable Network.

The History Channel's showing of the series drew a record audience and a corresponding increase in Winters' fan mail.

At about the same time the History Channel was renewing his fame, Winters was invited to the opening of the World War II monument on the Mall in Washington, D.C.

"The guy told me all expenses will be paid. We'll put you up first class," Winters remembered. "But I had some good counsel from the mayor of Media, Pennsylvania, who wanted to take me there. Later he said, 'Let's forget that. It'll be a madhouse. Stay away from it.' With the condition that I'm in, my health and all, he advised I attend something local, but stay out of Washington. That's what I did."

But even his reduced schedule soon proved too much.

On April 19, 2004, Winters, then eighty-six, was invited to meet President Bush, who was stopping by in Hershey during a reelection campaign swing through Pennsylvania. This was, in part, Bush's way to meet Winters after postponing their previous appointment the year before. Winters agreed, even though he had a previous engagement that evening to speak at a Lancaster County high school.

"I hope we make it through the day," Ethel told this author the day before the meeting.

They did, but in doing so Winters pushed himself too hard.

The veteran met the commander in chief as Bush alighted from Air Force One at Harrisburg International Airport. The two shook hands and exchanged a few words. They then got into limousines for the motorcade to the Hershey Convention Center, where Bush was to speak. In his speech, Bush took time to acknowledge Winters.

"I had the honor of meeting Major Richard Winters," Bush said. "Dick Winters is a World War II veteran. There's an HBO miniseries called *Band of Brothers*. He led the platoon in World War II. I told him when I got off the airplane, it was an honor to meet him. It's such a fine example that he and others have set for those brave souls who now wear our nation's uniform. Major Winters, I'm glad you're here. I also want to thank the other members of our military who joined us today as well. Thank you all for coming."

That same evening, Winters kept his appointment at Donegal High School in the Lancaster County town of Mount Joy, where he spoke before a standing-room-only crowd and showed clips from his video.

It was all too much. The strain led to an onset of atrial fibrillation that caused Winters' heart to beat erratically. His doctors ordered him into complete rest. Medications failed, and his heart problems continued for several weeks until shock therapy got it back on rhythm.

As of the writing of this book, Dick Winters, still battling a weak heart and worsening Parkinson's disease, keeps a much more sedate schedule. Still, he is bombarded by mail, phone calls and requests for interviews. When he goes out in public, he is frequently stopped and asked to give autographs.

"Everybody wants a piece of you," he said.

On September 24, 2004, and shortly after the sudden death by heart failure of his sister, Ann, Winters was part of a program at the Army War College at Carlisle, Pennsylvania, during the dedication ceremony for Ridgeway Hall, named for General Matthew B. Ridgeway. The new building, a library, will eventually hold 14 million historic items and documents. At that time Winters presented to the college some of his wartime papers. (The remainder of his collection is destined for the college upon his death.)

A month later, just prior to the 2004 presidential election, Winters again had an opportunity to meet President Bush during a campaign stop in Hershey. The aging veteran, his face revealing his weariness, introduced the president at a gathering at the Hershey Convention Center.

"Mr. President," he said. "You have a Band of Brothers in Pennsylvania."

Now eighty-seven and in frail health, Winters is hoping to at last put public focus behind him. Wanting his private life back, he told this author he very much hopes to recapture the peace and quiet he promised himself in Normandy, and lost—albeit, to some degree, voluntarily—amid the hubbub that followed the release of the miniseries.

These days, Winters can be mostly found in his home, answering his mail as best he can, and safeguarding the history and memory of the men of Easy Company. It's a task he takes "very conscientiously."

Likewise, his men still revere him and stay in frequent contact.

So do his friends. Every January 21, on Winters' birthday, a package arrives from Tom Hanks. Inside, carefully packed, are four half gallons of ice cream, the one treat Winters missed most during his time in combat. Winters also gets gifts from people he has never met, including an annual box of candy from a dentist and fellow F&M College graduate living in California. This same man also sends him a crate of oranges each year at Christmas. All of that, plus the piles of mail from all over the world, is proof positive that the deeds of Major Richard D. Winters, and a million men like him who served their country during World War II, will be remembered long into the future.

★ ★ ★

On October 13, 2002, noted historian and Dick Winters' friend, Stephen Ambrose, died of lung cancer in Bay St. Louis, Mississippi. He was sixty-six years old. Winters fondly remembers the man who told Easy's story so well and so eloquently. Above the front door of his Hershey home, Winters has mounted a brass plaque that is simply engraved "Steve Ambrose slept here."

Looking at the piles of fan mail in Ethel's downstairs office, the light blinking on his phone's answering machine and the *Band of Brothers* books that arrive in the mail with requests for autographs, and with the memory of his night at the Emmys still fresh in his mind, a gleam comes to the veteran's eyes.

Glancing up at the plaque, he said to this author, "It took a few years for all this to happen, but by gosh it happened. And it all started right here."

Dick Winters on Leadership

Major Richard D. Winters is an acknowledged leader of men, both on and off the battlefield. He is fair, yet determined, and he places high value on people who do their best.

Since the debut of the book, *Band of Brothers*, and the subsequent miniseries, Winters has been asked to speak at many places and before many groups. He has been interviewed by newspaper reporters, magazine writers and TV interviewers, and his message is always the same: leadership.

What follows are some of Winters' most poignant quotes on leadership, spoken in his own words:

- "I find that as I go through life, and I meet other people, what I am doing as I get to know them is I'm looking at them and I'm seeing if I find the same characteristics and same qualities in them that I have in the men that I fought with. That's what I'm looking for. If I can find in a man those characteristics, then I know what I'm dealing with."

- " 'Hang Tough.' That means you do your best every day."

- Once asked by a West Point cadet what aspect of his military service provided him the greatest satisfaction, Winters answered without hesitation, "Knowing I got the job done; knowing that I kept the respect of my men. The greatest reward you can have as a leader is the look of respect. The key to a successful combat leader is to earn respect not because of your rank, but because you are a man."

(Much of Winter's philosophy on leadership was revealed to writer Christopher J. Anderson for an August 2004 article in *American History* magazine.)

- "The qualities you are looking for in a leader include: Does the individual have the respect of the men? How do you get the respect of the men? By living with them, being a part of it, being able to understand what they are going through and not to separate yourself from them. You have to know your men. You have to gain their confidence. And the way to gain the confidence of anybody, whether it's in war or civilian life or whatever, you must be honest. Be honest, be fair and be consistent. You can't be honest and fair one day, and the next give your people the short end of the stick. Once you can achieve that, you will be a leader."

- "Sometimes leadership is a matter of adjusting to the individual, and you do this every day. You don't have just one way of treating people; you adjust yourself to who you are talking to. I might talk to one person one way, someone else another. Ambrose had spent a good deal of time thinking about leaders and leadership. He had it about right. If you have character, that means the guy you are dealing with can trust you. So when you get into combat, and you get in a situation such as we were in along the dike in Holland, when I gave the orders, 'Ready, aim,' and this cook who had been in the unit only a short time but was experiencing his first combat action interrupted and said, 'Don't talk so loud!' nobody else there was thinking about anything except what he had been told to do. They trust in you, have faith in you and they obey right now, no questions asked."

- "You get it done by making a decision quick, getting to it and getting the thing done. Don't sit back and let the other guy make a decision that will put you on the defensive. Make up your mind quickly and get it done, right or wrong."

- On Captain Ronald Speirs, Winters said:

"Speirs was very effective. He got the job done. But if you were around and talked to the men who worked under him, he was never liked. Now, he could turn around and walk away and talk to someone at my level and be a completely different guy. He could take orders. He was very likable.

"The stories about him are true. When I first heard, I was speechless. What he did was unbelievable, inexcusable. If you talk to somebody in today's Army, they would say, well, how come he wasn't court-martialed? Well, you needed every man you had. Those guys that goofed up, didn't measure up, you couldn't just get rid of them. You needed the body, because if you lose that body, then somebody else has to shoulder twice the burden. You needed every body you could get. At Foy, he was the first officer I saw when I turned around. It could have been anybody, but it was Speirs. I didn't ask, 'Would you mind taking over?' No, I just turned around, saw him and said 'take over.' It was just a roll of the dice that he was standing there when I needed someone."

- "You maintain close relationships with your men, but not friendship. You have mutual respect for one another, but yet you have to hold yourself aloof, to a degree. If you are too friendly, it works in a negative way when you need to discipline your men. You can have your men's respect and friendship, but there is a point where you have to rise above this relationship and make sure they are following the orders that are in effect for everybody. In leading groups effectively, you have to rise above camaraderie. You have to be fair to everyone. Everyone must know that they are treated equally."

(Winters acknowledges different styles of leadership and cites the ability of men to lead through fear, such as Speirs and E Company's first commander, Herbert Sobel. He asserts, however, that the most effective leader will have quiet self-confidence and self-assurance that ultimately command the respect of the men.)

- "In Sobel's case it was in training, and in Speirs' case it was in combat. It is impossible to imagine what would have been the result if we had been led into battle by Sobel. He had driven the men to the point of mutiny, and, more important, he had lost their respect. If he had been in command, more men would have died in battle. Speirs had the men's respect. He had my respect. We both knew he would get the job done."

- "I was fortunate enough to fall in with the Barnes family. They were wonderful people. For the nine months prior to the invasion, I was there and studied, developing my own personality, my own personal perspective on command. Most of the other officers never had that. It was a chance for self-analysis. If you listen and pay attention, you will find that your own self-consciousness will tell you if you are getting off track. Nobody will have to tell you that what you are doing is incorrect or ineffective. If you take advantage of opportunities for self-reflection, and honestly look at yourself, you will be able to be a better leader."

ACKNOWLEDGMENTS

A number of people helped make this book possible, and to them I wish to extend my thanks for their encouragement and support.

First and foremost, of course, is Dick Winters himself, who not only provided me with his reports, letters, photographs and his memories, but with his friendship. Likewise, I wish to thank his wife, Ethel, for putting up with my monopolizing her husband during our lengthy interviews. If Dick Winters deserves medals for bravery, Ethel should get one for her patience. I also wish to thank their daughter, Jill, who provided me with genealogical information on the Winters family.

None of this would have happened without my editor at the Lancaster *Intelligencer Journal*, Charles Raymond Shaw. It was Ray who assigned me to locate Dick Winters for a news story back in 2001, and it was he who suggested this book two years later.

The *Intelligencer Journal* also kindly allowed me to use an excellent photo of Dick Winters sorting through his fan mail. The picture was taken by *Intell* photographer Dan Marschka, who provided me with the copy that appears in this book.

I also wish to convey my appreciation to Robert Hoffman for his fine photograph of Dick and Ethel Winters, Grace Nixon and Tom Hanks, taken at the Emmy Awards celebration at Spago in 2002.

Other photo credits in this book belong to Dick Winters' cousin, A. Anthony Kilkuskie, and Susan Smith Finn, daughter of the late Robert Burr Smith, a member of Easy Company. Plus I want to thank my friend, Barry Kline, whose scanner proved invaluable. Thanks, too, to Tom Carter, an expert researcher on Winters' assault at Brecourt Manor, for his technical assistance on details of the German defenses.

Gratitude must also be expressed to the Lancaster County Library and Franklin and Marshall College for archival photos.

And let me not forget the enthusiastic support of Tony, BK and the folks on the Wild Bill Guarnere Website, all of whom have told me they are eagerly awaiting this book. I hope it meets their expectations and answers most of their questions about this remarkable man.

I can't forget to mention Bucky Simmons of the Stephens County Historical Society, who provided me with invaluable information on Camp Toccoa during the war, and for his eyewitness recounting of the premiere of the miniseries at Toccoa fifty-nine years later.

I am deeply grateful to my agent, Dave Robie, for his endless patience and help in a project that was more difficult than it had to be, and my editor at NAL, Doug Grad, who helped me wade through the strange waters of putting together a book.

Last but not least, I want to express my most sincere love, gratitude and appreciation to my wife, Barbara, and daughter, Sarah. For over a year, they both endured my taking time out from family activities while I put this book together. They cheered me on at the good times and helped me to keep my focus when things weren't going so well. A special thanks to Barbara, a printing professional, who listened with a critical ear as I read each chapter to her, and made her own suggestions and recommendations on how to improve the text.

GLOSSARY

CBI	China-Burma-India Theater of Operations
CP	Command post
DP	Displaced person. A name for the homeless civilians who flooded Europe during the war
Deuce-and-a-half	U.S. Army truck with a 2.5-ton load capacity. Used to carry troops and supplies
DUKW	Wheeled vehicle capable of traveling on land or water. Can carry up to 2.25 tons. D(1942) U(amphibious) K(all-wheel drive) W(dual rear axles)
ETO	European Theater of Operations
40 & 8	World War I term for a boxcar capable of carrying forty men or eight horses
Handie talkie	Handheld radio, also known as the SCR 536

MG 42	Standard German infantry machine gun, 7.62 mm, belt fed, capable of firing 1,500 rounds per minute
M1 Garand	Standard American infantry weapon, .30 caliber, effective range 500 yards, maximum range 3,000 yards, 9.5 pounds. Rate of fire: 20 rounds per minute (the average soldier could aim and fire an 8-round clip in 20 seconds).
M1 carbine	Shorter, lighter American infantry weapon, .30 caliber, 5.2 pounds, holds 15- or 30-round clips. Later versions had full automatic capability. The M1A1 had folding metal stock for convenience of airborne troops.
PIR	Parachute Infantry Regiment
PT	Physical training
S1/G1	Regimental/Division administration and personnel officer
S2/G2	Regimental/Division intelligence officer
S3/G3	Regimental/Division plans and training officer
S4/G4	Regimental/Division supply officer
S5/G5	Regimental/Division executive officer
S6/G6	Regimental/Division commanding officer
SNAFU	Situation Normal, All Fucked Up (slang)
Stick	A group of paratroopers, usually 17 or 18 men, assigned to one plane
Thompson submachine gun	The tommy gun. Popular American infantry weapon, .45 caliber, 10.5 pounds. Rate of fire: 600–700 rounds per minute

BIBLIOGRAPHY

Books

Ambrose, Stephen A. *Band of Brothers*. New York, Simon & Schuster, 1992.
Forty, George. *U.S. Army Handbook, 1939–1945*. Great Britain: Alan Sutton Publishing Limited, 1995.
Koskimaki, George E. *The Battered Bastards of Bastogne*. Bentonville, OH: 101st Airborne Assoc., 1994.
———. *D-Day with the Screaming Eagles*. New York: Vantage Press, 1970.
———. *Hell's Highway*. Havertown, PA: Casemate Publishing, 1989.
Rappaport, Leonard and Arthur Norwood Jr. *Rendezvous with Destiny: History of the 101st Airborne*. Old Saybrook, CT: Konecky & Konecky, 1948.

Periodicals

Anderson, Christopher J. "Dick Winters: Reflections on His Band of Brothers, D-Day and Leadership." *American History* (August 2004).
Kingseed, Colonel Cole C. "Captains Courageous." *Army* (January 2002).
World War II, Band of Brothers Special Collector's Issue (2001).

INDEX

Aar River, 94
Advanced Service Rating Score, 206
Aldbourne, Wiltshire, 39, 51–53, 59, 82–85, 210–211
Alley, James H., Jr., 116, 133, 145, 163
Almon, DeEtta, 31, 32, 34–36, 49, 50, 53, 76–77, 79, 84, 88, 90, 92, 93, 129, 133, 134, 157, 164, 165, 176, 180–181, 197, 200–201, 204–206, 209, 212, 216–217, 219, 250–251
Ambrose, Hugh, 269
Ambrose, Moira, 243, 247
Ambrose, Stephen E., 235, 241–250, 254, 265–266, 269–271, 273–275, 281
Angoville-au-Plain, 67
Ardennes Forest, 134
Arnhem, 94, 100, 126, 276
Arnhem Annie, 107
Austill, Ulysses E., 151

Bain, Roderick G., 115–116
Band of Brothers (Ambrose), 29, 244–250, 267, 273
Band of Brothers (miniseries), 254–271, 277, 279
Barlow, Sergeant, 54
Barnes, Francis, 40, 52–53, 83, 94–95, 129, 211, 239, 241, 285
Barnes, Louie May, 40, 52–53, 83, 95, 129, 211, 239, 241, 285
Bastogne, 85, 136–157, 161, 168, 176, 245
Bataan, 136
Battle of France, 9
Battle of Sedan, 135
Battle of the Bulge, 166, 167
Battle of the Marne, 135
Battle of Verdun, 135
Berchtesgaden, 187–195

Blaine, Blanche, 222–223, 225, 226
Blithe, Albert, 72, 77, 154, 239
Bois Jacques, 137–150, 247
Bonning, Charles W., 169, 176
Bormann, Martin, 190
Boyle, Leo, 59, 73, 82, 85, 116, 118, 120, 122, 123, 208
Bradley, Omar, 18, 79, 91
Braun, Eva, 191
Brecourt Manor, 9, 17, 18, 76, 78, 79, 86, 101, 154, 240, 242, 243, 248, 261, 263, 275
Brewer, Robert B., 85, 98–99, 110, 113, 242, 243
British 1st Airborne Division, 93, 126
British XII Corps, 114
British XXX Corps, 94, 100
British 43rd Division, 115
Brownlee, Les, 275
Burgess, Rick, 38, 219
Bush, George W., 279, 280

Camp Breckinridge, Kentucky, 50
Camp Croft, South Carolina, 29–32, 34–36, 38, 40, 53
Camp MacKall, North Carolina, 49
Camp Pittsburgh, France, 214
Camp Shanks, New York, 50
Camp Toccoa (Toombs), Georgia, 38, 40–42, 44–48, 262–263
Carentan, 67–73, 76, 78, 79, 83, 245, 248, 251, 252
Carson, Gordon F., 54
Ceniceros, Salvador G., 151
Chamberlain, Neville, 187
Channel Islands, 2–3
Chapman, Elbridge G., 202
Chase, Charles H., 50, 104–105, 109, 175, 212, 213

Christenson, Burt, 3, 4, 117, 124, 277
Churinski, Victor C., 151
Civil War, 115
Clemens, Herman W., 274
Cobb, Roy, 120, 171–172
Cole, Robert, 7, 8, 18, 79, 248
Collins, Herman F., 19, 82
Collins, Royal, 82
Compton, Lynn "Buck," 7, 8, 10–13, 15, 18,
    53, 65, 69, 78, 85, 102, 113, 141,
    154–155, 163, 208, 243
Concentration camps, 183–186, 190, 198
Corregidor, 136
Cotentin Peninsula, 15, 67
Cowen, Mark, 261, 270
Cowing, Robert H., 190
Cox, Lloyd, 168, 175
Cromwell tanks, 100–102
Cronin, Raymond E., 151
Cudlitz, Michael, 262
Culver Military Academy, 43, 249
Cumberland River, 50
Currahee mountain, 44, 45, 47, 263

D Day (June 6, 1944), 1–19, 76, 153–154,
    205, 240, 242
D-Day with the Screaming Eagles
    (Koskimaki), 240
Daladier, Edouard, 187
Desobry, William, 137
De Vallavieille, Colonel, 9, 261
De Vallavieille, Louis, 240–241, 261
De Vallavieille, Michel, 18, 240
Diel, James L. "Punchy," 43, 65, 74, 81, 87,
    104, 208
Dietrich, Marlene, 132
Dike, Norman S., 128, 135, 141, 156,
    158–160, 200
DiMarzio, Jumbo, 16
Dittrich, Rudolph R., 51–52
Doby, David, 126, 134
Dominguez, Joseph P., 114, 146, 147
Dommel Bridge, 99, 100
Dukeman, William H., Jr., 117, 124, 208
Dunkirk, 2

Easy Company (see 506th Parachute Infantry
    Regiment)
82nd Airborne Division, 6, 41, 43, 94, 100,
    207, 212
83rd Infantry Division, 78
Eindhoven, 94, 96, 98–100, 103, 110
Eisenhower, Dwight D., 61, 107, 161, 176,
    182
11th Armored Division, 164
Elliot, Helen, 82
Emmy Awards, 267–270
Esbenshade, Emma Neff Casky, 21, 23, 28
Esbenshade, Serenus Herr, 21, 23, 28, 220
Estoppey, Lilian, 238
Evans, William S., 19, 56, 65

Fassnacht, Hank, 23
Feiler, Samuel "Shifty," 91–92, 203
Firefly tanks, 111
First Parachute Battalion, 41
501st Parachute Infantry Regiment, 54, 126,
    138, 167
502nd Parachute Infantry Regiment, 7, 96,
    132, 148, 167, 175, 207
503rd Parachute Infantry Regiment, 42
506th Parachute Infantry Regiment (see also
    Winters, Richard D.)
  activation of, 41
  Band of Brothers (book), 29, 244–250, 267,
    273
  Band of Brothers (miniseries), 254–271,
    277, 279
  basketball team of, 53–54
  Bastogne, siege of, 85, 136–157, 161, 168,
    176, 245
  at Berchtesgaden, 187–194
  Carentan, attack on, 68–73, 76, 78, 79, 83,
    245, 248
  casualties, 78–79, 81–82, 103–104, 113,
    123–124, 129–130, 151–156, 164, 175,
    201, 208
  commander of, 41–42
  counterassault on (after Carentan),
    74–76
  D Day (June 6, 1944), 1–19, 76, 153–154
  end of war, 195–209
  equipment of, 62–63
  field rations, 131–132
  formation of, 41
  Foy, attack on, 157–160, 168, 247
  in Holland, 93–129
  at Moder River, 166–174
  motto of ("We Stand Alone"), 44
  at Mourmelon-Le Grand, 130–132, 134,
    164, 175–177
  NCO mutiny, 58, 86, 206
  Noville, attack on, 160–164, 168
  postwar, 212
  preparations for D Day, 59–64
  reorganization of, 85–88
  replacements, 88–89, 91, 169, 175
  in reserve, 78–80
  at Rhine River, 177–181
  training of, 44–49, 51–52, 54, 89, 91, 92
  unit patches, 43
  Vierville, attack on, 65–67
Foley, Jack, 275
Fort Benning, Georgia, 35–38, 48
Fort Dix, New Jersey, 231–232
Fort Eban Emael, 41
Fort Indiantown Gap, 215, 278
Fort Knox, Kentucky, 36
Fort Lawton, Washington, 234
Fort McClellan, Alabama, 35
409th Regiment, 168
4th Division, 17
Foy, 137, 138, 143, 152, 157–160, 168, 247

French 2nd Armored Division, 188
Frye, Max, 269

Gardner, Charles C., 22, 24, 238
Gardner, Charlotte Winters, 22, 24, 29, 224,
    226, 238
Gardner, Dutch, 235, 236
German 2nd Panzer Division, 138
German 6th Fallschirmjager Regiment, 66,
    67, 74, 247, 252
German 7th Army, 91
German 25th Panzer Grenadier Division, 168
German 107th Panzer Brigade, 101, 153
German 363rd Volksgrenadier Division, 114,
    124
Goering, Hermann, 190–193, 197, 199–200
Golden Globe Awards, 266, 267
Gordon, Walter S., Jr. "Smoky," 75, 99,
    144–145, 240, 241–244, 254
le Grand Chemin, 9
Grant, Charles E., 206, 278
Gray, Daniel, 82
Gray, Everett J., 79, 82
Great Depression, 24
Green, William, 168
Grimes, Scott, 262
Grogan, Kitty, 204
Gross, Jerre S., 8, 66, 67
Guarnere, Henry, 14
Guarnere, William "Wild Bill," 7, 8, 10,
    12–14, 18, 43, 74, 77, 86–87, 102, 110,
    135, 140–141, 153–155, 208, 241, 246,
    253, 259, 262, 270, 275
Guth, Forrest, 82, 241, 243–245, 273, 275

Hackman, Don G., 151
Hagenau, 168–169
Hall, John D., 14–16, 54, 240, 263
Hanks, Tom, 254–256, 258, 259, 263–264,
    267, 269, 270, 280
Harms, Donald, 54
Harper, Joseph B., 173
Harris, Terrence C., 58
Hashey, Lester, 277
Hawkins, Winifred "Wyn," 59, 85
Heffron, Edward "Babe," 140, 141, 156
Hell's Highway, 104, 112, 113, 115
Helmond, 100, 101
Hemmen, 115, 118
Hendrix, Walter, 10, 11, 18
Herron, A.P., 151
Hershey Foods, 237
Hess, Rudolf, 183
Hester, Clarence, 8, 10, 16, 42, 43, 47, 65,
    72, 93, 98, 100, 109, 129, 140, 278
Heteren, 115
Heyliger, Frederick T. "Moose," 51, 125–128,
    180, 278
Hickman, Chester, 152
Hicks, Len, 16, 17
Higgens, George R., 117

Higgins, Gerald J., 133, 175
Hill, Andrew, 15, 16, 83
Hitler, Adolf, 77, 183, 186, 187, 189,
    191–193, 199
Hoffman, Robert, 268
Hogan, Joseph E., 2, 61, 201
Holland, John R., 71
Hoobler, Donald B., 119, 155–156, 157, 208
Horton, Oliver, 8, 42, 59, 93, 109, 124, 125
Houch, Julian "Rusty," 16
Howard, John, 244
Howell, Clarence S., 54
Hudson, Charles A., 85, 113
Hughes, Frank John, 259, 262, 263, 270

Jackson, Eugene E., 115, 172, 173
Jagdpanzer III tanks, 74, 75
Janovec, John A., 206, 260
Jendresen, Erik, 256, 259, 260, 269
Jodl, Alfred, 193
Johnson, Frances, 31
Johnson & Johnson, 235, 236
Joigny, 209–210
Joint, Ed, 275
Jones, Hank, 169–171
Jordan, Joseph M., 79, 82
Jordan, Phyllis, 82
Julian, John T., 151

Kaprun, 195–199, 203–205
Kastner-Kirdorf, Gustav, 191
Keitel, Wilhelm, 193
Kelly, John, 9, 10
Kent, Louis, 185
Kesselring, Albert, 195, 199
King, Donald, 277
Kingseed, Cole C., 274, 275
Kinnard, Harry, 175
Kopecky, Michelle, 268
Korb, John R., 277
Korean War, 228, 234
Koskimaki, George, 240
Krochka, Al, 38, 179, 193, 203–204

La Prade, James, 98, 138
Lavenson, George, 9–10, 42, 68–69, 71, 79,
    208
Leach, William, 178–180
LeClerc, General, 183
Lee, William "Bill," 4, 41, 60
Leonard, Robert T., 62
Lesniewski, Joseph A., 77, 275
Lewis, Damian, 257–259, 262, 263, 267
Liebgott, Joseph D., 10, 11, 18, 67, 89–90,
    99, 121–122, 143–144, 170, 185
Lindbergh, Charles A., 199
Lipton, Carwood, 6, 8, 10, 11, 14–16, 18, 70,
    71, 81, 82, 87–88, 99, 105–107, 111,
    116, 141, 145, 155–158, 163, 169, 176,
    240, 241, 243, 244, 246, 262, 266, 274,
    275, 277

Livingston, Ron, 270
Lorraine, Gerald, 10, 12–14, 18
Lovell, George, 139
Lovell, George E., 151
Luz, George, 154, 158, 278
Lyall, Clancy, 273

Maas River, 94
Maas-Waal Canal, 94
MacArthur, Douglas, 228
Maginot Line, 92
Major Richard Winters...In His Own Words, 274
Malarkey, Don, 7, 10–13, 17, 18, 77, 86, 102, 110, 112, 115–116, 142, 156, 240, 244, 246, 262, 275
Mande St. Etienne, 136
Manry, Thomas W., 151
Mark IV tanks, 74
Marshall, George C., 132–133
Marshall, S.L.A., 78, 243
Martin, Elizabeth, 25
Martin, John W., 43
Mather, Gordon, 139
Mather, Gordon E., 151
Matheson, S.L., 47
Matthews, Jack F., 101
Mayhew, Alice, 249, 257, 266
McAuliffe, Anthony C., 133, 138, 147, 148, 200, 229–231, 246
McCallum, Walter, 78
McClung, Earl, 275
McCreary, Thomas, 171–172
McGrath, John, 75
McKenna, Bruce, 269
McMillen, Joseph F., 67, 139, 151, 161–162, 175
Meehan, Anne, 19, 82
Meehan, Thomas, 9, 18–19, 58, 61, 63, 65, 79, 82, 93, 208, 263
Mein Kampf (Hitler), 183
Mellet, Francis J., 151
Melo, Joachim, 56
Menze, Vernon J., 103
Mercier, Kenneth J., 85, 170–173
Metzler, Estaban, 82
Metzler, William S., 79, 82
Meuse River, 93
Mihok, Steve, 149
Miller, James W., 102, 103
Miller, William T., 103
Moder River, 166–174, 168
Montgomery, Bernard Law, 94
More, Alton M., 80, 184, 186, 190–191, 239
Morris, Willie A., 151
Mourmelon-Le Grand, 130–132, 134, 164, 175–177
Moya, Jesus, 82
Moya, Sergio G., 82
Muck, Warren H. "Skip," 86, 117, 118, 156, 208

Mulvey, Thomas, 66, 74
Murray, Elmer "Moe," 82
Murray, Nancy, 82
Mussolini, Benito, 187

Neavles, Jackson, 70–72, 104, 121–123, 252
Neill, Patrick, 159
Nijmegen, 94, 100, 114, 126
99th Division, 136
Nixon, Lewis, 8, 16, 17, 42, 44, 47, 51, 74, 77, 78, 83, 93, 94, 97, 100, 102–107, 110, 112, 115, 122, 123, 125–126, 129, 134–135, 137, 140, 141, 145, 149–150, 157, 158, 161, 168, 170, 173, 176, 184, 186–187, 191–192, 196–197, 200, 204–205, 208, 210, 212, 213, 220–221, 223–224, 234–235, 246, 253, 270
Nixon, Stanhope, 220, 221, 223, 226–228, 234
Norwood, Arthur, Jr., 193
Noville, 137, 138, 160–164, 168
Nuenen, 101–104, 153
Nuremberg, 198, 199

O'Brien, Francis L., 78
Officer Candidate School (OCS), 35–37
O'Keefe, Patrick, 277
Okinawa, 201
Oliver, Marshall Clayton, 239
Omaha Beach, 67, 252
101st Airborne Division, 18, 38, 59, 67, 212, 213 (*see also* 506th Parachute Infantry Regiment)
  declared inactive, 215
  first commander of, 4
  formation of, 41
106th Division, 136–137
Operation Beaver, 54
Operation Cobra, 91
Operation Eagle, 54
Operation Linnet, 92
Operation Market Garden, 93–94, 126, 276
Operation Tiger, 54
Operation Transfigure, 91, 92
Operation Varsity, 176
Opheusden, 115
Orloff, John, 269
Ott, Mel, 132
Owens, Dick, 19

Pacific theater, 197, 200–202, 205, 209, 210
Paris, 133–134
Patton, George S., 42, 91, 149
Peacock, Thomas A., 85, 86, 118–120, 129, 141, 207
Pearl Harbor, 31
Pegasus Bridge (Ambrose), 244
Penkala, Alex M., Jr., 117, 118, 156, 208
Perconte, Frank, 142, 184
Perdue, Lieutenant, 179
Perkins, Benjamin W., 110

Pisanchin, John G., 85
Plesha, John, Jr., 10, 11, 18
Poorbaugh Grain Inc., 236–237
Powers, Darrell "Shifty," 101, 206, 246, 275

Rachamps, 164
Rader, Robert J., 43, 54, 69, 70, 132
Randleman, Denver "Bull," 3, 43, 76, 85, 104, 184, 262, 277
Randwijk, 115, 116
Ranney, Myron "Mike," 10, 11, 14, 15, 18, 43, 58, 86
Rappaport, Leonard, 193
Reese, Frank, 118, 119, 158
Reese, Lavon P., 54, 86
Reims, 131, 132
Rendezvous with Destiny (Rappaport and Norwood), 193, 194
Renkum, 122
Revolutionary War, 20
Rhine River, 114, 118, 121, 122, 125–127, 177–181
Rhodes, Thomas A., Jr., 176
Rice, George C., 137
Richey, Ralph D., Jr., 174, 176, 185, 189, 198, 199, 214, 239
Ridge, Tom, 275
Ridgeway, Matthew B., 280
Riggs, Carl, 19
Robbins, Johnnie Spurgeon, 250
Roberts, Nancy, 82
Robinson, Thomas, 20
Roe, Eugene G., 71, 73, 145, 172, 278
Rogers, Paul C., 86, 145
Rohr River, 136
Rome & Hawes, 236, 237
Rooney, Mickey, 132
Roosevelt, Franklin D., 28, 107, 180, 224
Rousch, Warren, 65, 78, 85, 278
Ruhr pocket, 176, 182
Rumsfeld, Donald, 275

S.S. Samaria, 51, 216
Santorum, Rick, 275
Saverne, 175
Saving Private Ryan (film), 255, 256
Sawosko, Carl C., 151
Schmitz, Raymond G., 60, 85
2nd Armored Division, 75
17th Airborne Division, 207
75th Infantry Division, 213, 214
705th Tank Destroyer Battalion, 147
Shade, Earl V., 151
Shames, Ed, 141, 163, 275
Sherman tanks, 17, 66, 75, 105, 106
Shindell, John E., 151
Shuster, Charlie, 222, 226
Sink, Robert F., 10, 18, 41–42, 45, 47–48, 50, 51, 54, 55, 58–59, 61–62, 67, 72, 76, 78, 79, 97, 98, 115, 124, 125, 138, 139, 143, 147, 148, 159–160, 168, 170, 173, 174,

176, 182, 185, 187–189, 192, 199–200, 202, 205, 212, 213, 233, 239, 274
Skyline Drive, 136
Slusher, Sergeant, 30, 31
Smith, George H., Jr., 73
Smith, Robert Burr, 61
Smith, Robert T., 85
Sobel, Herbert M., 42–45, 48–49, 55–59, 93, 102, 175, 200, 206, 211–212, 246–247, 249–250, 274, 284–285
Son, 96
Son Bridge, 94, 96, 97, 100, 138
Sowerby, Keith, 278
Speer, Albert, 190
Speirs, Ronald, 16, 159, 160, 162, 169, 170, 173, 174, 189–190, 206, 213, 261–262, 267, 274, 283–285
Spielberg, Steven, 169, 170, 255, 256, 260
Spina, Ralph F., 71
St. Come du Mont, 67
St. Oedenrode, 96
Staplefeld, Barnard F. "Ben," 136, 168, 179, 184, 193, 198
Ste. Marie-du-Mont, 6, 9, 16, 18, 240, 248
Ste. Mere-Eglise, 6, 7, 19, 84, 251, 252
Stevens, Elaine, 52, 59, 83, 90, 95, 211, 278
Strayer, Robert, 8–10, 14, 15, 17, 18, 42, 57, 58, 65, 66, 68–72, 75, 77, 97, 98, 103, 104, 109, 115, 124–126, 129, 134, 137–140, 143, 144, 146, 152, 157, 159, 160, 175, 203, 206, 258, 274, 277
Streicher, Julius, 199
Strohl, Roderick J., 75, 82, 102, 116, 245
Sturzelberg, 178–180
Sweeney, Patrick J., 58

Talbert, Floyd, 54, 70, 73–74, 111, 118, 120, 193, 278
Taylor, Maxwell, 18, 60, 68, 76, 128, 132–133, 160, 161, 176, 185, 188, 203, 212, 246
Taylor, Ray, 16
Team Desobry, 137, 138
10th Armored Division, 147, 183
Thalham, 186–188
13th Airborne Division, 209, 210
32nd Guards Brigade, 109
37th Armored Tank Battalion, 149
Thomas, Ed, 138, 164
326th Engineers, 149
326th Medical Company, 142
Tiger tanks, 110, 111
Tipper, Edward J., 70, 88, 208, 251, 252
Tolsdorf, Theodor, 199
Toye, Joseph J., 7, 10, 12, 18, 43, 102, 142, 152–155, 208, 245, 253–254
Trenta, Triesta, 30–32, 35–37
Trout, Glenn, 237
Tuck, Andrew E., III, 206
Turner, Robert L., 66
28th Division, 136

Uden, 104–109, 113
U.S. Army Ranger school, 232–233
U.S. 3rd Army, 91, 149
USO, 132
Utah Beach, 9, 17, 54, 67, 79–80, 240, 245, 261

V-1 Buzz Bombs, 77, 84
Van Klinken, Robert, 102, 103, 208
Van Oer, Nel, 106
Van Oer family, 106, 107
Vaughn, J.W., 8
Veghel, 94, 104–106, 109
Vierville, 65–67
von der Heyte, Frederick, 66, 68, 247–249
von Luck, Hans, 18

Waal River, 94, 114, 115, 121
Wahlberg, Donnie, 262
Washington, George, 20
Webb, Harold B., 151
Webb, Kenneth J., 159
Webster, David Kenyon, 170, 172, 192, 239
Welsh, Harry F., 17–19, 44, 52, 61, 65, 69–71, 75, 76, 78, 85, 92, 99, 103, 105, 108–109, 118, 127–129, 140, 146, 164, 169, 176, 179–181, 188, 189, 200, 204, 208, 213, 214, 245, 254
We Stand Alone (documentary), 261
Whitmore Laboratories, 235–237
Wilhelmina Canal, 94, 96
Willems Canal, 94
Winn, Melvin W., 171–172
Winter, Alfred, 162, 169
Winters, Ann, 24, 29, 52, 90, 106, 129, 208–209, 224, 226, 278
Winters, Barton N., 21
Winters, Beatrice, 24, 238
Winters, Catherine A. "Kate" Shirk, 21, 22, 24, 28
Winters, Edith Esbenshade, 20–21, 24–26, 29, 34, 37, 46, 77, 90, 93, 100, 205, 209, 215, 216, 224, 226, 235, 237–239
Winters, Ethel Estoppey, 225–226, 234, 235, 238, 251–254, 267, 268, 270, 272–273, 278
Winters, Jill, 235, 238
Winters, Richard D. (see also 506th Parachute Infantry Regiment)
    in Army Reserve, 231–234
    Atlantic crossing and, 51
    Band of Brothers book and, 29, 244–250, 267, 273
    Band of Brothers miniseries and, 255–271, 277, 279
    basic training and, 30–31
    Bastogne, siege of, 85, 136–157, 161, 168, 176, 245
    as battalion XO, 125, 127, 129, 140, 160, 169
    at Berchtesgaden, 187–195
    birth of, 20
    birth of children, 226, 235
    at Camp Toccoa, 40–41, 44–48
    childhood of, 21–24
    code of conduct of, 37
    in command of 2nd battalion, 134, 160, 169
    concentration camps and, 184–186, 190
    courtship and marriage of, 225–226
    dating by, 27–28, 31
    D Day (June 6, 1944), 1–19, 153–154
    death of sister, 24
    dental problems of, 91–92, 203
    disobeys order, 173–174
    early jobs of, 24–26
    education of, 23–26, 29, 223
    at Emmy Awards, 267–270
    end of war and, 195–214
    in England, 39–40, 51–60, 82–95, 210–211
    enlistment of, 29
    fame and celebrity of, 264–266, 272, 274–281
    farm and animal nutrition business of, 235–237
    files of, 239–240
    finances of, 26–27, 30, 53
    at Fort Dix, New Jersey, 231–232
    hitchhiking by, 32–34
    in Holland, 93–129, 153
    on leadership, 282–285
    letters to DeEtta Almon, 31, 32, 34–38, 49, 50, 53, 60, 76–77, 79, 84, 88, 90, 92, 93, 129, 133, 134, 157, 164, 165, 176–177, 180–182, 197, 200–201, 204–206, 209, 212, 216–217, 219, 250–251
    lifestyle of, 53
    medals awarded to, 18, 76, 79, 203
    mountain climbing by, 202–203
    notice of callback and, 228–230
    Officer Candidate School and, 35–37
    personal reconnaissances by, 109–110
    postwar employment of, 220–228, 235–237
    postwar period and, 215–230
    promotions made by, 85–88
    promotion to captain, 79
    promotion to corporal, 36
    promotion to first lieutenant, 45
    promotion to major, 174, 176–177
    promotion to second lieutenant, 38
    relations with men, 54–55, 72, 73, 84, 140–141, 143
    religion and, 23, 30–31, 114, 164–165, 207–209
    revisits Europe, 240–241, 247–249, 251–253, 261–262

Sobel and, 42, 55–59, 93, 211–212, 246, 250
sports and, 25, 30
wounded, 71, 76, 77, 90
Winters, Richard Nagle, 20–27, 29, 34, 37, 53, 77, 90, 164, 209, 213, 215, 216, 224, 238
Winters, Tim, 226, 234, 235, 238
Winters, Timothy, 20
Winters, William Davis, 21
Wolf, Ed, 30
Wooster Victor, 214, 216

Worringen, 178
Wynn, Robert "Popeye," 10–14, 17, 18, 82, 100–101, 277–278

Yost, Graham, 269
Youman, Arthur C., 85
Young, Charles H., 63, 64

Zell-am-See, 195–196
Zetten, 115
Zons, 178, 179

About the Author

Larry Alexander is a reporter and humor columnist for the *Intelligencer Journal* in Lancaster, Pennsylvania. He is the winner of more than a dozen state-level awards for excellence in journalism, and a series he coauthored on sexual abuse and domestic violence among the plain Amish and Mennonite communities has been submitted for a Pulitzer Prize in 2005. A lifelong resident of Ephrata, Pennsylvania, he grew up in Dick Winters' boyhood neighborhood. He still resides in Ephrata with his wife, Barbara, and daughter, Sarah.